A CENTURY OF
DESIGN
DESIGN PIONEERS OF THE 20TH CENTURY

PENNY SPARKE

MITCHELL BEAZLEY

Dedicated to Molly, Nancy and Celia

A Century of Design

First published in Great Britain in 1998 by Mitchell Beazley, an imprint of
Octopus Publishing Group Ltd, 2–4 Heron Quays, London E14 4JP

Executive Editor	Alison Starling
Executive Art Editor	Vivienne Brar
Project Editor	Elisabeth Faber
Art Editor	Nina Pickup
Editorial Assistant	Stephen Guise
Picture Research	Wendy Gay
Directory	Emma Shackleton
Production	Paul Hammond
Index	Hilary Bird

ISBN 1 84000 213 1

A CIP record for this book is available from the British Library

Set in Baskerville and Futura

Printed in China

A C[...]

DESIGN

Contents

Introduction

This is essentially a book about people. It is also a book about things – things that would not exist, and would certainly not look the way they do, if someone had not imagined them first. We do not always realize that everything that surrounds us in our everyday lives – from the knives and forks we use for breakfast, to the bus we take to work, the computer we use, the chairs we sit on and the lamp-posts we pass on our way home – has been conceived of and designed, and that someone, or a team of people, has given those things the features that we see.

Conceiving things is perhaps not as simple a process as it may seem at first. It is not just of matter of a sketch on the back of an envelope but rather of imagining a need and then of trying to think what would fulfil it. That need may be defined in a number of different ways: it may be a functional need, something to cut your bread with, for example. It may be an aesthetic need, something to make your life more beautiful or more pleasant. It may be a social or a psychological need, something that makes you feel secure or in tune with your peers. Or, as is most often the case, it may be an economic imperative on the part of a manufacturer who needs a new product to sell. All these needs and more have to be considered by a designer before an object can even begin to be thought of as a possibility.

The responsibilities of the designer are many. Not only do they include making the components of the thing in question fit together properly, they also include being the interpreters of our dreams, our aspirations and our anxieties and creating the appropriate symbols for us. We form our identities, both individual and collective, through the things with which we surround ourselves, and designers have to take this into account as well. It is a complex task that in many ways demands superhuman qualities.

Designers work with an enormous number of constraints as well. If their object is to be mass-produced – which in this century is most often the case – they have to work with all the demands of the manufacturing industry, as well as, even more importantly in recent decades, with those of marketing and retailing. They have to understand production techniques and the possibilities and limitations of different materials. They also must have some insights into consumers and their needs, desires and tastes. Designers also have an important cultural role to fulfil. They are the creators of the material environment we inhabit, and must have a vision, therefore, of what that environment should be like and how it should affect our lives. Some have explored the limits of possibilities, imagined new forms and created new meanings for the designed object. Others have worked at theorizing the ideological framework for design, positioning its role within the greater cultural, economic and political picture. Still others have had personal visions that have coincided with the aesthetic and emotional needs of the public.

This book is about the pioneering individuals who saw in design a way of fulfiling both their own personal ambitions and their aims for society at large. It is impossible to design for industry without thinking about the social implications of that task. Designers in this century have faced that responsibility many times over.

At different moments design has been at the forefront of cultural, and indeed other forms, of change in this century. Designers have worked alongside, and been inspired by, among other people, fine artists, architects, politicians and technologists. They have been led by different forces, depending on current preoccupations. If political change was the order of the day, then that was the direction in which many designers looked. If a major shift in fine art sensibility took place, then as likely as not designers would have reacted to it in some way.

Designers have worked in groups to promote a single cause and as individuals fulfiling a personal project. Like all communities of professionals they have been influenced by the prevailing ideologies of their times. The dominant design ideology in this century has been that of Modernism, a movement in design which set out to translate the concept of modernity into the mass material environment. Taking its lead from technological advances, and aligning itself firmly with the principles of mechanized mass production, Modernism took it visual language from avant-garde abstract art, believing it to be the appropriate language for the modern age. Nearly all the leading Modernist designers were architects first and foremost, and they took the architectural theory of Functionalism – the idea that the outer form of a building should be determined by its internal structure – with them into the arena of design. So dominant was this approach that by the 1920s and 1930s all the institutions relating to design – educational establishments, museums – adopted Modernism as the legitimate design theory of the new century. Inevitably many designers worked outside its parameters but its influence was felt by all. Not until the 1960s did Modernism come under serious threat and even after its apparent demise it remained, and remains, the preferred option of many influential designers.

Who are the designers that this book has chosen to focus upon? They are mostly men, as is the case in the history of most professions in this century, although significantly several women enter the story either as interior decorators, or as assistants to the famous early Modernists. A handful made it on their own, and as the century has progressed so has the number of successful female designers.

The majority of these figures trained as architects. Inevitably they turned first to the objects of the interior but from there they moved on to the products of this century – the typewriters, the food-mixers and the automobiles. The exceptions to this general rule were mostly trained as craftspeople, graphic designers or fine artists. Not until after 1945 did product designers emerge trained for that specific role. The input of these related disciplines has added a richness to 20th-century design, lending it a diversity that is celebrated in the pages of this book.

In spite of this diversity these pioneers were, and in many cases, still are, motivated by the same thing: to create order out of chaos; to improve the quality of their own and other peoples' lives; and to put beauty and meaning into the everyday environment. That, in essence, is the story of design in this century and the achievement of these pioneering individuals.

The cover of The Architectural
Review *from June, 1952, featuring
a cluster of "cat's cradle" wire chairs
designed by Charles Eames for the
furniture manfacturer Herman Miller.
The elegant sculptural forms of these
minimal objects helped influence
public taste in the post-war period.*

The New Century

The New Century

The decades around the turn of the 19th into the 20th century witnessed transformations in the material world, and in patterns of living, the like of which had never been seen before. These were the years in which what we now call "the modern age" was born. The lives, not only of a chosen few but of the mass of people living in the western, industrialized world, were irrevocably changed. The advent of mass transportation, mass communication systems and the mass manufacture of goods was to alter things for ever. The dominant force behind those changes was technology, seen as rational, progressive and, above all, unstoppable. Many people put their faith in its unrelenting impact believing it to be the way forward, the means of moving positively from one century into the next. From it, they believed, would flow material progress, social equality and an efficient and rational approach to the problems of everyday life.

Architects and designers were amongst the first to respond to technology's seductive call. For nearly a century they had had to work within a very different climate, one that had favoured the safety of the past rather than the excitement of the future. Caution rather than a sense of adventure had determined the tastes of the new middle-classes and imperial powers of the mid-19th century, and Gothic Revivalism had vied with Neoclassicism to win their favour.

It was against the backcloth of this reactionary climate that modern design was born. Architects showed the way forward, transferring their ideas from the building to its interior spaces and finally to the objects within them, breaking down the hierarchy that had long divided these areas in the process. Architecture had long been the "queen of the arts", a respectable and powerful enough profession to influence the material world as a whole. Now it took on the responsibility of transforming it beyond recognition.

The task of renewal began in Great Britain. On the basis of ideas initiated by John Ruskin, and carried forward by William Morris, C.R. Ashbee, C.F.A. Voysey and others, designers began to question the chaotic sequence of revived styles repackaged by machines and mindlessly consumed. They sought a remedy in the pre-industrial world of craft manufacture that offered a means of purification and of re-establishing a link between makers and their artefacts. Although this reforming zeal was rural in essence and, in some ways, backward-looking, it marked an important transitional moment in which the practitioners of architecture and design were able to respond openly and sensitively to the new climate in which they found themselves.

While the rural ideal of the Arts and Crafts Movement spawned European counterparts in remote areas in countries seeking images for their national identities, Finland, Hungary and Sweden among them, it was in urban centres – Vienna, Paris, Brussels, Munich, Barcelona, and, to some extent, Milan and Glasgow – that modern design was really formed. Although it was expressed most forcibly in architecture it crossed over into the fine and decorative arts and interior decoration as well.

Art Nouveau, or *Jugendstil* as it was known in Northern Europe, represented the first real break with the past. It was a transitional movement inasmuch as it still leaned heavily on the world of nature, but it also exploited the possibilities of new materials – for example cast and wrought iron, aluminium and sheet glass – in its determination to be of the moment. It spanned a wide spectrum of stylistic possibilities, from the curves of Hector Guimard (see pp.20–21), Emile Gallé and Eugène Gaillard in France, to the those of Henri van de Velde (see pp.16–17) and Victor Horta in Belgium, and of Antoni Gaudí in Spain and Peter Behrens (see pp.30–33) in Germany, to the more geometric forms of Charles Rennie Mackintosh (see pp.26–9) in Scotland and of Otto Wagner and Josef Hoffmann in Austria (see pp.12–13 and 34–7). In all its facets Art Nouveau sought to bring decoration and structure more closely together. Buildings, interiors and objects began to be thought of as products of their materials, their principles of construction and their function, as much as meaningful components of the world of signs and symbols.

The role of the machine and the move towards greater rationalization and efficiency in modern life suggested a shift away from the world of nature towards simpler forms inspired by geometry. The *Jugendstil* designers in Austria and Germany became increasingly sensitive to this new imperative and sought an approach towards the construction of the material environment which acknowledged it visually.

Major exhibiitons held in the period displayed the transformations and mirrored their successes. The Universal Exhibitions held in Paris in 1889 and 1900 (see pp.22–3) paid homage to the impact of Art Nouveau while the Turin exhibition of 1902 brought the more geometric style of the Glaswegian Mackintosh to international attention. The spread of new decorative art periodicals such as *The Studio* and *Pan* also accelerated the movement of influences across national boundaries. Styles and ideas crossed the Atlantic and exotic influences from Europe's colonial empires played a vital part in this expanding melting-pot of possibilities.

While the new climate made things possible change could not have taken place without the personal initiatives of a body of far-sighted and courageous individuals. In Europe, as well as in the United States, practitioners of architecture, fine art, design and craft embraced the possibility of change. This was a change not only of architectural and design styles, but of a whole way of life. The idea of the *Gesamtkunstwerk* ("total work of art") justified designers working across creative boundaries. Soon a new relationship between the material environment and everyday life could be seen not just as a remote utopia but as a realistic possibility.

This was a masculine vision for the most part. Inspired by modern technologies, male architects dominated the search to transform the material environment. However, the areas of decoration and craft manufacture had not yet been relegated to the margins by what later came to be known as the "machine aesthetic", and they too played an important part in casting off the restraints of the past. Above all, as the architects and designers whose lives and work are discussed in this chapter firmly believed, anything was possible.

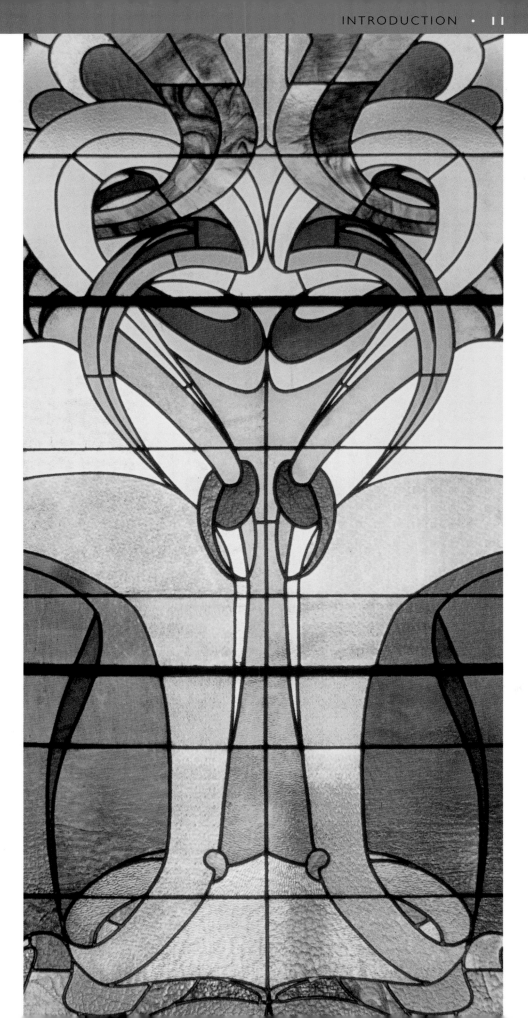

A stained glass window designed for the Hôtel Otlet in Brussels in the late 1890s by Henry van de Velde, who was responsible for the building's interior. The sinuous curves of this window design were echoed throughout the interior, marking it out as a characteristically fin-de-siècle creation.

The Viennese architect and designer Otto Wagner (1841–1918) was indisputably a key influence on modern architecture and design. As a teacher and writer as well as a practitioner, he was a catalyst for the ideas and work of many who came after him. He was among the first to respond in a practical way to the multiple forces of "modern life",

Otto Wagner

which included new materials and technology, and the specific demands made by the growing urban environment. He refined an approach toward creating buildings and objects that did not depend, as had those of so many of his earlier 19th-century predecessors, on inspiration from past architectural styles, frequently gathered from different periods and mixed together into a meaningless mélange.

Otto Wagner was the undisputed leader of the modern Viennese architectural and design movement. Through his teaching, his writing and, above all, through his architectural and design work, he played a seminal role in helping design to move seamlessly from the 19th into the 20th century.

A corner of the roof of Wagner's Karlsplatz Station (below) designed in 1898 for Vienna's urban rail system. The combination of attention to structural detail and to surface pattern characterized the transitional period of this designer's work as he shifted from the use of historical decorative styles to Functionalism.

TRAINING AND EARLY WORK

Wagner received a solid academic training in architecture, first from 1857 to 1860 at the Technical High School in Vienna (including a year spent at the Building Academy in Berlin). Between 1861 and 1863 he studied at the Academy in Vienna, where he became a Professor and Head of Architecture in 1894. His first forays into architecture were town houses with decorative and monumental features in historical styles, a taste that he moved away from as his career developed. He designed about forty such houses, including his own house at Rennweg 3 (1889), which had a façade embellished with Renaissance decoration. He also designed ornamented furniture for the interiors of these buildings, reminiscent of the Neo-Classical Biedermeier style that had been popular among the new Viennese urban middle-class that emerged in the mid-19th century.

TOWARDS FUNCTIONALISM

The first few years of the 20th century represented a period of transition for Wagner. During this period he began to develop the personal approach toward architectural design that derived its impetus from the modern age. For a brief period in 1889 he joined the Vienna Secession – a group of

A single wall-mounted light (right) designed in 1902 for the telegraph office of Die Zeit newspaper building in Vienna. Its utilitarian simplicity reflects Wagner's functionalist approach to product design at that time.

The interior of the Am Steinhof Church in Vienna (left), built between 1904 and 1907. The Church was one of Wagner's key achievements as a precursor to Modernism; although the surface of the building is richly patterned, its structure is forward-looking in its austerity.

TEACHING AND WRITING

While Wagner's own designs served as important examples of early Functionalism for other designers in Vienna and elsewhere in Europe, his progressive ideas were also disseminated through his writing and teaching. Wagner's commitment to meeting the demands of modern living were outlined in his book of 1896, *Moderne Architektur*, which helped to earn him the title of the "father of Viennese Modernism". In the book Wagner stressed the need to meet the requirements of function through practicality, construction and new materials. At the Academy's school of architecture in Vienna he had a strong influence on such students as Josef Hoffmann (see pp.34–7) and Joseph Maria Olbrich both of whom worked in his studio in 1896 and who went on to found the Secession group. Wagner's work embraced design of all kinds and on every scale, but it was unified by his unerring commitment to the concept of modernity.

artists and architects (est. 1897) that was formed in opposition to the Academy in Vienna, where the applied arts were considered inferior to painting. The Secessionists aimed to abolish the division between architecture, and the fine and decorative arts. At the end of the century Wagner produced a number of designs: for example, an exhibition stand with a cast-iron surround and accompanying furniture for the Paris Universal Exhibition of 1900 (see pp.22–3), displaying the characteristic curves of Jugendstil – the northern European version of the more florid French Art Nouveau style.

The aims of the Secession – that the disciplines of architecture and the decorative arts should move more closely together – were central to Wagner's work as a designer. From 1900 his architecture and furniture began to look more overtly functional; his chairs, in particular, derived their visual impact through an emphasis on construction. He also favoured new materials, such as glass and aluminium, which led him to abandon much of the decorative nature of his earlier work. The furniture for one of his most striking buildings from this period, the Post Office Savings Bank (1904–6) in Vienna, for example, consisted of simple cube shapes in dark-stained beechwood, some of it bent, with aluminium details that provided reinforcement and emphasized the functional role of the chair (see right). Holes punched in the seats of some of the chairs and stools both reduced their weight and echoed visually the aluminium circles covering the joints.

The same attention to detail that Wagner devoted to his architecture and furniture was evident in everything he designed. In 1902, for example, he worked on a range of Jugendstil silver pieces for the Viennese manufacturer J.C. Klintosch, exhibited at the Turin International Exhibition of that year. On a much larger scale, Wagner was involved in city planning in Vienna. As artistic adviser to the Vienna Transport Commission, he designed stations and bridges for the Vienna City Railway between 1894 and 1899, including the Karlsplatz station (1898; see opposite). From 1906 to 1907 he worked for the Commission for the Regulation of the Danube Canal.

The little bentwood armchair in stained and polished beech with a perforated seat (right) was designed between 1904 and 1906 for the interior of the Post Office Savings Bank in Vienna, perhaps the most lastingly significant of all Wagner's buildings.

Most of the pioneers who played a role in the formation of a modern design movement at the turn of the century worked in Vienna, Paris or Brussels – centres that witnessed the blossoming of a new style that looked forward rather than to the past. A few isolated individuals in other cities also made an international impact through the

Carlo Bugatti

display of their work at key exhibitions and through publication in the major art and design journals of the day. One such was the Milan-based designer and furniture-maker Carlo Bugatti (1856–1940). His unusual and highly personal style can be linked to trends in the decorative arts during this period: for example, the widespread interest in unusual materials and non-Western art. He combined them, however, in his own idiosyncratic way.

A photograph of Carlo Bugatti taken in front of an example of his work from the late 1890s. It shows details of the rich decoration that he used, as well as his trademark circular forms.

A casket (c.1902; below) made from parchment and gilded with bronze. The stylized floral motifs featured on the casket's patterned surface were frequently used by Bugatti to decorate his furniture.

TRAINING AND EARLY WORK

Unlike many other pioneering designers, Bugatti was not trained as an architect but as a painter. He studied first at the Brera Academy in Milan in the late 1870s and subsequently at the Academy of Fine Arts in Paris. He flirted briefly with the idea of becoming an architect. For nearly 30 years, however, he dedicated his energies to the design and hand manufacture of furniture for a wealthy Milanese clientele. His first attempt at furniture-making was a bedroom suite, made for his sister's wedding in 1880. The bed incorporated arches derived from Islamic architecture and was decorated

A bedroom (c.1900; above) designed for Lord Battersea's London home. The circular forms, exotic decorative details and claustrophobic arrangement of the space are all typical of Bugatti's work. This was one of the few complete interiors that he designed.

with Japanese-style imagery on the head and footboards. Bugatti made extensive use of inlaid wood in this project, and in 1888 he opened a commercial workshop in Milan dedicated to making wooden furniture.

In his commitment to high-quality craft manufacture Bugatti was indebted to the ideas of the reformers John Ruskin and William Morris in Britain, but the exotic stylistic influences in his work, such as Near Eastern and Arabian imagery, came more directly from the interests of the English Aesthetic Movement and of Parisian artists. His designs, which to many seemed highly eccentric, were realized in unusual materials, such as vellum and leather. Inlays and tassels were frequently used to enhance the exotic effect of these bizarre creations.

STYLISTIC DEVELOPMENT

Through the 1890s Bugatti moved away from his early interest in asymmetry toward more symmetrical forms. He increasingly used vellum to cover and disguise the joints of his furniture and repeatedly deployed a circle motif. In 1900 he won a silver medal at the Paris Universal Exhibition. (see pp.22–3) and in the same year

A display cabinet (right), inlaid in metal and wood with vellum and wooden panels, designed in the late 1890s. The symmetry of this highly ornate piece characterizes his earlier work. Japanese influences are evident in the floral and bamboo decorations, while the carved arches reflect the influence of Islamic art.

supplied furniture for a palace in Istanbul. His designs for furniture were always intended to form a part of complete interior settings, and he submitted designs for four rooms to the Turin International Exhibition of 1902, one of which, the "Snail Room", won first prize. This design, with curved fitted seating, chairs and a table based on the spiral form of a snail shell, marked a dramatic move to a sinuous, organic aesthetic more obviously linked to European Art Nouveau. It marked the peak of his creative career and was an achievement which did much to enhance his international notoriety as an innovative designer.

Despite its exotic influences and visual eccentricity, Bugatti's work can be seen as an Italian variant of international Art Nouveau. His primary aim was to avoid using historical European styles as a source of inspiration – especially in Italy, where the inheritance of the Renaissance still had considerable influence – and to reject traditional forms. In 1904 Bugatti, who had probably exhausted the possibilities allowed by his elaborate and laborious designs, turned his back on the pressures of running a workshop and sold his furniture business. He moved to Paris where, with the exception of a range of elaborately decorated silver items which he exhibited there in 1907, he re-dedicated his career to painting.

Along with Otto Wagner, Henry van de Velde (1863–1957) was one of the older generation of early Modernists who were highly influential in the development of 20th-century design. Like Wagner (see pp.12–13), van de Velde was a writer, theorist and teacher, as well as a practising architect and designer. In addition to his work, it was his

Henry van de Velde

ability to articulate, through his writings, the ideas of the early modernists that had such an impact on younger designers. While Wagner led the movement away from past styles towards a new design language rooted in the requirements of materials and structure, van de Velde was more committed to exploring line and form. No longer, he claimed, should the shape of an object symbolize the external world of nature but rather should reflect its inner structure: in his words, "utility alone can generate beauty."

Henry van de Velde seated at a desk that he designed in 1899 as part of a set of study furniture and fittings for the Secession Exhibition held that year in Munich. Behind him (just seen) is one of his early Symbolist paintings.

TRAINING AND EARLY WORK

Van de Velde first learned about line through painting. He trained as a painter in Antwerp from 1881 to 1884 and in Paris from 1884 to 1885; his early work was inspired by the Post-Impressionism of Vincent van Gogh and Paul Gauguin and the Pointillism of Georges Seurat. However, he was ultimately drawn to the rhythmic lines of Symbolist painting and from there to the decorative arts and the Art Nouveau style (initially in the form of posters and graphic design). In 1889 he joined the Belgian group of Symbolist painters, Les Vingt, and in 1894 wrote his tract *Le Déblaiement de l'art* ("Clearing the Way for Art"). Here he evolved a theory of line that he called "dynamographique" to reflect his aim to reveal the dynamic internal structure of an object. In his chair for the Villa Bloemenwerf (see right), for example, the wooden curves not only provided structural support, but also suggested a sense of upward movement.

THE VILLA BLOEMENWERF

Much of van de Velde's theorizing had a social reformer's moralistic dimension, in the manner of John Ruskin and of the members of the British Arts and Crafts Movement, such as William Morris. His first move away from graphic design into

Van de Velde's furniture designs were typified by their use of curved forms that were both decorative and structural. The subtlety and simplicity of the curves employed in this chair (right) – designed in 1895 for van de Velde's house, the Villa Bloemenwerf – show his commitment to an early form of modernism in design.

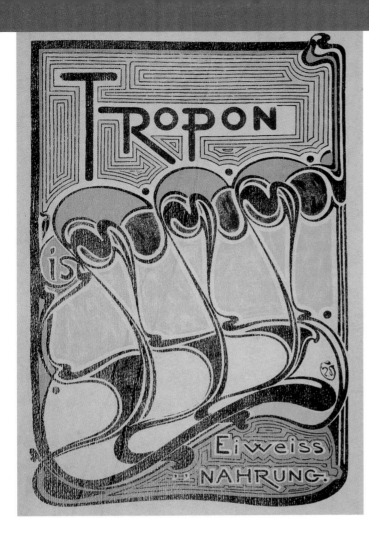

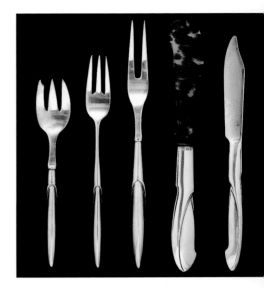

A poster (left) dating from 1897 designed for the Tropon food factory in Mülheim, Germany. In the early years of his career van de Velde moved from painting to designing posters. With its biomorphic shapes, abstract patterns and integration of typography into the image, this poster is typical of van de Velde's graphic work.

Van de Velde's designs for silverware demonstrated his commitment to the powerful "dynamographic" line, which was at once decorative and structural. These pieces of 1903 (right), made by the court jeweller Theodor Müller in Weimar, Germany, reveal the simple elegance typical of the designer's work.

architecture and the decorative arts came, just as it had for William Morris, through designing a house for himself and his family (1895). This house, the Villa Bloemenwerf in Uccle, Belgium, was clearly indebted to the curvilinear forms of French and Belgian Art Nouveau architecture. Its distinction lay in van de Velde's application of these organic forms to all aspects of the house and its contents to create a cohesively designed environment. The villa generated a number of commissions for its designer, most notably from the art dealer Siegfried Bing and from Bing's rival, Julius Meier-Graefe, owner of La Maison Moderne, to design furniture for their respective shops in Paris. Indeed, during the late 1890s and early 1900s van de Velde branched out into a wide range of decorative design, including interiors, book designs, metalwork, ceramics, wallpapers, textiles and – aligning himself to the Dress Reform Movement – women's dresses. His style in this period remained characteristically curvilinear yet restrained.

GERMANY AND LATER CAREER

In 1899 van de Velde went to Germany, where he stayed until 1917. In 1902 he was asked to design a new school of applied arts, the precursor of the Bauhaus, in Weimar, and in 1908 became its co-director. Until World War I he pursued a very active propagandist role within the German modern design movement, and was a co-founder of the Deutscher Werkbund, an organization formed in 1907 to bridge the gap between design and industry. Important design projects from these years included porcelain for Meissen, silver and metalwork for a range of manufacturers, and the interior of the Folkwang Museum in Hagen.

In 1914, however, van de Velde's somewhat romantic ideas about the role of the designer clashed with the more rigorously rational principles of Hermann Muthesius, a co-founder of the Deutscher Werkbund and a leading figure in German design circles. Muthesius was firmly committed to the idea that standardization was fundamental to design if the latter was to be appropriate to the new age of mass production, whereas van de Velde retained a belief, inherited from the crafts movements of the 19th century, in the importance of individualism. In the same year van de Velde gave up his teaching post, and in 1920 moved to the Netherlands and then to Belgium. The years until his death were occupied by a variety of projects, including those for the left bank of the Schelde in Antwerp (1926), the University Library in Ghent (1936) and the Kröller-Müller Museum in Otterlo (1937–8), but he became less and less central to the debate about the direction that modern design should take.

The breadth of van de Velde's work is large but united by a single vision – that "utility alone can generate beauty." The shape of this two-handled stoneware vase (below), designed for the Reinhold Hanke firm in the early 1900s, is determined mainly by the practical placement of the handles.

Most of the important breakthroughs in the story of the birth of modern design were achieved by progressive architects who felt compelled to transform not only the exteriors of buildings but their interiors as well. Their inspiration came from what was perceived to be the logical world of mass production, the spirit of which they tried to

Elsie de Wolfe

capture in their daring, abstract designs. At the same time, however, another equally innovative but less radical approach to modernizing the interior emerged from the newer profession of "interior decoration". This approach focused on the search for a fresh, light, modern "look" to replace the heavily furnished, overcrowded and overdecorated Victorian interior. The American Elsie de Wolfe (1856–1950) was a prime mover in the formation of the idea of the professional interior decorator who provided a whole look for an interior space, replacing the hitherto separate work of the upholsterer, the cabinet-maker and other related specialists. Guided by her maxim "simplicity, suitability and proportion", she set out, at the turn of the century, to modernize the homes of rich American clients who wanted to demonstrate their appreciation of beauty and their refined taste.

A portrait taken by Cecil Beaton of the American interior decorator Elsie de Wolfe. De Wolfe's legacy is considerable: a number of younger American women, among them Sister Parrish, followed her into the interior decorating profession, as did Syrie Maugham (see pp.54–5) and Sibyl Colefax in Britain. Their work was far removed from the rigorous interiors of the modern movement, which reflected the application of "machine-age" principles to design, but it remains, none the less, one face of the influence of modernity on 20th-century interior design.

An illustration from de Wolfe's book The House in Good Taste (1913; right), showing her love of floral chintz, which featured in many of her schemes. De Wolfe also placed great importance on setting aside a corner of a room for a "proper" writing desk, of which this is a typical example. Although she made extensive use of antique furniture, pieces were often painted in soft greys or greens and upholstered with bright fabrics to update the old-fashioned combination of dark wood and heavy brocades.

EARLY WORK

Although de Wolfe worked mostly for the wealthy "society" women with whom she mixed socially, she came from a somewhat different background herself. Her first career was in the theatre, as a professional actress, and she only moved into interior decoration as she was approaching 40. The change came about as a result of her decoration (1897–8) of her own home in New York, which she used as a kind of showhouse to encourage others to use her "eye" and her knowledge and skills. In 1905 her reputation was enhanced by the commission to decorate the interior of the Colony Club, the first all-women's club in New York, designed by the architect Stanford White. De Wolfe used this project to experiment with many of the decorating strategies that she believed would result in a fresh approach to the interior. These included an extensive use of flower-printed chintzes; a combination of soft, light colours, including rose pink, grey, pale blue and, most importantly, white; the use of stripes and trelliswork, inspired by 18th-century art; and design, and of French Rococo furniture. Antiques sat alongside new items, but the overall effect was one of lightness and modernity.

The Trellis Room (left), designed for the architect Stanford White's Colony Club, the first all-women's club in New York, built in 1905. The room was illustrated in de Wolfe's book, The House in Good Taste, in a chapter devoted entirely to the use of trellises in interior and exterior settings. De Wolfe also used this form of decoration for several of her projects for private homes, and was largely inspired by the trelliswork in the gardens at the palace of Versailles, near her house.

An interior (below) inside de Wolfe's house, the Villa Trianon in Versailles. She made extensive use of antique European furniture in this scheme, and, as ever, was very dependent on 18th-century French styles for inspiration. The striped wallpaper and light-coloured furnishings were also characteristic of her interiors.

CAREER SUCCESS

The widespread enthusiasm engendered by this project led to several other commissions, and de Wolfe was soon kept busy designing interiors for many of her wealthy social acquaintances. The decoration of her own homes continued to serve as an advertisement to attract other commissions. In 1905, with her former manager and companion Elizabeth Marbury, she bought a house in Versailles, near Paris, called the Villa Trianon (see right), and the transatlantic lifestyle that they led became an important aspect of de Wolfe's work. It enabled her to transport antiques to the United States for use in her interiors and also lent her work a European flavour.

THE HOUSE IN GOOD TASTE

In 1913 de Wolfe further enhanced her reputation through the publication of her book, The House in Good Taste. The book had previously been serialized in Good Housekeeping magazine, which allowed it to reach a wide audience, and was illustrated with photographs of her interiors. In the book de Wolfe described interiors that she had designed, with suggestions for readers on how to create their own modern schemes. In one chapter she advised the use of plain white muslin curtains instead of old-fashioned heavy lace, and was a keen advocate of modern bathrooms and electric lighting. In the 1920s and 1930s she spent an increasing amount of time in France, decorating the homes of expatriate Americans.

De Wolfe maintained her New York office until 1937, when her business was declared bankrupt, and she moved to California with her husband, the British diplomat Sir Charles Mendl, in 1940. Their new house in Beverly Hills, which she decorated with bold stripes, green lacquered walls and large mirrors, was featured in House and Garden magazine.

Like Antoní Gaudí in Barcelona and Victor Horta in Brussels, the Parisian Hector Guimard (1867–1942) can be said to represent the flowering of the Art Nouveau style, which had such a fashionable following among the urban middle class in Europe in the 1890s and early 1900s. Art Nouveau was also an important catalyst in the shift from

Hector Guimard

19th-century historical styles to 20th-century Modernism. Although the sinuous curves characteristic of the style originated in natural forms, in the hands of the best Art Nouveau designers, such as Guimard, they were not only realistic depictions of plants and flowers but also took on a structural and functional role. Guimard's work was only of stylistic interest for a limited period, but his achievements in aligning function and aesthetics were to have longer-lasting effects. His contribution to modern design lay in his consistently rigorous attempts to consider architecture, interiors and decorative art objects as forming a unified environment and to apply to them the same motifs and forms.

The French Art Nouveau architect and designer Hector Guimard, working in his studio. His organically inspired designs for both public and private commissions made a great and lasting impact on the appearance of turn-of-the-century Paris.

Guimard's designs for the Parisian Metro system (begun in 1903) are among his most dramatic and remarkable. Nowhere was the combination of natural imagery both with the object's function and with the structural possibilities of the material more complete than in his light fittings for the Metro stations; these were depicted as stylized buds emerging from the tops of long, sinuous stems. Many of the distinctive entrances survive to this day, and form one of the city's most dramatic features. This contemporary image (right) shows the ironwork at the entrance to the station on the Champs Elysées.

Le Style Guimard
Le Métropolitain
Station des Champs-Élysées

METROPOLITAIN

Hector Guimard
Arch[te] d'Art
Paris

Tous droits de Propriété et
reproduction réservées

EARLY WORK AND THE CASTEL BERANGER

Guimard trained from 1882 to 1885 at the School of Decorative Arts in Paris and for a year in 1889 at the School of Fine Arts in that city. His first commission (1888) was for an interior for the Grand Neptune restaurant on the Quai d'Auteuil in Paris, which featured curvilinear designs and a predominance of wood. From the outset he approached his task as an "ensemblier" – a maker of a set of items forming a whole interior. Guimard used the same approach in his creation of an apartment block, the Castel Béranger (1894–7), in rue La Fontaine in Paris. Here he designed the entire building – interiors, furnishings and architectural accessories – in such a way that they formed an integrated composition. Wrought-iron and copper features such as the grille over the main entrance (see opposite, top left) and the balustrades on the main staircase were striking, asymmetrical compositions of flowing lines, injecting a sense of movement into the otherwise static structure. Guimard's rigorous attention to detail and his desire to control the appearance of the whole building, both inside and out, led him to design such features as floor and wall coverings, lighting fixtures and a range of fitted and free-standing dark mahogany furniture, all characterized by asymmetrical, elongated forms or carved decoration.

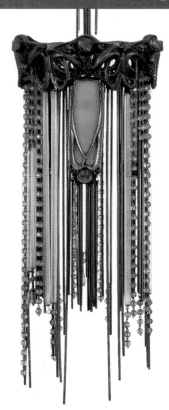

The decorative wrought-iron and copper gate at the entrance to Guimard's Castel Béranger (1894–7; above), an apartment block in Paris designed in the curvilinear style that was to become the trademark of Art Nouveau. The asymmetry of the gate and the motif of the attenuated line looping back on itself were features that Guimard repeated in the furnishings throughout the building, from staircases to wallpaper and carpets.

METRO STATIONS

At the Paris Universal Exhibition of 1889 Guimard worked on the Art Nouveau-style Pavilion of Electricity, a display of generating equipment. This commitment to designing for the modern age reached its height in his fantastic designs, begun in 1903, for stations for the Parisian Metro system. His use of cast and wrought iron combined with glass in this project demonstrated his dedication to modern materials, while his rejection of classical form and ornament showed the strength of his desire to move away from historical styles in architecture and design, leaving him free to create his own visual language, mainly inspired by organic forms.

LATER DESIGNS

Guimard's involvement with designing architectural accessories – for example, grilles, door-handles and window latches – preoccupied him throughout his career and he designed the ironwork for many of his projects. He also continued to design furniture – including chairs, tables and cupboards – for his own house, for Hôtel Guimard (1909) and for Hôtel Mezzura (1910). The dark mahogany of his furnishings for the Castel Béranger gave way to lighter materials such as pearwood. These elaborately carved pieces were covered with richly patterned upholstery.

In 1920 Guimard produced his first standardized range of furniture, but by then the Art Nouveau style had faded out of fashion, and although he showed some work at the Paris Decorative Arts Exhibition of 1925, his contribution to modern design was complete. Even though his style was supplanted by more geometric forms, it was Guimard's ability to create a new style, unencumbered by the influences of previous centuries, that gave a new sense of freedom to the designers who followed him.

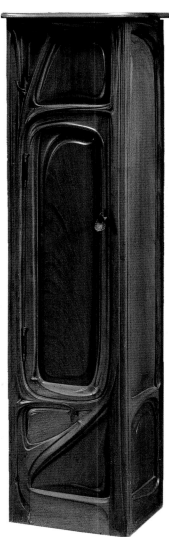

A ceiling light (above), made of bronze and glass, designed c.1908. The rich decorative detail of the light is combined with an underlying practicality in the designer's commitment to the modern power source, electricity.

A mahogany cabinet designed c.1902–3 (left). The asymmetrical, vegetal relief pattern carved into the surface is typical of Guimard's furniture designs, as are the framed panels. Although the inspiration for Guimard's swirling motifs came from nature, their clean lines lend these designs an almost abstract quality that signifies the designer's concern with the creation of modern forms.

Paris 1900

In the second half of the 19th century there was nothing to match the impact of the huge international exhibitions and world's fairs, which brought new technologies and mass-produced goods within the reach of a general audience for the first time. Their role in spreading taste was unprecedented. The Universal Exhibition held in Paris in 1900 followed an exhibition on a comparable scale that had been held in the same city 11 years previously, and which had established Art Nouveau as a specifically French achievement. The 1900 event set out to repeat the success of its predecessor; to reiterate the French origins of this ubiquitous style; and to celebrate success in Europe in the years after 1889, especially in the fields of interior design and the decorative arts.

LOCATION AND LAYOUT

The Paris Exhibition was constructed on the Champ de Mars, with the Esplanade des Invalides and the Champs Elysées constituting the central focus, and it included two palaces – the Petit Palais and the Grand Palais – in its scope. Lasting for several months, it attracted many thousands of visitors who passed through a dramatic entryway, called the Porte Binet (named for its architect), which sought to emulate the impact made by the Eiffel Tower at the 1889 event. At the top of this huge gate was a statue of a woman called the "Parisienne", a sign of the predominantly feminine nature of the fair, epitomized by the sinuous Art Nouveau forms and the stress on interior decor. The site was covered with pavilions, mainly French, but also representing other European countries such as the Netherlands. The Austrian presence was especially strong, with contributions from Viennese architects and designers Josef Hoffmann (see pp.34–7) and Otto Wagner (see pp.12–13); however, a little surprisingly, the work of the Belgian Henry van de Velde (see pp.16–17) and the Scotsman Charles Rennie Mackintosh (see pp.26–9), both leading designers of the period, was not represented.

THE PURPOSE AND IMPACT OF THE EXHIBITION

Paris 1900 served a number of functions, nearly all of them nationalistic. It set out to show that Art Nouveau style had reached a peak of popularity and was a specifically French invention, rooted in 18th-century artistic achievements and in 19th-century technological breakthroughs in iron manufacturing. It also aimed to demonstrate that the decorative arts held a pre-eminent position in France, thus helping to associate the idea of French design with "quality" in the eyes of the rest of Europe.

The main impact of the exhibition was, without any doubt, the success of French Art Nouveau as a style for the modern domestic interior and the decorative arts. The leading dealer, Samuel Bing, from whose Paris shop, the Maison de l'Art Nouveau, the style took its name, presented a pavilion featuring interiors with designs by Eugène Gaillard, Georges de Feure and

A carved mahogany vitrine (left), specially designed by V. Epaux for the Paris Exhibition of 1900. The curvilinear but symmetrical forms of the apple blossom relief carved into its surface reflect an 18th-century Rococo influence, which was considered an important factor in the development of French Art Nouveau at the time.

A bedroom suite (right) by the furniture designer Eugène Gaillard, exhibited in Samuel Bing's highly influential Pavilion of Art Nouveau, which contained six rooms with decoration and furnishings by French artists. The exhibits here showed the strong influence of 18th-century French design – a theme dominating the exhibition and also seen in the display of Rococo furniture in the Petit Palais.

A poster advertising the exhibition (below), designed by Georges Leroux. The image of a woman in draped clothing, shown here holding a moon, was a motif used throughout the event.

Edward Colonna. Other French exhibits, including the Pavilion of the Central Union of the Decorative Arts, displayed the work of the luxury ateliers, representing the close bond between fine art and craft production. Furniture, ceramics, metalwork and interior decor by leading contemporary artists and designers such as Hector Guimard (see pp.20–1), Louis Majorelle and Emile Gallé took pride of place. The display of products of the traditional French decorative art manufacturers, including the Sèvres porcelain factory and the Gobelins tapestry factory, also emphasized the strong sense of continuity between the past and present, which was such an important theme for the organizers of the exhibition. Simultaneously, there was also an emphasis on the modern age, exemplified predominantly by the role of electricity at the exhibition. This was expressed overtly in the Pavilion of Electricity but also more subtly through the use of electric power to drive the water fountains of the impressive Château d'Eau, which served as a complex façade to the pavilion. Because of such technological displays, the exhibition was characterized by a new sense of movement and energy.

THE DECLINE OF ART NOUVEAU

Although the next significant international exhibition, held in Turin in 1902, still paid considerable homage to Art Nouveau, the style was by this time less all-encompassing. This was partly due to the emphasis on elaborate hand-crafting, which meant that much Art Nouveau furniture could not be produced on any scale. Within a few years it had given way to the more machine-inspired geometric style associated with Vienna. Josef Hoffmann's offering at Paris 1900 – rooms designed for the Viennese School of Applied Arts and for the Secession, characterized by strong horizontals and verticals and without any references to the organic forms of Art Nouveau – were, in retrospect, perhaps the most prophetic displays of all.

A panoramic view of the Universal Exhibition site (below), along the banks of the Seine. The Eiffel Tower, built for the preceding exhibition of 1889, still provided a point of focus. Shown in the centre foreground is the distinctive exhibition entrance, the Porte Binet.

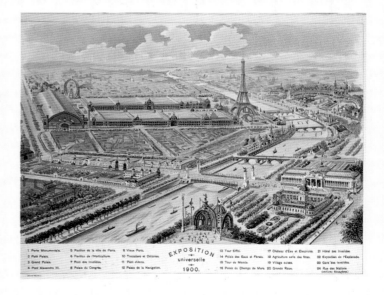

Although most pioneers of modern design active around the turn of the century were based in Europe, the United States also played a crucial part in bringing about the dramatic shift from styles inspired by the art of the past to design for the modern age. In both the United States and Europe architects played a leading role in this transformation,

Frank Lloyd Wright

working not only on building exteriors but also on the design of their interior spaces and contents – in the modern context, the interior was seen as an extension of the exterior. The American architect Frank Lloyd Wright (1867–1959) is most often linked with this change in the United States, and he had an incomparable influence on European design thought and practice before and after World War I.

Frank Lloyd Wright was one of the few 20th-century American architects whose influence was strongly felt in Europe right up to the years following World War II.

The "barrel" armchair was designed for the Darwin D. Martin House (1904–5; below). The use of wood combined with a strong rectilinear emphasis is a distinctive feature of Wright's early furniture designs.

EARLY WORK AND THE "PRAIRIE HOUSES"

Trained as an engineer at the University of Wisconsin (1885–7), but determined to excel at architecture, Wright practised as an architect in and around Chicago from 1887 onwards, most notably between 1889 and 1892 in the office of Dankmar Adler and Louis Sullivan. In 1896 he set up his own practice and began work on a number of domestic architecture projects. His approach to the design of these houses was influenced by Japanese beliefs regarding the lines between interiors and exteriors, and the symbolism of open spaces. The term "Prairie House" is widely used to describe the type of free-standing domestic residence that he designed from the mid-1890s to the early 1900s for a number of progressive clients. These were characterized by an emphasis on horizontal lines, asymmetrical plans and natural materials, especially wood.

Wright considered the internal space, furnishings and decorative details of a building intrinsic to the architecture and preferred to offer his clients an integrated building and interior designed entirely by him. He aimed to build what he described as "organic architecture" – buildings that seemed to grow naturally from the landscape. Furnishings, designed and placed by Wright, often took on the role of spatial dividers instead of walls. In the Ward Willitts House (1901–2) in Highland Park, Chicago, he added built-in seating with a horizontal emphasis around the fireplace to create a visual focal point in the interior.

FURNITURE DESIGN

Wright's preoccupation with geometric forms and intersecting planes in his architecture led him to develop a similar style for pieces of furniture. These were simple wooden structures, often rectilinear and box-like and with exaggerated elements – usually the back – to emphasize their role in creating internal space. Perhaps Wright's greatest achievements in this field were the metal desks and chairs that he designed for the Larkin Building in Buffalo, New York, in 1904: among the first metal items of furniture to be

"The Tree of Life", a leaded glass window (1904–5; below), designed by Wright for the Darwin D. Martin House in Buffalo, New York, and manufactured by the Linden Glass Company. The emphasis on verticals recalls the decorative work of Charles Rennie Mackintosh (see pp.26–9), and is characteristic of Wright's window designs from the first decade of the century.

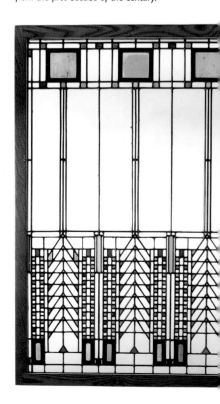

A porcelain plate setting, designed by Wright for the Imperial Hotel, Tokyo (1915–22; above). After his death the pieces were manufactured by the Japanese company Noritake.

A view (left) of Wright's Frederick C. Robie House (1909) in Chicago, Illinois. This view of the living-room terrace shows the strong horizontal emphasis of the design and its attachment to the land on which it was built.

The "Imperial Tokyo" armchair (below), created for the Imperial Hotel as part of Wright's integrated scheme. This design, like the "barrel" chair shown opposite, was reproduced by the Italian company Cassina (see pp.212–13) in the 1980s.

used indoors that did not set out to imitate wood. The chairs were made of painted steel with leather upholstered seats and swivelling steel bases on casters; the backs were rigidly geometric with square perforations. These were radical objects, in terms of the material used and of their minimal, geometric style, and set a new standard for the design of office furniture.

OTHER DESIGNS

In addition to designing built-in storage and seating, which he regarded as a direct extension of his creation of the building structure, Wright also designed stained-glass windows (see opposite, right), as well as glass, ceramics, metalwork and textiles. For the Imperial Hotel (1915–22) in Tokyo, for example, he provided a wide range of such decorative and utility objects (see right and above, right).

LATER CAREER

Following a period in Japan, Wright returned to the United States and continued to create such innovative buildings as "Fallingwater" (1935–9), built for Edgar Kaufmann at Bear Run, Pennsylvania. The house is fully integrated into the landscape, with stone vertical elements supporting a concrete structure cantilevered over a waterfall. While it is as a progressive architect and theorist that Wright is ultimately remembered, his impact on European design, especially the work of the Dutch De Stijl designers such as Gerrit Rietveld (see pp.98–101), should not be underestimated.

Perhaps no single architect-designer played as unique a role in the early formation of the modern design movement as the Scotsman Charles Rennie Mackintosh (1868–1928). In spite of living much of his life in what at the time was regarded as the somewhat marginal city of Glasgow – seemingly far from such centres of avant-garde

Charles Rennie Mackintosh

"The Four", with a group of their friends, photographed at Dunure in the mid-1890s. Frances Macdonald is at the top, her sister Margaret Macdonald is on the extreme left, and Herbert McNair (left) and Charles Rennie Mackintosh (right) are lounging at the front.

With the exception of a slightly different head-rest, this high-backed oak chair (right) of 1898–9 is identical to the one designed two years previously by Mackintosh for Miss Cranston's Tea Rooms in Argyle Street, Glasgow. Mackintosh often used high-backed chairs in his interiors to echo or enhance the architectural features of the rooms.

artistic activity as Paris, Vienna and Brussels – he made a dramatic and highly individual contribution to modern design. Mackintosh's greatest achievements date from his early career. In the years around 1900, with the help of his three close collaborators – his wife Margaret Macdonald, her sister Frances Macdonald, and Frances' husband Herbert McNair (the group referred to collectively as "The Four") – his name was celebrated across Europe as one of the most original and inspired designers of the day. By the time Mackintosh left Glasgow for London in 1913, however, he was suffering from depression and disappointment that his early successes and international reputation could not be sustained, and this was to overshadow the rest of his life.

A NEW STYLE

Mackintosh is perhaps best known for his radical architectural projects. The Glasgow School of Art, completed in 1909, and two houses near Glasgow – Windyhill (1900–1) and Hill House (1903) – were remarkably innovative in their clean, modern appearances and light-filled interiors. However, it was in his designs for furniture, stained glass, textiles and metalwork that much of his genius resided. He brought together new abstract forms, with an emphasis on horizontal and vertical lines, and heavily stylized designs with a symbolism derived from nature and the human body. Flowers were drawn in a simplified, stylized manner with elongated stems and tendrils to form abstract motifs that took on lives of their own in the context of his work. His was a unique combination of influences: interlaced Celtic forms and motifs, linear Japanese aesthetics and Arts and Crafts and Pre-Raphaelite imagery. While all these elements were present as sources for a new style, only Mackintosh merged them so effectively.

EARLY CAREER AND INTEREST IN SYMBOLISM

Mackintosh's early career was as an architectural apprentice in Glasgow. In 1889 he met the draughtsman Herbert McNair while working in the office of the architects Honeyman & Keppie. The two attended drawing

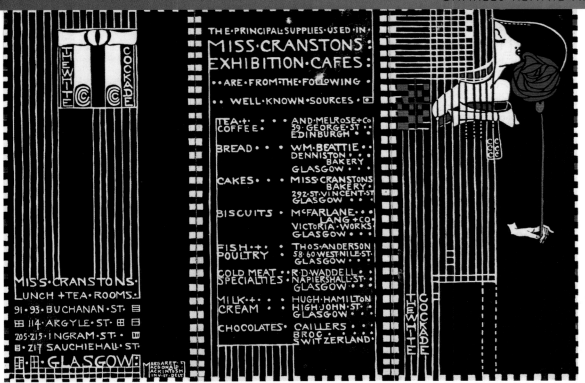

An illustration for a menu (left), designed by Margaret Macdonald in 1911 for Miss Cranston's White Cockade Tea Rooms and Restaurant – a project created for the Glasgow Exhibition of that year. Macdonald contributed her illustrative talents to many of her husband's decorative schemes, which typically involved elegant female figures and sinuous vegetal motifs.

A chest – originally made for Windyhill – and light fittings (below), all designed by Mackintosh. The circular flower motif and purple colour scheme are both typical of Mackintosh's decorative style.

classes at the Glasgow School of Art in the evenings and, along with their fellow students, Margaret and Frances Macdonald, began to work together on a number of projects, including posters and decorative art objects. Their work at that time – and the poster designs in particular – showed a strong fine-art emphasis, with echoes of the work of the illustrator Aubrey Beardsley and of Art Nouveau forms.

In the mid-1890s Mackintosh was clearly attracted to the artistic movement known as Symbolism, which incorporated familiar imagery – idealized women, flowing hair and garments, flowers and birds – suggesting universal, abstract themes such as love and death. In as early as 1893, he also began designing furniture. Most of his pieces from the mid-1890s were relatively simple oak cupboards or other storage items, created for individual commissions.

DEVELOPMENTS IN 1900

The year 1900 was crucial for Mackintosh and his collaborators. In that year he began work on Windyhill, the house he designed for William Davidson; he also exhibited at the Eighth Secession Exhibition in Vienna at the invitation of the architect-designer Josef Hoffmann (see pp.34–7), who was thus largely responsible for introducing Mackintosh's work to a Viennese and thence to an international audience. Mackintosh also married Margaret Macdonald in 1900, and their close collaboration was to underpin all his work from that date onwards. Margaret's sinuous depictions of elongated women and natural motifs (see above) embellished many of Mackintosh's interiors and furniture.

THEORIES OF INTERIOR DESIGN

Unlike William Morris, C.R. Ashbee, C.F.A. Voysey and other members of the British Arts and Crafts Movement, Mackintosh was less a social idealist campaigning for "Art for all" than a man with an artistic vision. Equally, he was less committed to the ethic of craftsmanship, epitomized in the maxim "Truth to materials", than to the creation of striking forms and images that communicated his new vision of integrated architecture and interior design.

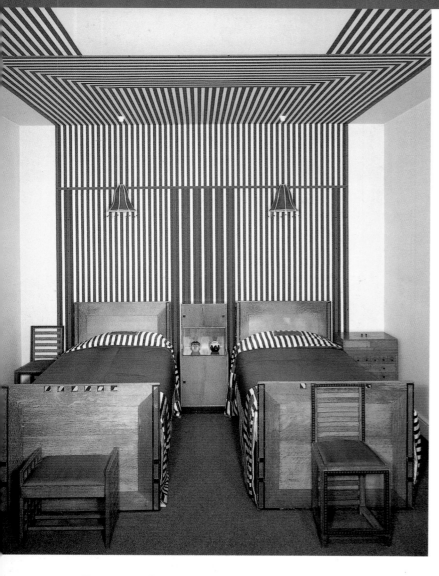

Inspired by German and Austrian design principles, he sought to unite buildings and their contents in the creation of "complete works of art" in which all the elements of an interior were linked to the exterior and to each other through a sense of visual harmony.

Two interiors stand out to demonstrate how Mackintosh created spaces in which the whole was ultimately greater than the sum of its parts. In his design of 1900 for the interior of 120 Mains Street in Glasgow, his first home with Margaret Macdonald, he emphasized the interplay between horizontals and verticals through the lines created by the backs of his tall chairs, the panels on the wall, a frieze rail positioned halfway up the wall and his suspended lights. Colours were muted – white, cream and soft grey – highlighted by spots of purple. The geometric effect of the basic structure of the interior was offset by dried flowers, arranged in a Japanese style, and by strategically positioned Japanese prints. The scheme was undoubtedly a collaborative effort on the part of the young married couple, the husband providing the geometric frame and the wife the decorative detail. In the famous "Rose Boudoir", exhibited at the Turin Exhibition of Modern Decorative Art in 1902, the Mackintoshes repeated this successful collaboration. Their design once again combined geometric structure and careful proportion with decorative highlights that stressed the organic and the natural – stylized women's faces, long flowing hair, curvilinear forms and simplified rose motifs. The furniture that Mackintosh designed around 1900 was also conceived as a series of elements within a whole, each piece playing a part in creating a sense of visual harmony. These included: his famous tall ladder-back chairs for Hill House; numerous pieces for Windyhill; those for Miss Cranston's chain of tea rooms in Glasgow (1898–9 and 1903; see below), the interiors of which he also designed; and the painted and stained cupboards, desks, beds and items of fitted furniture.

The guest bedroom (above) at 78 Derngate, Northampton, a house adapted for W. J. Bassett-Lowke and his wife (1916–1917). Mackintosh gave the house a new rear elevation and a new interior with specially designed furnishings. He abandoned the floral motifs of earlier interiors for a simpler, linear style.

A painted settee (right) designed in 1917 for the Dug-Out – a basement room in Miss Cranston's Willow Tea Rooms in Glasgow – named after the trenches in World War I. The geometric effects created by the use of horizontal and vertical lines were particularly evident in Mackintosh's later designs and also much favoured by his contemporaries at the Wiener Werkstätte (see pp.38–9).

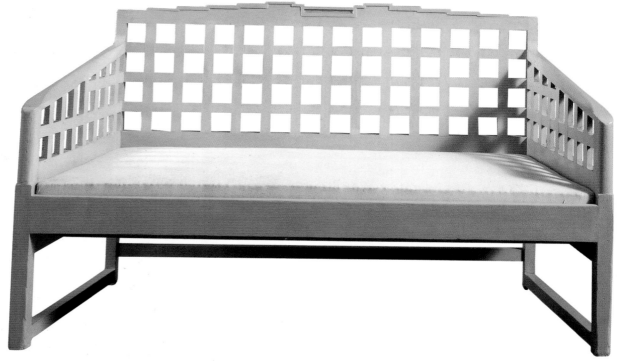

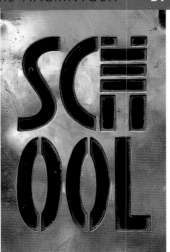

Hill House, Helensburgh, 25 miles west of Glasgow, is seen from the south-east in this drawing (left). Commissioned by the publisher Walter Blackie, the house, designed in 1903, was stunningly modern, but nevertheless drew upon Scottish Baronial architectural traditions.

INTERNATIONAL SUCCESS AND ARCHITECTURAL DESIGN

The years 1900 to 1906 were Mackintosh's most prolific. He exhibited widely, gaining a pan-European reputation. A number of commissions arose directly from the success of his exhibited work. In 1902 he was asked by the Viennese banker (and financial backer of the Wiener Werkstätte), Fritz Wärndorfer, to design a music room. As with the interiors described previously, Mackintosh introduced white panelling on the walls, a frieze rail, hanging lights and a selection of tall-backed chairs.

One of Mackintosh's greatest achievements was the Glasgow School of Art, built in two phases from 1897 to 1899 and from 1907 to 1909. It ranks highly, not only as an exercise in which function – rather than decoration – determines form, but also as a "Gesamtkunstwerk": a total work of art, in which even the smallest features – down to the iron brackets outside the windows to hold the window cleaner's ladder – play a vital part. Every interior and exterior detail reveals the designer's hand.

LATE DESIGNS

Within a few years, however, the requests for work started to come less frequently, and Mackintosh left Glasgow for London in 1913. His notable works in the years during and after World War I included a house for the industrialist W.J. Bassett-Lowke (1916–17; see opposite, above) and, through the 1920s, textile designs using stylized motifs such as flowers and stems.

The tea rooms, interiors and major architectural works mark Mackintosh as one of the group of designers whose sensibility enabled them to be at the forefront of design during the transition of the 19th to the 20th century. Mackintosh's sharp awareness of the need for a new approach to architecture and design, one that recognized the importance of structure but also took into account the role of decoration, has made his work one of the richest early contributions to modern design.

The Glasgow School of Art, designed by Mackintosh and constructed between 1897–9 and 1907–9, was one of the architect's greatest achievements. He was responsible for all aspects of the exterior and interior, down to the last detail. Pictured here is an example of the innovative graphics and dramatic interior spaces created for the project, in the form of a metal panel (top right), and the library (right).

Despite the wide variety of his achievements in modern design, architecture and visual culture, Peter Behrens (1868–1940) is often simply described as the first designer for industry in the modern sense. While many credit the 19th-century English designer Christopher Dresser with this achievement, Behrens was probably the first artist

Peter Behrens

to apply his skills to the creation of an entire visual identity for a manufacturer of modern, standardized technological products. As a consultant designer for buildings, products and graphics for the German electrical company AEG between 1907 and 1914 he enhanced the company's reputation as design-oriented, progressive and, above all, coordinated. In this he anticipated the work of later industrial consultant designers such as Walter Dorwin Teague (see pp.116–17), Norman Bel Geddes and Raymond Loewy (see pp.120–23), who performed a similar role for large American corporations during the 1930s. Behrens saw himself as something of a cultural reformer and sought, through mass production, to introduce good design into the lives and everyday environments of ordinary people.

A portrait of Peter Behrens painted in 1913 by the German artist Max Liebermann when the sitter was 45 years old and had achieved a great level of success as both an architect and an industrial designer.

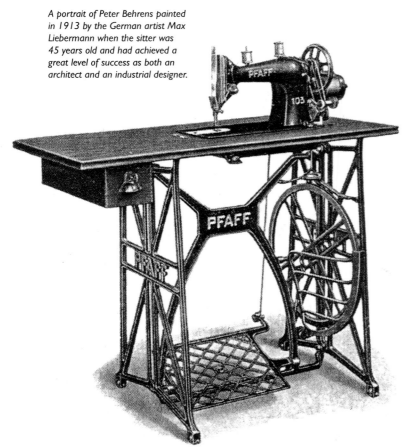

TRAINING AND EARLY WORK

Behrens trained as a painter and devoted his early career in the 1890s to this art. He became involved with a succession of modern artistic movements, including Impressionism and Symbolism, as if in search of an appropriate form of personal expression. He participated in the first Munich Secession Exhibition of 1893 – an event dominated by artists who, like their counterparts in the later Vienna Secession, wanted to move away from academic painting – and received a positive response to the work he showed there. During the 1890s he exhibited more work at these annual events, and his reputation grew as a result. At the end of the decade he moved into producing woodcuts: a notable work in this medium was *The Kiss* (1898), featuring stylistic echoes of the work of the Englishman Aubrey Beardsley and clearly following the international Art Nouveau style in its use of flat, sinuous lines.

In the 1890s Behrens also designed furniture, porcelain, metalwork and glass in a restrained Art Nouveau style, demonstrating his growing interest in the craft process. In 1897 he helped form the United Workshops for Art in Crafts, a Munich-based organization devoted to raising the status of craft to that of fine art. After this he produced several designs for German manufacturers including wine glasses made by Benedikt von Poschinger of Oberswieselau (1898), jewellery by Schreger of Darmstadt (1901) and cutlery by Ruckert of Mainz (1902; see opposite, top right). Behrens also

Behrens designed this sewing machine in 1910 (left) for the German company Pfaff. The commission came following his successful work for AEG, which proved his skill in designing goods of a technical nature while also taking aesthetic concerns into account.

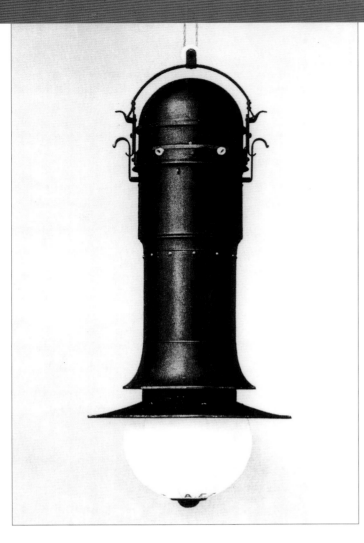

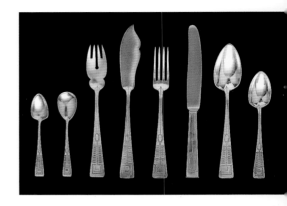

A hanging arc lamp designed for AEG in 1907 (left). The lamp, which beamed light straight through the reflector, was intended for use in interiors with low ceilings.

Silver cutlery (right) designed by Behrens in 1902 for his own house, and manufactured by Ruckert in Mainz. The softly geometric patterns on the handles are characteristic of the way in which Behrens simplified Art Nouveau decorations.

During his time in Darmstadt, Behrens was also involved with theatre production and design, writing the booklet "Feste" (1900), in which he described the ideal theatre. He subsequently worked on three interiors for the Turin International Exhibition of 1902. The major shift in his career came when he left the artists' colony, became Director of the School of Applied Arts in Düsseldorf in 1903, and began to earn a reputation as an architect and designer in the modern style with his work for the German electrical company Allgemeine Elektricitäts Gesellschaft (AEG).

A side chair (below) designed by Behrens in 1903 for the Hamburg home of his friend, the poet Richard Dehmel. The curved Art Nouveau silhouette is very restrained in this piece, a quality also present in the work of Behrens's Belgian contemporary, Henry van de Velde (see pp. 16–17).

presented woodcuts and bookbindings in the German pavilion at the Paris Universal Exhibition of 1900. During the first decade of his career he had established himself as a significant figure in international art and design.

DARMSTADT

The year 1900 was an important one for Behrens. He moved to Darmstadt to become a member of an artistic colony, modelled partly on the British Arts and Crafts Movement. The colony was founded in 1898 and included among its members Hans Christiansen, a designer of furniture, ceramics and glass; Rudolf Bosselt, a sculptor and medallist; and Patriz Hüber, who designed interiors, furniture and metalwork. In 1901 Behrens built a house for himself in Darmstadt. This ambitious project was an impressive "Gesamtkunstwerk" (total work of art): he was responsible for the design of every detail, and the house represents the full range of his skills as designer and self-taught architect. It was still in the Art Nouveau style, although a new simplicity was in evidence in the subtly curved forms of the exterior.

The house was more than an artistic achievement alone – it was also a statement about Behrens as a family man, as it was conceived as an ideal family home. At the age of 21 Behrens had married Lilli Kramer, and they had two children: Josef (b.1890) and Petra (b.1898). Behrens' desire to build a home for himself and his family represented, perhaps, an idealistic and optimistic statement about a better way of life in the new century. The reformist designers William Morris and Henry van de Velde (see pp. 16–17) had also built homes for their families, and this link between progressive theory and practice was to remain strong within 20th-century design.

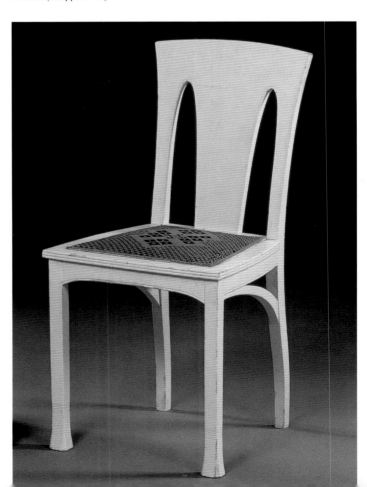

A "Synchron" double-sided electric clock (c.1910; above), with a brass case and sheet steel face. The functional simplicity of this easy-read clock reflects Behrens' concern that mass-produced items for factories and offices should be as standardized as possible.

WORK FOR AEG

The commission from AEG provided Behrens with an opportunity to move from the design of hand-crafted goods and domestic architecture to that of mass-manufactured goods and industrial buildings. From 1907 the company's managing director, Walther Rathenau, employed Behrens to design a range of products, from arc lamps, electric kettles and fans to brochures and cutlery for the workers' canteen. The functional and technological nature of such items encouraged Behrens to abandon the ornate curves of Art Nouveau in favour of much simpler, more utilitarian forms.

He did not, however, reject decoration and references to craft entirely: his designs for electric kettles, with their soft lines and woven cane handles, looked as much like traditional teapots as electrical appliances (right). This link between traditional forms and modern design was also apparent

Behrens designed a range of electric kettles for AEG in 1909, which were available in a choice of three shapes and several finishes. These examples (right) are both nickel-plated, with hammered surfaces to give the impression of hand-crafting. Other versions had a plainer, mass-produced appearance.

in Behrens' graphic work for AEG, whereas his designs for fans and arc lamps (see p.31, top left), destined to be used in factories and other public buildings, were much more assertively "machine-like" and made no concessions to decoration. The strongly industrial idiom was also evident in the famous AEG turbine factory, designed by Behrens between 1908 and 1909. At the same time, however, his concern was to "beautify" the AEG products as much as was practically possible, if only through attention to their proportions; he maintained that "a motor ought to look like a birthday present." This statement in many ways anticipated what was to become one of the key ambitions of later professional industrial designers in their emphasis on styling.

Behrens' work for AEG, based on a functionalist approach, was more radical than anything else in the design world at this time. It was the first time that a designer took on the role of creating a visual image appropriate for the modern age, with all its accompanying demands and innovations.

LATER CAREER AND INFLUENCE

Although Behrens' work for AEG was one of the earliest examples of modern industrial design, in his own career it was an isolated episode, although he went on to design some very simple pieces of furniture for working-class families in 1912. He dedicated most of the rest of his life to architecture, moving into a neoclassical style after 1907. He was also deeply committed to the German programme of design reform initiated by the Deutscher Werkbund, an organization (est. 1907) that numbered manufacturers, architects, designers and politicians among its members and which campaigned strongly for a design movement appropriate to the new industrial age. Behrens also played an important role in fostering new ideas among the next generation of architects; for a period in 1910, three men who were to become "heroes" of the Modern Movement in architecture – Le Corbusier, Walter Gropius and Ludwig Mies van der Rohe (see pp.94–7, 88–9 and 92–3) – all worked in his office at the start of their careers.

EIN LANDHAUS IN SCHLACHTENSEE

Von PETER BEHRENS

Mich leitete dieser Gedanke: Wenn man für einen Menschen ein Haus baut, so muß es sein wie ein Porträt, ihm ähnlich und sein Wesen abspiegelnd. Mit diesem Ziel war es mir eine besondere Freude, Herrn Universitätsprofessor Kurt Lewin zu einer Wohnstätte behilflich zu sein. Die Aufgabe war interessant, weil es sich hier darum handeln mußte, ohne Aufwand großer materieller Mittel, nach der Gesinnung des Bewohners die Einfachheit seines Wesens auszudrücken und von meinem eigenen Standpunkt aus die Formidee zu finden, die ihr gemäß sei.

Solche Erwägungen wurden mir erleichtert durch überlegte Wünsche des Bauherrn, der das Haus nicht allein mit seinen nächsten Angehörigen, sondern mit einem Verwandten bewohnen wollte, der seinen eigenen Kreis beanspruchte. Das bedingte eine klare Zweiteilung des Grundrisses und ergab sich in der äußeren Erscheinung die deutliche Gliederung der Baumasse mit einem abgeschlossenen Flügelanbau, auf dessen Terrasse sich aber, wie im gemeinsam benutzten Garten, alle Familienmitglieder nach Wunsch zusammenfinden können.

P. B.

A page from Die Neue Linie *(The New Line; published 1932)* with text by Behrens, illustrating a country house in Schlachtensee designed by him (above). The house's clean lines and functional forms became the trademarks of the great Modernist architects Le Corbusier, Gropius and Mies van der Rohe, all of whom worked briefly in Behrens' architectural practice.

The entrance hall (left) at the headquarters of Höchst AG in Höchst am Main (1920–24). The monumental concrete forms and textural surfaces in this example had been used by Behrens for earlier industrial commissions, most notably the AEG Turbine Factory in Berlin (1908–9).

JOSEF HOFFMANN

By the turn of the century the Austrian city of Vienna was playing a key role in defining a new architecture and design that was rapidly becoming internationally significant. The pioneering work of Otto Wagner (see pp.12–13) and the artists and designers of the Vienna Secession had created a climate of innovation and an optimistic sense of

Josef Hoffmann

progress in their rejection of historical styles. The architect and designer Josef Hoffmann (1870–1956), a founder member of the Secession, played an important part in both the creation and the dissemination of progressive ideas in design. He produced a vast body of work, from buildings to furniture to flower vases, which was to prove hugely influential on the next generation of architects.

Josef Hoffmann is shown here seated on one of his own designs. His influential and widespread design ethic was based on the theories of the Arts and Crafts Movement developed by John Ruskin and William Morris in Britain. However, while Morris' ideas of social reform were based on hand-crafting, Hoffmann sought to bring good design to the public through more modern, industrialized channels. Hoffmann's monogram is shown above, top; the other members of the Secession and the Wiener Werkstätte had similar logos, which were sometimes used as marks to sign their work.

APPROACH TO DESIGN

In all his work Hoffmann deliberately rejected historical models and applied decoration derived directly from the natural world. Instead, he concentrated on abstract and geometric shapes, which had a strong symbolic impact in a world dominated by the advent of mass production and rationalized, systematic manufacture. This is not to say that Hoffmann rejected decoration. Rather, he succeeded in making it subservient to and dependent on the dominant geometric structure that he believed should determine the form of buildings, interiors and objects. This was clearly visible in his early interior designs, many of which were included in the Secession exhibitions from 1898 to 1900. In these designs, the rectilinear, cube-shaped furniture pieces, often built into the room and frequently elongated in form to emphasize visually their structural role, were usually offset by decorative items and pattern, such as vases of flowers, and sinuous lines and motifs on rugs and walls (see opposite, left). Hoffmann relied on the power of this visual contrast between decoration and geometric form throughout his creative career.

TRAINING AND THE VIENNA SECESSION

Born in Pirnitz – now part of the Czech Republic – Hoffmann studied architecture initially in Brno and, from 1892 to 1895, at the Vienna Academy, where he was taught by Otto Wagner. He appears to have been a serious man and was clearly ambitious and highly motivated. His work as a teacher, from 1899 to 1936, and his continuous commitment to group endeavours suggest, however, that he shared his ideas willingly with others.

Hoffmann worked in Wagner's studio from 1896 to 1897. In 1897 Hoffmann also co-founded the radical group, the Vienna Secession, with the artist Gustav Klimt and the designers Koloman Moser and Joseph Maria Olbrich. From then on he designed prolifically and acted as a spokesman in Vienna for ideas he saw emerging elsewhere. Between 1897 and 1900 he worked on numerous interiors, among them the "Ver Sacrum" room in

In Hoffmann's side chair, model 371 (c.1906; below), the stark vertical lines of the back are relieved by the small wooden balls – a recurring feature in Hoffmann's seating furniture – that were also used to strengthen joints.

An 1899 sketch (above) for an early
interior by Hoffmann. The furniture
items are part of a total ensemble,
dominated by a characteristic use of
vertical and horizontal lines. The use of
some restrained curves – for example,
in the chair – was replaced by a much
stricter geometrical emphasis in his
later designs.

A view of the entrance area in the
sanatorium at Purkersdorf in Austria
(right), designed in 1904. The influence
of neoclassical structure can be seen
both in the monumental pillars and
in the strict symmetry of the hall,
but the simplicity of the interior is
strikingly modern. The entrance area
incorporates armchairs designed by
Koloman Moser, a fellow founder
member of the Wiener Werkstätte.

The Palais Stoclet in Brussels, designed by Hoffmann between 1905 and 1911 (right), was one of the architect's most significant achievements. While its exterior shows his mastery of rectilinear form, the interior demonstrates his ability to combine function and decoration harmoniously without detriment to either.

Joseph Maria Olbrich's Secession building and, in 1899, a scheme for the house of the industrialist Paul Wittgenstein in Vienna. Hoffmann was also chosen to be one of the Viennese representatives at the Universal Exhibition in Paris of 1900 (see pp.22–3). The starkly geometric room installations he presented stood out from the flamboyant French exhibits characterized by the curves of the Art Nouveau style. He established links with the Glaswegian architect Charles Rennie Mackintosh (see pp.26–9), asking him to exhibit at the Eighth Secession Exhibition of 1900 and, in 1903, was a major force behind the formation of the Wiener Werkstätte (see pp. 38–9). By the early 1900s Hoffmann was established internationally as one of the most promising young architects and designers of the day.

ARCHITECTURAL PROJECTS

Hoffmann began his architectural career in 1900, designing four villas in a suburb in Vienna, which were constructed between 1901 and 1905. In 1904 he designed a sanatorium in Purkersdorf (see p.35), for which he developed his famous "cubistic" language of form with its emphasis on straight, unadorned lines; this startlingly modern-looking building, complete with interior fittings, was hugely influential on later modern architecture. Like

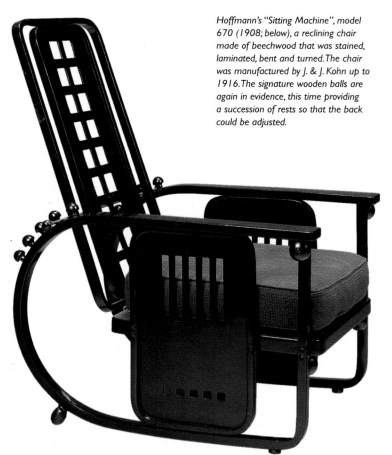

Hoffmann's "Sitting Machine", model 670 (1908; below), a reclining chair made of beechwood that was stained, laminated, bent and turned. The chair was manufactured by J. & J. Kohn up to 1916. The signature wooden balls are again in evidence, this time providing a succession of rests so that the back could be adjusted.

Wagner's, Hoffmann's early architectural and interior projects were conceived from the start as *Gesamtkunstwerke* (total works of art) – an idea promoted by the Secession. Outstanding examples include the Palais Stoclet (1905–11; see above) in Brussels, where he collaborated on the interior with Gustav Klimt, and the Fledermaus Café in Vienna (1907).

FURNITURE DESIGNS

Like Wagner, Hoffmann regarded a building as being inseparable from its contents. Furnishings played a key part in his work, and he produced many pieces, both built-in and free-standing, for his interiors. Once again, the idea of geometric structure dominated these designs, whether they were cabinets, chairs, tables or stools. Hoffmann is perhaps best known for the strikingly simple dining chairs, several intended for cafés, that he designed in the first decade of the 20th century. These "sitting machines", as Hoffmann called them, were characterized by structural simplicity and restrained decoration (see left). The repeated use of small balls positioned at stress points in a number of chair designs was Hoffmann's way of using a decorative feature to emphasize the construction of the object rather than simply as a superficial extra. The manufacturing company J. & J. Kohn put a number of Hoffmann's furniture items into production, so that his designs became influential throughout Europe and the United States.

CERAMICS, METALWORK AND GLASS

Hoffmann's designs for other decorative arts, including ceramics, metalwork and glass, followed the same principles as his architecture: in other words, they were based on an approach that emphasized his interest in structure. These designs were exhibited widely, including at the Turin International

Exhibition of 1902. Glass, ceramics and metalwork each presented a different challenge to Hoffmann, who followed the belief that designs should reflect the nature of the materials used; each material dictated the resulting forms. For the Austrian glass manufacturer Lobmeyr, for example, he designed a wide variety of drinking sets and glasses, and flower bowls in cut and blown glass. Blown glass naturally resulted in more organic forms, while more hard-edged, geometric shapes could be achieved by carving a solid block of glass. Clay resisted such hard edges, and Hoffmann's ceramics had a certain softness, although their surface patterns were geometric. Open grids featured heavily in his metalwork, especially his widely manufactured pierced metal baskets, and in the patterns of his textile designs.

A double-handed bowl made of hammered gilt metal (1920; left). The bowl exemplifies the more decorative face of Hoffmann's work which, somewhat conversely, ran parallel to his commitment to Functionalism in structure. This increasingly decorative quality is characteristic of the work of many Wiener Werkstätte designs produced in the 1920s.

LATER CAREER

Hoffmann's working career was a relatively long one, and he continued to design architecture and to teach and exhibit widely into his old age. He was responsible for the design of the Austrian Pavilion at the Paris Decorative Arts Exhibition of 1925, and his geometric motifs became one of the key influences on the Art Deco style of the 1920s and 1930s. His influence spread beyond Europe to the United States; in 1928 his work was seen at an exhibition, "Art and Industry", held at the New York department store, Macy's, and it had an especially strong impact on the Viennese émigrés Joseph Urban and Paul Frankl, as well as on the American Donald Deskey (see pp.62–3). By this time Hoffmann's strikingly modern designs were widely familiar, and he was seen internationally as one of the seminal figures in the modern decorative art movement of the first half of the 20th century.

A bathroom in the Palais Stoclet (1905–11; below); the use of marble on the floors and walls illustrates the way in which Hoffmann successfully created luxurious interiors without sacrificing a sense of functional simplicity.

Wiener Werkstätte

The Wiener Werkstätte (Vienna Workshops) were established in 1903 with the aim of sustaining high-quality craft manufacture in the face of expanding industrialization. The Werkstätte were a development of the Vienna Secession, formed in 1897 to break down the division between the fine and decorative arts; the workshops' founders, Josef Hoffmann (see pp.34–7) and Koloman Moser (the latter was also artistic director), were leading members of the Secession. Financial support was provided by the banker Fritz Warndorfer, who had acted as secretary to the Secession. Based on earlier British Arts and Crafts initiatives – especially C. R. Ashbee's Guild of Handicraft and the ideas of John Ruskin and William Morris – the workshops did not look back to past styles for inspiration but sought to create new forms appropriate to the modern world. The aim was, in the words of Hoffmann, to develop "an intimate relationship between the public, the designer and the craftsman and to create good, simple things for the home".

A glass vase (above) designed c.1905 by Jutta Sika, one of the prominent women members of the Wiener Werkstätte. Its chequerboard pattern and ball feet are typical of early Werkstätte designs.

A silver-plated inlaid mantel clock (right), designed in 1906 by Joseph Urban for the Paul Hofner Restaurant in Vienna. The clock's ornamental style reflects the more commercial aspect of the Werkstätte.

EARLY DESIGNS

The designs of Hoffmann, Moser and others – such as Otto Prütscher, Michael Powolny, Carl Czeschka and Joseph Urban – dominated the production of the workshops and were at the forefront of progressive design in Vienna during the years leading up to World War I. Their distinctly modern style was characterized by abstract patterns and geometric motifs such as chequerboards, squares, grids and spheres. The small studios (each devoted to a particular medium) produced objects in a wide range of media, including jewellery, metalwork, toys, glassware, ceramics and bookbinding. From 1910, dresses and fashion accessories joined the list of products. The expensively hand-crafted goods, all bearing the marks of the designer and the master craftsman, inevitably became luxury items, affordable only to the wealthy.

ORNAMENTAL DESIGNS

After about 1915 Werkstätte designs began to display a more ornamental quality, with overt references to such past decorative fashions as the ornate 17th-century Baroque style and the Neo-Classical Biedermeier style favoured by the Viennese "nouveaux riches" of the mid-19th century. This new sense of opulence was dictated by the demands of buyers and was especially obvious in the work of Dagobert Peche, whose interiors, furniture and decorative items were richly ornamented (see opposite, top right).

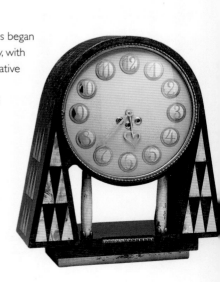

A reception room (left) at the Wiener Werkstätte Exhibition in Neustiftgasse, Vienna, c.1904. The interior contains a small hanging lamp designed by Josef Hoffmann, one of the founding members of the group.

A giltwood-framed mirror (right), designed c.1925 by Dagobert Peche. The suggestion of luxury combined with an overt modernity (somewhat akin to the decorative style popular in Paris at that time) was characteristic of products from the last decade of the Werkstätte.

for the wealthy, although such manufacturers as J. & J. Kohn and Thonet played a part in popularizing the Werkstätte style by manufacturing furniture by Hoffmann and Moser (for example, see below). In 1919 the Werkstätte opened a sales headquarters on Fifth Avenue in New York, with a showroom designed by Joseph Urban. This move to the United States enhanced the commercial aspect of the operation at the expense of social reform, and the designs came to reflect this more and more. The new Viennese style was soon visible all over New York, from theatre and packaging designs to shop window displays. Eventually, however, the increasingly opulent Werkstätte style became indistinguishable from Art Deco, which, by the 1930s, had become the prevailing fashion. The Vienna workshops were disbanded in 1932, probably due to the dominance of Art Deco combined with a lack of financial support.

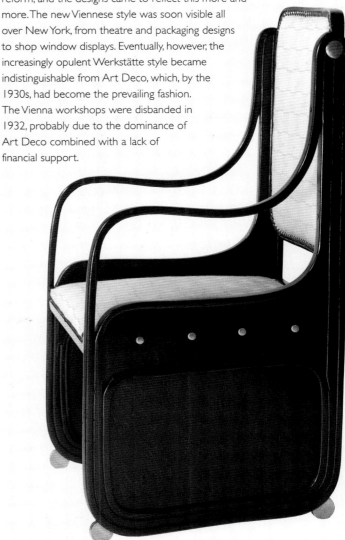

THE ROLE OF WOMEN

By the 1920s a number of women had become involved in the workshops, where the focus on the production of domestic objects was regarded as a respectable way for them to express their creativity. Several of these women had trained under Moser at the Vienna School of Applied Arts; among them were Therese Trethan and Jutta Sika (see opposite, left), whose later work – respectively, painted furniture and ceramics and glass – was included in the range of commercial Werkstätte goods.

LATER DEVELOPMENT

The ideal of social reform that underpinned Hoffmann's aim of producing simple, high-quality objects for the home was never realized by the Werkstätte. Instead, its products became fashionable decorative arts

A bentwood chair (right), designed by Koloman Moser in 1901 and manufactured by J. & J. Kohn, a company that collaborated with members of the Wiener Werkstätte on a number of innovative furniture projects.

Conservative Modernism

Conservative Modernism

In many ways World War I was a watershed in the evolution of a modern design movement. By 1914 the body of ideas that had crystallized around the turn of the century had either vanished from view entirely or come more sharply into focus. Art Nouveau (especially in its curvilinear manifestations), for example, had ceased to be a full-bodied design movement and become little more than a fashionable style, and a dated one at that. The masters of that style had either vanished with it or sunk into repetitiveness and old age.

On the other hand the approach to design, rooted in British Arts and Crafts thinking – which sought a new simplicity and a rational attitude, and which took materials and their demands as their starting point – blossomed, after World War I, into the highly influential architectural and design theory known as Functionalism (which will be the focus of the next chapter, Progressive Modernism). The years after 1918 saw this approach become the basis of a rationale for a radically new architecture and design movement which, by World War II, had had a great international impact. Two faces of Modernism emerged in fact – one overtly progressive and the other more historically oriented and conservative in nature.

Within this climate craftspeople and interior decorators such as Jean Dunand, Eileen Gray and Jacques-Emile Ruhlmann (see pp.44–51) found a sympathetic audience and, along with others such as Pierre Legrain, Jean Puiforcat, the decorating team of Süe et Mare, and Jean Michel Frank, rose to prominence in the 1920s. Each one followed their own individual trajectory but, at the same time, played a part in a bigger picture. The highly influential Exhibition of Decorative Arts, held in Paris in 1925 (see pp.52–3), provided a focus for their efforts (as well as a name for the new style – Art Deco) and an opportunity for the rest of the world to see what was happening in France. Inevitably visitors from abroad, among them Keith Murray from Britain and Donald Deskey from the United States (see pp.60–63), were strongly influenced by what they saw there, while many others saw images from the exhibition in periodicals around the world and were affected by the designs. In Britain the interior decorator Syrie Maugham (see pp.54–5) was determined to combine tradition with novelty in an interior setting, while the Austrian designer Josef Frank (see pp.56–7) also believed that the modern interior should combine references to the best designs of the past with a commitment to the present.

While Art Deco promoted an élitist notion of luxury and an idea of quality that derived from craft skills and the use of expensive materials, like Art Nouveau before it, it was gradually transformed into a popular aesthetic which, by the 1930s, had penetrated the mass environment in an unprecedented way. From its presence in the luxurious French ocean-liners it changed gear to adorn the exteriors of skyscrapers, factories and cinemas thus becoming a popular style across the globe. It also featured widely in the design of cheap, mass-produced plastic goods from dressing table sets to picnic ware. What started life as an exclusive phenomenon had, ironically, by the onset of World War II, become a popular style for the modern age.

The same did not happen, however, to the other face of conservative Modernism, the face that manifested less in a visual style than through an approach to making which sought continuity with the past. The Scandinavian countries – for example Sweden, Denmark and Finland – all had strong indigenous folk traditions but were also, at this time, keen to find a form for the new decorative art objects – ceramics, glass, furniture and textiles among others – for which they were well known in the international marketplace. Added to this ambition, however, was a strong commitment to the idea of an egalitarian society within which modern design, allied with mass production industry, could help provide an opportunity for everybody to improve the material conditions of their lives.

The Modernism that emerged from Sweden, through the work of individuals such as Wilhelm Kåge (see pp.66–9), Edvard Hald, Simon Gate, Gregor Paulsson, Gunnar Asplund, Bruno Mathsson (see pp.80–81) and others, was made possible by the efforts of an organisation called the Svenska Slöjdföreningen (Society of Industrial Design, see pp.70–71), which highlighted the importance of combining craft traditions with industrial manufacture and social reform. In Denmark furniture featured strongly in that country's attempt to blend tradition, modernity and social idealism. Kaare Klint (see pp.64–5) did much pioneering work there in a programme that was to be carried into the post-war years through the efforts of a later generation. Finland was equally socially oriented in its desire to develop its own form of modernity and once again the decorative arts industries featured strongly. A sense of continuity with the national past was also important and, as in Sweden and Denmark, this was represented by a strong desire to retain the use of traditional materials. The achievements of Alvar Aalto (see pp.74–7) and his pioneering work with bent plywood demonstrates one important way in which Finnish designers succeeded in looking backward and forward at the same time. This success was mirrored by other designers in the areas of glass and metalwork.

The impact of this soft version of Modernism was highly influential in Britain, another country for which tradition had strong resonances, both in terms of its 19th-century Arts and Crafts heritage and of its national identity as a whole. In the 1920s and 1930s this was reflected in numerous attempts to come to terms with modernity. Furniture designers – including Ambrose Heal and Gordon Russell (see pp.72–3) – sustained the efforts begun by men such as C.R. Ashbee and Ernest Gimson before them, while English folk culture or popular art was referred to in the work of designers and artists such as Enid Marx (see pp.82–3), Eric Ravilious and Paul Nash. Although frequently described as idiosyncratic, their work did represent a determination to combine the past with the present in yet another way.

Where 20th-century design is concerned it was this somewhat reactionary brand of Modernism, which allowed for decorative additions and the incorporation of traditional, familiar materials, rather than its more rigid branch, which has most influenced, and continues to influence, our lives as they are lived on an everyday basis.

This design for a lacquered screen was created between 1945 and 1950 from a sketch by Jean Dunand by his son, Pierre Dunand. It is in the manner of the French painter known as Douanier Rousseau, and combines primitivism with sophistication in a way that is characteristic of Jean Dunand's Art Deco designs of the 1920s and 1930s.

Among the decorative artists who were active in France in the early 20th century, the Swiss-born Jean Dunand (1877–1942) was without doubt one of the most outstanding craftsmen. Nearly all of his work was created according to the traditions of fine craftsmanship, yet his mastery of decoration and colour was unequalled. He was a

Jean Dunand

prolific designer of interiors and maker of furnishings and decorative objects, such as vases, chairs, screens and jewellery; he was also skilled in working with a range of materials, from metal to wood and lacquer. Dunand's son described his father as "self-willed and resolute", and his career, which lasted for over 40 years, bears witness to that description; from humble beginnings in a sculpture workshop, Dunand was running his own workshop by the mid-1930s, with over 100 employees producing furnishings for France's ocean liners.

Jean Dunand was one of the most skilled craftsmen amongst the French decorative artists who came to the fore during the 1920s. His lacquerwork, in particular, was outstanding both for its artistic originality and for its high quality.

The dramatic colouring of this lacquered metal bowl (c.1925; below) is a typical example of how Dunand explored the expressive possibilities of lacquerwork. The elegant form of the object is also characteristic of his designs.

SCULPTURE AND EARLY DECORATIVE PIECES

Jules-John Dunand, as he was originally called, was born in Geneva and trained there as a sculptor at the Ecole des Arts Industriels (1891–6). In 1897 he was awarded a scholarship by the City Fathers of Geneva to study in Paris, where he was soon employed in the workshop of the sculptor Jean Dampt. Dunand spent his early career as an assistant helping with the production of traditional pieces of sculpture in wood and metal. At the Paris Universal Exhibition of 1900, however, he exhibited a bronze of his own, entitled *Quo Vadis*, for which he won a Gold Medal. It was only in 1903, when he worked on an interior for the Comtesse de Béarn in Paris – carving furniture and door frames – that he turned his attention to the decorative arts and established his own studio there. Around 1905 he committed himself entirely to this field and began making copper and brass vases. In their use of stylized plant motifs and asymmetrical imagery, many of these showed the influence of Art Nouveau and Oriental art, both of which were widely publicized in exhibitions of this period.

LACQUERWORK

Another departure in Dunand's career came in 1909, when he turned to lacquerwork and changed his name to Jean. From 1912 he was trained, like Eileen Gray (see pp. 46–9), by the Japanese immigrant Seizo Sugawara. Dunand embraced the medium enthusiastically, and it remained an important part of his work for the rest of his career. Initially he used lacquer for purely practical purposes – as a protective layer for metalwork – and only after World War I did he use it as a creative medium in its own right.

A lacquered screen by Dunand from the 1920s (right). The abstract pattern at the top right of the screen and the stylized fish reflect his strong interest in the arts and crafts of Japan, as well as his devotion to natural imagery, especially to the exotic flora and fauna that are visible in many of his pieces.

He began to make highly finished lacquered panels and screens decorated with scenes from nature and stylized animals – such as herons, frogs, monkeys and deer – that owed much to Japanese art. From about 1919, however, he increasingly began to favour brightly coloured geometric patterns, which became the hallmark of Dunand's designs from this time onwards. In 1924 he added fashion accessories to his list of designs, including jewellery and vanity cases.

SUCCESS IN THE 1920S AND 1930S

The 1925 Paris Exhibition was the culmination of the first phase of Dunand's career. Among his exhibits was a smoking room in the section called "A French Embassy Abroad"; this scheme, featuring lacquered walls, geometric designs and Cubist-inspired armchairs, was received with enthusiasm and ensured that Dunand was offered numerous commissions for furniture and interiors over the next decade. During this period Dunand's workshop expanded rapidly, and in 1928 his work reached the United States, with an exhibition held at the Lord & Taylor department store in New York.

A lacquered wooden "coiffeuse" (above), or dressing table, designed by Jean Dunand for the boudoir installation at the Salon des Artistes Décorateurs in Paris in 1930. By this date Dunand's style had evolved away from the highly decorative to incorporate simpler, geometric forms reflecting the influence of Cubist art.

It was undoubtedly his designs for the French ocean liners commissioned by the Compagnie Sud-Atlantique – the *Atlantique* (1931) and the *Normandie* (1935) – that brought Dunand the most attention. The enormous lacquered panels with figurative decoration, interior settings and furniture that he designed for the *Normandie* represented the continued strength of French traditions of fine craftsmanship and manufacture of luxury items, which had dominated Europe since the turn of the century.

This tradition did not, however, endure after World War II. Dunand's work was always exquisitely crafted and therefore expensive, but its popularity invited an upsurge of cheap imitations – especially jewellery, dressing-table items and other small, decorative objects; these limitations caused the final demise of the Art Deco style. In the 1920s and early 1930s, however, Dunand's internationally recognized projects for the 1925 Decorative Arts exhibition and the French ocean liners defined him as a key contributor to the style originally associated with quality and good taste.

An "ensemble" made up of five necklaces (right), designed by Dunand in 1927. These five concentric circles are decorated with geometric motifs in red and black lacquer, revealing the inspiration that he took from African jewellery.

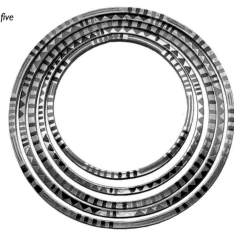

It is difficult to fit the Irish-born architect-designer Eileen Gray (1878–1976) into a category: in both her work and her life she stood defiantly outside the mainstream, and the design historian Philippe Garner has described her as a "quiet but determined loner". As she was difficult to categorize or to place within a particular group, recognition of her

Eileen Gray

contribution to design came as late as the 1970s, but she is now considered to be one of the most important designers of the first half of the 20th century and is certainly among the handful of women who have influenced the course of modern design. Her output ranged widely, from luxury decorative items in exotic materials to successful modernist architectural projects. Unlike Charlotte Perriand, however, who began her career with Le Corbusier (see pp.94–7), and Lilly Reich, who worked closely with Ludwig Mies van der Rohe (see pp.92–3), Eileen Gray was not associated with a heroic figure of modern architecture and for the most part worked alone.

Eileen Gray has only recently received the praise she deserves for her innovative work, in which she explored shapes and materials to create distinctive objects and interiors. She is seen here in Paris in 1926, photographed by Berenice Abbot.

TRAINING AND EARLY WORK

Although in Gray's later career her work was almost indistinguishable from that of her forward-looking modernist counterparts, in her early years she allied herself very closely with the decorative traditions of French design. She trained in fine art at the Slade School in London from 1898 to 1902, and in 1900 made her first visit to Paris, with

A lacquered wood day-bed designed by Gray c.1920–2 (below). Lacquer was the first material she explored as a designer, and she used it to great effect on a range of objects. The luxurious upholstery and Oriental-inspired motifs in the frame are characteristic of the work produced in the first phase of Gray's career.

her mother, to see the Universal Exhibition. The city made an enormous impact on her, and, supported by family funds, in 1907 she moved into a flat at 21 rue Bonaparte, which she inhabited on and off until her death.

In 1910 Gray abandoned fine art for lacquering, which she had learned first at a workshop in London and subsequently in Paris, with the Japanese master Seizo Sugawara. Her hand-made pieces of furniture were impeccably finished and restricted to a palette of black, brown and other dark shades, which gave her work a strong tonal harmony. Her screens and other furnishing items incorporated either stylized figures from mythology or, from around 1913, abstract patterns inspired by Cubism.

Gray first showed her work in 1913 at the annual exhibition of the Société des Artistes Décorateurs, and her first significant commission, from the couturier and collector Jacques Doucet, was a direct result of his seeing her work there. Among the pieces she made for him was a small, red-lacquered table with hanging black tassels. This piece was clearly inspired by 18th-century French furniture, an interest that Gray shared with a number of other decorative artists of the time, such as Jacques-Emile Ruhlmann (see pp.50–1) and Maurice Dufrène.

INTERIOR-DESIGN PROJECTS

In the 1920s and 1930s Gray worked on interiors for a range of Parisian clients, including Suzanne Talbot (Madame Mathieu Levy) and the Vicomtesse de Noailles. She approached these projects as an "ensemblier",

Le Destin, a four-panel lacquered screen designed in 1914 for the couturier Jacques Doucet. The front (right) shows an allegorical scene of two youths, one of whom carries an old man, while the back is covered with an abstract pattern of swirling lines.

A living-room designed for Suzanne Talbot's Paris apartment in 1933 (above). It contains Gray's famous "Serpent" (centre left) and "Bibendum" (far left and far right) chairs, as well as the signature animal skins that injected an exotic component into her work.

The hammock-style "S" chair (above) was designed between 1932 and 1934 for Gray's second house in France. Typically, Gray combined a functional laminated wooden frame, which can be folded in two, with a comfortable, lightly upholstered canvas seat.

using a wide variety of unusual and exotic materials and objects, including parchment and ostrich eggs on the walls of the interior for Talbot. Lacquer featured abundantly, covering the walls and many of the furnishings (screens in particular), but perhaps her most innovative design was a day-bed decorated in bronze lacquer and silver leaf, shaped like a canoe and supported on six sturdy legs. Named "Pirogue" (see below), this totally original type of furniture reappeared in Gray's later interiors. She also designed rugs with stylized abstract patterns for all her interior projects;

these show the strong influence of traditional art from France's colonies in Africa and the Pacific, also found in the work of many fine artists of the day, particularly the Cubists.

THE GALERIE JEAN DESERT

In 1922 Gray opened a shop in Paris, named the Galerie Jean Désert, from which to sell her work. Inevitably the prices for her interior schemes and furnishings were high, as they involved craft manufacture. Rugs were less expensive to make and proved a great commercial success (see opposite, above). During the gallery's eight years of operation, Gray became increasingly interested in Cubist art and contemporary functionalist architecture and design. This was particularly visible in her designs for furniture: examples include a small table of 1923 made up of intersecting planes and clearly indebted to the geometric work of the De Stijl designer Gerrit Rietveld (see pp.98–101), and a small dressing-table from the mid-1920s with a more open tubular steel structure, wooden drawers suspended from one side and a small wooden top. Even the lacquered pieces of the early 1920s became simpler in outline as she abandoned the decorative elements (such as tassels) that were found in her early work.

A MOVE TOWARDS MODERNISM

Gray's "Bedroom-Boudoir for Monte Carlo", exhibited at the 1923 Salon of the Société des Artistes Décorateurs in Paris, marked a transition from a decorative to a functional style. It was sparsely furnished with such simple furniture as two free-standing screens, consisting of white-lacquered blocks articulated on rods (these were also available in black), as well as a decorated rug and an animal skin thrown casually across a sofa. In the second half of the 1920s Gray increasingly embraced geometric forms, new materials such as tubular steel and the idea of mass production. Her furniture designs moved far away from her earlier decorative and exotic style and the craft-based tradition, and had more in common with pieces

The lacquered day-bed known as the "Pirogue" (below), designed c.1920 for Suzanne Talbot, one of Gray's most important clients. The hand-crafted appearance of the bed, combined with its resemblance to an African dug-out canoe, probably reflects the widespread interest among the Parisian artistic community in non-Western art.

A small woven woollen carpet (above) designed by Gray in the early 1920s. It was bought by the couturier Coco Chanel (whose initials it bears) and used in her house in Roquebrune, in the South of France. Gray often used simple, geometric graphics in her rug designs, which looked forward to the pared-down style of her later Modernist work.

designed in Germany and the Netherlands, and in Paris by the group surrounding the modernist architect Le Corbusier and his partner Charlotte Perriand. In many ways, however, her designs from these years were characterized by a subtle softening of the more austere Modernism found in Germany and the Netherlands – thereby rejecting the idea held by many Modernists that the user should serve the design, rather than the other way round. The "Transat" armchair of 1925–30, for example, combined comfortable upholstery and an adjustable wooden frame with a strikingly simple modern profile. Originally designed for the seaside holiday house, "E.1027" (see below), the chair perfectly served the dual requirements of comfort and flexibility, and was also sold in the Galerie Jean Désert.

ARCHITECTURE

The last phase of Gray's career took yet another new direction. She was persuaded in the mid-1920s by the critic Jean Badovici to experiment with architecture, a challenge she approached with confidence and enthusiasm. Her first attempt was a house for herself (1926–9), designed with Badovici, in Roquebrune in the South of France. Named "E.1027", it was strikingly modern, with a flat roof, white-washed walls and strip windows. Gray developed some new furniture designs especially for the house, among them the famous "Bibendum" chair (illustrated on p.47; top), and a tubular steel and glass bedside table (see right). After Badovici took

over "E.1027", Gray designed a smaller house (1932–4) for herself in Castellar, also in the South of France. It was equally radical in appearance, with the same flat roof and strip windows, and as rigorously furnished. The most significant item designed for it was the folding "S" chair (see opposite, above).

Gray's career as a designer culminated in the mid-1930s. Although she contributed some work to Le Corbusier's pavilion (a project for a holiday centre) at the 1937 Paris Exhibition, her greatest successes, among them the "Bibendum" and "Transat" chairs, had been achieved by that date.

A steel and glass bedside table (right) designed c.1927 by Gray for the "E.1027" house in Roquebrune in the South of France. The table was one of a set of pieces in tubular steel that Gray designed for her own use. The height of the table can be adjusted using a key hidden at the back.

Among French Art Deco designers and decorators, Jacques-Emile Ruhlmann (1879–1933) is perhaps mostly closely associated with notions of elegance and luxury. As he explained, "the luxury object is a stallion which helps improve the standard of mass-produced objects." Unlike Jean Dunand (see pp.44–5), he was not a craftsman

Jacques-Emile Ruhlmann

Jacques-Emile Ruhlmann was a leading figure within the French Art Deco Movement. Less a craftsman than an influential "eye", his work was aimed at the luxury market. His contribution to interior design was the concept of the "ensemble", in which furniture and decorative objects were blended together.

but rather a tasteful "eye", concerned with the design of furniture, light fittings, wallpapers, carpets and other elements of the interior and, above all, with the idea of the decorative "ensemble" – a concept that emerged in the late 19th century. The idea of "harmony" underpinned Ruhlmann's search for a modern decorative style that borrowed from the past (he was most strongly influenced by the Neo-Classical and Empire styles of the late 18th and early 19th centuries) while blending with contemporary geometric forms.

EARLY FURNITURE AND INTERIORS

Ruhlmann was not trained as a cabinet-maker but from 1901 gained experience in working with sumptuous materials – a distinctive feature of his later work – in his father's Parisian painting, wallpaper and mirror-making business. When his father died in 1907, Ruhlmann took over as manager of the business, renovating interiors for wealthy middle-class clients. He was married in the same year and, like so many other designers and decorators before and after him, designed furniture for his family home mainly in a simple Neo-Classical style. Ruhlmann's working method throughout his relatively short career was to make sketches and pass them on to a craftsman to execute the design.

"Ducharmebronz" was the name given to this rosewood and gilt bronze day-bed (below), designed by Ruhlmann in the 1920s. The use of luxurious materials and sumptuous colour is characteristic of his designs for furniture items, as is the combination of modern features – simple Cubist forms, for example – with historical references, such as gilt metal decorations and tubular upholstered cushions.

A bathroom interior (c.1925–30; left), illustrating the striking way in which Ruhlmann combined old-fashioned luxury with modernity. The extensive use of veined marble recalls the opulent styles of the past, while the simple forms of the basin and the exposed pipes show a commitment to utility.

La Chasse (The Chase), a lacquered and gilded panel (c.1934; right). The flat, stylized imagery of a huntsman and his dog reflects the way in which many Art Deco designers chose to interpret the art of Japan, and of Ancient Greece and Rome, all of which were popular sources of inspiration in the 1930s.

In 1911 Ruhlmann exhibited one of his wallpapers at the Salon des Artistes Décorateurs, and his reputation was enhanced by the favourable reaction to the furniture that he showed at the Salon d'Automne in 1913. These pieces consisted of wooden desks and tables with Neo-Classical motifs and long, tapering legs (a favourite motif). In 1919 he established a new business called Ruhlmann & Laurent, with the painter and decorator Pierre Laurent. From this time Ruhlmann developed a highly distinctive style that brought him enormous success in the 1920s. He concentrated on combining luxurious materials – including silk, velvet, ebony and ivory – with decorative woodworking techniques reminiscent of the 18th century. He also used bold, simple forms, resulting in richly ornamented and coloured decorative schemes with a modern twist to suit current bourgeois taste.

THE PARIS 1925 EXHIBITION AND COMMERCIAL SUCCESS

The peak of Ruhlmann's creative career came at the 1925 Paris Decorative Art Exhibition. There, with the help of his friend, the architect Pierre Patout, he designed and furnished the "Hôtel du Collectionneur" (House of a Collector), often considered among the greatest achievements of the Art Deco Movement. It combined simple, modern, Cubist forms with Neo-

Classical motifs such as friezes. The room settings featured patterned carpets and wallpapers, and tapered furniture with decorative upholstery (see p.53).

After the success of 1925 Ruhlmann worked on numerous prestigious commissions, among them the tea room for the ocean liner, the Ile de France; a meeting room for the Chamber of Commerce in Paris; and furniture for the Elysée Palace (1926). By the end of the decade his designs had become even more sumptuous and expensive, and he began to combine expensive woods with modern materials such as tubular steel.

Ruhlmann continued to exhibit his work widely, especially at the annual Salons des Artistes Décorateurs. His last furnishings, shown at the 1932 Salon, were strikingly simple and almost rustic in comparison with his earlier work. A year before he died, Ruhlmann closed his business, which had gone into decline as a result of changing fashions. Though his success lasted only a decade, Ruhlmann's high-profile work for important international exhibitions and public commissions placed him at the centre of French Art Deco.

A carved and gilt wood occasional table with a marble top (c.1929; right) designed for the Hôtel Ducharne in Paris. After the success of his "Hôtel du Collectionneur" in 1925, Ruhlmann was much in demand among wealthy Parisians, who liked his ability to combine modern forms wirh the luxury and craftsmanship associated with antiques.

Paris 1925

The term Art Deco, widely used to describe the modern architectural and decorative arts style that emerged in France in the 1920s, takes its name from the "Exposition Internationale des Arts Décoratifs et Industriels Modernes", held in Paris in 1925. Conceived back in 1912, this ambitious international event was intended to take place in 1915 but was delayed for a decade because of World War I. The 1925 Exhibition was organized as a follow-up to the enormously successful Paris Universal exhibition of 1900, which had confirmed France's pre-eminence in the creation of the Art Nouveau style. The government-sponsored 1925 Exhibition aimed to show France's continued leadership in the design and manufacture of high-quality decorative arts and was clearly intended to challenge the success of exhibitions of the work of German designers associated with the Deutscher Werkbund, an influential body formed to unite industry and design.

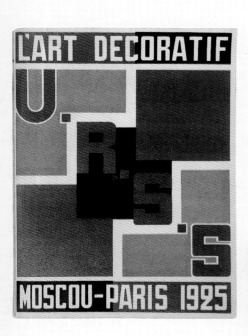

A cover of L'Art décoratif (1925; left), the catalogue for the Soviet Pavilion, designed by Konstantin Melnikov for the Paris Exhibition. The hard-edged typographic and graphic style shown here mirrors the abstract Constructivist aesthetic of the pavilion itself.

The Oasis, a wrought-iron and brass screen (below) made by the metalworker Edgar Brandt, was the centrepiece of his stand at the exhibition. The screen's stylized natural imagery and overt sense of luxury typified most of the modern decorative objects that were on display.

THE MODERN STYLE OF THE EXHIBITION

By the time the huge exhibition was actually realized, a new style had replaced Art Nouveau; it combined forms and motifs from a plethora of sources, among them 18th-century French Rococo interior and furniture styles, Cubist painting and African art. The brief for exhibitors made clear that direct copying from past styles was unacceptable, so all exhibitors strove to be as "modern" as possible in their use of abstract and stylized geometric forms. Many nations participated — among them Great Britain, Italy, Turkey, Denmark, Switzerland, Greece, Japan, Sweden, Poland and Austria — but two were notable by their absence: Germany, for political reasons, and the United States, whose government felt that it had not produced any designs worth exhibiting, and was not ready to take part.

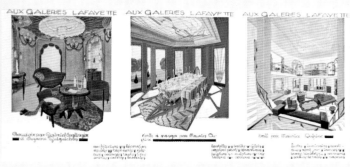

A catalogue of interior decorative schemes shown in the Galeries Lafayette Pavilion (above). It includes a drawing room and hall by Marc Dufrène. The schemes were executed in the decorative and luxurious style that became the signature of the exhibition.

Melnikov's Soviet Pavilion (left) was a rare instance of Russian avant-garde architecture at the event. The use of glass and metal, the grid pattern and the dramatic intersection of diagonals were all features of the Constructivist contribution to Modernism.

relegated to the margins of the exhibition. The architect Le Corbusier's "Pavillon de l'Esprit Nouveau" (Pavilion of the New Spirit; see p.95) was an example of French Modernism that had more in common with the functionalist, machine-age approach of German designers. This pavilion was conceived not as a decorative fantasy, but as a modular unit that could be replicated to construct a standardized apartment block.

The Paris 1925 Exhibition achieved its aim of confirming France's leadership in the luxury manufacturing trades, and the Art Deco style that it featured enjoyed international popularity through the 1930s. The streamlined geometric style was soon to be seen all over Europe and the United States in everything from factories and cinemas to skyscrapers.

A bedroom interior designed by Jacques-Emile Ruhlmann for the "House of a Collector" Pavilion (below). Ruhlmann's expensive hand-crafted furnishings exemplified the French exhibitors' emphasis on quality and luxury rather than mass production.

THE FRENCH PAVILIONS

The 1925 Exhibition covered a large area of Paris along the banks of the Seine. Stucco pavilions and other temporary buildings containing decorative arts and furnishings acted as the highlights of the Exhibition. Dominant among these buildings were the pavilions of the Parisian department stores – Bon Marché, Printemps, Louvre and Galeries Lafayette. Each employed an important decorator to take charge of their contribution. Maurice Dufrène, for example, was responsible for the Galeries Lafayette exhibit (see top right), housed in the spectacular Maitrise Pavilion, designed by the architects Jean Hiriart, Georges Tribout and Georges Beau. Other key French displays included Jacques-Emile Ruhlmann's "Hôtel du Collectionneur" (House of a Collector; see right and pp.50–51) and the architect Pierre Chareau's study in the "Pavillon de l'Ambassade Française" (Pavilion of the French Embassy).

INTERNATIONAL AND MODERN EXHIBITS

Among the notable foreign exhibits were the Austrian Pavilion designed by Josef Hoffmann (see pp.34–7), containing an interior designed by Josef Frank (see pp.56–9), and the Russian architect Konstantin Melnikov's pavilion (see above). One French contribution rivalled it, however, although it had been

By the 1920s the modern interior decorating movement, founded in the United States in the early years of the century by Elsie de Wolfe (see pp.18–19), had become established in Europe. In Britain, interior decoration was regarded as a suitable profession for society women who wanted to utilize their artistic skills; for wealthy clients, employing

Syrie Maugham

interior decorators was a means of enhancing their social status and showing their "good taste". Syrie Maugham (1879–1955), Sybil Colefax and Nancy Lancaster were three such fashionable society decorators. Maugham was, in many ways, the British equivalent of de Wolfe, and, in fact, the two women became close friends between the World Wars.

Syrie Maugham was one of a handful of professional interior decorators working in Britain in the 1930s. She contributed significantly to the fashionable interior style of the day, which combined comfort and elegance with modernity.

The hallway of Maugham's flat in London (below). The Neo-Regency stripes, the ornate stools, sculptural torch-bearers and Rococo mirror evoke the luxury of the past, while the light spaciousness of the interior gives it a sense of modernity.

EARLY CAREER

As did so many of her counterparts, Syrie Maugham took up interior decoration as an extension of her social life. For Maugham, however, her career was probably also a form of compensation for her failed marriages. She married and divorced twice, the second time to the novelist and playwright W. Somerset Maugham. Through him, she was introduced into intellectual and creative circles in London, many of whose members subsequently became her clients.

Syrie Maugham began her career, like a number of other professional female society interior decorators of the time, by opening a shop in London (on Baker Street in 1922) and selling "knick-knacks" – plaster casts, fabrics, paintings, candlesticks and other decorative furnishings. She also sold painted furniture that she adapted herself; these were illustrated in *Vogue* magazine in the following year and introduced a new fashion for stripping furniture and painting it in pale colours. Maugham found pleasure in adapting antique items throughout her working life, and the resulting pieces became characteristic features of her interiors. Her shop was so successful that she opened an outlet in Chicago in 1926 and another in New York a year later. In London her shop changed locations several times in order to meet the requirements of her expanding clientele.

INTERIOR STYLE

Like de Wolfe's, Syrie Maugham's vision of the modern interior was both progressive and conservative, though Maugham was more overtly modern in her use of new materials. Her style, fashionable among the wealthy and artistic, was distinguished by a unique combination of period and modern items and features that created both striking and comfortable interiors. Her work was frequently published in prestigious magazines, such as *Harpers Bazaar*, *Vogue* and *House and Garden*, in the second half of the 1920s and through the following decade, bringing her more and more customers. Her hallmarks – mirrored glass, bamboo furniture, shell flowers and flower arrangements, and cut crystal – became equated with elegance and taste.

Maugham's own dining room in Home and Garden *magazine (1949; above). The eclectic furnishings include her hallmarks: Rococo mirrors and painted furniture.*

A 1930s' bathroom in the London house of Margaret Argyll (left). Characteristically, Maugham combined antique items with more modern features, such as the large bath and the mirrored panel behind it.

THE "WHITE ROOM" AND OTHER SCHEMES

While Maugham strongly favoured white and muted tones of beige – the most distinctive feature of her designs – her interiors were far from austere. The mixture of textures and shades that she combined created variety in a single interior space. Some of her most outstanding creations were carried out, as were de Wolfe's, for herself. Among these, the Villa Eliza in Le Touquet, France, completed in 1926, and the drawing room of her house on the King's Road, London, decorated in 1927, stand out as two of her most uncompromising designs. The latter, although usually described as the "White Room" (see right), was far from a sterile, monotone environment. Its subtle combination of textures and shades of white in the upholstery and carpeting made it an extremely rich and varied space, exuding elegance and beauty. Although Maugham claimed that "elimination [was] one of the secrets of interior design", she never excluded flowers and period details from her rooms, using them as a visual contrast to the absence of colour. In 1933, Maugham moved away from muted tones towards more dramatic schemes characterized by the use of pink, green and blue.

At the end of the 1930s, with the approach of war, the taste for interior decoration subsided. Syrie Maugham closed her Bruton Street shop in 1938 and in 1940 left for New York with her daughter Liza, staying there for most of the war. Although she returned to Britain in 1944, her role as a leading interior decorator was, by the 1950s and 1960s, filled by others – most notably Osborne & Little, David Hicks and Jon Bannenburg.

The famous white drawing room in Maugham's own London house (1927; right). Her skill in combining modernity – shown here in the use of mirrored panels and an all-white colour scheme – with soft and comfortable furnishings proved extremely popular with Maugham's wealthy, fashionable clientele.

The Austrian-born architect and designer Josef Frank (1885–1967) made a distinctive contribution to the development of "conservative" modern design. He began his career in Vienna, at a time when the Secessionists and the Wiener Werkstätte were developing radical and progressive designs for the modern age. In the early 1930s,

Josef Frank

however, he moved to Sweden, where his work became part of the more tradition-based Swedish Modernism that dominated international taste in domestic interior design after World War II. By virtue of his Jewishness, his strong individualism and, in Sweden, his Austrian nationality, Frank was always an "outsider". Ironically, because his work received a large amount of exposure abroad in the 1930s, his role in the formation of the notion of "Swedish Modern" design was more central than that of many native Swedish designers.

The work of the Austrian Josef Frank ranged from functionalist product design to a new eclectic approach to interior decoration. For this reason his impact has been felt in a number of areas, most notably the formation of the design movement known as "Swedish Modern".

A bent-wood chair, model "A811F" (below), designed in the early 1930s for the Travel Company. Although the chair is sometimes attributed to Josef Hoffmann (see pp.34–7), contemporary magazines credited it to Frank. The chair's elegant proportions and simple structure are both typical of Frank's furniture designs.

ARCHITECTURE AND INTERIORS BEFORE 1914

Frank's father was a Jewish textile manufacturer and wholesaler, and Frank retained a strong interest in textile design throughout his career. His early training was in architecture at the Technical High School in Vienna. His education instilled in him a respect for past traditions by stressing the importance of the history of architecture, and his thesis was on the early Renaissance Italian architect Leon Battista Alberti. On graduation Frank set up an architectural practice with two colleagues, Oskar Strnad and Oscar Wlach, and undertook a number of interior design projects displaying a range of influences, from chinoiserie and 18th-century English furniture to 18th-century French silks and folk culture. In a room designed in 1910 for his sister in Vienna, for example, Art Nouveau-influenced elements were combined with more personal features.

From the beginning of his career it was clear that Frank did not have an allegiance to the Viennese avant-garde idea of the "Gesamtkunstwerk" (total work of art) but valued a less self-conscious notion of domestic design with more emphasis on comfort. Other early projects included an interior for the East Asian Art Museum in Cologne (1912) and for a Swedish school in Vienna, both executed in a neoclassical style. While working on the school, Frank met Anna Sebenius, the Swedish teacher whom he married.

POST-WORLD WAR I

After World War I Frank became a teacher at Vienna's Applied Art School from 1919 to 1927 and also continued to practise as an architect and interior designer in the city. He had two distinct preoccupations in this period: firstly, good-quality public housing, for which he designed several schemes in a rigorously Functionalist style (see opposite, top), with the backing of the city's socialist government; and, secondly, interior decoration. With Oscar Wlach in 1925 he formed Haus und Garten (House and

The Wiedenhofer-Hof (1923–4; left), a high-density housing block for workers. Frank was responsible for a number of social housing projects in Vienna in the 1920s, but on the whole he preferred more individualized low-density housing.

A table light (below) designed for the shop Svenskt Tenn in the 1950s. Unlike the more progressive Modernists who favoured steel and glass in their lighting designs, Frank often used more traditional materials such as brass and fabric.

Garden), a decorating company catering for Vienna's wealthy middle class and with its own retail outlet. Frank also designed furniture and textile patterns in this period; notable among the latter were "Primavera" and "Mirakel" (see p.59), which he created especially for Haus und Garten.

EXHIBITIONS IN THE 1920S

Frank's designs were first publicly displayed at the 1925 Paris Exhibition of Decorative Arts, where Haus und Garten showed a small, simple interior with white walls and wooden furniture. Among those it impressed was Estrid Ericson, owner of the fashionable Stockholm design shop, Svenskt Tenn, who became an important figure in Frank's career. In 1927 the

A sketch by Frank (right) of the installation he designed for the San Francisco Golden Gate Exhibition in 1939. Frank reused a number of pieces for this project, including the decorated screen and the bed, the three-mirrored dressing-table and the multi-directional floor light. The interior is typically light, airy and highly patterned, and helped to establish Frank in the United States as the founder of the Swedish Modern Movement.

A modern Svenskt Tenn interior (above) with items designed by Frank. The combination of the patterned rug, the elegant tapered-leg table and the comfortable sofa suggest a soft yet modern image of domesticity that is still popular in Sweden today.

From the 1930s to the 1950s Frank designed many variations on the theme of a cabinet on a stand – all of them covered with patterned veneers (right). The form was inspired by both 18th-century English and Asian furniture, but simplified and updated by Frank. One version of the cabinet was exhibited in 1952 at the National Museum, Stockholm.

architect Ludwig Mies van der Rohe (see pp.92–3) asked Frank to contribute to the "Weissenhofsiedlung", a housing scheme in Stuttgart featuring buildings and interiors designed by leading international Modernist architects. Frank's inclusion in this exhibition was to enhance his reputation as an exponent of Functionalism, but the interiors of his duplex housing showed a less austere and more human approach towards the design of living space, with comfortable furnishings, cushions and upholstery.

WORK IN SWEDEN

In 1932 Estrid Ericson asked Frank to design some pieces of furniture and textiles for Svenskt Tenn. In the following year, with the rise of the Nazi regime, Frank was forced to leave Austria for Sweden, and by 1934 he

had become Svenskt Tenn's chief designer. From this time onwards he concentrated more on the design of furniture, textiles and the domestic interior and less on architecture.

Frank's work in Sweden in the 1930s was characterized by a strong commitment to the use of colour and pattern, and to the idea of elegance, proportion and comfort in the domestic interior. Working closely with Ericson, whose role was that of an "arranger" rather than a designer, he designed corpulent sofas, elegant chests of drawers decorated with inlay and marquetry, brass standard lamps providing soft lighting, and brightly coloured and patterned fabrics for curtains and upholstery. Certain furniture types – an Egyptian-inspired three-legged stool, a dressing table with three mirrors and serving trolleys – became the hallmarks of his style. Following on from his publication in 1930, *Architecture as a Symbol*, in which he argued that architecture was about more than function and technology, he also published articles in the Swedish design magazine *Form*.

INTERNATIONAL INFLUENCE

Frank not only formulated a new design style in the 1930s, but his work was increasingly used to represent Swedish design at international exhibitions. At the 1937 Paris Universal Exhibition, for example, he and Ericson presented a light, airy design for a terrace furnished with cane seating and pot plants. Critics saw in this display a new sensibility that was less austere than

The "Mirakel" textile pattern (above) was designed by Frank in Vienna for his decorating firm Haus und Garten before he left for Sweden in 1934. It is typical of his exuberant flower patterns and it remained popular as a household textile right up until the 1960s.

"Vegetable Tree" (1944; right), an Oriental-inspired textile designed in the United States and sent back to Sweden on the occasion of Estrid Ericson's 50th birthday. The design shows Frank's predilection for colour and pattern at its most intense.

Functionalism, and dubbed it "Swedish Modern". At the New York World's Fair and the San Francisco Golden Gate Exhibition (both 1939), Frank's distinctive humanistic interiors were described by critics as "a movement towards sanity in design". His design for New York combined a bold chequerboard floor with a kidney-shaped desk, a floral upholstered fireside chair, bookcases and a coffee-table, while in San Francisco his display featured screens with a printed wild flower pattern, the familiar dressing-table with three mirrors and a flexible standard lamp.

WARTIME WORK

With the outbreak of World War II Frank left Sweden for New York, where he took up a teaching post in architecture at the New School for Social Research. In 1944, on the occasion of Ericson's 50th birthday, Frank sent his collaborator 50 new textile designs. These showed Frank's characteristically evocative depiction of birds and flowers and provided the basis of his post-war career after his return to Sweden the following year. Designs from this period, such as "Vegetable Tree" (see right), have become classics and are still popular today in Sweden.

POST-WAR "SWEDISH MODERN"

In the 1950s Frank's reputation was at its highest point. One of his most memorable projects from this period was a set of simple, light interiors furnished with patterned fabrics for the sculptor Carl Milles, which became known as "Anne's House". Increasingly, it was Frank's approach towards designing comfortable and pleasant living spaces that became linked throughout the world with the idea of "Swedish Modern". Toward the end of his life Frank returned to architecture, but by then his work in this field consisted only of visionary schemes, which had more influence on the later generation of Postmodernists than on his Modernist contemporaries.

The British decorative-art industries – as well as public taste – were notoriously conservative in their approach to design following World War I. In this reactionary climate the New Zealand-born architect and designer Keith Murray (1892–1981) came to work with British ceramics, glass and metalwork manufacturers between the wars, with

Keith Murray

the aim of modernizing their output and so bringing it in line with that of other countries, particularly France, where design was more progressive. His pioneering modernist designs received much critical acclaim, both at the time and in later years. He also helped to define a new British profession, that of the consultant designer to industry.

Keith Murray played a key role in modernizing the products of Britain's decorative arts industries in the 1920s and 1930s. Working on a freelance basis, he helped manufacturers, such as the ceramics maker Wedgwood and the glass company Stevens & Williams, to inject a new minimalism into their designs.

A silver-plate cocktail set (c.1935; below) designed for Mappin & Webb. Its distinction, when compared with other sets of the period, lies in Murray's rigorously controlled minimalist detail.

TRAINING AND EARLY CAREER

Murray's family came to Great Britain in 1906, and, following service in the Royal Flying Corps during World War I, he trained in architecture at the Architectural Association in London. After graduating, he visited the Paris Exhibition of Decorative Arts of 1925 and was impressed by what he saw there. Although he had long been fascinated by antique glass, a visit to the exhibition of "Swedish Decorative Arts" held at the Royal Academy in London in 1931 – where he saw simple, lightly engraved pieces by Edvard Hald and Simon Gate – reinforced his growing interest in modern glass.

Through connections with the Committee on Art and Industry, a government-backed body set up in 1931 to investigate the relationship between artists and manufacturers, Murray was introduced to Whitefriars Glassworks in London, for whom he produced a number of experimental designs with simple geometric forms. In 1932 he was given an introduction to another glass manufacturer, Stevens & Williams, based in the Midlands. In the same year Murray began his association with the Staffordshire ceramic manufacturer Wedgwood. As at Stevens & Williams, he was hired on a part-time basis and invited to study the company's production facilities. Although he was not a trained craftsman, the success of Murray's designs was largely the result of his understanding of materials and manufacturing processes.

Engraved glass vases (left) designed for Stevens & Williams (1935–9). The simple yet effective cactus motif provides a minimal amount of surface decoration that does not detract from the strong shapes of the vases.

A jug and a pint mug in celadon green and cream-coloured slipware (c. 1935; below), designed for Wedgwood. The only decoration on the pieces is provided by the concentric circles at their bases, a device that Murray used again and again.

GLASS AND CERAMIC DESIGNS

Until 1939 Murray provided many designs for Stevens & Williams and for Wedgwood. For Stevens & Williams, he created a wide range of glass, from table services for mass production to free-blown forms and engraved and cut vessels. For Wedgwood he was equally prolific, providing designs for vases, jugs, bowls, tableware and many other useful and decorative ceramics. He brought a radically new approach derived, on the one hand, from his architectural training and his commitment to a modern style and, on the other, from his respect for materials and Neo-Classical design traditions, especially those of 18th-century Britain. This was particularly apparent in his elegant cut-glass vessels decorated with repeated, small, flat-cut faceted motifs, both geometric and naturalistic. His ceramic designs depended strongly for their visual impact on form and structure, but the forms were dramatically enhanced by such integral decorations as simple ridges or

An earthenware vase covered with a matt green glaze (right) designed for Wedgwood by Murray to a shape that he named "Annular". The use of a lathe to create the formal ornament on this piece has resulted in a typically Art Deco design.

ribbing around the body of the piece. Colour was another important factor in Murray's glass and ceramics. His ceramics spanned a range of muted tones, from matt blue to grey, white straw, and, above all, green, while black was used for both ceramics and glass. The subtle colours were intended to enhance rather than overpower the minimalist forms.

Murray's work was publicized through exhibitions in London, among them "British Industrial Art in Relation to the Home", held at Dorland Hall in 1933, and "British Art in Industry", held at the Royal Academy in 1935. It was judged to be one of Britain's strongest contributions to Modernism. In the mid-1930s he also ventured into the design of metalwork for the manufacturer Mappin & Webb, for whom he designed luxury items such as cocktail sets (see opposite, left). In 1936, returning to the career for which he originally trained, he set up an architectural practice with C.S. White. Their first commission was for a new factory for Wedgwood, opened in 1940. He designed one more range of ceramics for Wedgwood in 1946 (in a softer, less aggressively geometric style than his earlier designs) but spent the rest of his career working on architectural projects.

Of the dozen or so American pioneer industrial designers who came to prominence in the 1920s and made their fortunes in the 1930s, Donald Deskey (1894–1989) was the one most strongly influenced by the modern decorative traditions of Vienna and Paris – in particular, the geometric Art Deco style. He was also the designer who

Donald Deskey

exploited most fully the decorative potential of new and unconventional materials, among them cork, aluminium, linoleum and chromed steel, and was responsible for the formulation of a distinctly American style known as "Streamlined Moderne".

Donald Deskey was instrumental in introducing the streamlined forms of European Art Deco to American industrial design. His New York-based design firm, Donald Deskey Associates, became one of the most important in the United States.

An upholstered aluminium chair (below), designed in 1929 for the Abraham and Strauss beauty parlour in New York, and produced by the Ypsilanti Reed Furniture Company. The minimal geometric form is typical of Deskey's work from this period.

EARLY CAREER

Born in Minnesota, Deskey spent his early career looking for a direction. He trained initially as an architect at the University of California (1915–19); his studies, however, were interrupted by World War I, and he never returned to that profession. Although he never went overseas during the war, Deskey trained as a master gunner and after the war took various jobs including helper to ship-fitters and junior highway engineer. These experiences, followed by travels to Chicago in 1920 – where he worked as a graphic designer – and then to Paris in 1923, introduced him to engineering and painting. He eventually settled in Paris, where he met his wife, Mary Campbell Douthett, and began to work as a lithographer and graphic designer. These varied early experiences were typical of this generation of artists and designers, who were being encouraged to apply their skills, for lucrative reward, in the commercial world. The benefits were mutual, as manufacturing industries increasingly regarded the incorporation of artistic designs into products as a way of gaining prestige and advantage over competitors.

SUCCESS IN NEW YORK

Deskey and his wife returned to the United States in late 1923, where they stayed until the lure of Paris and the 1925 Exhibition took them back across the Atlantic. The radically new designs at the exhibition clearly affected Deskey, and he was significant in bringing this modern decorative style to the United States, and especially to New York. In 1926 he started work in the city as an industrial design consultant and, the next year, began designing furniture, lamps and textiles for Deskey-Vollmer, a company set up with business partnerPhillip Vollmer which remained active until 1931. At this time Deskey also began to design screens in a range of materials, including linoleum, cork, copper and Bakelite, and displaying bold geometric Art Deco patterns. One of his screens was bought by Paul Frankl, a Viennese émigré designer, and displayed in his New York gallery; another appeared in a window display that Deskey created for the Saks Fifth Avenue store.

In the late 1920s Deskey concentrated on designing exclusive furnishings and interiors for wealthy clients. One of his first important commissions was for John D. Rockefeller's apartment at West 54th Street,

Deskey was well known for the lighting objects he designed in the 1930s. The example shown below (c.1935) was constructed from thin aluminium tubing topped by a simple white shade. Its design is as clean as anything that came out of the German Bauhaus, and typifies Deskey's signature "industrial" style.

Among the many New York interiors that Deskey designed in the 1930s was the International Casino Bar (1939; above). The stylish setting resembled something out of a Hollywood musical, and appealed to a consumer public hungry for glamour.

Deskey designed a number of simple modern furniture items for both private and public interiors in the 1930s. This little aluminium "bridge-framed" coffee table (below) shows his technical virtuosity and his eye for novelty.

New York, in 1930. This featured a muted colour scheme and a radical use of Deskey's favourite new materials. Reflecting the growing relationship between design and industry, he also became interested in working for mass manufacturers. An early example of such a collaboration was a small tubular steel chair, mass-produced by a furniture manufacturer in Grand Rapids, Michigan. However, his biggest break came when he won the competition to design the interiors of the Radio City Music Hall in the Rockefeller Center, New York, in 1932–3. This was a prestigious and demanding job, and Deskey needed to bring in a large team of draughtsmen and assistants. He invited artists such as Stuart Davis to contribute Modernist murals for the scheme, and he worked closely with the artists involved. The resulting interiors reflected Deskey's love of abstract forms and varied materials.

EXHIBITIONS AND LATER WORK

Like that of many of his contemporaries, Deskey's reputation was enhanced by the presence of his work at key exhibitions in the 1920s and 1930s, such as the Paris Universal Exhibition of 1937 (where he won a Grand Prix and a Gold Medal), and the New York World's Fair of 1939. By the end of the decade he had worked with a number of manufacturers, including Widdicombe Furniture, Libby Glass and Froehler Manufacturing, designing everything from industrial equipment to household appliances. He also continued to work on interiors. A particularly exciting project from the late 1930s was for New York's International Casino Bar, a night club with a bar that ran up the side of a dramatic staircase (see above). In the 1940s Deskey established his own design firm, Donald Deskey Associates, designing products and packaging for, among others, Procter & Gamble. He remained active until 1970.

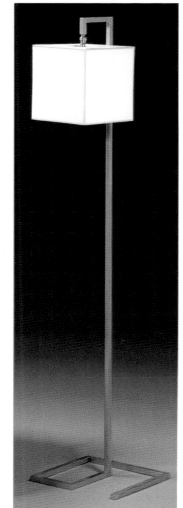

Throughout the 20th century Danish designers have played a vital role in developing modern furniture, consistently combining the "old" with the "new" in a fresh and original way. While this contribution was acknowledged in the 1950s, when such designers as Hans Wegner (see pp.160–61), Børge Mogensen and Finn Juhl were fêted internationally,

Kaare Klint

its origins can be found in the writings and designs of Kaare Klint (1888–1954) back in the 1930s. Klint was committed to bringing the values of traditional furniture and cabinet-making to pieces that also fulfilled the demands of modern living. He combined careful analysis of countless pieces of furniture from the past and from different cultures with the study of the proportions and requirements of the human figure to design practical, beautiful and modern items. His approach anticipated later attempts to create "functional" furniture, and by the 1930s his method was widely used by designers in several countries.

The Danish designer Kaare Klint was firmly committed to functional modernity. His approach was to design simple furniture as working pieces of equipment rather than as sculptural objects.

Klint's remodelling of the 19th-century deck-chair reflected his interest in the relationship between furniture and the human body. This version (1933; below) has the added comfort of upholstery.

DESIGNS BEFORE WORLD WAR I

Klint trained as an architect and designer at the Technical School in Copenhagen under his father, P.V. Jensen Klint, and Carl Petersen, both architects. In 1914 Petersen invited Klint to work with him on designing fixtures and fittings for the Art Museum in Fåborg, Denmark. Even in this early project, Klint was already aware that his main concern in designing furniture was to adapt the best features of historic pieces to contemporary requirements. A wooden chair for the Fåborg Museum, for example, combined classical proportions with details from 18th-century English furniture – such as elegantly tapering legs – and traditional materials and manufacturing techniques, but the design had an overall simplicity that was distinctly modern (see opposite, below). From c.1916 Klint began his lifelong personal study of human proportion in relation to furniture, which formed the basis for all his later designs.

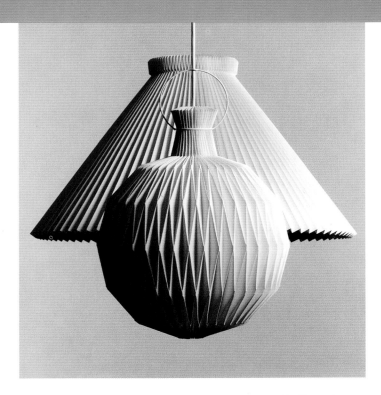

A pair of plastic-coated, folded paper lampshades (above) designed by Klint in the mid-1940s with his son Ebsen for the firm Le Klint. They fulfil Klint's aim of achieving function by minimal, and in this case, inexpensive means, and are still made by Le Klint.

The "Safari chair" (1933; right), Klint's reworking of the folding safari chair, produced by Rudolf Rasmussen. Klint was inspired by the utilitarianism and simplicity of traditional vernacular furniture, and exploited these qualities in his own designs. This example, still in production, has remained popular with consumers of Scandinavian design.

TEACHING AND WORK IN THE 1920S AND 1930S

Klint continued to work on furniture and fittings for museums, among them the Thorvaldsens Museum (1922–5) and the Danish Museum of Decorative Arts (1924–54), both in Copenhagen. In 1920 he opened his own design and architectural office and by the middle of the decade had also become a highly influential teacher; he was responsible for the formation in 1924 of the Department of Furniture in the Academy of Art in Copenhagen and 20 years later became Professor of Architecture there.

Above all, Klint is remembered for the simple and durable pieces of furniture that he designed from the late 1920s. They were all based on traditional furniture types but modified to suit early 20th-century lifestyles. The "Safari chair" (see above), for example, was inspired by a standard British military officer's chair but transformed into a practical, comfortable, well-proportioned, lightweight object.

INFLUENCE ON FUTURE DESIGNERS

Although committed to traditional methods of cabinet-making – his furniture was hand-made, mostly by the small family firm of Rudolf Rasmussen – Klint was also attracted to the idea of mass-producing inexpensive designs, such as folded paper lampshades (see above, left). Later Danish furniture designers – such as Ole Wanscher and Børge Mogensen, both of whom worked with Klint – were influenced by his adaptation of historic forms to modern use, as well as his concern for human needs.

An oak and woven cane chair (left), inspired by 18th-century examples, designed by Klint and Carl Petersen in 1914; it was manufactured by N.M. Rasmussen. Originally intended for public seating at the Fåborg Museum, the chair is still in production.

More than any other European country in the early 20th century, Sweden embraced modern design as a means of establishing a distinctive political, social and cultural identity. In many ways this was an extension of "National Romanticism": a movement focusing on the revival of folk art and culture that had dominated Scandinavian culture

Wilhelm Kåge

in the last decade of the 19th century and was linked with moves towards political independence in the early 1900s. However, modern Swedish design attempted to combine tradition with innovation, most notably in the new Swedish ceramic and glass industries. Although using mechanized production methods, these manufacturers set out to improve the aesthetic quality of everyday objects for all by inviting fine artists such as Wilhelm Kåge (1889–1960) to design for mass production. Kåge's relationship with the ceramics manufacturer Gustavsberg was among the most influential and successful of these "art into industry" experiments.

Wilhelm Kåge played an important role in the formation of the Swedish Modern style in design. Through his work for the ceramics firm Gustavsberg, he realized the ideals of many early 20th-century Swedish designers, who sought to create well-designed domestic products that were inexpensive to manufacture and affordable for ordinary people.

Kåge originally designed the "Blue Lily" service (below) for the 1917 Home Exhibition. The design's dependence on traditional folk colours and motifs, coupled with its simplicity, reveals the way in which Kåge developed a design approach that he felt could be integrated easily into mass manufacture and everyday domestic life.

EARLY PAINTING, POSTER DESIGN AND CERAMICS

Kåge's early career was as a painter and poster artist in the Art Nouveau style. He studied in Stockholm (1908–9) and Copenhagen (1911–12), and his exposure to the work of avant-garde artists in these countries – including the Swedish painter Carl Willhelmsson and the Danish sculptor Johan Rohde – led him to experiment with contemporary styles, and in particular with Symbolism. His move from painting to poster design, just prior to the outbreak of World War I, marked his first incursion into the world of commercial design.

GUSTAVSBERG AND THE HOME EXHIBITION

Kåge was approached in 1917 by Gustavsberg to replace Gunnar Wennerberg as Artistic Director. In his earliest designs, Kåge continued his predecessor's interest in simple, naturalistic motifs representing birds and flowers, inspired largely by Swedish folk art. His first challenge came in 1917 with a commission for a table service for the Home Exhibition at the Liljevalchs Art Gallery in Stockholm, an event organized by designers and manufacturers featuring 23 fully furnished interiors intended as model dwellings for the average working-class Swedish family (see opposite, top). Kåge's "Blue Lily" service, designed to be inexpensive and mass-produced in glazed earthenware, was decorated with a stylized transfer-printed surface pattern that was based on traditional Swedish designs, yet was modern in its bold simplicity (see left). "Blue Lily" proved too progressive, however, for Gustavsberg's customers at that time, who rejected it in their preference for more highly decorated models. Gustavberg's aim of producing simple decorative design for a mass audience was temporarily abandoned during

the 1920s in favour of a more neo-classical style and exclusive, one-off pieces. Like Simon Gate and Edvard Hald, fine artists who designed for the glassmakers Orrefors, Kåge responded to this new trend, winning a "Grand Prix" for a unique piece in this comparatively ornate style at the 1925 Paris Exhibition of Decorative Arts (see below right). He also experimented widely with using coloured glazes and more complex shapes in this period.

THE 1930 STOCKHOLM EXHIBITION

The next turning point in the evolution of Sweden's modern design movement and in Kåge's creative career came with the 1930 Stockholm Exhibition. For the first time, leading Swedish architects – including Gunnar Asplund and Sven Markelius – embraced fully the radical style of Functionalist modern architecture. This modern Swedish architecture and design was closely related in style to its French and German counterparts and yet – uniquely – had strong links with social democratic politics, and with the accompanying concern for public housing and mass-produced but well-designed household items.

An interior from the influential Home Exhibition (above), held in Stockholm's Liljevalchs Gallery in 1917. The event reflected Swedish designers' concern about the everyday environment of ordinary people. The "Blue Lily" service sits atop the shelf on the right.

A bowl designed for Gustavsberg (below), which won a prize at the 1925 Paris Exhibition. In the 1920s Swedish ceramics in general, and Kåge's in particular, temporarily took on an élitist approach that favoured one-off pieces decorated in the Neo-Classical style.

The "Praktika" range (above), designed in response to the Functionalist ideals put forward by Sweden's leading architects at the 1930 Stockholm Exhibition, included these simple bowls that could be stacked neatly inside each other. The design proved too austere for the Swedish public, however, and as a result it was a commercial failure.

Once again, however, the Swedish population lacked enthusiasm for this experiment in radical design, especially in relation to the decorative arts. This was evident in the commercial failure of Kåge's most innovative ceramic design for the Exhibition: a simple, white-glazed earthenware table service – undecorated, save for a green line around the edge – in oval, stackable or multi-purpose forms that could be mixed and matched. Named "Praktika" (see above) as a reference to its functional style and heat-treated durability, the service was first manufactured commercially in 1933 but, just as had been the case with "Blue Lily", it proved too purist for the Swedish market and failed to sell.

However, Kåge produced another design in the same year called "Pyro" that proved to be an enormous economic success for Gustavsberg, and was displayed at the Paris exhibition of 1937. This service was still very simple but had softer lines, with a warmer, cream-coloured background, and was decorated with a brown, stylized folk art-inspired floral motif (see below, right). At the other extreme, in the same year he also created the "Argenta" range (see below, left), a much more sophisticated Art Deco-inspired design embellished with silver neo-classical figures and animals. This range was also shown at the 1930 Stockholm Exhibition.

WARTIME AND LATER CAREER

In the 1940s Kåge continued to design tableware for the purposes of mass production, developing increasingly soft, fluid, sculptural forms with minimal decoration that became enormously influential in the arena of European ceramics after 1945. One set of tableware, which he produced in 1944 – on which five lines in grey provided the only embellishment for each piece – recalled "Praktika" (see left), although its profile was more rounded and organic. The early 1950s saw the appearance of "Praktika II", an all-white service based on soft, simple forms.

Kåge also produced sculptural and highly expressive "art" ceramics; by the 1940s he had moved away from Swedish peasant culture as a source of inspiration for these ceramics towards more international influences, such as Mexican and Chinese art. These influences resulted in such designs as his "Farsta" stoneware. An exhibition that was held in Stockholm's National Museum in 1953 included an enormous range of highly expressive items designed by Kåge, from fish-shaped vessels to vases covered in dramatic abstract marks and images executed in a freehand manner. These objects were a long way away from his mass-produced utility wares of earlier years, and demonstrated the full range of his artistic ability. Other pieces from the 1950s bore a resemblance to the sculptural ceramics created by Pablo Picasso during the same period, while earlier pieces, from 1940, collectively titled "Surrea", made obvious references to the work of the Surrealists and to Cubist sculpture.

Kåge remained in his position as Art Director at Gustavsberg until 1947, when he was replaced by Stig Lindberg, although he continued to design ceramics for the company until his death in 1960.

The silver-decorated "Argenta" range of vases (c.1930) was the last group of pieces that Kåge designed in the Neo-Classical style, which was so popular in Sweden in the 1920s. The simple form of this example (left), however, looks forward to his later, functional designs.

The oven-to-tableware service "Pyro", first shown at the 1930 Stockholm Exhibition and manufactured by Gustavsberg, was an enormous commercial success. The cream and brown colouring and the stylized floral motif recalled traditional folk designs, but the practicality and wide availability of the pieces was distinctly modern.

IMPACT ON A NATIONAL STYLE

Although he had worked in a single medium for over 40 years and in collaboration with only one manufacturer during that time, Kåge's ability to create designs that were traditional and yet modern proved highly significant in the formation of the domestic style known as "Swedish Modern". The style dominated both popular and critical taste on a wide international scale in the immediate post-war years.

Kåge's long career exemplified the way in which the Swedish design and manufacturing industries succeeded in combining comfort and accessibility with innovation in a way that appealed to the consuming public, while also evolving a specifically 20th-century modern design style that recognized the political and social requirements of the day. The range of Kåge's output — from exotic, one-off pieces that he produced purely to satisfy his own creative needs, to the inexpensive, commercial, mass-produced items with their attractive surface patterns — demonstrated how as a fine artist he had the ability to channel his visualizing skill into the design arena and create items that came to symbolize the taste of a whole nation.

The Gustavsberg display (above) at the highly influential Stockholm Exhibition of 1930. Among the pieces is a wide range of designs by Kåge.

The feathery blue decoration on the surface of this vase (right), designed in the 1920s, recalls motifs from Swedish folk ceramics. The lightness of the design, however, distinguishes it from the heavier patterns found on the more traditional items that were being produced at this time.

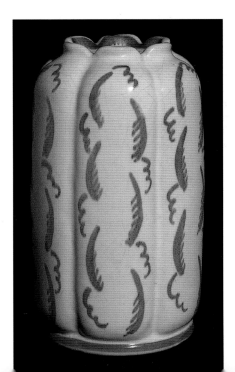

Svenska Slöjdföreningen

Many of the efforts made throughout the 20th century to formulate a modern design movement were made by national design associations, established either by governments or independent groups. Their role was to promote and improve standards of design, usually for political, economic, cultural or ethical purposes. The origins of these bodies can be found, for the most part, in the mid-19th century, when the growth of industrial mass manufacturing threatened to lower the standards of design found in traditional craft production. The Svenska Slöjdföreningen (Swedish Society of Industrial Design), established in 1845, is one of the oldest of these bodies.

EARLY HISTORY AND EXHIBITIONS

The Society was founded to "bring about improvements in the products of Swedish handicraft and industry through co-operation with artistic forces, better the household culture and work to raise the general level of taste". Around the turn of the 20th century, under the secretaryship of Erik Folcker, the Society took its lead from Germany, and the writings and work of Hermann Muthesius; he was a founder and leading member of the Deutscher Werkbund, an organization established in 1907 to bring design and industry closer together. In the same spirit, the Society organized an exhibition of Swedish design in Stockholm in 1909. It featured the work of pioneering artists and designers collaborating with manufacturing industry: Alf Wallander, who worked with the ceramics manufacturer Rorstrand, and Gunnar Wennerberg, who designed pieces for Sweden's other leading ceramic producer, Gustavsberg. However, their hand-made work was still Art Nouveau in style and was essentially élitist in nature.

A vase (1918; left) designed by Simon Gate for the Orrefors glassworks. Trained as a fine artist, Gate was introduced to Orrefors in 1915 as part of the Society's campaign to bring artists into contact with the manufacturing industry.

An interior (right) designed for the 1939 New York World's Fair by Josef Frank (see pp.56–9), acting for the the shop Svenskt Tenn. This interior style, termed "Swedish Modern" by the Americans, was a newer, more human domestic design approach. The Swedish exhibit at the Fair was organized by the Svenska Slöjdföreningen.

An interior at the 1930 Stockholm exhibition (left). The use of tubular steel and undecorated surfaces betrays the strong influence of the designs of the Bauhaus and Le Corbusier in Sweden at that time.

Edvard Hald's "Fireworks" glass vase (right), designed for Orrefors in 1921. The artist Hald, like Gate, was introduced to Orrefors in 1915 as part of the Society's project to unite art and industry.

THE 1930S AND THE POST-WAR PERIOD

Although little progress was made in the 1920s, the enormously influential 1930 Stockholm Exhibition, organized in part by the Society, proved not only that Swedish designers were participating in international Modernism but that they could combine progressive design with a radical social programme. The coming to power of the Social Democrats in Sweden in 1932 enabled the this idealism to be realized. Through the decade the Society played a central role in promoting Swedish design and the concept of "Swedish Modern", the light, simple style made famous by Josef Frank's entries at the 1937 Paris Universal Exhibition, the 1939 New York World's Fair (see opposite and pp.119) and the 1939 San Francisco Exhibition.

After World War II there was again a shift in the direction of the Society's activities. Immediately after 1945 it dedicated itself to gathering information for designers concerning the ideal measurements of furniture. In 1955, under the leadership of the critic Åke Huldt, it set out to revive the spirit of 1930 with a similar event called "Hålsinborg '55". This was less successful than its predecessor, however, partly due to the emergence of other international shows such as the Milan Triennales. By the 1970s the Society had lost its previous authority but, under the name "Föreningen Svensk Form" (Swedish Craft and Design Society), it continues to publish its influential journal *Form* and to represent Swedish design at home and abroad.

THE "HOME" EXHIBITION

Around 1915, under the influence by its new secretary, the critic Erik Wettergren, the Society set out to promote more aggressively modern design, to bring more artists in contact with manufacturing industry and, most significantly, to link its programme with that of social democracy. The "Home Exhibition", organized by the Society in 1917 in Stockholm's Liljevalchs Art Gallery, was a conscious attempt to fulfil the last aim. The exhibition consisted of 23 furnished interiors intended as model dwellings for Sweden's working class. Wilhelm Kåge, Art Director of the Gustavsberg ceramics factory, exhibited his "workers' service" there (see pp.66–9).

The achievements of the exhibition were sustained by the ideas of the critic Gregor Paulsson, who became the Society's head in 1917. In his influential book, *Vackra Vardagsvaror* ("More Beautiful Everyday Things"), published in 1919, he explained that it was necessary to "achieve a definitive change from the isolated production of individuals to the conscious work of a whole generation for a culture of form on a broad social basis". These radical ideas of social and design reform underpinned the Society's work through the many years of Paulsson's leadership.

In 1909, the Svenska Slöjdföreningen organized an exhibition of Swedish design in Stockholm. The event highlighted the products of artists working within the manufacturing industry. This ceramic plate (right), designed by Gunnar Wennerberg for the Gustavsberg factory, was influenced by natural colours, patterns and shapes such as those found in fungi. This sophisticated brand of abstract naturalism was Sweden's distinctive contribution to the international Art Nouveau movement.

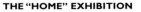

The ideals of the 19th-century British Arts and Crafts designers – the importance of "truth to materials" and hand-craftsmanship – were carried into the 20th century in part through the efforts of the British furniture-maker and designer Gordon Russell (1892–1980). Although he had no formal education in design, Russell absorbed and

Gordon Russell

treasured the ideals of the Arts and Crafts Movement as a consequence of working in the Cotswolds in the West of England, where the architect–designers C.R. Ashbee and Ernest Gimson had established medieval-style guilds and rural communities to promote craftsmanship. At the same time, Russell was also aware that the 20th-century designer could not ignore mechanized production; he considered, however, that the machine could be a useful, democratizing tool when combined with traditional craft values.

Gordon Russell's furniture designs and writings were dedicated to reconciling hand and machine manufacture and to creating a balance between Arts and Crafts tradition and modern innovation.

An oak dining table (below) designed by Gordon Russell in 1923 and made by hand by G. Cooke in Russell's workshop in Broadway, Worcestershire. Its almost rustic simplicity is typical of the late Arts and Crafts furniture of this period.

TRAINING AND EARLY WORK

In 1906 Gordon Russell started working in his father's small antiques-restoration workshop in Broadway, in the Cotswolds; he began designing furniture in 1910, and established his own craft workshop. Examples of his work were shown at a one-man exhibition in Cheltenham, Gloucestershire, in 1922; at the British Empire Exhibition at Wembley, London, in 1924; and at the Paris Exhibition of Decorative Arts in 1925. At the last of these he won five medals, thereby establishing an international reputation. By 1927 he had created Russell Workshops Limited (which in 1929 changed its name to Gordon Russell Limited) in Broadway, dedicated to the manufacture of simple wooden furniture, inspired by the work of Gimson. These pieces recalled 18th-century English furniture but were none the less innovative, and the workshop itself was semi-mechanized.

LATER FURNITURE AND COMMISSIONS

Russell was occupied by two important projects in the second half of the 1920s. While he continued to expand his business, opening a shop in London in 1929 (managed by the art historian Nikolaus Pevsner), he also began work on the furnishings for the house that he had built for his family at Kingcombe in the Cotswolds.

The 1930s were important years in Russell's career. Visiting the Stockholm Exhibition of 1930, he was particularly impressed by the decorative arts on display – by designers such as Simon Gate, Wilhelm Kåge (see pp.66–9), Edvard Hald and Carl Malmsten – which successfully combined

elements of traditional crafts with modern forms and manufacturing methods. With his brother W.H. Russell and the craftsman Eden Minns, he continued to design and manufacture furniture, which became plainer under the influence of the Modern Movement as the decade progressed.

INFLUENCE IN THE DESIGN WORLD

Russell also played an important role as an advocate of design reform, through his membership of the Design and Industries Association – an organization founded in 1915 to promote links between design and industry – and his affiliation with the Good Furniture Group of the late 1930s. He resigned as Managing Director of Gordon Russell Limited in 1940, a year after he became involved with the wartime Utility Scheme for furniture and textiles, promoting the need for low-cost design and manufacture. From 1947 until 1959 he was a powerful advocate of design reform in the role of Director of the Council of Industrial Design, a government body formed in 1944 as part of the Board of Trade to increase British exports. Russell's unique vision was of a world in which the best of craft and of machine manufacture should be combined, much as they had been in Scandinavia, to create a formidable and competitive modern British design movement.

The "Cirencester" bedroom suite (above) in English walnut with inlay of yew and ebony, designed by Gordon Russell and made in 1926 in his Broadway workshop. The items in question are examples of fine, British craftsmanship combined with a simplicity that was inherited from the Arts and Crafts ideals of the previous century.

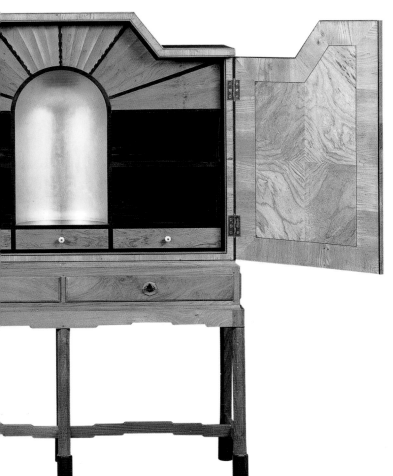

A collector's cabinet of fine walnut and burr-elm (left), designed by Gordon Russell and made by H. J. Holloway in 1929. The sun-ray motif and the use of inlay shows the way in which French Art Deco styles influenced Russell in the late 1920s.

A rosewood-and-ebony inlaid bookcase and cabinet (right), designed by Russell and made by F. Shilton in 1928. Although the careful attention to the use of wood veneers and the Gothic-style shapes at the top of the glass panels recall 18th-century English furniture, the overall simplicity of the design typifies Russell's own conservative brand of Modernism.

One of the greatest architects of the 20th century, the Finn Alvar Aalto (1898–1976) can also be considered one of the most significant figures in modern design. His approach, although rational, avoided the mechanical, and, although embracing modern demands for practicality and mass-production, favoured continuity with the past. Aalto

Alvar Aalto

has been called a "humanistic rationalist"; although he approved of advances in technology, he only considered them useful when they enhanced the comfort and ease of everyday living, and he retained a respect for natural materials and organic forms. He never strove to be part of the avant-garde but chose rather to undertake each project as an exercise in the use of materials and in creating designs that could be adapted to the widest variety of possible environments. His success in achieving these aims is proved by the fact that many of his designs are popular around the world and still in production today.

Alvar Aalto was Finland's most important modernist architect–designer. He merged the softness of organic materials and shapes with a purely 20th-century approach to design and manufacture.

The "Armchair 39" chaise-longue (1936–7; below). Made of laminated birch with a webbed seat, the design was created by Aalto especially for the Finnish Pavilion at the 1937 Paris Exhibition.

TRAINING AND EARLY WORK

It is significant that Aalto was born in rural Finland, in the small town of Kuortane, near Jyväskylä, where he designed his earliest buildings. The influence of the Finnish landscape – with its rugged, dramatic coastline – was a recurrent theme in his work, as was Finland's most abundant natural resource: wood. The route to visual abstraction for Aalto was through the model of the natural world rather than the geometric imagery derived from the world of mechanization. In this, Aalto allied himself with the organic design of the American pioneer Modernist Frank Lloyd Wright (see pp.24–5), rather than with the industrial aesthetic of the European Modernists, such as Le Corbusier in France (see pp.94–7) and Walter Gropius in Germany (see pp.88–9).

Aalto went to Helsinki to study architecture between 1916 and 1921 under the Swedish masters Armas Lindgren and Lars Sonek, and on completing his studies travelled extensively in Scandinavia, Central Europe and Italy; this last country, with its classical tradition, had the greatest impact on his early architectural career. Other influences to emerge in his later work were the writings of the British Arts and Crafts designer William Morris – who promoted the ethic of "truth to materials" – and the biomorphic Art Nouveau designs of the Belgian architect and designer Henry van de Velde (see pp.16–17). From the beginning of his career Aalto thought of himself

A row of Armchairs (left), in bent plywood and laminated wood, designed by Aalto for the Paimio Sanatorium (1931–2). The one-piece plywood seat and back units are suspended from the birch frames in a manner that is both practical to produce and comfortable to sit in. After 1935 the chair was produced by Aalto's retail company Artek.

The "900" tea trolley (below) designed by Aalto for Artek in the mid-1930s. Based on a modification of the laminated wooden frames developed for his "Paimio" armchairs, the designer has added wheels, a tiled tray and a basket to create a useful and highly appealing domestic object.

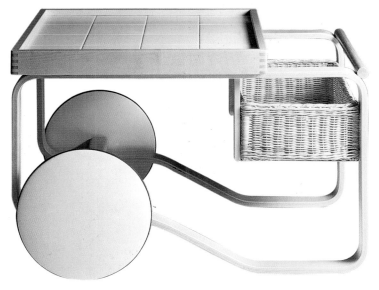

as a part of international Modernism, although, ironically, he has come to be thought of as the archetypal Finn. This is partly because he worked in his native country throughout his career; he opened an architectural office in Jyväskylä in 1922, moved to Turku in 1927 and then to Helsinki in 1933, where he lived until his death.

FURNITURE DESIGNS IN THE 1920S AND 1930S

In 1924 Aalto married Aino Marsio, a fellow architect, and collaborated with her through the 1920s on experiments with the new techniques of laminating and bending wood to create soft, organic forms. It was through working on equipment for his two major architectural projects of the late 1920s – the Viipuri Library, begun in 1927, and the Paimio Sanatorium, begun in 1929 – that he made his greatest design breakthroughs.

The seat and back of Aalto's "Paimio" chair (see above), designed for the Sanatorium in 1929 (although not perfected until the early 1930s), were made out of a single piece of curved birch plywood attached to two side components, made of the same material, for the chair's frame and armrests.

The "Savoy" glass vase (above) was originally designed by Aalto in 1937 as part of his project for the Savoy Restaurant in Helsinki. The designer has extended his use of organic forms from wood to glass, and it is said that the profile of the case was inspired by Finland's complex coastline. The vase is still produced by the Finnish glassmaking company Iittala.

Made initially by a Turku-based company called Huonekalu-ja Rakennust-yotehdas, it was a highly imaginative design that had no direct antecedents, although experiments with tubular steel by German and Dutch Modernist designers, such as Marcel Breuer (see pp.108-11) and Mart Stam (see pp.112-13), clearly influenced the elegant, minimalist curved form.

The "Paimio" chair inspired Aalto to design from 1930 onwards an impressive range of plywood chairs, stools, trolleys and tables, most of which are still in production today. His stacking stool, model number 60, is perhaps the best-known piece, having graced many a modern interior and been widely reproduced (although copies are often of inferior quality). From

1929 Aalto's furniture designs were executed by a skilled joiner in Turku, called Otto Korhonen. In the early 1930s Korhonen developed the "L", "Y" and "X" joints, which featured in Aalto's subsequent furniture designs. Aalto regarded these technological breakthroughs as extremely significant, comparing them to the discovery of the column in architecture.

WORK FOR ARTEK

Most of Aalto's designs for furniture, lighting fixtures, textiles and glass were conceived as "architectural accessories" – integral elements of a particular building – but were also produced commercially, especially after the formation of the company Artek in 1935. The company was established by Alvar and Aino Aalto and Marie Gullishsen and her industrialist husband, Harry, to manufacture and sell inexpensive, well-designed furniture made from Finnish wood. The Artek shop in Helsinki made all Aalto's designs available directly to the Finnish public for the first time. In addition to wooden furniture, Artek sold versions of pendant lights originally designed by Aalto for his various architectural projects. Suspended over tables for dining or chairs for reading, these were designed with the visual requirements of the user in mind.

Other items sold under the Artek name included textiles with a simple linear pattern printed in black on white (see opposite, below) and "Savoy" glass vases (see left), designed originally in 1937 for the Savoy Restaurant in Helsinki. The undulating forms of these objects, executed in clear and opaque glass by the Iittala glassworks, echoed those of Aalto's bent-wood furniture and many of his buildings.

Aino Marsio-Aalto, on whose creative input Aalto clearly depended enormously, was responsible for designing relatively inexpensive beakers and water-jugs, manufactured by Karhula in ribbed, moulded glass in the early 1930s and sold by Artek. They remained in production until the late 1950s and were revived at the end of the 1970s. Aalto collaborated on

The result of Aalto's experiments with bent wood, these stacking stools (below) were originally designed for the Viipuri Library (1927–35). The simplicity and practicality of this much-imitated design has yet to be surpassed and the stool is still made by Artek.

A small table lamp (left) designed by Alvar Aalto in the early 1930s. Unlike the Bauhaus light fittings, which emphasized materials and production methods, Aalto's experiments with lighting focused on the quality and variety of the light to be produced.

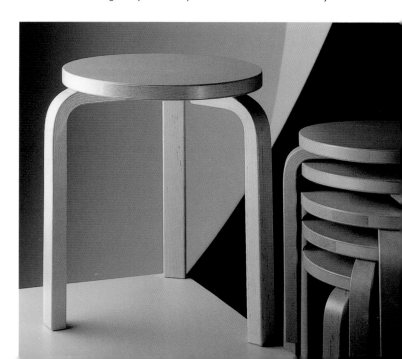

architectural projects with his second wife, Elissa Makiniemi, whom he married in 1952, in a similar way until his death. In 1954 Artek moved to larger premises in the centre of Helsinki, where it still produces and sells Aalto's designs and, in the spirit of its founder, supports craft and design around the world.

INTERNATIONAL REPUTATION

Through the 1930s Aalto represented Finland at numerous international exhibitions, thereby establishing his country – even though geographically on the margins of Europe – as a key force within 20th-century Modernism. In November 1933 his "Paimio" chair was displayed at London's Fortnum & Mason department store, in an exhibition sponsored by the progressive magazine, *Architectural Review*. Companies were subsequently established in Britain (Finmar, est. 1934–5) and the United States to import Aalto's furniture pieces. He designed the Finnish Pavilions for the Paris Universal Exhibition of 1937 and the New York World's Fair of 1939, and in 1938 he held a one-man show at the Museum of Modern Art in New York.

Most significantly, much of Aalto's work continues to be produced, and is valued as highly today as it was when first made. Finland's kindergartens, libraries and social-welfare institutions, for instance, still contain many of his original furniture pieces that look as good and function as well as when he conceived them. Indeed, Aalto's designs have an ageless quality that derives from his essential humanism and from his ability to keep tradition in touch with the requirements of the modern world.

A room (above) in the Baker House dormitory (1949), designed by Aalto for the Massachusetts Institute of Technology, Cambridge. The wooden furniture was also designed by Aalto, who sought to create a practical and comfortable unified interior.

A textile pattern (below), yet another example of the "architectural accessories" that Aalto designed for Artek in the 1930s and that are still made today. Characteristically, these textiles combine naturalness and comfort with a strictly minimalist pattern.

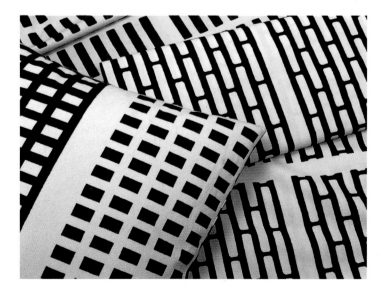

Bent wood

Modern design in the 20th century has not simply been the result of artistic innovations by far-sighted individuals, but has also depended on advances in materials technology, including the development of bent and laminated wood veneers and, later, plywood. This innovation made possible the construction of furniture in fewer separate elements, so that designs gained a new visual unity and fluidity. Laminated woods and plywood were light yet strong and provided comfort with a minimum of bulk. These technological breakthroughs provided designers with the opportunity to create potent visual symbols of the modern machine age for both public and private spaces.

THONET AND EARLY BENT-WOOD FURNITURE

The Viennese furniture-making company founded by Michael Thonet was the most important innovator in the field of bent-wood furniture-making. In c.1830 Thonet developed ways of bending under heat several layers of wood veneer glued together and laminated, for which he took out a patent in 1841. He used this material for curved back-rails on chairs and head- and base-boards for beds and sofas, and later developed components for the sides and legs of chairs. Thonet's aim was to reduce the necessary number of parts to a minimum. Inevitably this method of manufacture was less expensive and laborious than hand-carving, and by the second half of the 19th century he had introduced into his factory a system involving the division of labour and the use of machines to bend the wood.

EARLY MODERNISM

Thonet evolved a method of bending solid as well as laminated wood, and his innovations were taken up by progressive designers. By the turn of the century designers such as Josef Hoffmann (see pp.34–7), Otto

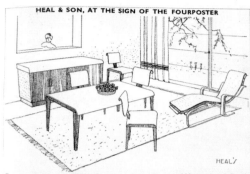

An advertisement (above) for the London furniture retailer Heal & Sons, produced to promote plywood furniture items manufactured by Isokon. The lightness and rigidity of plywood are emphasized in the text that accompanies the image.

A bent beechwood and bent plywood chair (left) made by the Thonet company in 1907. Wood-bending methods had become widely used in the United States by 1900 and Thonet exploited them to mass-produce inexpensive, simple utility items.

A nest of stacking tables (right) designed by Marcel Breuer for the British company Isokon in 1936. The design visually exploits the bends in the plywood, showing the tops and legs to be part of the same flowing surface.

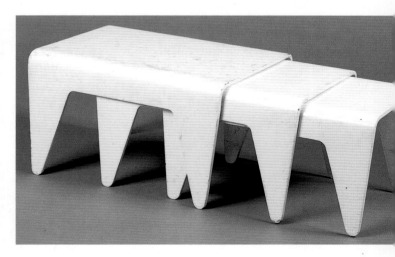

Wagner (see pp.12–13) and Adolf Loos were designing for Thonet and its competitor Kohn. Later, Le Corbusier used Thonet furniture in his "Pavillion de l'Esprit Nouveau" (see p.95) at the 1925 Paris Exhibition.

FINNISH AND BRITISH INNOVATIONS

The qualities of bent wood enabled several designers to develop radical furniture forms in the 1930s. While the use of wood linked such designs with nature and with earlier furniture traditions, the lightness, strength and flexibility of the material offered a means of producing designs suitable for modern lifestyles. Among the designers to take the greatest advantage of this was Alvar Aalto (see pp.74–7). His "Paimio" chair (see p.75) combined bent laminated wooden side components with a bent back and seat made from a single piece of plywood – a form of processed wood made up of several very thin layers of wood mechanically compressed and glued together, with the grain running crosswise in alternate layers for strength and durability. The result was the first cantilevered plywood chair.

Aalto's achievements were influential in other countries, especially in Great Britain, where – as in Scandinavia – designers valued the role of tradition in modern design. In 1931 the engineer Jack Pritchard founded the company Isokon, which specialized in the production of modern plywood furniture. Key Isokon designs include a 1936 chaise-longue, and the "Penguin Donkey" for holding paperback books, both designed by Marcel Breuer (see pp.108–11). Walter Gropius (see pp.88–9) also made designs for Isokon.

The British designer Gerald Summers designed such plywood items as round coffee-tables and cantilevered seating, which were manufactured by his own company, Makers of Simple Furniture (1931–40). After 1945, however, bent plywood was replaced by newer technologies such as moulded plywood (see pp.152–3) and plastics.

An exhibition was held in 1937 at London's Bowman Brothers store, showing an interior (above) with furniture made of bent laminated wood and bent plywood, and designed by Alvar Aalto. The plywood chair seats combined lightness and flexibility with strength.

The "DA Chair"(c.1948; below) by the Danish craftsman-designer Hans Wegner. The dramatically bent curves of the laminated wood used for the seat and the back give the chair a modern, organic appearance.

nlike many designers included in this book whose reputations depend partly on their prolific output, the Swedish designer and architect Bruno Mathsson (1907–88) is known only for a small number of furniture designs created from the 1930s to the 1960s. None the less, some of his original and visionary pieces have

Bruno Mathsson

become "classics" of 20th-century design and remain in production today. Mathsson belongs to the generation of designers who were responsible for creating the "Swedish Modern" style before World War II, and for many people his designs exemplify this style.

Bruno Mathsson is known for designs that have successfully incorporated his ideas about technology, aesthetics and lifestyle, thus epitomizing the style that became known as "Swedish Modern".

The "Miranda" armchair and "Mifot" footstool (1942; below) were variations on the "Eva" chair (1934). The chair and stool are produced today in a number of versions by the Swedish firm, DUX Mobel.

EARLY WORK

Born in Värnamo, Sweden, Mathsson was trained there from 1923 to 1931 as a cabinet-maker and designer by his father, Karl Mathsson, who ran the family furniture business that later manufactured most of Bruno's designs. While Mathsson lived and worked far from such centres of progressive design as the Bauhaus in Germany, his experiments in bending and laminating wood in the early 1930s linked him with the work of other European Modernists such as Alvar Aalto (see pp.74–7) and Marcel Breuer (see pp.108–11). This innovative tendency was evident in those of his works that were shown at the 1930 Stockholm Exhibition, and later at his one-man show in Gothenburg in 1936. Like the Danish designer Kaare Klint (see pp.64–5), Mathsson was concerned with redefining the chair in its simplest sense: as an object for sitting in. Unlike Klint and his Swedish contemporaries

An interior (left) in the summer house that Mathsson designed for himself. The room contains a number of his own furniture items, among them a version of his 1934 "Eva" armchair. The lightness and informality of the interior typifies many examples of the "Swedish Modern" style, which dominated international domestic design in the 1940s and 1950s.

Carl Malmsten and Josef Frank (see pp.56–9), however, Mathsson did not draw inspiration from traditional styles but sought totally new solutions to the problem of creating modern furniture. The famous "Eva" chair, designed in 1934, is a light, minimal structure made of two simple bent beechwood components fitting together to create a frame. Added to this is a strong and flexible woven fabric seat. As Mathsson explained, his main aim in this design was comfort: "comfortable sitting is an "art" – it ought not to be. Instead, the making of chairs has to be done with such an "art" that the sitting will not be any "art"." The curving, highly organic form of the "Eva" chair was defined more by the imagined body sitting in it than by the properties of the materials from which it was made.

MATHSSON AND "SWEDISH MODERNISM"

The "Eva" chair was made in a number of different versions: arms and a foot stool were added (see opposite), the back was heightened and different fabrics were used for the seat. The idea behind these variations was to produce a comfortable modern chair that could be adapted for all. This, and the softness and fluidity of the design, were distinctive characteristics of Swedish Modern furniture and interiors. More humanistic than German Modernism, this style preferred the use of natural materials such as wood to tubular steel, and was widely popular after World War II. The presence of Mathsson's chairs in Paris in 1937, and at the Golden Gate Exhibition in San Francisco and the New York World's Fair of 1939, reinforced the growing dominance of the style internationally.

LATER CAREER

After World War II Mathsson continued his career as an architect and furniture designer. Between 1945 and 1958 he concentrated on architectural commissions, working on simple structures such as glass, concrete and wood summer houses, although he also produced a notable table design in 1946. From 1958 he worked on the creation of new furniture forms with the Danish scientist Piet Hein, and the result of this collaboration was the oval "Superellipse" table (1964). It is for the "Eva" chair, however, that he is most remembered. Equally suitable for domestic settings, reception areas and conference rooms, it is a lasting symbol of the idealism that underpinned Swedish design in the mid-20th century.

The uncomplicated look of this wooden table (1935; right) is matched by the ease with which it can be folded away. Swedish design during the 1930s and 1940s was characterized by this lack of pretentiousness.

The British designer Enid Marx (b.1902) has been responsible for the appearance of a vast range of everyday goods – for example, textiles, book jackets and illustrations, carpets, stamps and plastic laminates – that have subtly influenced the form of the modern environment. Throughout her long career she has retained a consistent approach and an

Enid Marx

unmistakable personal style, including a light use of pattern with a stylized and modern appearance. She has succeeded in bringing together in her work aspects of folk art and Modernism, coupled with a strong understanding of both hand-craftsmanship and design for industrial manufacture.

Enid Marx has played an important part in 20th-century British design through her work for such bodies as the Advisory Committee on Utility Furniture, London Transport and the Royal Mail.

A book jacket originally designed in the 1930s (below) for Chatto & Windus. The stylized fleur-de-lis motif exemplifies Marx's skill at abstract pattern-making and her ability to combine references to the past with a fresh, modern style.

EARLY HAND-BLOCK FABRIC DESIGNS

Enid Marx trained as a fine artist at the Royal College of Art in London between 1922 and 1925, when she became interested in wood engraving. After her training she abandoned painting for hand-block fabric printing and worked as an apprentice in the workshop of the textile designers Phyllis Barron and Dorothy Larcher in Hampstead, London, where she created patterns with naturalistic motifs. She left to establish her own London workshop in 1927 and, for the next 12 years, produced a wide range of fabrics for a broad clientele. She was mainly influenced by English folk art, but also by the machine-inspired style of the early English Modernists.

A design for a 1½-pence postage stamp (below) marking the accession to the throne of Queen Elizabeth II in 1952. While respecting the necessary confines of stamp design, Marx styled and arranged the traditional symbols of England, Scotland, Wales and Northern Ireland – the rose, thistle, daffodil and shamrock – in a lively, informal way. (Actual size: 24 x 20.5mm; 1 x ⅞in)

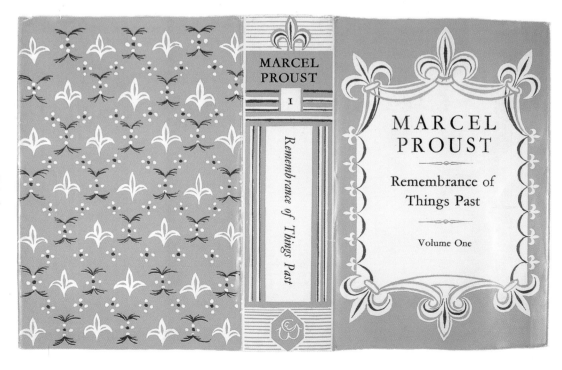

A design for a linen-fold patterned fabric (1949; above) entitled "Door". Created by the block-printing method, this fabric demonstrates Marx's strength as a designer of abstract repeated pattern, and also illustrates the traditional, hand-crafted side of her work.

A view of the interior of a London Underground carriage (1949; left) with upholstery fabric designed by Marx. The moquette, called "Shield", combines a modern pattern with an awareness of the practicalities of designing a textile for mass production and heavy wear.

INDUSTRIAL DESIGN

The same combination of tradition and modernity was also apparent in Marx's working methods. While she was drawn to the idea of hand-craftsmanship, she was also committed to industrial manufacture and designed patterns for machine-made textiles. One example of her ability to adapt designs for industrial manufacture was her set of moquettes for seating on London Transport buses and trains, from 1937. These strongly textured fabrics featured repeats of a geometric pattern in bold, contrasting colours. Her aim, she claimed, was to produce something visually appealing that would not date and would also wear well. Another of Marx's more industrially oriented commissions was the design of patterns for plastic laminates produced by ICI and, in the mid-1930s, fabric linings for luggage.

UTILITY FURNITURE AND POSTWAR DESIGNS

Between 1944 and 1947 Marx worked for the Utility Scheme, set up by the British Board of Trade to produce high-quality, low-cost furniture and textiles during wartime. She was careful to meet the demands of the brief – to create as varied a range as possible from limited resources – and designed a number of fabrics with small patterns and repeats for the scheme.

In 1945, as a mark of her special contribution to British design, Marx was made a Royal Designer for Industry, the highest recognition bestowed in Britain on international designers. Much of the rest of her long career has been dedicated to graphic design, including books, stamps and wrapping paper. Through her ability to design such a variety of basic everyday items, Marx has quietly become a central figure in the world of British design.

Progressive Modernism

Progressive Modernism

The dominant metaphor for modern design in the first half of this century was, without doubt, the machine. Perceived as a powerful symbol and perpetrator of progress, democracy and control over the unruly world of nature, the machine stimulated the imaginations of many architects and designers living in industrialized countries who responded to the pressing call to renew the appearance of the everyday environment. At no time was this more apparent than in the reforming efforts of the first three decades of the 20th century. Within the changing cultural, political, economic and technological climate of that period both the idea and the fact of mechanization inspired experimental work of an unprecedented nature.

In the aftermath of World War I the leading countries of Europe were galvanized into action, spurred on by the need to create a new democratic world in which the material environment was to play a vital role. Many architects and designers saw an opportunity of applying their visualizing and intellectual skills to the task of creating a new way of life for the mass of the population. To this end they combined the innovations made possible by mass production – as pioneered by American automobile manufacturers such as Henry Ford – with the stylistic innovations that progressive architects and designers had been working on since the early century based on the principles of simplification and geometric abstraction.

Brought together for the first time these forces added up to a powerful formula for a new movement in design. It was a movement that was essentially idealistic in nature and that was based on the need for change and renewal. The Soviet Union and the Netherlands were the first countries to attempt to realize these ideals, the first stimulated by the need to find a post-revolutionary role for architecture and design, and the second by a commitment to develop a new language of design that combined spirituality with social idealism. In the pages of the Dutch magazine De Stijl, first published in 1917, the work of Piet Mondrian, Theo Van Doesburg, Bart Van Der Leck, Gerrit Rietveld (see pp.98–101) and others combined vertical and horizontal lines with a simple palette of colours to reach what they believed to a pure style that could be applied to buildings, chairs and paintings alike. In the Soviet Union artists, architects and designers worked together in a similar way in pursuit of a similar goal – though their concern was less about idealistic reconstruction than about creating a new material world. They produced posters, workers' clothing, buildings and other tools of propaganda for practical as well as ideological purposes. The result was a much more dynamic movement, which led artists and designers such as Kasimir Malevich, Vladimir Tatlin, El Lissitzky and Alexander Rodchenko (see pp.102–105) to produce innovative abstract forms and images.

It was at the Bauhaus (see pp.90–91) in Germany that the design theory that came to be known as Functionalism achieved its most sophisticated and clearly thought-out level of expression. Once again inspired by political and cultural idealism, this experimental school for architecture, design and craft, formed in 1919, set out to create a universal language of form for the designed object. By the 1920s that ambition had been realized. The theory of Functionalism, which was rooted in the principles of mass production and of geometric simplification, held that an object's outer appearance should be defined by its inner structure. The Bauhaus teachers developed a system of design education that emphasized the belief in "truth to materials" and the importance of function.

France also developed its own brand of progressive Modernism in the 1920s. The work of Le Corbusier, Charlotte Perriand (see pp.94–7) and others was also aligned to the machine and to geometric abstraction. The high cultural aspiration of this movement was reinforced by its close links with the world of fine art, especially post-Cubist painting and sculpture.

These approaches to design moved through architecture into the applied arts – furniture, ceramics, glass, metalwork and textiles – and, eventually, product design. By the end of the 1920s Modernism had become an international ideal, represented at numerous events, such as the 1927 Weissenhofsiedlung exhibition and the 1930 Stockholm exhibition.

Inevitably the movement's idealism meant that the individual efforts of its protagonists failed to affect the mass environment in a significant way. Its broad influence was felt, however, in a number of tangible ways, for example in the presence of tubular steel furniture in schools and hospitals around the world. Modernism's influence was more important on a theoretical level, where it dominated international magazines, museum collections and educational curricula.

Although most pioneering efforts were made in Europe, the United States was not immune to the effects of what came to be known as the Modern Movement in architecture and design. In 1932 a major exhibition of work in this area entitled "The International Style" was held at New York's Museum of Modern Art. The United States was also the home of a more commercially oriented movement in design that was to have as much, if not more, of an international impact in the post-war years. While the Europeans limited themselves mainly to architecture and the applied arts, the American "industrial designers" dramatically refashioned the world of refrigerators, cash registers, cameras and, last but not least, automobiles.

With backgrounds in advertising and shop-window display, these designers were neither high-minded nor ideologically driven like their European counterparts. Their mission was the modernization of the mass environment. The aim of Norman Bel Geddes, Raymond Loewy (see pp.120–23), Walter Dorwin Teague (see pp.116–17), Henry Dreyfuss (see pp.130–31), Lurelle Guild and others was to embue consumer goods with a new attractiveness that would give them a competitive edge. They worshipped speed and modernity and nowhere were these themes more in evidence than at Chicago's Century of Progress Exhibition in 1933 and the dramatic New York World's Fair in 1939 (see pp.118–19). By that year the modern machine dominated modern life, both in factories and in the new labour-saving home, enabling everyone to believe that they could participate in the future. In making that dream a possibility the progressive modern designers played a fundamental role.

A piece of graphic design created at the Bauhaus in Germany by P. Keler and W. Molnar in 1923. The abstract, geometric composition was formulated to represent the system of movement through a service route that ran underneath a building.

The architect Walter Gropius (1883–1969) was a significant figure in the promotion of the Modern Movement in design, as a practitioner, an influential teacher and a theorist. His designs for mass-produced objects, such as ceramics, wallpaper and furniture, were all governed by the idea of a unified, functional style, derived from the rules of

Walter Gropius

architectural construction – where form is determined by structural requirements. "Mastery of space" – the emphasis on an object's spatial role rather than its decorative qualities – determined the approach to design of Gropius and other Modernists.

By forming the Bauhaus school in 1919, Walter Gropius successfully inculcated into those who studied there the ideal of many early 20th-century design reformers: the unification of the worlds of art and manufacture. He spread his ideas across Europe and the United States via his teaching, his writings and his own designs.

EARLY ARCHITECTURE AND INDUSTRIAL DESIGN

Gropius trained in architecture in Munich and Berlin from 1903 to 1907. In 1908 he began working in the office of the architect and designer Peter Behrens (see pp. 30–33), becoming his chief assistant on a number of important projects including the office interiors and furnishings for the Lehmann department store in Cologne. Two years later he opened his own architectural office in partnership with Adolf Meyer and rapidly gained a strong reputation as an innovative modern architect through his design for the Fagus shoe factory in Alfeld in 1911. The pure cubic form, flat roof and unprecedented all-glass curtain wall façade of this factory showed that even in his earliest designs Gropius had an original contribution to make to modern architecture. In 1913 he began to design industrial equipment, including a diesel locomotive and a motor coach. His interior for a train sleeping-car was shown at the 1914 Deutscher Werkbund exhibition in Cologne (opposite, right), alongside the dramatic model factory that he designed with Meyer, which used industrial materials such as glass and metal. By this date he had also begun to design interiors, including steel furniture (with Meyer) for the battleship Von Hindenburg.

A ceiling light (1923; below) from the Haus am Horn, a showhouse designed by members of the Bauhaus. The severely geometric glass and metal light was made in the Bauhaus metal workshop.

Gropius designed the "TAC 1" tea-set (left) for the German porcelain company Rosenthal in 1968, a year before he died. Its atypically organic forms marked a move away from the rigorously geometric style that he pioneered in the 1920s and with which he is usually associated.

Gropius' office at the Bauhaus (1927; opposite, below). As Director, his office was as much a showplace as a working environment. It contained many examples of Bauhaus design and manufacture, including items made in the weaving, wood and metal workshops. The overhead light was designed by Gropius himself and was influenced by the Dutch designer, Gerrit Rietveld (see pp.98–101).

THE BAUHAUS

A key turning point for Gropius came in 1915, when he was invited to take up the post of Director of the School of Applied Art in Weimar. The progress of World War I put this appointment on hold, but in 1919 he took up the position and also became Director of the Weimar Academy of Art. He persuaded the local government authority to merge the two schools into a single institution, which became known as the Staatliches Bauhaus Weimar (later called simply the Bauhaus; see pp.90–91).

The development of the Bauhaus was Gropius' main preoccupation in the 1920s. As Director of the school, he was responsible for determining the philosophy behind its teaching; he believed that the divisions between fine art, craft and architecture should be broken down and that artists should be trained specifically to work with industry. He continued to work on his own design projects, producing a simple, geometric door handle in 1922 and a ceiling light used in the Haus am Horn (see opposite, right), a showhouse specially designed and furnished by Bauhaus staff and students, in 1923. When the Bauhaus moved from Weimar to Dessau in 1925, Gropius designed a new building in the Modernist style for the school (see p.90), as well as houses for himself and other staff. In 1926 he created the interior of his own office, featuring a simple, functional glass tube and metal light fitting and a cube-shaped armchair (see below).

A train sleeping-compartment designed in 1914 (above). The emphasis on function and the clean lines of the interior fittings, in addition to the abstract patterns on the seats, show that Gropius was already as progressive a designer as he was an architect.

DESIGNS AFTER THE BAUHAUS

In 1920 Gropius re-established his architectural practice with Meyer and dedicated much of his energy to designing modular furniture for mass production. After resigning from the Bauhaus in 1928, he again became involved in transport design, in this case car bodies for the Adler company. His progressive ideas on architecture and design were not tolerated by the Nazi regime, however, and in 1934 he moved to London, where he set up an architectural practice with Maxwell Fry and designed furniture for the Isokon company (see p.79). In 1937 he emigrated to the United States, becoming Professor of Architecture at Harvard University. He lived and worked in that country until his death, although one of his last design projects was for the German ceramics company Rosenthal (see opposite, below).

Bauhaus

Although there have been many different modern design styles in the 20th century, the work of the Bauhaus is perhaps most closely associated with the idea of "Modernism". The Bauhaus was a German design school based from 1919 to 1925 in Weimar, from 1925 to 1932 in Dessau, and briefly in Berlin until its closure in 1933 by the Nazis. Its enormous significance derives from its influential staff and students, who included many of the 20th century's most notable designers; its functional product designs, many of which are still manufactured today; and the theory of design developed there. The inspiration of the school and its members can be seen in the work of such designers as Dieter Rams in Germany and Kenneth Grange in Britain (see pp.184–9).

The Bauhaus moved from Weimar to Dessau in 1925, to a purpose-built headquarters (above) designed by the school's Director Walter Gropius. With its rigorous geometry and glass façades, the building quickly became a prominent example of architectural Modernism.

An electric table lamp (1923–4; right) designed by Wilhelm Wagenfeld with K.J. Jucker at the Weimar Bauhaus, and made in the metal workshop there, where Wagenfeld was a student. Its use of transparent and opalescent glass and of metal, along with its geometrically shaped components, made it a "classic" modern design that is still in production today.

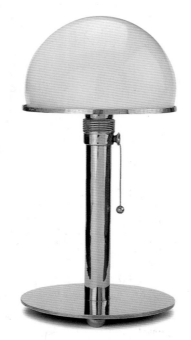

TEACHERS, STUDENTS AND THEORIES

The Bauhaus (construction house) was founded in 1919 in Weimar, Germany, by the architect Walter Gropius (see pp.88–9), with the merger of the Academy of Art and the School of Applied Art, of which institutions he was Director. The school's main aim was to train artists to design for industrial production, although in the early years its organization was similar to that of a medieval guild. Gropius' foresighted approach meant that avant-garde artists, such as Paul Klee, Wassily Kandinsky, Lyonel Feininger, Johannes Itten, László Moholy-Nagy and Josef Albers, were employed to teach the basic course introducing students to the handling of materials and the study of natural forms; they then studied specific crafts in special workshops.

Among the many well-known names to emerge from the school were Otto Lindig and Gerhard Marcks (ceramics); Wilhelm Wagenfeld and Marianne Brandt (metalwork; see pp.106–7); Marcel Breuer (furniture; see pp.108–11); Anni Albers (textiles); and Oskar Schlemmer (theatre and costume design). After Gropius' resignation in 1928, Hannes Meyer became Director but was replaced in 1930 by Ludwig Mies van der Rohe (see pp.92–3). With the unstable political climate in Europe in the 1930s many of its members moved to the United States, thus spreading Bauhaus theories.

The impact of the Bauhaus on modern design was rooted in its radical philosophy, which, according to Gropius, extended the ideas of the British Arts and Crafts leaders John Ruskin and William Morris into a new age dominated by machine production. It sought to combine the idea of "truth to materials" (that the forms of objects should reflect the materials from which they are made), with the rule that "form follows function" (the construction and form of an object or building should reflect its structural requirements). By using abstract forms free from historical references and mechanized production, Bauhaus designers aimed to create standardized, functional objects with universal appeal.

PRODUCT DESIGNS

This theory of design, often referred to as "Functionalism", underpinned the teaching programme at the Bauhaus, particularly after the school moved to its new headquarters in Dessau in 1925 (left, above). At this time the influence of the geometric forms and rational aesthetics of the Dutch

The metal workshop (right) at the Weimar Bauhaus in 1923, when the "form master" was László Moholy-Nagy. The school's emphasis on traditional manufacturing at that time is clear from this image, which shows individual wooden work benches and a range of hand-tools.

The cover of a catalogue of work by staff and students at the Weimar Bauhaus in the first four years of its existence (below). It was designed by Herbert Bayer using a characteristically simple, "sans-serif" typeface. The publication was created to accompany an exhibition.

A wall hanging (1926–7; below) designed by Gunta Stölzl at Dessau and made in the weaving workshop. Its abstract pattern shows how the ideas about geometric form that were taught in the preliminary course were translated into two dimensions. Most of the women who studied at the Bauhaus were based in the weaving workshop.

De Stijl movement and Russian Constructivism replaced the crafts-oriented curriculum. Materials and the process of mass manufacturing itself were seen as the determining factors in the creation of form. Bauhaus products include a large number of the "classic" designs of this century, among them Marcel Breuer's tubular steel chairs (see pp.108–113), Wilhelm Wagenfeld's electric table lamp (1924; opposite, below), Marianne Brandt's hemispherical teapot (1924; see p.107) and Anni Albers' geometric tapestries. It is simple, in retrospect, to identify a Bauhaus "style" in spite of the fact that the protagonists of the period believed that they were creating objects without a deliberate "style". Bauhaus objects, the result of a disciplined programme of design education, are still admired enormously for their usefulness and simplicity, and continue to inspire designers today.

Ludwig Mies van der Rohe (1886–1969), one of the greatest figures in Modern Movement architecture and design, was enormously influential in creating the image of the modern city with his designs for towering glass and steel skyscrapers. His chair designs of the 1920s, however, are equally significant for his use of refined details,

Ludwig Mies van der Rohe

daring minimalist forms, unerring sense of proportion and visual harmony, and, above all, for his creation of a universally appealing style, which makes his work as relevant today as when it was created. In many ways, his chairs are architecture in miniature — exercises in the use of space and of new materials — and were an intrinsic part of the interiors for which they were originally designed.

Although his influential furniture pieces were designed in the 1920s, Mies van der Rohe's career as a leading architect in the United States continued into the 1950s.

The cantilevered "Brno" armchair (1930; below) was originally produced both in tubular steel (shown here) and in flat steel. Like many of Mies's chair designs, it is now manufactured by Knoll Associates.

EARLY ARCHITECTURAL CAREER

Throughout his career Mies was known less as a theorist than as a practical designer, and he himself described his work as "thoughts in action". Born in Aachen, Germany, he first worked as a stonemason in his family's business (1900–2). He studied architecture in Berlin, where he was strongly drawn to the early 19th-century Neo-Classical architecture of Karl Friedrich Schinkel. His earliest experience of working as an architect was in the studio of Bruno Paul (1905–7) and, like the other Modernist architects Le Corbusier and Walter Gropius, in the office of Peter Behrens (1908–11; see pp.94–7, 88–9 and 30–33). Mies set up his own architectural practice in Berlin in 1914.

FIRST TUBULAR STEEL CHAIRS

From the beginning of his career Mies designed furniture for many of his buildings, and in 1920 created a very simple rosewood dining table and chairs for his own apartment in Berlin. It was only from the mid-1920s

A small glass-topped coffee-table with an "X"-shaped frame of flat steel (1929). Its structural originality, use of new materials and bold modernity characterized all of the furniture designs that Mies created with the assistance of Lilly Reich at this time.

The interior of the Farnsworth House in Fox River, Illinois, built between 1946 and 1950 (left). Mies designed the minimalist interiors, incorporating wood panelling and marble, to reflect but not distract from the natural surroundings that were visible from every part of the house.

The interior of the German Pavilion (below), designed by Mies and built for the 1929 Barcelona International Exhibition. His famous "Barcelona" chair first gained international recognition at this event.

that he began to design the chairs that became "classics" of 20th-century furniture, even though they had been conceived for particular interiors. In 1927 he met the architect-designer Lilly Reich, a Bauhaus alumnus who had served as the first female member of the Deutscher Werkbund board in 1920. They collaborated on Mies's first version of a cantilevered chair with a tubular steel frame. Unlike the slightly earlier rectilinear designs of Mart Stam and Marcel Breuer (see pp.108–11), Mies's chair had a curved frame, which emphasized his interest in the aesthetic possibilities as well as the structural virtuosity of this new material. The chair was shown at the 1927 Weissenhofsiedlung in Stuttgart (see pp.112–13): an exhibition, directed by Mies, of model dwellings by leading Modernist architects.

THE BARCELONA AND TUGENDHAT PROJECTS

Just two years later Mies and Reich designed their next important chair for Mies' German Pavilion for the Barcelona International Exhibition. Mies' small building – exceptionally simple in form but making use of rich materials such as brass and marble – also functioned as a reception area for King Alfonso XIII of Spain. The chair, intended as a modern throne, was made of a simple curved metal "X" frame inspired by Classical furniture, with black leather upholstery for the seat and back rest. As with everything Mies designed, the "Barcelona" chair and its matching stool and table were perfectly proportioned, with an air of elegance and authority (see right). Unlike other Modernist furniture of the time, the chair was not originally made for mass production; the frame was welded and polished by hand.

Between 1928 and 1930 Mies worked on the Tugendhat house at Brno, now in the Czech Republic, and, again with Reich, conceived two chairs for its interior. The "Tugendhat" chair (1929–30) featured a skeletal steel frame, constructed of chrome-plated bars screwed and welded together, and leather upholstery supported by leather straps. The "Brno" chair (see opposite, left) was another exercise in creating graceful forms with steel tubing, although a variation was also made with solid steel bars.

LATER CAREER IN THE UNITED STATES

After 1930 Mies gave up designing tubular steel chairs, but the items that he had created over the previous decade, particularly the "Barcelona" chair, all attained the status of "classics" in later years – they were, and continue to be, produced by the American firm Knoll Associates. After a short period spent as Director of the Bauhaus school at its final headquarters in Berlin (1930–32), Mies moved to Chicago in 1938. The rest of his career was dedicated to promoting the Modernist style of architecture in the United States, resulting in such celebrated and rigorously Modernist buildings as the Farnsworth House (1946–50; see above, top) near Chicago, and the Seagram Building (1954–8) in New York.

There can be little doubt that Le Corbusier (1887–1968) is considered by many to be one of the most revolutionary and influential architects of the 20th century. To him we owe some of the most radical and well-articulated ideas about an architecture that set out to meet the needs and aspirations of a modern, democratic society, dominated by the

Le Corbusier & Charlotte Perriand

machine. In his work, which encompassed urban planning, mass housing blocks and individual villas, Le Corbusier developed not only a theory of architectural form but a vision of a society that had broken its links with the decorative excesses of the previous century and in which the forces of reason, simplicity and order would prevail. Le Corbusier produced many of his most famous and influential furniture designs in collaboration with the designer Charlotte Perriand (b.1903) – who worked both in his studio and independently – and with his cousin, the architect Pierre Jeanneret.

Le Corbusier and Charlotte Perriand are pictured here in 1927 in the "Bar Sous le Toit" (Bar Beneath the Roof) – an interior designed by Perriand for the Salon d'Automne of that year.

The "B301" chair (1928–9; below), by Le Corbusier and Perriand. The design was not originally suited to mass production because of the cutting and welding needed to make its steel frame.

TRAINING AND EARLY ARCHITECTURE

Le Corbusier was born Charles-Edouard Jeanneret in the Swiss watch-making town of La Chaux de Fonds, but changed his name in 1920 after moving to Paris. In spite of his enormous contribution to modern architecture, Le Corbusier did not train as an architect but as a metal engraver like his father. In 1902 a watch case engraved by him won a prize at the Turin International Exhibition. He supplemented a fine-art training at the local art school with work in two important architectural practices: Auguste Perret in Paris (1907–8) and Peter Behrens in Berlin (1910–11; see pp.30–3). Perret introduced him to the use of reinforced concrete in building and Behrens taught him industrial processes, the concept of standardization and the alliance between geometric forms and machine design. In 1914 Le Corbusier developed the first of his revolutionary architectural ideas: the reinforced concrete structural frame supported by steel pillars. In this type of construction, there was no need for supporting, load-bearing walls, so interior space could be unrestricted. The idea featured in his unrealized designs for the "Dom-ino" houses in 1915.

ARCHITECTURAL THEORIES AND THE "ENGINEER'S AESTHETIC"

In 1917 Le Corbusier moved to Paris and quickly became part of the avant-garde community there. After meeting the painter Amedée Ozenfant, he turned to painting in a post-Cubist style that became known as Purism. Le Corbusier and Ozenfant painted everyday, mass-produced items such

An interior in Le Corbusier's L'Esprit Nouveau pavilion, one of the most innovative of France's contributions to the Paris 1925 exhibition. Seen here is the architect's commitment to the use of readily available furniture in interiors of this kind, among them the bent-wood chairs produced by Thonet (see pp.78–9) and the leather club armchair.

as bottles, which they believed represented a pure, undecorated "universal" aesthetic. Le Corbusier admired objects such as cars (he was a proud owner of a Voisin model), aeroplanes or door-handles as the "ultimate" solution to a practical design problem.

In 1920, however, Le Corbusier committed himself to architecture and over the next decade dedicated his efforts to perfecting his radical modern architectural theories. He published these in his influential books *Towards a New Architecture* (1923), in which he famously declared that "the house

Charlotte Perriand is shown (below) reclining on the "B306" chaise-longue (1928–9), on which she collaborated with Le Corbusier and Pierre Jeanneret. The position of the tubular steel chaise could be adjusted on the "H"-shaped steel base.

is a machine for living in", and his *Five Points of a New Architecture* (1926), which set out the principles of his architectural design approach: the use of a "free plan" unrestricted by internal walls; a roof terrace; large, continuous windows; a plain façade; and "pilotis", or columns, on which the building should be supported. These theories were demonstrated in his numerous designs for minimal dwellings: villas, including the *Esprit Nouveau* Pavilion (named from the progressive art journal that he edited), shown at the 1925 Paris Exhibition, the Villa Stein at Garches (1927) and the Villa Savoye at Poissy-sur-Seine (1929–30). All were conceived in the spirit of what he called the "engineer's aesthetic" – a visual language resulting from the most rational and efficient solutions to design.

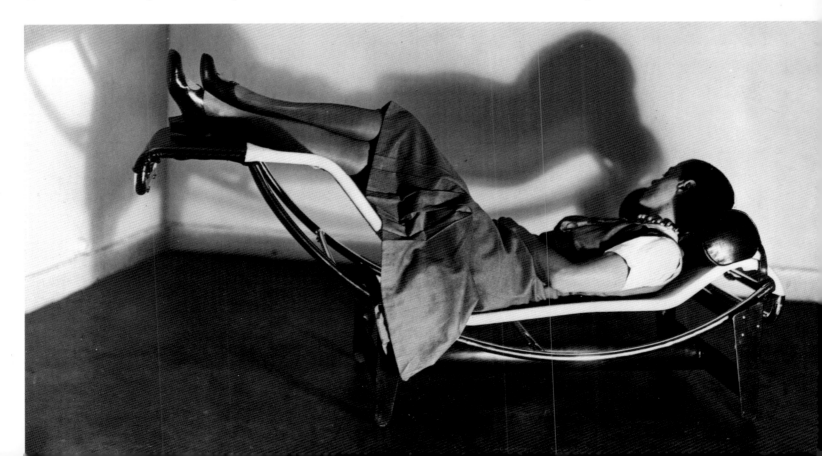

EARLY FURNITURE DESIGNS

Le Corbusier focused his attention on the interior but also on the building itself. For him the interior of a building was essentially determined by the exterior, and in accordance with his idea of the "free plan", his interiors generally consisted of a single, open space that could be divided with sliding partitions. Furniture formed part of the structure – for example, in the form of cantilevered concrete tables – or consisted of anonymous, factory-made products such as Thonet bent-wood chairs or more expensive leather club chairs from the Maples furniture store in London.

Before 1920 Le Corbusier had designed his own Arts and Crafts-style furniture for some of his architectural projects, but by the early 1920s the way in which he transformed interiors through his radically new approach to architecture demanded a new style for furniture such as chairs, on which he collaborated with Charlotte Perriand and his cousin Pierre Jeanneret. Le Corbusier regarded furniture as functional pieces of equipment, an idea first demonstrated in the standardized, geometric storage units ("casiers") designed for the *Esprit Nouveau* pavilion.

CHARLOTTE PERRIAND

Designs for tubular steel-framed chairs followed a couple of years later, when Charlotte Perriand joined Le Corbusier's studio. She had studied decorative art in Paris between 1920 and 1925 but, rejecting the luxurious Art Deco style of her teachers, the designers Maurice Dufrène and Paul Follot, she exhibited a radically minimalist bar at the Salon d'Automne in 1927; this made extensive use of steel tubing and chromed metal as a decorative wall covering. Between 1927 and 1929 she worked with Le Corbusier on the chairs that became icons of modern design: the "Grand Confort" armchair (below), a reworked version of a club armchair from the

A view of the living area in the Villa Savoye (1929–30; above) in Poissy, just outside Paris. Le Corbusier's idea of furniture being "built in" to the architectural structure is exemplified here by the table in the foreground – it embraces one of the structural columns and has a single tubular steel leg for support.

A two-seater version of the "Grand Confort" club armchair (1928–9; left), designed by Le Corbusier, Perriand and Jeanneret. The idea of exposing the tubular steel frame by putting it outside the leather cushions was a revolutionary tactic that transformed a traditional chair-type into a modern object. It is still made today by Cassina (see pp.212–13).

Maples store in London; the swivel-back chair (right), modelled on a British officer's chair; and the "B306" chaise-longue (see p.95, bottom), a reworked version of the Thonet rocking-chair. Each of these pieces presented, in Perriand's words, "confrontations" between new industrial materials such as tubular steel and natural materials such as cowhide.

FURNITURE PRODUCTION

Unlike the designs of Marcel Breuer (see pp.108–11) and Ludwig Mies van der Rohe (see pp.92–3), these chairs were not especially innovative technically but were explorations of a new image for modern furniture. The designs were originally rejected by the bicycle and automobile manufacturer Peugeot, eventually being produced by Thonet-Mundus. This firm was known for its mass production of low-cost pieces, but Le Corbusier and Perriand's designs proved difficult to manufacture in large quantities, as had been intended; as a result they were only produced in limited numbers and remained expensive. In the 1929 Salon d'Automne, Le Corbusier and Perriand showed their designs in a display called "Equipping a Living-Space". In addition to the chairs, the display included chrome and glass storage walls; it is less likely that Perriand was involved with this aspect of Le Corbusier's work, as similar designs had been created before her arrival in his studio.

THE 1930S AND LATER WORK

In 1930 Le Corbusier, Pierre Jeanneret and Perriand designed a plywood display stand for an exhibition in London, showing their renewed interest in natural materials. After 1930, however, furniture ceased to play a major role in Le Corbusier's work, and he concentrated more on architecture and urban planning. By the 1950s the severe style of his pre-war designs softened and became more organic and sculptural. Perriand worked in

Le Corbusier and Perriand's tubular steel revolving chair (1929; right). The chair type derives from the bent-wood Thonet "B.9" model, and was manufactured by Thonet with other tubular steel pieces.

Le Corbusier's studio until 1937 and later became more interested in architecture, although she also spent some years in Japan as an adviser to the government on arts and crafts. In 1946 she designed furnishings for a holiday resort at Méribel-les-Allues, France, and, in 1950, a prototype kitchen for Le Corbusier's housing block in Marseilles, the Unité d'Habitation. Perriand continued to work on interiors in the 1950s and 1960s, designing items for the Air France office in London (1957) and students' rooms for Le Corbusier's Cité Universitaire in Paris (1959).

THE 1960S' REVIVAL

The furniture designed by Le Corbusier and Perriand in the late 1920s was revived in the 1960s by the Italian manufacturer Cassina. The 1928 colonial chair (see p.94) and the chaise-longue (see p.95), for example, were reproduced in 1965 and the revolving armchair (above) a little later. Like the originals, the reproductions were available in different versions using a range of materials for the upholstery. In the 1980s Perriand acted as a consultant to Cassina, giving advice on the way in which the original pieces had been made. Only recently, however, has she been given full credit for the part she played in creating these important modern furniture designs.

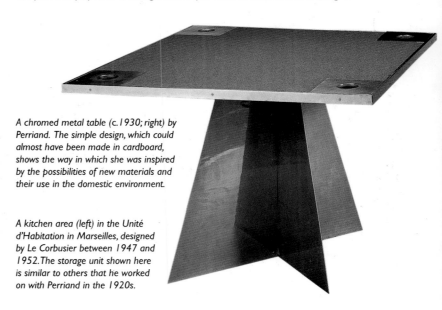

A chromed metal table (c.1930; right) by Perriand. The simple design, which could almost have been made in cardboard, shows the way in which she was inspired by the possibilities of new materials and their use in the domestic environment.

A kitchen area (left) in the Unité d'Habitation in Marseilles, designed by Le Corbusier between 1947 and 1952. The storage unit shown here is similar to others that he worked on with Perriand in the 1920s.

If there is one example of modern design that stands out above all others, it is most probably the uncompromisingly abstract "Red/Blue" chair of 1918 (opposite, below) designed by the Dutchman Gerrit Rietveld (1888–1964). A familiar image in design books and lifestyle magazines, its strictly geometric structure is frequently presented as testimony

Gerrit Rietveld

to the idea that Modernist design and physical comfort have very little in common. The chair is perhaps the best-known work by one of the 20th century's most innovative designers, who succeeded in radically reformulating the language of furniture and the interior, and whose interest in the way structure dictates form influenced many later important figures in modern design.

Gerrit Rietveld is shown with a model of the Magnette-Core House, which he designed in 1947. For Rietveld, designing for furniture, interiors and buildings were inseparable. His aim to make the viewer aware of the basic structure of a piece as well as the space around it was innovative and highly influential on later Modernist designers.

TRAINING AND EARLY WORK

Rietveld was born in Utrecht and, apart from a few visits to other European cities and later to the United States, he worked there all his life. Despite his great influence on modern design, there is little information about the way in which he developed his radical theories; trained until 1912 as an apprentice in his father's cabinet-making shop after leaving formal education, he never became skilled in the art of rhetoric or in expressing his ideas in manifestos or treatises. His radicalism was expressed instead in his creations and his practical approach to the act of design; he worked out his ideas by making prototypes directly in cardboard or solid wood.

This wooden sideboard (1919; right) was among the first furniture items with which Rietveld experimented between 1910 and 1920. Basing it on the same constructional principles as the "Red/Blue" chair, Rietveld set out to make the piece's essential geometric structure obvious to all. This example was manufactured by G. Van de Groenekan in 1983.

A corner of the office (left) that Rietveld designed in 1920 for Dr Hartog in Maarssen. The chair is a variation of the "Red/Blue" chair of three years earlier. The hanging light, desk and set of drawers are all designed along similar lines; the geometry underlying their structure has been made visually explicit.

The "Red/Blue" chair (1918; below). Through the use of form and colour, Rietveld deliberately exploited, rather than concealed, the joints created by the chair's wooden elements, and in this way introduced a new level of self-consciousness into designing chairs.

From 1906 to 1908 Rietveld attended evening classes in design, and from 1908 to 1911 he worked as a designer for the jeweller Cornelius Begeer. Over this period he also studied architectural draughtsmanship. He opened his own furniture-making business in Utrecht in 1911. For the next four years he attended an advanced architectural course and produced solid, rustic-looking, wood furniture based on that designed by his teacher P.L. Klaarhamer or in the style of the influential Dutch architect–designer H.P. Berlage. Rietveld's early furniture also displayed vague references to the work of the British designers Charles Rennie Mackintosh (see pp.26–9) and E.W. Godwin, which he could have seen in *The Studio* magazine, as well as that of Frank Lloyd Wright (see pp.24–5). Rietveld became familiar with Wright's work through his friend the artist Robert Van't Hoff, who had met the pioneering American architect.

THE "RED/BLUE" CHAIR AND DE STIJL

In 1917 Rietveld designed a chair that had no real precedents (see right). It consisted of geometric, standardized wooden components – flat, rectangular panels and listels with a square section – assembled in such a way that the pieces overlapped, emphasizing the chair's simple construction. The oak was originally left unpainted, but in the following year Rietveld

The "Zig-Zag" chair (below) was designed for Metz & Co. in 1934. Although constructed from several pieces of wood, it reflects Rietveld's experiments with producing chairs made from a single piece of material, and looks forward to the moulded plastic chairs of the 1960s.

The slat-constructed red spruce "Crate" armchair (c.1935; below), made by Metz & Co., was originally sold as a kit for home assembly and has a crude look not seen in Rietveld's earlier work.

modified the form slightly and painted the components, using black for the frame, yellow for the ends of the listels and red and blue (hence the chair's name) for the back and seat panels respectively. The origin of this design – which can be seen as a skeletal version of the traditional armchair as well as an exercise in manipulation of space – lay in Rietveld's connections with the group of artists, designers and architects who had come together in 1917 under the banner of a new journal called *De Stijl* (The Style). Building on the discoveries of Cubism, the members of De Stijl (as the group was later known) aimed to break down the divisions between fine and applied arts and to create a new, pure form of art and architecture. In painting, for example, Piet Mondrian and Theo van Doesburg reduced their palette to the simplest tones and to primary colours. Form was represented by straight horizontal and vertical lines that did not reveal the artist's hand.

DE STIJL FURNITURE AND THE SCHRÖDER HOUSE

This rigorous painting system, known as "Neoplasticism", was translated directly into three dimensions through the architectural experiments of van Doesburg and J.J.P. Oud. Rietveld searched for an equivalent in furniture in his designs over the next six years, including a buffet (see p.98) and "High Back" chair (c.1919); a range of children's furniture, such as a wheelbarrow and cart (c.1923); a variation on the "Red/Blue" chair (1919), designed for an interior by van Doesburg; and others, including a suspended ceiling light, for Dr Hartog's clinic in Maarssen (1920; see p.99). In all of these strikingly innovative compositions he used the same minimal language of intersecting lines and planes as in the "Red/Blue" chair.

In 1924, in collaboration with his client Truus Schröder-Schräder, with whom he had worked since 1921, Rietveld created an equally radical work of architecture in Utrecht. The compositional, structural and spatial concerns that Rietveld had already been experimenting with in his furniture were the basis for the design of the Schröder House, in which exterior, interior and furnishings were fully integrated through a restricted colour scheme and the use of lines and planes (see opposite, below). In the innovative open plan of the upstairs part of the house, sliding partitions were used to divide working, sleeping and living areas.

LATER ARCHITECTURAL WORK AND LEGACY

With these enormous achievements behind him and still only a young man, Rietveld went on to become known internationally through his role in the formation of the CIAM (the International Congress of Modern Architecture) in 1928 and in the Viennese Werkbund exhibition of 1931, where all the major Modernist architects exhibited. He continued to create innovative furniture, from his experiments with tubular steel and bent plywood in the "Beugelstoel" of 1927; to his simple "Zig-Zag" chair of 1934 (see top left), which recalled his links with De Stijl in its cantilevered design of wooden panels; and his "Crate" furniture of the same date (see above left), a low-cost, mass-manufactured, self-assembly design. He also experimented with aluminium and plywood in his search for a chair that could be made from a single sheet of material, and, in 1924, created a chair with a seat and back made from one piece of bent plywood. He anticipated by almost two decades the breakthroughs that Charles Eames (see pp.148–51) was to make with moulded plywood after World War II.

A wall-mounted coat rail in wrought iron (1924; right), which was used both in the Schröder House and in a Dutch apartment building. The coat rail is just one example of the way in which Rietveld took responsibility for even the smallest details in his projects for interiors.

After 1945 Rietveld received more public attention as an architect, although he did not abandon furniture design. Before the war he had built a row of houses (1930–31), on the Erasmuslaan opposite the Schröder House, and the Vreeburg Cinema (1936) in Utrecht, while after 1945 significant projects included the Netherlands Pavilion at the Venice Biennale

A view across the upper floor of the Schröder House (1924; below) in Utrecht. The house was an exercise in which the architectural frame, interior space and furnishings were all seen as part of the same visual challenge to be treated together.

and the sculpture pavilion in Amsterdam's Sonsbeek Park (both 1954). He worked on the Institute of Applied Arts (1956–67) and, with the architect Van Tricht, on the Van Gogh Museum (1963–74), both in Amsterdam.

There can be little doubt that, regardless of his reputation and skill as an architect, Rietveld will ultimately be remembered as the designer of the "Red/Blue" chair. In 1971 the Italian furniture company Cassina brought the chair back into production, and it quickly became a symbol of the purity of early Modernist design.

The Russian artist and designer El Lissitzky (1890–1941) formed an important link between the avant-garde in his native country – where radical ideas about the function of art emerged after the 1917 Revolution – and in Western Europe. Through his connections with members of the De Stijl group and the Bauhaus, for example, the

El Lissitzky

principles of Constructivism – a movement of progressive Russian artists, architects and designers who abandoned fine art traditions after 1917 with the aim of creating art to serve the new social and political order – spread to Europe. Lissitzky worked in many fields, including photography, interior design, exhibitions, and typography and graphics.

El Lissitzky, photographed in around 1919 in his studio in Vitebsk. He was one of a group of influential figures who helped develop an entirely new visual language for the generation of post-revolutionary, avant-garde Russian artists, designers and architects.

The bent plywood "Leipzig chair" (1930; above) has a crudeness not seen in bent-wood pieces that were being produced elsewhere at this time.

EARLY WORK AND TEACHING

Like so many other pioneers of modern design in the first decades of the 20th century, El Lissitzky – born Lazar Markovich Lissitzky in Polschinok – trained as an architect: from 1909–14 at the Technical High School in Darmstadt, Germany, and from 1915–16 in Russia. He was also, in common with many of his contemporaries, a committed teacher. From 1917 onwards he gave classes in a range of disciplines; in 1918, for example, he was invited by the artist Marc Chagall to teach graphic design at the art school in Vitebsk, where he stayed until 1919; from 1925–6 he taught furniture and interior design in the department of metalwork and woodwork at the Vkhutemas, the new school of art and design in Moscow.

In 1919 the avant-garde artist Kasimir Malevich became Director of the art school in Vitebsk and renamed it "Unovis" (College of the New Art). Malevich developed the concept of Suprematism: a form of "non-objective" painting realized through pure, geometric forms in plain colours. Under Malevich's influence, Lissitzky abandoned the traditional figurative Jewish style of his illustrations for children's books and moved towards developing a modern form of typography. In 1920 he designed the celebrated poster *Beating the Whites with the Red Wedge* (see opposite, centre), using the diagonal lines and asymmetry familiar in Malevich's art.

"PROUN" STUDIES AND LATER WORK

In 1919 Lissitzky had introduced his concept of "Proun" – a Russian acronym for the "Project for the Affirmation of the New": an installation described by the artist as a combination of painting and architecture (see opposite, top). In his "Proun" studies (1919–21), Lissitzky combined the principles of Suprematist and Constructivist art, which he also applied to a wide range of media. Graphic design and typography, often incorporating photomontage, were his primary preoccupations. However, in the early 1920s he also made convincing attempts at exhibition – for example, the 1927 Cologne Exhibition – and at architectural design. He collaborated with the Dutch architect Mart Stam on an unrealized project for a cantilevered office block,

The "Proun Room" (right), designed for the Great Berlin Exhibition in 1923. For this project Lissitzky used wall-mounted geometric elements to create a sense of movement and dynamism that is missing in his two-dimensional compositions, although he used the same red, black and grey Suprematist colour scheme.

El Lissitzky's most famous Suprematist poster (below), Beat the Whites with the Red Wedge (1920). It shows the artist's skill in using abstract signs and minimal colour, in conjunction with typography, to convey an ideological message — the Red Army's destruction of the anti-Revolutionary White Army.

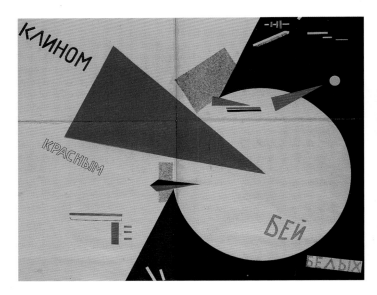

A book-cover design (below) for a publication entitled Die Kunstism (The Isms of Art), designed by Lissitzky and the Alsatian artist Hans Arp in 1925. Dramatic typography and minimal but strong colour are combined to create a visually arresting effect.

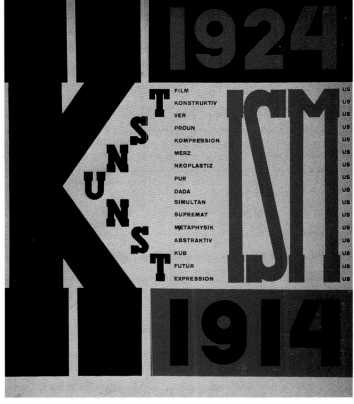

called the "Cloud Props" project (1924–5). Like other artists of the period, Lissitzky also provided props for the new political regime, including a crane-like steel speaker's platform for Lenin in 1920.

During the 1920s Lissitzky visited Germany, France, the Netherlands and Switzerland and established links with designers such as Theo van Doesburg and Ludwig Mies van der Rohe (see pp.92–3). His ideas were well known at the Bauhaus, and in turn Bauhaus theories of design (see pp.90–91) had an influence on Lissitzky, as his only known chair design of 1930 clearly demonstrates (see opposite). In the 1930s he concentrated on photography, but in 1941 – the year he died – he designed another notable poster, also abstract and geometric in concept, entitled Provide More Tanks.

The ideas of Russian avant-garde designers such as Alexander Rodchenko (1891–1956) were of great importance in the evolution of modern design. Rodchenko was one of the youngest members of a new generation of artists and designers associated with the Constructivist Movement that emerged in Russia after the 1917 Revolution.

Alexander Rodchenko

The Constructivists sought to renew the material environment and all areas of cultural activity in a way deemed appropriate for the new, democratic society in which they lived. In the visual and applied arts, this was to involve the use of pure, geometric forms that represented the "universality" of human experience. Many Western designers, especially those associated with the Bauhaus, were enormously influenced by Constructivist art.

The breadth of Alexander Rodchenko's avant-garde work – including posters, book-covers, interiors and stage sets – made him one of the most influential Russian designers of his generation.

EARLY CONSTRUCTIVIST WORK AND TEACHING

Rodchenko trained as an artist between 1911 and 1916, first in his home town of Kazan and subsequently in Moscow, where he spent the rest of his life. In 1914 he met the radical poet Vladimir Mayakovsky, who campaigned in 1918 for the separation of art and the state and for the self-government of art institutions in his treatise *The Manifesto of the Flying Federation of Futurists*. In 1915 Rodchenko met another avant-garde artist, Vladimir Tatlin, who had seen Cubist painting in Paris and was also associated with Constructivism. The influence of these two artists can be seen in Rodchenko's early abstract paintings and three-dimensional constructions.

From 1917 onwards, however, together with his wife and fellow designer Varvara Stepanova, Rodchenko dedicated himself to developing a new visual language for everyday objects. Over the next decade he worked on a range of projects covering industrial and graphic design, stage sets and theatre design, fashion and costume, and architecture. Although

A design for the interior of the Workers' Club by Rodchenko (above). It was shown in the Soviet Pavilion at the Paris Exhibition of 1925, and was highly praised for its simplicity, practicality and, above all, its uncompromising modernity.

The set design and costumes from Scene Six of The Bed Bug by Mayakovsky (1929; right). The play was staged at the Moscow Theatre of Satire, where Rodchenko's minimal Constructivist sets proved highly successful.

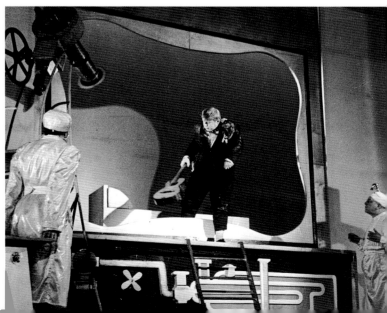

A photomontaged film poster (left), designed for Sergei Eisenstein's film The Battleship Potemkin *(1925); Rodchenko also designed the cover of the programme that accompanied the film. Both film and theatre were important forms of propaganda art for the Constructivists.*

A set of book covers (1924; below), designed for the Mess Mend *or A* Yankee in Petrograd *series written by Jim Dollar (the pseudonym of Marietta Sanginyan). These covers are typical of the way in which Rodchenko combined bold graphics and typography with photomontage to dramatic effect.*

little of his work – with the exception of his graphic designs – was ever mass-produced, its radical approach was highly influential within the international Modernist Movement.

One of Rodchenko's first projects was a series of lamps in abstract forms for the Café Pittoresque in Moscow in 1917, and in 1919 he designed a Cubist-inspired kiosk for the distribution of newspapers and propaganda. Also in 1919, he produced a set of architectural compositions, and the following year designed a building consisting of geometric elements with a scaffolding-like structure at the top, but none of these designs was executed. Rodchenko played a key role within post-Revolutionary cultural politics in Russia; he was an active member of the Inkhuk (the Institute of Artistic Culture, formed in 1920 to investigate the basic questions of art) from its beginnings until 1923, while from 1920–30 he taught composition at the Vkhutemas, the new art and design school in Moscow. He worked with his students on various designs for domestic goods, among them lights and tableware. Although these never got past the drawing-board stage, they were highly original compositions of abstract, geometric elements.

WORK IN THE 1920S

In the early 1920s Rodchenko applied his skills to two-dimensional design, including textiles, book covers, posters, trademarks and packaging. The challenge confronting graphic designers in post-revolutionary Russia was to introduce an arresting and easily understood graphic style for a general public with a high rate of illiteracy. Rodchenko's response to this challenge is demonstrated by his use of very simple graphics and type coupled with photomontage. Abstract concepts were illustrated using basic geometric shapes or symbols such as arrows. His numerous advertising posters from these years – among them a famous example for galoshes (1923), designed in primary colours and depicting a realistic-looking rubber shoe protector – featured a strong element of geometric abstraction in their imagery and a commitment to modern typography. Returning to three-dimensional

design, he created an interior for a workers' club, with simple wooden furniture such as chairs and bookshelves, which was exhibited at the 1925 Paris Exhibition (see opposite, left).

Rodchenko was particularly drawn to the worlds of film and theatre, where his inventive designs could come to life, even if only for a limited time; his sets and costumes for various theatrical productions, among them the abstract, Constructivist set for *The Bed Bug* (1929; see opposite, right), were stunningly original. He was also interested in dress, on which he worked closely with his wife. Stepanova designed for her husband a pair of overalls, indicating their role as "workers" within the new Soviet state.

From 1927 to 1930 Rodchenko was the Dean of the Faculty of Metalwork at the Vkhutemas, but he increasingly saw photography as his ideal medium of creative expression. Once again he collaborated with Stepanova in this field, and dedicated most of the rest of his career to it.

The metal workshop was among the most productive of all those at the Bauhaus school, both in terms of the designs for mass production created there and of the significant industrial designers who trained there. These included Wilhelm Wagenfeld, who became one of Germany's leading product designers, and Marianne Brandt (1893–1983).

Marianne Brandt

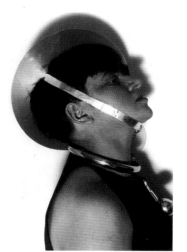

Brandt is an important figure in the history of modern design, not simply because she created some of this century's most beautiful and durable metalware, but because she did so as a woman. She later explained how difficult it was to enter the male-dominated domain of metalworking at the Bauhaus and described how the men gave her dull, repetitive work for a considerable amount of time before they accepted her. She eventually became one of the most celebrated designers associated with the Bauhaus and one of its very few female students not based in the textile workshop. Her designs are still produced today by the Italian manufacturer Alessi.

The Bauhaus-trained metal designer Marianne Brandt. The picture is a self-portrait and Brandt is wearing jewellery that she designed herself, which she called "Jewellery for a Metal Festival".

A metal and plexiglass "smoker's companion" set (mid-1920s; below). Brandt's designs incorporated both new and traditional materials and were all intended for practical use in everyday life.

EARLY YEARS AT THE BAUHAUS

Born in Chemnitz and trained as a painter and sculptor in Weimar for a short period from 1911, Brandt established her own studio in 1917 but spent much of the next few years travelling. She was married in Norway in 1919, and in the following year she went to Paris to study for several months. In 1923 she entered the Bauhaus as a student on the "Vorkurs" (preliminary course). The artist László Moholy-Nagy had taken over the role of "form master" in the metal workshop a year earlier and, impressed by the new student's work, encouraged her to specialize in this medium.

In spite of the restrictions she encountered because she was female, between 1923 and 1924 Brandt designed a range of innovative yet functional tableware – including a tea- and coffee-service and a tea-infuser – made in silver or brass with ebony handles and finials (see opposite, centre). Their pure geometric forms – spheres, hemispheres and cylinders – were inspired by the Constructivist aesthetic principles that Moholy-Nagy had introduced into the workshop. Although these pieces were originally executed by hand by a skilled craftsman, Brandt fully

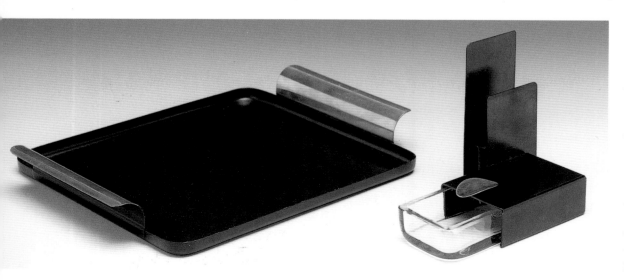

embraced the Bauhaus philosophy of designing for industrial production, in theory at least, and wrote later that "the task was to shape these things in such a way that even if they were to be produced in numbers, making the work lighter, they would satisfy all aesthetic and practical criteria and still be far less expensive than any singly produced item."

DESIGNS FOR MASS PRODUCTION

Over the next couple of years a large number of designs for domestic metalware, including bowls and ashtrays, emerged from Brandt's drawing board. Her early crafts-influenced approach was gradually replaced by a more direct focus on the problems of mass production. From around 1927 she turned to designing electric lamps and lighting fixtures, for which there was an ever-expanding market. These practical, economic and modern items, combining chrome, aluminium and glass, were produced under a Bauhaus licence by two companies: Körting & Mathiesen and Leipzig Leutzch. Among the best known was the "Kandem" table lamp (1928; right).

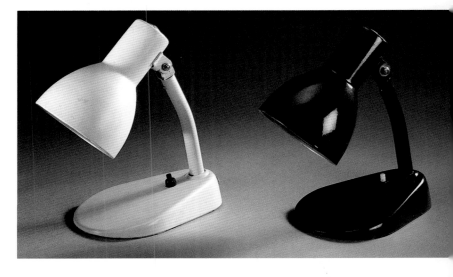

Brandt designed model "702" or the "Kandem" flexible bedside light (above) in 1928, at a time when she had become interested in the idea of mass production. Made of metal, the nickel-plated and lacquered light was designed as a class project at the Bauhaus with the help of Hin Bredensieck. It was first manufactured by the firm of Körting & Mathiesen.

A tea- and coffee-service (left) designed by Brandt just after she had entered the Bauhaus (1924). Realized using silver, ebony and plexiglass, the set is aggressively modern but remains one of her more élitist designs. The Italian metalworking company Alessi put the design back into production in 1985.

With its flexible stem, single colour-scheme (it was available in either black or white) and sturdy base, the lamp had a simple, functional quality that has made it a design "classic".

AFTER THE BAUHAUS

When Walter Gropius (see pp.88–9) and Moholy-Nagy left the Bauhaus in 1928, Brandt also wanted to leave, but was persuaded to remain as head of the metal workshop for a further year. In 1929 she worked for a brief period in Gropius's office in Berlin and spent the next three years with the Ruppelwerk metalworking factory in Gotha. For the rest of her career she combined painting and sculpture with teaching at the College of Fine Arts in Dresden (1949–51) and at the School for Applied Art in Berlin (1951–4). She never repeated the design successes of her youth, but her objects from the 1920s have remained inspirational to many designers.

An ashtray in German silver and bronze (right) designed by Brandt (1923–4) and made in the Bauhaus metal workshop. In keeping with Brandt's formal interests at this time, the ashtray is an abstract composition – consisting of a hemisphere with a hole, small feet and a lip – as well as fulfilling a practical function.

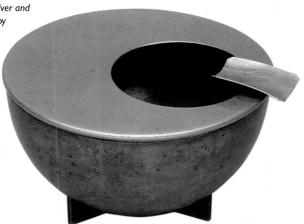

Marcel Breuer (1902–81) enjoyed a long and successful career at the forefront of modern architecture and design. However, his most celebrated contributions to 20th-century design were created at the Bauhaus in Germany when he was still in his twenties, and he ranks equal to his mentors Walter Gropius and László Moholy-Nagy

Marcel Breuer

in his achievements. By the 1930s his simple, light and functional furniture, intended for mass production, came to represent an ideal of modern life that embraced new technology and the concepts of reason, function and progress.

Marcel Breuer as a student at the Bauhaus. An influential furniture designer at that time, who made key breakthroughs – especially in the area of new materials – Breuer went on to become a leading modern architect in the United States.

A version of the chair designed by Breuer in 1921 when studying at the Bauhaus (below); the interest in structure, and in construction made visible, reveals the strong influence of the designs of Gerrit Rietveld in this early, formative phase of Breuer's career.

EARLY TRAINING AND BAUHAUS EXPERIMENTS

Unlike Gropius, Breuer was not a philosopher but a practical designer, as reflected in his prolific output; he was without doubt highly organized and driven to succeed. Born in Pecs in Hungary, he spent his early years far away from the cosmopolitan world of avant-garde designers in Germany, Austria and France. On discovering modern art through magazines, however, he was determined to become a painter and went to Vienna to study art. He soon heard about the new art and design school established in Weimar and in 1920 moved there to become a student at the Bauhaus.

From the outset it was clear to Gropius, the "form master" in the furniture workshop at the time, that Breuer was an exceptional student, and he encouraged him to take up furniture design. Breuer's early designs

A domestic office desk designed by Breuer for Gropius' house in Dessau (1925–6). The metal-framed swivel chair – the "B7" – was a piece manufactured by Standard-Mobel (1926). Breuer designed other pieces for this house, including a sofa for the living room.

An interior of Moholy-Nagy's house at Dessau (above). It contains a number of furniture items designed by Breuer, among them his famous tubular steel club chair (1925) – the designer's first foray into this new material – and a tubular steel side-table.

A table and chair set for children (1923; right), with plywood seats and backs on the chairs. The influence of Rietveld and the De Stijl movement is still in evidence here. The rug was designed by Benita Otte and made in the Bauhaus weaving workshop.

were in wood with fabric upholstery. His liking for primitive art was manifested in a design of 1921 for what he called his "African" chair, which resembled a chair from that continent and was decorated with abstract wooden carving. However, this interest was quickly replaced by experiments with geometric forms and horizontal and vertical planes – clearly influenced by the work of the Dutch De Stijl designers Gerrit Rietveld (see pp.98–101) and Theo van Doesburg – which represented the chair in its simplest form.

TUBULAR STEEL FURNITURE

A breakthrough came in 1925, when Breuer suddenly abandoned wooden structures and, inspired by the lightness and strength of the frame of his new bicycle, turned to tubular steel for furniture. His first experiments resulted in his revolutionary design for a modern "club" armchair (above);

A bent plywood chair (1935–6; left), designed for the British furniture company Isokon. The chair shows an understanding of the human form that is absent from Breuer's earlier Bauhaus designs, which were more materials-oriented.

all Breuer's designs through a Bauhaus franchise; however, it came to an end a couple of years later when Breuer made a new agreement with Thonet (see pp.78–9), who took on the manufacture of the "B32" chair and all his subsequent furniture designs.

WORK IN BERLIN

In around 1926 Breuer began to wish for independence and to disassociate himself from the Bauhaus; what had been the ideal environment in which he could experiment had turned into an atmosphere of conflict and negativity. His brief marriage to a student named Marta Erps in 1927 took him away from the campus, and in the following year he resigned his post, following Gropius (who had left in the same year) to Berlin to set up an architectural practice. Although Breuer continued to design furniture, he became more involved in interior design; his interiors for houses by Mart Stam and Gropius had been shown at the Weissenhofsiedlung in Stuttgart in 1927.

Between 1928 and 1931 Breuer redefined the notion of the modern interior in such commissions as the De Francesco apartment (1929) and the Leum house, both in Berlin, explaining that "a few simple objects are enough, when these are good, multiuse and capable of variation. We avoid thus the lavish pouring of our needs into countless commodities that complicate our daily lives instead of simplifying them and making them easier." He also designed the Werkbund exhibit at the 1930 Salon des Artistes Décorateurs in Paris, while in 1932 he received his first commission as an architect for a house for Harnismacher in Wiesbaden.

its cubic form and light yet strong skeletal frame was the antithesis of heavy and bulky traditional furniture, and provided an ideal counterpart to the new architecture with its emphasis upon space, light and structure.

Over the next five extraordinarily productive years Breuer produced more designs for tubular steel chairs in addition to beds, desks, tables and stools. When the Bauhaus moved to Dessau in 1925, Gropius asked Breuer – appointed form master of the furniture workshop in the same year – to provide furniture for the new canteen, auditorium and masters' houses. In around 1926 Breuer created his second best-known design – the "B32" cantilever chair (known since 1960 as the "Cesca" chair after his daughter Francesca) – and signed a contract with a furniture manufacturer, Standard-Möbel, to put his designs into mass production. This relationship displeased Gropius, who wanted to produce

WORK IN SWITZERLAND AND BRITAIN

By the early 1930s Breuer had achieved an international reputation and had what would have been for some a full career behind him. The political climate of the period in Germany, with the rise of Fascism, was undoubtedly deeply unsettling for him as both his parents were Jewish. Between 1932 and 1935 he travelled around Europe, ending up in Zurich. There he redesigned the interior of the Wohnbedorf department store – one of the few Swiss retail outlets for modern furniture – and developed aluminium

A reclining chair in aluminium and wood (left), designed when Breuer was working in Switzerland. It clearly demonstrates his preoccupation with the requirements of the materials and of the reclining human body at this time. As with so many of his designs, he developed a number of versions of the chair; they were manufactured by Embru and retailed through the Wohnbedorf department store.

The "B26" table (1928; right), part of a series made of glass and tubular steel that exploited a range of formal possibilities. Many of these items were manufactured by the Thonet company at the end of the decade.

Breuer and his wife sitting on the wooden outdoor furniture that he designed for his own home in New Canaan, Connecticut (1947; above). In spite of his earlier experiments with new materials, Breuer returned to wood in his later American architecture and design.

furniture. Extensions of his earlier experiments in tubular steel, these designs – for example, a lounge chair of 1933 – placed greater emphasis than his earlier pieces on the user's relaxation and comfort.

In 1935 Breuer once again followed Gropius, this time to Britain, where he stayed for two years. He worked with the architect F.R.S. Yorke on a number of architectural projects in the south of England, and played a significant role in Britain's somewhat unfulfilled foray into Modernism by designing bent plywood furniture for Jack Pritchard's progressive design company, Isokon. The best-known of these pieces was his lounge chair (1935–6; opposite, above), which closely resembled the earlier aluminium type, and a set of nesting tables of 1936, based on Breuer's tubular steel stool designed for the canteen at the Bauhaus.

CAREER IN THE USA

With a career in three different countries behind him, Breuer left Britain for the United States, once more following Gropius, in 1937. The two men set up an architectural practice in Cambridge, Massachusetts, and taught at

Harvard University. Their differences led to the end of their partnership, however, and in 1941 Breuer set up on his own, moving in 1946 to New York, where his architectural practice was based for the next two decades.

In 1940 Breuer remarried, and in 1947 and again in 1951 designed houses for himself and his family in New Canaan, Connecticut (above). These houses and several other of his American architectural and interior designs – including the Pittsburgh glass house (1945) and the house in the garden of the Museum of Modern Art in New York (1949) – showed a softer, more sculptural and tactile sensibility; simple wooden furniture was offset by the texture, colour and pattern of stone and concrete. Breuer's contribution to modern furniture design came to the fore again in the 1960s, when the Italian company Gavina revived production of a number of his pieces from the 1920s, showing how his designs continued to be popular almost half a century after they were created.

Tubular steel

Advances in materials technology have played a key role in many of the most significant innovations in design this century. Perhaps none has more dramatically encouraged change than the application of steel tubing to the design of furniture items, especially chairs. Bent to form the essential elements of seating furniture and related items – dining-tables, coffee-tables and trolleys – tubular steel helped create a radically new profile for furniture, and set the tone for the modern interior. It totally transformed expectations of the domestic environment from one characterized by bulky comfort to one representing space, light and simplicity. Heavy upholstery was replaced by the open silhouette of the new metallic forms, helping to bring the aesthetic of Functionalism, with its emphasis on clean lines, into the home.

THE ORIGINS OF STEEL

The 19th century had already witnessed the huge impact on the material world that had been made by the development of steel – a malleable yet strong metal that facilitated the manufacture of a vast range of products from sewing machines to locomotives. Pressed and stamped steel quickly entered the environment. In extruded tube form the new metal was particularly light and strong and was soon used in bicycle manufacture.

Since the 1830s furniture had exploited the availability of iron tube, in the form of bedframes, and of bent wood, which was popularized by the European firm Thonet from the mid-century. Bent steel also appeared in the first decades of the 20th century. It was a small step forwards, therefore, to see tubular steel as a material that could be used in furniture design, although its use in the manufacture of domestic items was revolutionary.

INNOVATION AND DEVELOPMENT

It was at the Bauhaus in Germany in the mid-1920s that the designer Marcel Breuer (see pp.108–111) – inspired by the handlebars of his Adler bicycle – set out to create a radically new version of the traditional club

The British firm PEL (a shortening of Practical Equipment Limited) specialized in the manufacture of tubular steel furniture in the 1930s. The "Model SP9B" steel and black leather dining chair (above) is from the PEL catalogue, 1937.

The "Model B3" (later the "Wassily" chair) was designed in 1925 by Marcel Breuer, while a teacher at the Bauhaus. The photograph (right) illustrates how, as a result of Breuer's ingenious design, the sitter appears to be suspended inside a steel cube. The model wears a mask designed by the painter and stage designer Oskar Schlemmer, who also taught at the Bauhaus. The "Model B3" went into production in 1927, and is manufactured today by Knoll.

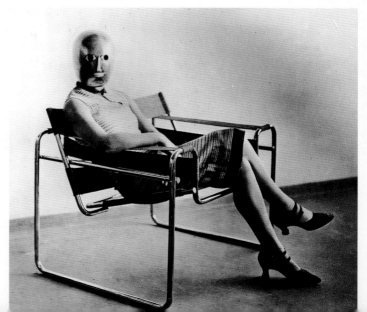

The furnished interior of Haus 16 (shown right) formed part of the experimental housing estate created by the Deutscher Werkbund for the 1927 Weissenhof Exhibition. Including the work of Marcel Breuer, Ludwig Mies van der Rohe and Le Corbusier (see pp.108–11, pp.92–3 and pp.94–7), the exhibition was devoted to promoting mass-produced design for the domestic market.

Ludwig Mies van der Rohe's "Chair No. MR20" (below), which was first seen at the Weissenhofsiedlung held at Stuttgart in 1927, was by far the most daring and elegant of all the chair experiments in cantilevered tubular steel. It came with or without arms.

Mies van der Rohe (see pp.92–3), who designed his more stylized version in 1927 (above and left). By the end of the 1920s, tubular steel – nickel-plated or chromed, and combined with black fabric or leather – was synonymous with Modernism and was used by all the leading figures in that movement, from Le Corbusier in France to Giuseppe Terragni in Italy (see pp.114–5).

INTERNATIONAL SUCCESS

In Britain, the PEL company produced tubular steel chairs for public venues such as cinemas and village halls (opposite, above), while in the United States Gilbert Rhode and Wolfgang Hoffmann designed a wide of models that were used both in public and private spaces. True mass accessibility was not realized until after World War II, however. It reached its peak in the 1960s and 1970s with, in Great Britain for example, the Habitat store producing its own versions of the modern classics and design groups such as OMK and Plush Kicker bringing early Modernism to a new consumer group.

A table with chromed metal legs (c.1935; below) designed by Eileen Gray (see pp.46–9). Although Gray used tubular steel extensively in her furniture designs, she combined it with organic materials – natural pine here – to offset the metal's cold, hard quality.

armchair, the structure of which was entirely made from pieces of seamless tubular steel, welded together. In so doing he moved the experiments in wooden furniture that he and the De Stijl designers – Gerrit Rietveld (see pp.98–101) among them – had carried out one stage further. His chair was refined through the late 1920s. Around 1962 (when it was reproduced and marketed widely) it became known as the "Wassily" chair (opposite).

While Breuer had established the way forward for designers to use the new material in pursuit of the ultimate modern chair, it was the Dutch designer Mart Stam who first developed the idea of a steel chair bent into a cantilevered form (in which the weight at the back of the chair was distributed at the front). This solution eliminated the need for so many joints and allowed the flexibility of the material to come into its own. The side chair that Stam made out of gas pipes and plumbers' elbow joints in 1927 had an in-built comfort that no longer relied on bulky upholstery. Breuer produced his own cantilevered tubular steel chair the following year, as did

Although primarily an architect, the Italian Giuseppe Terragni (1904–43) frequently designed objects – especially furniture – for his buildings. Terragni, like many other Modernists, approached the design of furniture as essentially a set of planes suspended in space and as such a continuation of architecture. His unique contribution to modern

Giuseppe Terragni

design was to show how an idiom that had been established elsewhere – for example, the bent tubular steel furniture developed at the Bauhaus in Germany – could be successfully adapted to another culture and political climate. Contemporaries described Terragni, a devout Catholic who remained unmarried throughout his short life, as an obsessive character committed to his profession and religion, and, it appears, to the ideology of Fascism. Although the Fascists in Germany derided the Modernists, Mussolini embraced the movement to a certain extent, and several of Terragni's commissions undoubtedly came through his membership of the Party, which he joined in 1928.

Giuseppe Terragni was among Italy's most prominent modern architects of the 1920s and 1930s. He applied the same rigour that characterized his buildings to the furnishings inside them, many of which he designed himself.

In 1936 Terragni was commissioned to design the Sant'Elia school in Como (below); it was built in a radically modern style using concrete and glass. He also designed the furniture, all of which was constructed from wood and tubular steel.

WORK IN THE 1920S

Associated with Rationalism, the name given in Italy to the architectural and design Modern Movement, Terragni was a founder member of a group of seven architects – the Gruppo Sette (Group Seven) – formed in the late 1920s and sympathetic to the work of other Modernists in France, Germany and the Netherlands. After studying at the Technical School in Como and at the Polytechnic of Milan he opened an architectural office in 1927; in that year he gained international recognition when his designs were included in the Weissenhofsiedlung, organized by the Deutscher Werkbund, in Stuttgart.

One of Terragni's first architectural commissions (1927–9) was for a five-storey apartment block, the "Novocomum", in Como (opposite, below). This strikingly minimal composition attracted a great deal of attention, as it was among the earliest examples of Modern Movement architecture in Italy. His work throughout the 1930s tended, however, to combine an element of Neo-Classicism with a more radical Modernism. Although Terragni opted for architecture as a profession, he painted, in a modern figurative tradition, until well into the 1930s. He was also interested in graphic design, as seen in the Art Deco-style chromed lettering he created in 1930 for the façade of the Vitrum glass and china store in Como.

THE CASA DEL FASCIO

Without doubt, Terragni's best-known building is the Casa del Fascio in Como (1932–6), now called the Casa del Populo. Like Le Corbusier (see pp.94–7) and other Modern Movement designers of the 1920s, Terragni considered the design of interior fittings and furnishings as important as the exterior of a building, and was also committed to using new materials: for

The boardroom of the Casa del Fascio (1932–6; above), the headquarters of the local Fascist Party in Como. Terragni also designed the furniture for the building, including tubular steel chairs with a novel reverse cantilever, which gave them extra flexibility.

The entrance to the "Novocomum" apartment building (1927–9; right) in Como. It was nicknamed the "Transatlantic" because, with its curved ends, it resembled an ocean liner. Terragni delighted in playing with contrasting geometric forms for dramatic effect.

example, bent tubular steel, which was combined with black leather for the chairs of the Casa del Fascio (above). However, Terragni's interpretation was more sensual and decorative than designs in the same materials by Marcel Breuer (see pp.108–11) and Ludwig Mies van der Rohe (see pp.92–3); he played with soft curves in his tubular steel frames and modified the cantilevered form so that there was a space between the seat and the back, a daring detail also applied to his "Larina" chair and "Benita" armchair (1936). Terragni also designed tables and lights for the building's interior.

Later commissions included the Sant'Elia school (see opposite), for which he supplied child-size desks of painted wood and metal with black tops and tubular steel legs. By 1938, however, he was receiving fewer commissions and in 1939 left for the Balkans to join Mussolini's war effort. Within four years he was dead, having suffered a nervous collapse.

From finding clients and working with architects, engineers and draughtsmen to undertaking market and materials research, making models and presenting new product concepts, the activities of the industrial designer of the inter-war years played a crucial role in the modernization of the United States. Walter Dorwin Teague (1883–1960)

Walter Dorwin Teague

was the "elder statesman" of the pioneering group of American industrial design consultants who began their careers as freelancers at the end of the 1920s and who, by the 1930s, had become almost household names. More than any other, Teague helped to establish the status and define the parameters of this new profession.

Walter Dorwin Teague, known in his day as the "Dean of industrial design", headed the generation of American consultant designers for industry in the years of the Depression. He pioneered the profession and worked with many large corporations, among them Kodak and Ford.

Unlike many of his colleagues, Teague worked on decorative as well as industrial objects. His designs for Steuben glass included these delicately engraved pieces (below) in the evocatively named "St Tropez" pattern designed c.1932.

ADVERTISING WORK

In many ways Teague presented himself more as a businessman than as an artist. He was often described as being more practical than spectacularly creative, but his achievements in visualizing new products and environments – such as retail interiors and exhibition spaces – were impressive. Born in Indiana, Teague came to New York in 1903 to study at the Art Students League, where he concentrated on typography and lithography. From there he moved into the world of advertising and, until 1908, was employed in the art department of a well-established New York advertising agency, Calkins & Holden. There, Teague excelled at, and earned a reputation for, highly decorative borders for printed advertisements. He discontinued this work after leaving the agency to set up on his own on a freelance basis, soon acquiring a number of regular clients, including Phoenix Hosiery.

THREE-DIMENSIONAL DESIGNS

Teague's career expanded along with the general growth of advertising in the United States, and in 1911 he opened his own office on Madison Avenue, New York. At first his work was dominated by "grotesque" decoration, but in 1925 he travelled to Paris where he saw the Exhibition of Decorative Arts, as well as buildings designed by Le Corbusier (see pp.94–7). As a result of this exposure to Modernism, Teague decided to abandon his traditional style and to take up the design of mass-produced consumer goods reflecting the requirements of the machine age. When the photographic company Eastman Kodak approached him in 1926, he eagerly accepted the opportunity of redesigning the "Box Brownie" camera, which had not been done for a number of years. For this project he created an innovative, soft-edged plastic body-shell that gave the camera a truly modern identity for the first time (opposite, below left). Later designs from Teague's office included the Marmon automobile (1930); the "Baby Brownie" Kodak camera, which was launched in 1933; radios for the Sparton Corporation (1933–6); glassware for Steuben (left); ovenware for Pyrex; a pen for Scripto in 1952 (opposite, right); and gas ranges and boilers.

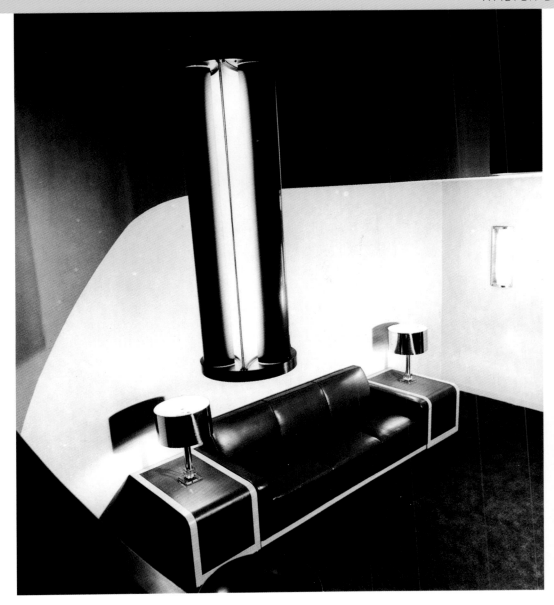

The executive lounge (left) designed for the Ford Exposition at the 1939 New York World's Fair. Teague humanized the streamlined interior with warm brass light fittings, green carpeting and tan walls.

An advertisement for Scripto pens and pencils (1953; below). The pen on the right shows how Teague gave these writing instruments a streamlined style.

This telescopic camera with a hinged plastic case (below) was just one in a series of designs created by Teague for Eastman Kodak from the early 1930s.

CORPORATE IDENTITIES AND LATER CAREER

Although consumer goods remained a crucial part of Teague's career until his death, he was also involved in creating corporate identities, including shop interiors and exhibition stands. For Eastman Kodak and the Ford Motor Company, for example, he put as much energy into their images and into the retail and marketing of his products through their logos and packaging as the products themselves. He also designed interiors for public transport, including Pullman coaches for the New Haven Railroad Company in the 1930s and, after 1946, the Boeing 707 and 747 aeroplanes.

Teague's position as Chairman of the Board of Design for the New York World's Fair of 1939 (see pp.118–19) consolidated his growing influence and senior status in the industrial design profession. His building for the Ford Motor Company at the Fair (all of the buildings there were temporary) showed the maturity of his design style and his vision of a clean and modern environment, which was nevertheless less austere and more openly popular than its European counterpart (see above).

Following World War II Teague's office expanded, and he continued to work with many of his long-term clients, among them Kodak and Boeing. He did very little designing himself but instead became the director of a large and extremely successful design consultancy that still exists today.

ollowing the success of the Great Exhibition in Hyde Park, London, in 1851, the idea of exhibitions providing an opportunity for designers to demonstrate their skills to an international audience was well established. While Europe had led the way, the United States had also organized important exhibitions, in particular the Centennial Exhibition in Philadelphia (1876), and the Columbia Exhibition (1893) and the Century of Progress Exhibition (1933), both held in Chicago, the home of modern architecture. In 1939 it was the turn of New York; the spectacular show in Flushing Meadows Park in Queens bore witness to the imaginative power of a few individuals – including Walter Dorwin Teague (see pp.116–17), Norman Bel Geddes, Henry Dreyfuss (see pp.130–31) and Raymond Loewy (see pp.120–23) – whose success during the 1930s as industrial designers had given them the confidence and authority to show others their vision of the future.

A poster (below) by the American graphic artist Joseph Binder promoting the New York World's Fair of 1939. The two most prominent buildings of the event – the Trylon and the Perisphere – provided the subject matter for this dramatic, modern image and became the fair's trademark.

SITE AND LAYOUT

The fair, which opened on 30 April 1939, was divided into seven zones: Transport, Communications, Food, Government, Production, Health and Science. These were organized in a formal layout, with avenues and vistas emanating from two central, dominant constructions: the spherical Perisphere and the 200-foot-high Trylon (both designed by the architectural firm of Harrison & Fouilhoux). Like most of the fair's structures, these temporary buildings were constructed from gypsum board, wire lath and stucco. Painted dead white, they formed the beginning of a colour scheme which changed from light to dark shades of red, yellow and blue from the central to the peripheral structures on the 1200-acre site.

INDUSTRIAL DESIGNERS

The theme of the fair was "Building the World of Tomorrow"; in the vision of the future being presented, new technology, humanized by the industrial designer, played a vital role. American industrial designers were without doubt the stars of the fair. Walter Dorwin Teague (see pp.116–17), Chairman of the Board of Design set up in 1936 to mastermind the event, designed the interior of the "Ford Exposition", which consisted of a dramatically winding half-mile "Road of Tomorrow" on which visitors could test-drive Ford automobiles. Norman Bel Geddes created the popular "Futurama" exhibit housed inside the General Motors building where, seated high up on a moving chair, the visitor could get a panoramic, bird's-eye view of a small-scale "world of 1960", featuring skyscrapers and seven-lane roads with a 100-mile-per-hour (160 kph) speed limit.

Henry Dreyfuss (see pp.130–31) was responsible for the AT&T building housing the "Demonstration Call Room", which enabled selected visitors to make a free telephone call anywhere in the United States, as well as the "Democracity": a model of an ideal city of the future situated inside the Perisphere. Raymond Loewy's (see pp.120–23) key contributions were a futuristic rocket ship that could take passengers from New York to London and a streamlined locomotive for the Pennsylvania Railroad Company.

A view of the New York World's Fair at night (above), showing the all-white "theme-center", with the Perisphere and the Trylon dominating the picture. In front of these, the domed building for United States Steel, with its illuminated ribs, also stands out.

A weekend sitting-room (left), designed by Elias Svedborg and Astrid Sampe for the Swedish Pavilion at the World's Fair. It was at the fair that the epithet "Swedish Modern" was coined to describe a soft, modern domestic style that had little in common with the utopian, technology-driven, streamlined aesthetic that dominated the American entries.

OTHER EXHIBITS

In addition to the important buildings dedicated to the large automobile corporations, there were also those of many other companies which had commissioned buildings as three-dimensional advertisements for their products, demonstrating how even architects were embracing commerce. The "Wonder Bakery", for example, had holes in its façade to suggest rising dough, and the General Electric Company's building was topped by a large flash of steel "lightning". Although many other countries exhibited at the fair – examples included a Turkish Pavilion, comprising a blend of traditional and modern elements; a British Pavilion with a replica of the Crown Jewels; and the Swedish Pavilion with its influential domestic interiors (above) – its lasting message was, undoubtedly, the strength of American corporations and their exploitation of industrial design as a marketing tool.

A powder compact commemorating the New York World's Fair (left). Made of yellow metal and covered with blue enamel, this was among the many souvenirs available for sale and depicted the dramatic buildings at the event.

The National Cash Register Company's building (right), one of several rather fantastical exhibition constructions designed to evoke their products with large-scale replicas.

Among American industrial designers of the 1930s the French-born Raymond Loewy (1893–1986) was undoubtedly the most stylish. Throughout his long career in the United States he retained a strong French accent and, with his well-trimmed moustache, presented himself as a chic, style-conscious, cosmopolitan European, keen to transform

Raymond Loewy

what he regarded as the chaotic and styleless material environment of the United States. By removing all links with the past in his designs, he played a key role in the formation of modern American "styling": making products more attractive so that they had "added value" in the eyes of consumers. Loewy was to become an almost mythical figure, with a reputation as a man whose designs could move products that would otherwise not sell in the increasingly difficult economic climate of the Great Depression of the 1930s. His later designs for such items as Coca-Cola bottles, jukeboxes and cars became inextricably linked with the idea of 1950s' American exuberance and prosperity.

Seen here in 1934, Raymond Loewy was by far the most stylish of the American consultant designers for industry from the 1930s to the 1960s. French by birth, he worked in the United States from the 1920s onwards for large corporations such as Gestetner, the Pennsylvania Railroad Company and Sears Roebuck.

Loewy's design for a steam locomotive – the "K4S" – for the Pennsylvania Railroad Company (1936; below). The train's speed is emphasized by the bullet-shaped engine with its chromed highlights; this visual style, known as "streamform", was applied to moving and static objects alike in the 1930s.

EARLY COMMERCIAL WORK

Much of the Loewy myth was self-created; he described his early life in an autobiography entitled *Never Leave Well Enough Alone*, published in 1951 at the height of his success. Born in Paris, Loewy was dedicated to a career in design from an early age, apparently designing a model aeroplane in 1909, for which he won a prize. His early love of steam locomotives was also realized in his designs for the Pennsylvania Railroad Company in the 1930s. Loewy's education in electrical engineering was interrupted by World War I, during which he served in the French Army and was awarded the

The "Super Six" Coldspot refrigerator (left), designed for Sears Roebuck in 1935 and the first of a series of three annual models created by Loewy for the company. The monolithic character of the refrigerator was achieved through the use of large, curved steel panels.

A pencil sharpener designed in 1933 (right). The chromed surface of this object, combined with the use of the "teardrop" form, demonstrates the fact that streamlining and a sense of speed were as common in designs for static items as they were for moving objects.

FIRST INDUSTRIAL DESIGNS AND COMMERCIAL SUCCESS

In 1929 the Gestetner Duplicating Company, headed by Sigmund Gestetner, invited Loewy to redesign and modernize its duplicating machine. Loewy replaced the cabriole legs with smaller, less obtrusive ones and encased the mechanism in a moulded plastic shell. The new design looked more hygienic, more stylish and, above all, more modern than its ageing predecessor and consequently had more consumer appeal.

The Gestetner project was rapidly followed by others, so that by the mid-1930s Loewy had established himself as one of the leading industrial designers of his day. In 1934 he was asked to exhibit a mocked-up setting of his office at the annual industrial design exhibition held at the Metropolitan Museum of Art in New York. The stark interior of his office – created using newly fashionable materials such as chrome and bakelite – was every bit as streamlined as his own physical appearance; Loewy thus presented himself as a designer and his work as a complete stylistic package, developed strategically to enhance the desirability of the products he designed as well as the manufacturer's image. His name went on every single drawing that came out of his office, regardless of whether he had created it or not.

Croix de Guerre. In 1919 he set off for the United States and, on the basis of a sketch made for an auction, decided to try his luck as a commercial artist when he landed in New York.

Loewy's arrival coincided with the boom years of American advertising in the mid-1920s; he was energetic in finding work and good at persuading clients of his skills. He designed window displays for Macy's department store, and graphics and lift-attendant uniforms for Saks of Fifth Avenue. He also produced fashion illustrations for Harper's Bazaar and worked on other projects in the fashion industry, including making drawings of models.

A Coca-Cola dispenser (above), known as the "Dole Deluxe" model (1947). As with most of his commissions, Loewy's brief in this case was to restyle and modernize an existing object; his contribution here was to clean up the surface and to add subtly curved radii.

The design for the "United UPA 100" jukebox (1957; right) characterized the designer's post-World War II approach to form creation; sharp radii and straight lines were emphasized, while the bulbous, streamlined shapes of earlier years were played down.

As a businessman and head of a large design studio Loewy developed highly sophisticated processes of design and presentation to clients, and was a master of self-advertisement and the hard sell. Not only the United States but Britain and France benefited from his skills; between 1936 and 1952 he ran a London office and in 1951 opened the Compagnie de l'Esthétique Industrielle (CEI) in Paris, an independent industrial-design firm, and produced some significant designs for cars and sewing machines as well as graphic work. He lived on both sides of the Atlantic and always retained an aura of cosmopolitanism.

TRANSPORT AND PRODUCT DESIGN

Another important client for Loewy in the 1930s was the Hupp Motor Company, for which he designed the "Hupmobile", launched in 1934. Loewy initially financed the prototype of the project with his own money in order to gain the commission. Fortunately the design was highly acclaimed and won prizes at many international automobile exhibitions. Although the automobile was elegant and modern in its unified, refined style, it lacked the dramatic and adventurous streamlining seen in the work of other American industrial designers such as Norman Bel Geddes, and in the Chrysler Company's futuristic "Airflow" automobile of the same year.

The same could not be said, however, of two major Loewy projects of the mid- to late 1930s: the "Coldspot" refrigerator for Sears Roebuck (1935) and the locomotives for the Pennsylvania Railroad Company (1936). The "Super Six" Coldspot refrigerator (see p.121, above left), epitomizing the bulbous, curving fridges associated with mid-20th-century American kitchens, was designed with annual model changes like an automobile to stimulate consumer demand. The resemblance did not stop there, as the stamped metal components came off production lines similar to (and indeed sometimes the same as) those for automobiles; the recessed handle, used to allow a flush surface, was also borrowed directly from automobile design. The locomotives designed for the Pennsylvania Railroad Company represented the high point of Loewy's aesthetic of streamlining; their curvaceous and dynamic forms were accentuated by horizontal chromed metal strips to enhance the impression of speed (see pp.120–21).

The Lucky Strike cigarette pack (left) is among Loewy's best-known designs of the mid-century. In this instance he decided simply to change the colour of the existing pack from green to white, and to put the circle motif and brand name on to the back as well as the front of the pack.

Among Loewy's most celebrated projects were those for the Coca-Cola Company and Lucky Strike cigarettes (1940–42). For Coca-Cola he redesigned the famous bottle, giving it a more subtle, curved profile. He also designed related products for the company, including the "Dole Deluxe" dispenser in 1947 (opposite, above left). For Lucky Strike he changed the colour of the packet from green to white, as wartime restrictions meant that the manufacturers could no longer use the original green ink because of its high metal content. Loewy also made the new white packet – which he felt had connotations of freshness – more striking by putting the logo on both front and back so that it could be seen at all times, and by adding an extra ring around the bull's-eye motif. These minor modifications had a significant commercial impact, and the design remains one of the most instantly recognizable logos to this day.

POST-WAR CAREER

Raymond Loewy Associates worked on several important projects after World War II. From 1947–62 Loewy dedicated much of his energy to working for the Studebaker Company, designing a range of automobiles stylistically far more advanced than other American models (below). The 1947 "Champion" had distinctively simple and elegant lines, while the 1953 "Starline" and 1962 "Avanti" models owed much to sophisticated European influence in their restrained styling. This influence also came to the fore in his work for the Greyhound bus company – the distinctive streamlined buses have become one of the most ubiquitous and well-known transport designs in post-war America.

For the 1939 New York World's Fair (see pp.118–19), Loewy had contributed a mock-up of a futuristic rocket ship that could travel across the Atlantic. Between 1967 and 1972 he was involved in a real-life space project when he was asked by NASA to help design the interiors for the Skylab, to ensure that the space capsule in which the astronauts would live and work for long periods was as habitable as possible. Loewy himself felt that his work for NASA was one of his most important achievements.

Unlike some of his earlier, more fantastic projects, Loewy's more minimal designs of the 1960s and 1970s displayed a renewed elegance, demonstrating that he could adapt to changing fashions. By the 1970s his reputation as a key designer of the 20th century was fully acknowledged internationally and confirmed by a retrospective exhibition of his work held in 1976 at the Renwick Gallery in Washington, D.C.

The Studebaker "Commander" (1950; above), one of Loewy's most influential post-war designs. In comparison with many of its bulbous, chrome-laden contemporaries, the Studebaker epitomized a European-derived stylishness and restraint.

To a great extent Britain was marginal to the development of modern architecture and design in the 1920s and 1930s, as, compared with Europe, it was largely resistant to new ideas. Nevertheless, a few progressive architects and designers (many of them immigrants), including Raymond McGrath, F.R.S. Yorke, Berthold Lubetkin, Maxwell Fry,

Wells Coates

Serge Chermayeff, and, in particular, Wells Coates (1895–1958) promoted the aims of the Modern Movement in a design world strongly influenced by past traditions. Although Coates was less prolific than others, the scope of his work – covering architecture, interiors, furniture and a range of industrial products – was impressive and influential.

Wells Coates was among the most progressive of Britain's inter-war designers. He applied his skills to a range of buildings, interiors and objects, producing a number of highly original designs that still look modern to contemporary eyes.

The Ekco "AD65" wireless (below), designed for E.K. Cole Ltd (1934). The dramatically modern appearance of the bakelite body-shell of this object helped to transform the look of the radio from a domestic item into a piece of equipment.

JAPANESE BACKGROUND

Although Canadian by nationality, Coates was born and spent his first 18 years in Tokyo, where his father was a missionary. The Japanese love of minimalist design and pure forms influenced his particularly austere brand of modern design. He trained as an engineer at the University of British Columbia, Vancouver, Canada, from 1913–15 and from 1919–21, and studied for a Ph. D in engineering at the University of London from 1922–4. This rigorous scientific and technical background provided him with a detailed knowledge of structural principles and technical processes that greatly enriched his approach to architecture and design.

EARLY INTERIORS

Although ready to enter the architectural profession on his graduation, Coates worked as a journalist, mainly in London on the *Daily Express* during the mid-1920s. In 1925, however, he was working in Paris and visited the Exhibition of Decorative Arts. There, he was particularly taken by the work of Le Corbusier on display in the *Esprit Nouveau* pavilion (see pp.94–7); this was to have an enormous influence on him in later years.

In 1928 Coates married Marion Grove, and decided to settle in London and to concentrate on architecture and interior design as a career. One of his early commissions was for shop fronts and interiors for the Crysede Silks company in 1928 and for its subsidiary, Cresta Silks, in the following year. His designs for Cresta shops in London, Bournemouth and Brighton displayed a daringly modern and minimal aesthetic, influenced by avant-garde American and French Art Deco design, with dramatically austere window displays and lettering that was strikingly novel in its simplicity and modern styling, some of which was designed by the modern graphic artist Edward McKnight Kauffer (opposite, below).

In 1931 Coates was asked, along with his fellow Modernists Raymond McGrath and Serge Chermayeff, to design interiors for Broadcasting House, the new London headquarters of the BBC. Coates rose to the challenge of creating designs specifically for a new communications medium with typical

An interior in the Lawn Road Flats, London (1943; above). In keeping with the building's exterior, Coates used furniture designed for Isokon by Marcel Breuer (see pp.108–11) – the plywood lounge chair and side-table – as well as items that he designed himself.

enthusiasm. His interiors for the dramatic control room, the news studios and the dramatic-effects and gramophone-effects suites (see p.127) were technologically sophisticated but minimal in design, based on fundamental requirements only and using new materials such as tubular steel.

ARCHITECTURE

In the 1930s Coates designed a number of key Modernist architectural projects in Great Britain, among them the Lawn Road Flats, Hampstead, the London residence of Marcel Breuer (see pp.108–11) and Walter Gropius (see pp.88–9); the flats were commissioned by the entrepreneur Jack Pritchard in 1932 and completed by 1934 (above). Other projects included the Embassy Court Flats in Brighton (1935) and an apartment building at

Coates's "minimum kitchen" (above) was first exhibited in London's Dorland Hall at the "British Industrial Art as Applied to the Home" show (1933). He went on to use the kitchen in the Lawn Road Flats and an apartment block on Brighton's sea-front.

A Cresta Silks shop-front in London (left), designed in the early 1930s. Coates used metal-framed windows, supplied by the Crittall company, to create the large areas of plate glass that were integral to the "open" effect that he wanted to achieve.

10 Palace Gate, Kensington, London (1936). Coates always conceived the exterior and the interior as unified in terms of practicality and function. The Lawn Road Flats, for example, were based on the idea of the "minimal dwelling", influenced by the ideas of Le Corbusier and Coates' experiences of Japanese culture. At the 1933 "Exhibition of British Industrial Art as Applied to the Home" at Dorland Hall in London, Coates exhibited what he described as the "minimum flat", containing the bare requirements for civilized living. The kitchen (above) consisted of functional storage and appliance units that made the most efficient use of limited space. The small living/dining area boasted plain walls and carpet, a sofa, an armchair, a

bookcase, a small dining-table and two tubular steel dining chairs in a strictly Modernist style. This minimalism was particularly progressive for a designer working in Britain, which was slower to accept the severity of Modernist interior design than many European countries.

FURNITURE

It was not only architecture and interiors that preoccupied Coates during the 1930s; he was also developing radical ideas about the design of mass-manufactured furniture. Inspired by the work of Marcel Breuer and others, Coates regarded bent plywood and tubular steel as the appropriate materials for modern furniture. Indeed, for Coates, as for other Modernists, furniture became almost an extension of architecture. In 1932 he and Jack Pritchard founded the company Isokon (Isometric Unit Construction) to design and manufacture modern furniture – for example, shelving systems – intended for the "minimum interior" (see pp.78–9). In 1935 Coates worked with the

The "Telekinema" (below) designed in 1951 for the Festival of Britain, held in London. Coates's interest in broadcasting stemmed from his background in engineering, his work on radios and television sets, and his work for the BBC in the 1930s.

The catamaran that Coates, a keen sportsman, designed for his own use (above). He loved speed, and considered it an important facet of modern life. This preoccupation motivated his designs, which were intended as essential accessories for "modern living".

British furniture manufacturer PEL (Practical Equipment Limited) to produce a range of tubular steel furniture – similar in style to that of Breuer – for the interiors of the Embassy Court flats in Brighton.

DOMESTIC EQUIPMENT

Coates went one step further than many of the European Modernists: from designing furniture to working on the new domestic technology that preoccupied American industrial designers. With his engineering background, he conceived radios and television sets less as pieces of domestic furniture (as they had traditionally been designed) than as technological equipment. His work for the British manufacturer E.K. Cole from 1932 was particularly important in this respect. Coates, Chermayeff and Misha Black all worked on designs for their Ekco line. Model "AD65" (1934; see p.124), the result of Coates's successful entry in a competition run by E.K. Cole, represented

The Ekco "Princess-Handbag" radio (right) designed for E.K. Cole Ltd (1948). This slim, "feminine" radio, clearly intended for use by the housewife, was, with its colourful cellulose acetate body, an innovative example of post-war British design.

a milestone in modern radio design. In addition to its innovative use of bakelite, a newly developed plastic, it showed how the Modernist principle that "form follows function" could be applied to new consumer products; the circular form of the body-shell was determined by that of the loudspeaker behind it. The radio's round shell had an added advantage in that it required less material and was therefore cheaper to manufacture than square shapes. Its affordability, coupled with its exciting streamlined design, made it extremely popular with the British buying public.

LATER DESIGNS

Following the resounding success of the "AD65", Coates designed another radio for Ekco, the "AC76" (late 1930s); the Thermovent electric fire series, also with bakelite cases (1937); and a television set with a lift-up top (1946). These last two designs, which were set on small feet, had stronger affiliations with traditional forms of furniture; at the same time, however, they were minimal, somewhat monolithic objects with no decorative surface detailing. A particularly novel design produced during the immediate post-war years, again for Ekco, was the "Princess-Handbag" radio of 1948 (opposite, below

right). Compact and portable with a transparent plastic handle and a strap, this product was clearly aimed at women in the home, in need of entertainment as they undertook domestic chores.

In the 1940s and 1950s Coates was employed by a number of other companies as a design consultant, among them the aircraft manufacturer De Havilland, the British Overseas Air Company (BOAC) and the recording company EMI. In 1944 he was made a Royal Designer for Industry; he was given this award in recognition of his pioneering role in the new profession of industrial design consultancy.

His career entered a decline, however, after 1951 – the year in which he designed the "Telekinema" (a futuristic cinema; opposite, left) for the Festival of Britain at London's South Bank. By 1955, Coates had left Britain for the United States to lecture at Harvard University; in the following year he returned to Canada, where he died of a heart attack.

Studio 6D (below), designed in 1932 for the BBC headquarters in Great Portland Street, London. Although the BBC also asked Raymond McGrath and Serge Chermayeff to work on interiors, those designed by Coates were the most overtly functional in appearance.

nlike many of his fellow American industrial designers of the inter-war years, who
dedicated much of their time to designing cars, aeroplanes and other machines,
Russel Wright (1904–76) focused exclusively on domestic goods – in particular furniture,
ceramics and metalware. Although he specialized in what might be traditionally termed

Russel Wright

the "decorative arts", his designs were aggressively modern, displaying a preoccupation
with minimalist, organic forms that turned his utilitarian pieces into abstract sculpture.
At the same time, he was a populist at heart, determined to transform and modernize
the lives of everyone through his designs.

*Russel Wright was responsible for
bringing affordable modern design into
the ordinary American household. With
his keen eye for the changes in modern
living habits, he designed cups and
saucers, cooking equipment and items
of furniture to suit the new demands
of the mass marketplace.*

*The "Residential" range of melamine
tableware (below) was introduced in
1953 and manufactured by the Northern
Industrial Chemical Company of Boston.
These low-priced, colourful and cheerful
place settings, employing non-traditional
forms, were intended to make up the
first set of tableware for young married
couples who could not yet afford ceramic
services. Like the "American Modern"
wares of the late 1930s, the pieces came
in a range of colours that could be mixed
together, a concept that underlined
Wright's preference for a more informal
domestic environment.*

EARLY CAREER

Like Norman Bel Geddes and Henry Dreyfuss (see pp.130–31), Wright
began his career in theatre design. He trained initially as a painter in his
home town of Cincinnati and subsequently, in 1920, at the Art Students'
League in New York. After a brief period that was spent studying law at
Princeton – under the orders of his father, a Quaker judge – he moved on
to architecture at Columbia University and thence to stage design in 1924,
undertaking some commissions – including *The Miracle* and *King Lear* –
in collaboration with Bel Geddes. This was a short-lived career, however:
following his marriage in 1927, his wife Mary encouraged him to design
small housewares for retail outlets. The commercial success of such items
as bun warmers and ice-buckets in spun aluminium prompted him to
open his own workshop in New York in 1930.

DESIGNS IN THE 1930S

The 1930s proved both a productive and profitable decade for Wright.
His designs included flatware in 1930 and a table-radio for Wurlitzer in
1932 (opposite, above right). In 1931 he was asked to exhibit at the annual
"Industrial Art" show at the Metropolitan Museum of Art in New York, and
in 1933–4 he was producing chrome-plated kitchenware for Chase Brass
and Copper. The somewhat ad hoc nature of his operation was subsequently
transformed when his "Modern Living" furniture range – designed to be
simple yet practical – was mass-manufactured by Conant-Ball and sold
through Macy's department store from 1935 (opposite, below).

TABLEWARE

Wright's most famous range of ceramic tableware, "American Modern", was
designed in 1937, produced by the Steubenville Pottery and launched two
years later in 1939; it featured in countless American homes through the
1940s and 1950s, becoming one of the most popular household wares
of its time, especially among young married couples. The unusual tapered
forms and curled edges of the pieces reflected vegetal shapes, and they

Mary Wright, Russel's wife and close collaborator (left), demonstrating how easy it was to be a modern hostess with the assistance of the items of informal cooking and serving equipment designed by her husband.

A tabletop radio (right), designed by Wright for Wurlitzer in 1932 and evocatively named "Lyric". Its neatness and small size represented an enormous step forward from the earlier types of console sets, which had been considerably more bulky.

world, although he continued to work on a number of other designs for the same ranges of ceramics and furniture over the next 15 years. He did achieve successes on a smaller scale with his "Casual China" range (1946), produced by Iroquois China, and with the inexpensive melamine "Residential" tableware range in 1953 (opposite), an early example of the use of plastics for dining rather than just storage. In 1955 he became a consultant to manufacturers in South East Asia, initiating ideas for cottage industries, and continued in this role in 1965 in Japan, where he designed over 100 products. After 1967 he retreated from New York City to a house he had built for himself in Garrison, New York State, called Dragon Rock, and from there acted as a planning consultant to the United States National Parks Service, thereby breaking his link with the world of industrial design.

came in a range of dusky, muted shades that could be mixed and matched. The popularity of the "American Modern" range also spawned a number of related wares, including cutlery, glass and table linens.

Wright's mass-produced furniture and ceramics were successful not only because of the functional simplicity and organic beauty of their design, but also because they were appropriate for the growing informality of living and entertaining in American middle-class homes. Wright described this concept as "informal hospitality" in *A Guide to Easier Living*, written in collaboration with Mary Wright in 1951.

LATER CAREER

Wright never repeated the unprecedented and unexpected success of the "American Modern" products, and his next project – the "American Way" range of furnishings – was a total commercial failure, so much so that production ceased by 1942. Following this setback, and the death of his wife a decade later, Wright began to fade from prominence in the design

A room set with pieces from Wright's "Modern Living" range (1935; right); this was an ultra-modern design made of solid maple, available either in a reddish tone or in an unstained "blonde" finish (shown here). The line was a great commercial success.

Of the generation of American industrial designers who emerged in the late 1920s and early 1930s, Henry Dreyfuss (1904–72) was the least publicly celebrated; yet he probably did more than his contemporaries to give the profession respectability through his rigorous approach to design as a form of "problem-solving" for human needs.

Henry Dreyfuss

For Dreyfuss the solution to a design brief had to address all social, ethical, aesthetic and practical requirements, and he spread his views on this subject through his writings and through his consultation work for many large American corporations.

Henry Dreyfuss, pictured here in 1951 (above), was one of the generation of American pioneer consultant designers for industry who radically changed the face of the mass environment in the inter-war years. His special contribution was to keep "man" at the centre of things and not to let the rush of technology trample him in its wake.

EARLY PRODUCT DESIGNS

In spite of his somewhat sober image Dreyfuss began his career, like the designer Norman Bel Geddes (with whom he served a brief apprenticeship in 1923), in theatre design. He had previously studied at the Ethical Culture School in New York and worked briefly in his grandfather's theatrical supplies store. Unable to support his family on the meagre proceeds gained from working on Broadway, Dreyfuss turned to commercial design from 1929 onwards, initially for packaging, then to work for department stores (on window displays and products) and finally, having been approached by the manufacturers, on product design. One of his early clients, from 1930, was Bell Telephone Laboratories, and Dreyfuss was responsible for one of the first modern telephone designs, the "300", launched in 1937; this model, combining mouth- and earpieces in a single black bakelite body-shell, was subsequently updated and sold for over a decade (left).

Through the 1930s Dreyfuss worked with numerous firms, always approaching his commissions with the same rigorous discipline. Key long-term clients included the Big Ben alarm clock company (from 1932); Sears Roebuck (also from 1932), for whom he designed the "Toperator" washing machine; General Electric (from 1933), for whom he created the "Flat Top" refrigerator; the Hoover company (from 1934); and Deere & Co. (from 1937), for whom he redesigned tractors. His products were similar to those of other American industrial designers in their forms, styles and materials, although they showed comparatively less evidence of streamlining.

The Polaroid Corporation's "Automatic 101 Land Camera" (1964; below). Intended to be cheaper than its predecessor, the camera was also designed to be neat and portable; it is hardly any bigger, in fact, than a cigar case. The controls were marked to aid easy use, another example of Dreyfuss's concern that his designs should serve the consumer.

The "Model 300" telephone (left) was produced in 1937 by Bell Telephone Laboratories. Its bakelite body-shell and simple forms were the results of intensive research into materials and the human form.

Show-off.

This is the finest automatic camera Polaroid has ever produced.

It's a terrible show-off.

Worse yet, it will turn you into one. Like all Polaroid Color Pack Cameras, it will deliver a color print in 60 seconds. A pretty flashy act in itself.

But this model has a few other tricks up its sleeve. (It's all done with a sensitive electric eye and a remarkable transistorized shutter.)

For instance. Load the camera with black and white film. Turn off all the lights, except perhaps a candle or night-light near the subject. *Without flash*, it will give you a perfect time exposure. Automatically. (Great for portraits of dinner guests, sleeping kids, pretty girls by the fire.)

This one's pretty impressive too. Load with color film, add the flash and start shooting. The electric eye will read the light of the flash and set the exposure. Automatically. You

never have to worry about special distance settings.

What else? It produces bea close-ups with the close-up and po attachments. It has a triplet le superimposed-image, coupled r finder, 2 exposure ranges for co for black and white. It's light. Com Fast-loading.

But don't say we didn't warn Once it's in the house, you've goi be unbearable.

The prefabricated Consolidated Vultee Aircraft Company project (1942; above) in Pasadena, California, was a collaboration with the architect Edward Barnes. In addition to simple housing, Dreyfuss also designed interiors for the company's aeroplanes.

DESIGN FOR THE USER

For the New York Central Railroad Company, Dreyfuss designed the "Mercury" locomotive in the late 1930s; this model for the later "20th Century Limited" train – launched in 1941 – was a totally unified product, even down to the coffee cups in the buffet. The streamlined exterior of the locomotive gave way in the interior to an innovative informal clustering of seats, intended to provide a more relaxed travelling experience. As was the case with all his designs, here Dreyfuss combined his commitment to a modern style with concern for the consumer.

Nowhere was this concern more evident than in his 1955 publication *Designing for People*. At the beginning he explained that "We bear in mind that the object worked on is going to be ridden in, sat upon, looked at, talked into, activated, operated, or in some other way used by people individually or *en masse*." This led on to Dreyfuss's invention of "Joe and Josephine" – two model consumers or users – and to a discussion of anthropometrics – the science of human measurements – as a starting point for the design process. This concept had originated in studies by the Danish designer Kaare Klint (see pp.64–5) in the 1920s and had been developed through wartime aircraft design. Dreyfuss helped to establish anthropometrics as an essential element in the design of everyday objects.

LATER DESIGNS

Through the 1950s and 1960s Dreyfuss continued to work with a range of industrial clients, some long-standing, others new. The Polaroid Corporation, for example, commissioned him in 1960 to create the "Automatic 100 Land Camera" (a later version shown opposite, right), designed to fit into a pocket. Here, as in all his other projects, Dreyfuss' lack of detailed technical knowledge meant that his imagination was unfettered by limitations of manufacture, enabling him to envisage solutions that others could not. He retired in 1969, but his firm, Henry Dreyfuss Associates, is still in operation.

This well-known insulated carafe (right) was designed for the American Thermos Company (1936). Dreyfuss claimed that its form was inspired by an Ancient Greek jug but, with its smooth contours and chrome and plastic detailing, it is also a prime example of American streamlining.

Sixten Sason

The profession of consultant designer for industry – which had developed in the United States in the 1930s – was gradually introduced to Europe in the 1940s, particularly to Britain, France and Italy, providing an alternative to the more traditional European roles of the designer as architect or craftsman. Somewhat surprisingly, one

exceptional designer for industry, Sixten Sason (1912–69), emerged from the crafts-oriented world of modern design in Sweden. Sason came from a family of sculptors and lived in a Swedish artists' colony in Paris in the 1920s; he trained, like many designers in the crafts tradition, in fine art. His family name was Andersson, but for artistic purposes he changed it to Sason by simply adding "son" to his initials.

Sixten Sason was Sweden's version of the American consultant designer for industry. His work for Saab on streamlined automobiles, as well as his designs for Hasselblad and Electrolux, mark him out as one of the 20th century's most successful industrial designers.

The "Saab 92" (1947; below). The integration of its form, achieved by the streamlined body-shell, made this one of the most modern cars of its time. The inspiration came from aeroplanes – an area of production very familiar to the Saab company – and it was Sason who succeeded in transferring those ideas into the new arena of automobile design.

ILLUSTRATION WORK

Like earlier designers such as the Belgian Henry van de Velde (see pp.16–17) and the Swede Wilhelm Kåge (see pp.66–9), Sason first made a living as an illustrator. However, he began his career in the 1930s, at a time of increased mass manufacturing, and of unparalleled technological development and commercialization in Europe. As a result of his sketches of motorcycles, he was first employed as a draughtsman in the engineering department of Husqvarna, a manufacturer of motorcycles and small arms.

Sason served as a pilot in the Swedish Air Force during World War II, but was wounded in a crash. A four-year convalescence provided him with an opportunity to study engineering by correspondence, and, on recovering, he continued to work for Husqvarna on a freelance basis, as well as undertaking illustration work in a representational style for advertisements in motoring, religious and romance magazines.

PRODUCT DESIGNS

In the immediate post-war period, Sason set up independently under the name of Sason Design AB and rapidly gained a reputation as Sweden's pioneer industrial designer. Commissions came from manufacturing companies such as Electrolux, for whom he designed a vacuum-cleaner; he also continued to work with Husqvarna on its expanded product range of sewing machines, irons and kitchen appliances. Other commissions included designs for buses and trains for the ASJ company, while

in 1955 he worked with Victor Hasselblad on the design of a new camera. Sason's skills in drawing and engineering enabled him to create innovative products that were technologically advanced yet, in their overtly "modern" appearances, owed much to the American streamlining of the 1930s.

WORK FOR SAAB

It is for his automobile designs for Saab, the Swedish company founded in 1937 by private capital but on a government initiative to manufacture military aircraft, that Sason is best remembered. At the end of World War II, when the company decided to move into automobile manufacture, Sason was asked to submit a design, which was immediately accepted. His vision of a light yet powerful, eminently futuristic and streamlined automobile underpinned the whole project in the late 1940s for the "Saab 92" (opposite) led by the company's engineer, Gunnar Ljungström. Sason's designs evoked

A Saab aeroplane, the "1A37 Viggen" (1971; above), demonstrated the company's continued commitment to aeroplane production as well as to incorporating a strongly modern image into its products.

a vision of modernity that was as much about lifestyle as about engineering; the nylon-clad women who populated his drawings represented a new age in which speed and sophistication were all-important.

In line with the practice of American industrial designers, Sason was involved in all stages of the design process, from initial concept sketch to wind-tunnel model; as a result, his original vision is clearly evident in the final production models. From his work on the "Saab 92" to the "Saab 99" (below, left), which was launched in 1969, Sason was responsible for the enormous success that the company enjoyed — not only in Sweden but internationally. Unfortunately he died just too soon to see the final result of his labours in full production.

The instrument panel of a "Saab 99" (left), an automobile that was designed by Gunnar Ljungström and Björn Envall on the basis of ideas established by Sixten Sason; it was launched in 1969, six months after the designer's death.

The famous SLR camera (right) produced by the Swedish family camera company Hasselblad. The company employed Sason as a consultant when the camera was being designed. Its appearance remained unchanged for several decades after it was launched in the late 1940s.

The New Modernism

The New Modernism

By 1939 and the outbreak of World War II the modern design movement, in its variety of manifestations, was fully formed and its influence was felt internationally, on the levels both of the real and the ideal. Its beliefs were fully articulated and its pioneers widely recognized. Designers working after 1945 had a modern tradition to work with or against, and a set of leaders to either follow or reject. The most sophisticated way in which post-war design progressed was as an outlet for a variety of national identities. Many of the countries that set out to reconstruct themselves after World War II wanted to project a new image of themselves in the international marketplace, and design was one of the ways in which they could do this.

In Europe this was most visible in the Scandinavian countries, Italy, Germany and Great Britain. Outside Europe the United States and Japan also used modern design as a showcase for their progressive economies and cultures. That of the United States was represented by the streamlined goods that were exported to many countries around the globe. In response many European countries harnessed their own traditions in an effort to differentiate themselves. Sweden and Denmark, for instance, reformulated their craft traditions in the light of the requirements of modernity as a means of creating their own identity, while Italy looked to its heritage of quality and good taste to create its marketable image.

All the countries in question sought to promote their own images of good design in this period and many different strategies were adopted to make this possible. A number of design reform bodies – some were new, such as Britain's Council of Industrial Design formed in 1944 and Germany's Rat für Formgebung of 1951, while others were inherited from the pre-war period, such as Denmark's Den Permanente and Sweden's Svenska Slöjdföreningen – encouraged manufacturers and the public to reform their tastes. The Museum of Modern Art in New York was especially active in this context, organizing internationally popular competitions on the subject of good design. Exhibitions were used as showcases once again; particularly important in the 1950s were the Milan Triennales, where the cream of international design was exhibited at one venue. Prizes at this event were coveted and careers were made on the basis of them. Many leading designers also made a significant impact at the Festival of Britain in 1951.

Post-war modern design stood for the various brands of democracy that were set up after 1945. Pre-war Modernism had set the tone and after 1945 modern design and the ideal of well-designed goods that were available for all still went hand in hand. Countries responded differently to their own pasts however: Italy, for instance, rejected some pre-war architectural styles because of their links with Fascism, whereas Germany reinstated its Modernist design programme because the Bauhaus school was closed by the National Socialist Party in 1933 and its development was perceived as incomplete.

Italy's post-war design movement embraced organic forms as an alternative modern aesthetic, and evolved a highly sophisticated modern design style for itself that was visible in furniture, products, ceramics and glass. The expressive Italian lighting objects produced at this time were featured in international magazines and came to stand for a new post-war lifestyle associated with affluence and sophistication.

In contrast Germany set out to revive its pre-war efforts after 1945. The standardization of the machine style was reinforced by advances in engineering. A systematic approach was favoured by designers and manufacturers alike and the country quickly came to be associated with the idea of neofunctionalism, a design movement that was linked with Germany's technologically advanced and visually minimal electrical goods.

The 1950s saw consumer booms across Europe and the United States. They were matched by a huge growth of interest in goods made of modern materials, which were seen as signs of a new affluent lifestyle. Increasingly consumers across the globe sought to represent their personal aspirations through their domestic interiors. Their unprecedented interest in the varieties of modern style available in the marketplace encouraged designers to evolve more and more choices for them, and manufacturers to produce a greater variety of goods. In Great Britain, for example, the Contemporary style in furniture, interior and product design was characterized by its use of surface pattern and expressive colour. It showed how modern designers had learnt to respond to market demands.

As in the pre-war years the decade after 1945 saw the international success of a number of pioneering individuals. Both the dominant stylistic possibilities – the organic Modernism formulated by men such as Charles Eames in the United States, Arne Jacobsen in Denmark, Robin Day in Great Britain, and Marcello Nizzoli in Italy (see pp.148–51, 142–5 and 168–72) – and the more austere Neo-Functionalism of Dieter Rams in Germany and Kenneth Grange in Great Britain (see pp.184–9) – were disseminated internationally. New materials, moulded plywood in particular, made it possible for objects to exhibit a new expressiveness while advances in electronics freed the consumer machine to become as stylistically sophisticated as its applied art counterparts. While objects related to the decorative domestic interior tended to move in the direction of the organic, rejecting the machine in favour of abstract forms derived from the human body and the world of nature, consumer electronics, in the hands of manufacturers such as the German firm Braun, and the newly formed Japanese company SONY (see pp.180–81), defined themselves, increasingly, as items of equipment, characterized by their technological virtuosity.

In this way two worlds of design existed alongside each other. Designers became more and more adept at constructing these new styles for material objects, conscious that it was the meaning of objects, not just their underlying principles, that mattered. With the mass consumption of the modern style that had occurred by the late 1950s, the ever-expanding technological possibilities open to designers, and the global nature of the marketplace, it was clear that modern design was fully integrated into the late 20th-century capitalist economy and had become one of the major cultural forces of the period.

An interior created by the American
designer George Nelson, featuring his
whimsical "marshmallow" sofa of 1956.
The modern interior style of the 1950s
was much more brightly coloured and
generally more expressive than its
pre-war equivalent.

Although never associated with one particular ideology or movement, the architect and designer Gio Ponti (1891–1979) was motivated by a single idea, which he expressed in the exhibition catalogue for the 1925 Paris Exhibition of Decorative Arts: "Industry is the style of the twentieth century, its mode of creation." For him, this did not

Gio Ponti

refer to dogmatic use of a "machine aesthetic" but rather an awareness of the implications of mass production. He embraced both tradition and modernity; worked with craft workshops and industrial manufacturers; and was involved in all areas of design, from town planning, buildings and interiors to furniture, domestic machines and ornamental items.

Gio Ponti was an influential figure in Italian design from the 1920s to the 1950s. His work in architecture, decorative arts and design set a standard for others to follow, while his writings provided an intellectual framework for design in his native country.

At the 1936 Milan Triennale, Ponti reconstructed the interior of his own home (below). This contained many examples of his work, including furniture – from the "spare" and modern to the more traditional – and ceramic and glass pieces with a distinctly contemporary feel.

ARCHITECTURAL WORK

Ponti studied architecture at the Polytechnic of Milan from 1918–21. Throughout his career he undertook several important architectural commissions, working from his studio in Milan in partnership with architects such as Emilio Lancia and, later, Antonio Fornaroli, Eugenio Soncini and Alberto Rosselli. For his first proposal for the office building of the Montecatini company in Milan (1936) Ponti designed all the interior fittings, from door handles to tubular steel chairs; this unequivocally modern design – based on a grid, with prefabricated elements and lack of decoration – marked him out as a key architect of the day. Another landmark in his career was the Pirelli tower in Milan, completed in 1958 and one of the first European skyscrapers. The tower's distinctly un-boxy faceted shape supports Ponti's claim that the architecture of Brazilian cities – with their unusual skyscrapers and elegant forms – rather than that of New York, had inspired this building.

EARLY APPLIED ARTS

Alongside his architectural work Ponti devoted himself tirelessly to the applied arts, in particular ceramics, glass, metalwork and furniture. His first employer in this field was the ceramics company Richard Ginori, based in Doccia, for whom he designed a vast range of objects between 1923 and 1930. Characterized by Ponti's distinctive reworking of classical motifs (such as the mythological imagery to be found in friezes and on pottery) in a fresh, modern spirit, these highly decorative pieces won a prize at the 1925 Paris Exhibition (see pp.52–3). Although he designed one-off "art" pieces for the company, he also reorganized its production systems to make large-scale manufacture more efficient.

In 1930 Ponti was employed by the Fontana Arte lighting company. As he was now dealing with a firm associated with newly developed technology – electricity – he took a different stylistic approach, designing a range of ultra-modern lights made of metal and glass. However, Ponti did not relinquish his commitment to producing luxurious objects; for the fourth

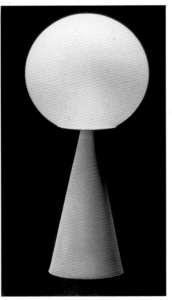

The "Bilia" table lamp (1931; above), made of laminated wood and opalescent glass, and manufactured by Fontana Arte. The geometric forms of this simple design show Ponti's ability to work without reference to the past, dealing exclusively with the problems of form, function and materials.

The stairwell and hallway of Ponti's own apartment in via Brin, Milan, photographed in 1935 (left). The bare walls, open balustrade and fitted shelving reveal his commitment to the functional and spatial concerns of European Modernism, while the use of wood and the inclusion of flowers for decorative effect suggest a softer approach.

A 1950s sketch for a textile design (above), for the JSA company in Como. Many of Ponti's designs for textiles were abstract, but this example shows his skill at figurative work. The emphasis is on a restricted colour range and a complex pattern repeat.

Triennale exhibition of 1930 he designed for Fontana Arte a large table with a black crystal top and cut crystal legs. At the sixth Triennale of 1936 he reproduced the interior of his own home, describing it as a "demonstrative dwelling", which showed how the many different aspects of his work could be combined successfully (see p.138).

POST-WAR DESIGNS

Ponti remained as prolific a designer in the early post-war period as he had been before World War II. In the 1950s he became increasingly influential both in industrial design and in the decorative arts. His interest in the latter

was expressed in his designs for furniture lavishly decorated by Piero Fornasetti, one of his protégés; these included pieces playfully decorated with images of playing cards, created for the interior of the San Remo Casino on the Italian coast. Ponti also designed neo-classical ornamental bronze objects such as pots and candlesticks for De Poli, a metal-goods manufacturer. Representing his interest in industrial design were the stunningly modern coffee machine for La Pavoni and the innovative "Superleggera" chair (1956) for Cassina: while clearly in the the modern furniture style of the 1950s, this cane-seated chair – with its elegantly tapering legs and open form – also made references to traditional Italian village furniture. It was inspired, in fact, by a vernacular chair type from the fishing village of Chiavari on the Italian coast, but with a pared-down, lightweight wooden frame (hence the chair's name, which means "superlight"). The chair's lightness and simplicity made it a lasting favourite, and it it still manufactured by Cassina.

Above all, it is Ponti's uncompromising sanitary equipment for Ideal Standard, designed in 1953, which numbers among his most progressive designs. Ponti's concept of Modernism allowed him to work on what he considered the appropriate style for different objects. While furniture belonged within the decorative arts tradition along with ceramics and glass, sanitary equipment was, above all, utilitarian, and was to be designed, therefore, with a functional approach. The sculptural forms of the toilets and sinks reflected not only the shapes dictated by their internal plumbing, but were also designed to accommodate the needs of the users – for example, Ponti provided wide edges and flat surfaces on some items to allow space for toiletries or other objects to rest.

TRIENNALE EXHIBITIONS

In addition to practising architecture and design Ponti took on an important role as a spokesman for Italian design, especially in the 1930s, by organizing the early Triennale exhibitions in Monza and Milan. In this role he refused to take sides, either with the Rationalist architects and designers (who allied themselves strongly with progressive Modernists in Germany and France) or with the Italian "Novecento" architects and decorative artists (who favoured a simplified neoclassical style that was more decorative and nationalistic than the austere style associated with Rationalism). For example, at the fourth Triennale of 1930 in Monza (it moved to Milan in 1933; see pp.166–7), Ponti exhibited the highly rational "Electric House" designed by Luigi Figini and Gino Pollini, while he himself showed the neo-classical "Vacation House", designed in collaboration with Emilio Lancia. He also contributed domestic product designs, for example a minimalist set of stainless steel flatware designed for Krupp Italia, shown at the sixth Triennale in 1936 (for illustration, see p.167).

A glass-topped coffee-table with splayed gilt-bronze legs (above), manufactured by Fontana Arte in the 1950s and attributed to Gio Ponti. An aggressively modern-looking object, using modern materials as well as strong forms and colours, the table has a flower-pot well at its centre.

The dining area (left) in the Parco dei Principi hotel just outside Sorrento on Italy's Amalfi coast, designed by Ponti in 1960. The soft patterning of the mosaic floor and ceramic plaques on the walls offset the tapering legs and cantilevered arms of the overtly modern chairs.

An ebonized, ladder-back chair designed by Gio Ponti in the 1950s (below). In common with several of his designs from that decade, it is a modernized version of a vernacular country chair; the wooden frame and rush seat belong to the past, but the subtly angled back and tapered legs reveal Ponti's aesthetic response to the period in which he was working.

After World War II Ponti gained wider recognition through his active roles in setting up the Compasso d'Oro design award and the Associazione per il Disegno Industriale – the Italian designers' professional body – and represented Italy abroad in numerous exhibitions.

DOMUS MAGAZINE

Ponti also documented and determined the course of Italian design through the century in his role as founder and editor of the leading Italian architecture and design journal *Domus*. He set up the magazine in 1928 and edited it until 1940, when he launched a new journal, *Stile*; intended as a general magazine of art and culture, this also featured articles on design. In 1947 Ponti took over as editor of *Domus* once again from the architect Ernesto N. Rogers, who took a radical position advocating the Rationalist style. On Ponti's return, however, the focus of the magazine turned to the importance of "the good life" – social and economic stability – in post-war Italy. His essentially middle-class values and espousal of a craft-based approach to design played a strong part in the direction that Italian design took through the 1950s and early 1960s, from a politically radical position towards an acceptance of the importance of luxury in everyday life. He was responsible, more than any other designer in Italy, for pulling together all the

aspects – tradition, craftsmanship, new materials and, above all quality – that formed the character of Italian design in the mid-century. He took this approach in his own work, for example his 1960 interior scheme for the Parco dei Principi hotel near Sorrento (see above), in which he combined such decorative elements as colourful mosaic work with simple, modern furniture pieces. If there is one achievement for which Ponti will be remembered it is his ability to synthesize these themes and to combine them into a single, recognizable style.

Ponti was never a political ideologue nor a stylistic hard-liner. Instead he embraced a humanism that is embedded within Italy's cultural tradition and that defined his career as a key designer.

In the years following World War II, Denmark played an important role in the international evolution of modern design. The crafts roots of so many of the country's industries – including ceramics, glass, metalwork and furniture-making – were enhanced by the innovative contributions of individuals such as the gifted metalworkers Georg Jensen

Arne Jacobsen

Arne Jacobson brought post-war Danish design international recognition by allying it with modern architecture rather than with crafts and hand-making.

and Kay Bojesen, and the furniture designers Kaare Klint (see pp.64–5), Hans Wegner (see pp.160–61), Børge Mogensen and Finn Juhl to create an environment in which change could take place. The essential humanism and softened modern forms of the Danish-designed object was also of enormous popular appeal in the immediate post-war years. From this background emerged the architect and designer Arne Jacobsen (1902–71), ready to build on Denmark's modern design heritage and to take it into a new era.

TRAINING AND EARLY WORK

Born in Copenhagen, Jacobsen studied first as a mason at the Technical School in Copenhagen and subsequently, in the 1920s, as an architect at the Royal Danish Academy of Arts in the same city. Here he worked under the tutelage of Kay Fisker, an architect and designer who combined tradition with modernity and who was well known for the silver pieces he created for the Danish company, A. Michelsen, in the mid-1920s. Jacobsen graduated from the Academy in 1927. For the next three years he worked in the architectural office of Paul Holsoe, and in 1930 he opened his own architectural office in Hellerup, which he headed until his death.

Influenced by the achievements of Modernists such as Le Corbusier (see pp.94–7), Ludwig Mies van der Rohe (see pp.92–3) and the Swede

The "Swan" chair (left), designed for Fritz Hansen and produced in 1958, was upholstered with latex foam and mounted on a cast-aluminium base, demonstrating the designer's commitment to new materials.

The famous three-legged "Ant" chair (right), so named because of its resemblance to the insect's body, was designed between 1951 and 1952 and manufactured by Fritz Hansen. Since that time it has remained a best-seller and a favourite of many modern architects, and is now available in a range of vivid colours.

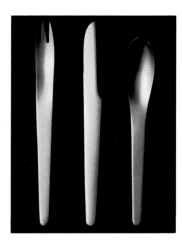

Jacobsen's 1957 stainless-steel cutlery (left), originally designed for A. Michelsen, characterized the sleek elegance of many of his 1950s designs. The cutlery pattern is now manufactured under the designer's name by the Danish metalware company Georg Jensen.

The "Egg" chair (right) was designed alongside "Swan" in 1958 and is also manufactured by Fritz Hansen. Jacobsen created the chair for the interior of the SAS Hotel in Copenhagen, which he also designed. As with "Swan", the inner structure of "Egg" consisted of a moulded fibreglass shell.

Gunnar Asplund, Jacobsen embraced the functionalist approach to architecture from the outset: that is, the idea that the appearance of a building – and indeed of its interior contents – should be arrived at through an analysis of its structure and intended use. In practice, this meant that the design of an object was dictated by the materials and industrial processes employed in its manufacture (as well as by its intended use) rather than by what were considered to be unnecessary decorative details. Jacobsen demonstrated these principles in his first major architectectural project, the Bellavista housing scheme, built in Copenhagen between 1930 and 1934.

FURNITURE DESIGNS AND WORK FOR HANSEN

The year 1950 marked Jacobsen's decision to bring furniture and products under the umbrella of his creative activities, and he began working with the Danish furniture manufacturer Fritz Hansen. Jacobsen had originally made contact with Hansen back in the 1930s, but it was not until after the war that the technology became available for him to take his furniture design dramatically forward into the modern age. The collaboration of these two men resulted in the production of a trio of chairs that put Denmark on the international design map: namely, the "Ant" chair (1951–2; below) and the

more ample "Swan" and "Egg" chairs (1958; opposite and above). These were accompanied by other less successful but equally important projects – including, in 1955, the "Series 7" group of chairs which had moulded plywood seats mounted on tubular steel legs – but it was the three chairs in particular that established their designer as a potent modern force.

Jacobsen's use of the new techniques involved in furniture design (the moulding of plywood and fibreglass to create unified sitting shells), as well as his new organic aesthetic, owed much to the American designer Charles Eames and his work with the Herman Miller company in the immediate post-war years (see pp.148–51). However, Jacobsen made these techniques and this aesthetic his own. His chairs had a refined sculptural elegance that immediately distinguished them as products of a Scandinavian sensibility.

The office version (below) of the "Oxford" chair was based on an original designed for St Catherine's College, Oxford, and produced by Fritz Hansen. This leather-covered example has castors and arms for office use.

A metal table lamp (right; 1956) designed for the Copenhagen lighting manufacturer Louis Poulsen. The minimal elegance and sculptural form of the lamp characterize the designer's work from this productive decade.

The "Ant" chair, for example – one of the first of a series of chairs consisting of a moulded plywood shell mounted on three chromed tubular steel legs – was strikingly original. The novelty of form of the moulded ply component, with its rounded upper half and "hips" below, narrowing in the middle to a slim "waist" (the characteristics that gave rise to its name), imbued the chair with a personality that made it more than a mere technological achievement. "Ant" was awarded a Grand Prix at the 1957 Triennale of Milan (see pp.166–7) – an achievement further confirming Jacobsen's status as a designer of international repute. Although the original was only available in a teak finish (the wood most widely associated with Danish furniture in the 1950s), it was later manufactured in a range of evocative colours, including red, various oranges, yellow, lime green, several blues and black. "Ant" remains a familiar element of modern interior environments – both public and private – to this day. The "3107" office chair of the 1950s, also produced by Fritz Hansen, was an adaptation of the design, but with castors and arms added to it.

NEW MATERIALS FOR NEW FORMS

The "Swan" and "Egg" chairs – first used in Jacobsen's glass-sheathed SAS Hotel in Copenhagen – were more complex structures than "Ant", and in many ways more sophisticated objects. The ovoid, womb-like shape of each of the two chairs was achieved through the manufacture of a moulded fibreglass shell, mounted on a base of cast aluminium, while the comfort of the upholstery derived from latex foam combined with leather, vinyl or fabric (as selected by the customer).

The chairs' organic appearance provided an ideal foil for the clean lines of the architectural spaces for which they were designed, and they quickly became widely used in such environments. Although abstract in form and in keeping with the image of modernity, they none the less provided a degree of comfort in what were often otherwise fairly austere settings, and were a favourite choice among modern architects for their interiors.

A COMPLETE VISION

Jacobsen's lasting vision was of a building, its interior and the items within it as one complete, harmonious environment. This concept underpinned his design for St Catherine's College, Oxford (1960–4; opposite, above), where he designed not only the building but also the furniture, lighting, textiles and cutlery that went into it. The college itself was created as a series of geometric planes, with straight lines serving to highlight the organic, curved shapes of its furniture. Jacobsen's "Oxford" chairs – like "Ant" before them – were made of moulded plywood, but this time he gave them exaggeratedly high backs in response to the tall ceilings of the college dining hall.

The "3300" sofa (1956; below). Its tubular steel frame, splayed legs and foam upholstery were in tune with the style of the decade, while its minimalism derived from earlier modernist thinking.

The reading-room/refectory in St Catherine's College, Oxford (above; 1960–64). Jacobsen designed all of the interior furnishings and fittings, including the tables, benches and the various types of lighting (both concealed and direct).

Although furniture played a key role in Jacobsen's achievement, it represented only one face of the "architectural accessories" (to borrow a term from Alvar Aalto; see pp.74–7) to which he devoted his attention. His lighting for the Louis Poulsen company (opposite, right), his bathroom fixtures for I.P. Lunds, his textiles for C. Olesen, his cutlery for A. Michelsen and his metal tableware items for Stelton (below) are all individual designs with their own group (or family) traits; at the same time they are all characterized by their dual commitment to abstract organic form and to the clean lines of Modernism.

Whether he was working with wood, plastics, fabric or metal, Jacobsen's extensive knowledge of mass-production techniques was such that he knew how to achieve the results he wanted. Unlike the Modernists of the 1920s, he also had the satisfaction of seeing his designs mass-produced in his lifetime, and of watching them become favourite items in sophisticated households all over Europe and the United States. In 1969, his 1957 flatware (designed for A. Michelsen and now produced by Georg Jensen; see p.143, above left) featured in Stanley Kubrick's science fiction film *2001: A Space Odyssey*, establishing beyond doubt that his vision of the future was one that penetrated the popular imagination as a whole.

The "Cylinda" line of stainless-steel tableware — including a jug, teapot, sugar bowl, ice bucket and ashtray (below) — was designed by Jacobsen for Stelton in 1966. Its strict geometry marks it out as an example of 1960s "neomodernism".

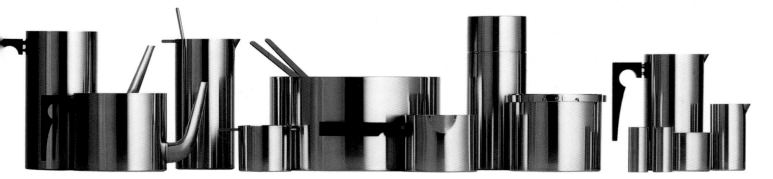

Few of the 20th century's influential designers were as enigmatic and individualistic as the Italian Carlo Mollino (1905–73). He is known for his furniture and interior designs for clients in his home town of Turin and elsewhere in Italy, especially during the 1940s, but he was also involved in designing fashion, film-sets, car-bodies and shop-fittings, as well as

Carlo Mollino

with photography. Obsessed with speed, he was skilled at aeronautics, car-racing and downhill skiing, while his interests in the occult and the erotic revealed themselves in his work. His penchant for curved, undulating forms and luxurious, brightly coloured materials set him apart from many of his Italian Modernist contemporaries.

Carlo Mollino was among the most innovative and idiosyncratic of Italy's designers. His exaggerated, organically curved furniture pieces – made possible by advances in wood production techniques – express his own personal preoccupations rather than the ideals of any group. Mollino's designs have recently enjoyed an upsurge of popularity.

A desk (below) designed by Mollino for the offices of Società Reale Mutua di Assicurazioni in Turin (1946). It is a simple, elegant and light structure, based on two "Y"-shaped supports, with a single central drawer and a top made of polished natural Fibrosil; the cabinet of drawers at the side is removable.

REPUTATION

It was not until the 1980s that Mollino's contribution to modern design, and his unique sensibility, were appreciated. He remained on the margins of the Italian design world during his lifetime because his work was far removed from that of the widely documented and celebrated Neo-Modern Italian design movement that emerged in Milan in the 1950s and 1960s. While these designers were strongly influenced by pre-war Rationalism (the Italian version of Modernism), Mollino was inspired by the earlier movements of Italian Futurism and Art Nouveau. The organic style that he developed in the 1940s was more sensual and idiosyncratic than that of his Milanese counterparts, and therefore its impact at the time was less widespread.

PRE-WAR ARCHITECTURE AND INTERIORS

Mollino trained initially as an engineer but went on to study architecture at the University of Turin, graduating in 1931. For the next five years or so he worked in the architectural office of his father, Eugenio Mollino, in Turin, but by 1937 he was working independently and designed his first significant building: an equestrian centre, the Ippica, in Turin. The following year, Mollino created an interior for the Miller house (also in Turin; see opposite, left), for which he designed, among other items, a small coffee-table with three turned-wood legs and an organically shaped glass top. His pre-war work was characterized by voluptuously curved forms and a careful juxtaposition of objects in a style described as "Streamlined Surrealism" (the term "Surrealism" was used because of the objects' biomorphic or "living" quality) or "Turinese Baroque". The considered use of lighting, draped fabric and sensuous materials – he frequently employed padded velvet for upholstery – enhanced the strange, almost decadent ambience of many of his interiors, which seemed to have been designed as settings for living out fantasies rather than as living machines in the Modernist tradition.

1940S DESIGNS

Through the years of World War II and immediately following, Mollino gained many more commissions for interiors and furniture. His chairs and tables were inspired by natural forms, such as skeletons, tree branches and deer antlers, and recalled models by the Art Nouveau architect Antoní Gaudí. Many of his pieces were unique and produced in the Apelli & Varesio joinery in Milan. Items designed for the Ada and Cesare Minola house of 1944 included a radio-gramophone and a table combined with a magazine rack, both with the familiar curved silhouettes, while for his own apartment, fitted out in 1946, he created a table-cum-writing desk with a dramatically curved rolling shutter.

The Miller House interior (below; 1938) contained many Mollino designs, including (shown here): a mounted light fixture with its own curved track, a glass showcase based on an asymmetric metal tripod, and chairs covered with topaz-coloured velvet.

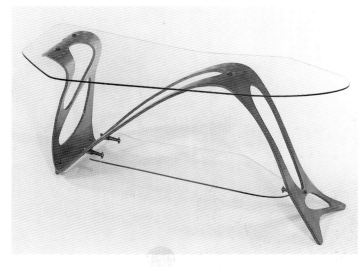

The "Arabesque" table (above; 1950) designed for the interior of the Singer store in Turin. It was made of moulded and perforated plywood with two glass surfaces and brass spacers, and one of the curved sections was intended for use as a magazine rack.

LATER CAREER

In the late 1940s and early 1950s Mollino worked increasingly on individual pieces. Important examples included a glass-topped table with a moulded plywood substructure for the "Italy at Work" exhibition, which toured the United States in 1950–51; another table, the famous "Arabesque" design, with a voluptuously curved piece of plywood topped by a piece of shaped glass for the Singer store in Turin (above); and a range of items including desks and a chair with a flexible plywood seat, consisting of two elements that moved independently of one another, for the Underwood offices in the same city. Following the death of his father in 1954, Mollino moved away from design for about a decade to pursue his other interests. In his final years he created a few more designs, including a desk for Ada Minola.

A side-chair (right) manufactured in the Apelli & Varesio workshop in 1945. It was created for the offices of the Società Reale Mutua di Assicurazioni in Turin (completed the following year), and is made of moulded plywood with brass ties and spacers.

"I think of myself officially as an architect. I can't help but look at the problems around us as problems of structure – and structure is architecture." In spite of this description of himself, the American Charles Eames (1907–78) is best remembered as one of the most influential furniture designers of the 20th century. He was one of a group of progressive

Charles & Ray Eames

furniture designers and manufacturers that first brought to the rest of the world's notice the fact that by the 1950s the United States – where so many radical European designers had settled and where mass production and mass media were at their most sophisticated – had replaced Europe as the dominant force in innovative design. Eames's ground-breaking and highly influential designs exploited technological breakthroughs in wood, plastics and metal. His charismatic personality, good looks and stylishness, combined with his skills as a graphic artist and film-maker, as well as his articulate championing of design, marked him out as one of the designer "super-stars" of the late 20th century.

Ray and Charles Eames provided a new post-war vision of the modern furniture object and interior that soon spread internationally. The use of new materials and the concept of the open living-space inspired a new relationship between design and lifestyle.

A pair of chairs in moulded and bent birch plywood (below; 1946), designed for Evans Wood Products; and a moulded ash plywood screen with canvas joints, made by Herman Miller in the same year. These pieces owe much to advanced American woodworking techniques.

THE CRANBROOK ACADEMY

Charles Eames was trained as an architect in his home town of St Louis, Missouri, between 1924 and 1926, set up in private practice in 1930 and returned to architectural education on a Fellowship at the Cranbrook Academy of Art in Michigan in 1936. At the Academy, where he was invited by the Finnish architect and designer Eliel Saarinen to head the department of experimental design from 1937–40, Eames encountered two individuals who were to become very important in his life and career. The first was Eero Saarinen (see pp.156–7), the son of Eliel, who asked Eames to collaborate with him on a number of design and architecture projects, and the other was a woman who was studying in the weaving department, Ray Kaiser (1912–88). She had worked with the painter Hans Hofmann in New York between 1933 and 1939 and had been a founder member, since 1936, of a group called the American Abstract Artists.

In 1941 Charles and Ray married and moved to California; in 1944 they set up a practice that remained active until Charles's death. Although the role that Ray played in his work is only now being uncovered, it is clear that her contribution should not be underestimated. It seems that they worked collaboratively on many projects, and that Ray was involved in all of the decorative aspects of their work.

COLLABORATION WITH SAARINEN

Before Charles and Ray left for California, however, Eames and Eero Saarinen produced an important range of moulded plywood furniture. In 1940 Eliot Noyes (see pp.174–5), the Curator of Design at the Museum of Modern Art in New York, announced a competition entitled "Organic

A living room containing a number of Eames pieces (above), including a long, elliptical table from the late 1940s; a sofa on a steel frame, designed in the early 1950s; a small metal-legged folding table; and a moulded plywood screen. Characteristically, the items are united by decorative items that soften and domesticize the space.

The Eames house in Pacific Palisades, California (left), constructed in 1949. The simple, pre-fabricated exterior was geometric and minimal, but the open-plan interior – arranged by Ray – contained many decorative items and houseplants that gave it a "lived-in" feel.

Design in Home Furnishings". Eames's and Saarinen's designs were awarded first prize in the storage category, and their work was exhibited at the museum the following year as a result. The pieces exploited technological advances in moulding plywood to create seating shells, and also used a new process known as "cycle-welding", developed by the Chrysler Corporation, which enabled wood to be joined to rubber, glass and metal. In applying new technology to the problem of evolving new structures for furniture, Eames was directly following earlier experiments with tubular steel by Mart Stam and Marcel Breuer (see pp.108–11). However, the 1941 furniture – including lounge and dining chairs, tables of various sizes and storage objects (the types of item on which Eames concentrated for the next three decades) – could not be manufactured in the way that they had planned, and eventually the pieces were fabricated entirely from wood.

MATURE DESIGNS

In California Eames continued to experiment with moulded plywood and, in 1942, was commissioned with Saarinen by the United States Navy to research the use of this new material for equipment such as leg splints (for illustration, see p.153). The advances made over the next two years working on wartime projects allowed Eames to develop new structural and aesthetic possibilities when he returned to furniture design in 1944. In the same year he established a company in California – Evans Manufacturing, an offshoot of the Evans Products Company – to produce his new designs, but

A storage unit (right) designed by Charles and Ray Eames in 1949–50. Based on a simple grid and composed of metal and wood, the structure combines closed cupboards and drawers for storage purposes and open elements to display decorative items.

A rocker version of Charles Eames's low armchair (above; 1950), with a moulded polyester seat on a steel wire base. Eames's foray into plastics reinforced his decision to create shell seats and bases as two distinct components made of contrasting materials.

The lounge chair and ottoman (1956; below), made from three moulded rosewood shells, with leather upholstery and a cast-aluminium base. Its image of comfort and sophistication have made this a classic 20th-century chair design.

in 1946 was introduced to the Michigan-based Herman Miller furniture company by George Nelson (see pp.154–5). Miller acted as a patron of Eames's work, and thus began a relationship that was to transform modern furniture in the second half of the 20th century.

In 1946 Eames was also asked to mount a one-man show at the Museum of Modern Art in New York. This time he was able to create furniture with steel legs welded to a moulded plywood frame, with rubber shock mounts positioned at the joins to allow for flexibility. The exhibition featured a number of experimental side-chairs, including one with a single front or back leg, which was not put into production because of its instability. The most successful pieces in the show were a range of side-chairs with steel-rod frames, a coffee-table, a bent-plywood screen, and all-wooden chairs and storage items. Within a short period these objects appeared in countless design journals; in Italy, for example, they were enormously influential on the country's designers – including Marco Zanuso (see pp.196–7) – over the next decade as a result of their publication in *Domus* magazine.

HERMAN MILLER FURNITURE

After the New York show Herman Miller put a number of Eames's pieces into production; they proved just as successful commercially as they had been when exhibited. Over the next two decades Eames designed a sequence of equally innovative pieces, including a chair with a fibreglass shell (1948), which spawned a number of related versions (left) and anticipated many later creations in plastic by other designers. Eames's famous lounge chair and ottoman, designed in 1956 as a one-off birthday present for the film director Billy Wilder, and made of three rosewood moulded shells and black leather upholstery (later also produced in tan and white), became an icon of modern living (below). Pieces with aluminium frames combined with upholstered black leather produced in 1958 were also widely used in modern offices, while in the early 1960s Eames transformed the airport environment in a similarly radical manner with the minimalist pieces (incorporating lightweight but hard-wearing materials such as aluminium and vinyl) that he designed for O'Hare Airport in Chicago and John Wayne Airport in Orange County, California (opposite, above). Such furniture has now become the standard in airports around the world. Today the German company Vitra holds the rights to manufacture all Eames's furniture.

ARCHITECTURE

Although Eames is less celebrated for his architecture than for his furniture, he did create one notable building in 1949: his own house in Pacific Palisades, California. The house is probably the best-known product of the progressive Case Study House programme, instigated by the editor of the California-based magazine *Arts and Architecture*, John Entenza. The contributors to the project, including Eames and Eero Saarinen, sought to tackle the post-war housing crisis in the United States by commissioning low-cost houses that could be built using mass-produced pieces in the Los Angeles area. The Eames house, with its reliance on prefabricated panels,

John Wayne Airport in Orange County, California (above) with tandem sling seating, designed in 1962. The seven-seat units are made of polished aluminium with vinyl upholstery, and have had an enormous influence on the appearance of public spaces.

represented an exercise in advanced design techniques that helped to consolidate his reputation as being technologically progressive, but at the same time the house was approachable and humanized. The interior was crammed full of decorative objects from Mexico, Africa and elsewhere, arranged by Ray, and contrasted with the austerity of the building's external structure (see p.149). Eames even made their home and its contents the subject of his own documentary film, entitled *House*.

These walnut stools (right) were designed as variations on a theme by Ray Eames in the late 1940s, and were manufactured by Herman Miller. Their references to traditional non-Western designs and decorative detailing contrast sharply with Charles Eames's much more technology-oriented work, once again demonstrating that the couple's success lay in their ability to complement one another creatively.

Moulded plywood

From the mid-19th-century developments of the Austrian furniture company Thonet in bending laminated wood to the bent-plywood chair designs of Alvar Aalto (see pp.74–7) and Marcel Breuer (see pp.108–11) in the 1920s and 1930s, progressive designers and manufacturers had sought to find methods of processing wood to make it lighter, more suitable for mass production and adaptable to the human form. Before World War II Aalto had made some radical advances in bending wood in not only two but three dimensions; his developments in wood-bending techniques were patented in 1933 and used to lasting success in the manufacture of such pieces as his stacking stool from the mid-1930s, the legs of which fanned out at the top to join the seat. However, the method used to bend the wood still involved steam and arduous manual work. The major technological breakthroughs in bending and moulding wood came during World War II in experiments in the aeronautical industry; new synthetic resins were used for bonding the laminates, creating a stronger material, while the wood was bent using electrically driven machinery. As a result, plywood could be moulded more easily, effectively and, above all, inexpensively into organic and sculptural forms more sympathetic to the shape of the human body.

AMERICAN DISCOVERIES

Adapting moulded wood to the human form was at the heart of experiments in designing new equipment undertaken by the American Charles Eames (see pp.148–51) for the United States Navy in the early 1940s. The furniture that he designed with Eero Saarinen (see pp.156–7) for the 1940 "Organic Design in Home Furnishings" exhibition at the Museum of Modern Art in New York featured moulded plywood "shells", but at that time there was no cheap method of producing them. Eames spent a considerable amount of time and energy experimenting with layering and moulding thin wood veneers, and with mass producing the results without heavy investment in precision machinery. His discoveries found their first practical application in traction splints, used in their thousands during World War II. From there Eames moved on to

Danish designer Arne Jacobsen made the seat and back of his "3107" chair (left; 1955) from a one-piece moulded plywood shell, in a development of the American Charles Eames's ideas. (Eames had made similar proposals back in 1940, although his wooden pieces had two or more elements.) Jacobsen had concentrated on the single plywood shell from the early 1950s, bringing it to a high level of visual sophistication by the middle of that decade.

Ernest Race's wartime experiences in the British aeronautical industry brought him into contact with plywood moulding, which he later used for the seat of the "Antelope" chair (above), designed for the Festival of Britain in 1951.

Carlo Mollino experimented extensively with bent and moulded plywood, combining elements in complex ways to create unusual shapes – as shown in this laminated ten-ply ash chair (below).

making sections for training planes and army gliders. Towards the end of the war the Moulded Plywood Division of Evans Manufacturing produced his 1946 collection of furniture using mass-produced plywood shell forms.

EUROPEAN DESIGNERS

Eames's breakthroughs coincided with similar developments across the Atlantic. The British designer Ernest Race (see pp.162–3), for example, also transferred the techniques he had learned in the wartime aeronautical industry to furniture manufacture. His "Antelope" (above) and "Springbok" chairs both had moulded plywood seats.

Other European designers and manufacturers exploiting the revolutionary aesthetic, economic and ergonomic possibilities of moulded plywood – with chair designs, which, like those of Charles Eames, had plywood shell seats and steel legs – included the Arflex, Cassina (see pp.212–13) and Gavina companies, and Carlo Mollino (see pp.146–7), Carlo di Carli and Roberto Mango in Italy. Influenced by Eames, whose work was featured in the Italian magazine *Domus* in the mid-1940s, di Carli and Mango produced chairs with curved and moulded plywood seats and backs, frequently mounted on steel legs in the style of the day.

THE ARRIVAL OF PLASTICS

Many designers had experimented with the idea of a chair made from a single piece of moulded plywood since Gerrit Rietveld (see pp.98–101) had attempted this in 1927 with his "Birza" armchair. In 1952 the Danish architect/designer Arne Jacobsen (see pp.142–5) succeeded in making the attempt a reality with the "Ant" chair (in creating a chair with a one-piece moulded plywood seating shell). However, when moulding fibreglass and other plastics became feasible in the 1950s and 1960s, the moulded plywood chair was quickly displaced by exciting designs in these newer materials.

In 1942 Eero Saarinen and Charles Eames used advances in wood-moulding technology to make contoured leg-splints (above) for wounded servicemen.

British designer Robin Day created the "Hillestak" chair for Hille (1950; right) as a one-piece plywood seat and back on a tubular steel base. This simple chair could be stacked and picked up easily, and was soon seen in public interiors all over the country.

The American George Nelson (1908–86), although trained as an architect, built very little but made a significant impact through his designs and his documentation and promotion of the Modern Movement. Nelson studied architecture at Yale University (1924–31) and at the American Academy in Rome (1932–4). In Europe he discovered

George Nelson

The American architect and designer George Nelson enjoyed a long and influential career throughout the middle years of the 20th century, helping to consolidate a new modern landscape for the home and office.

Modernism and, on his return home, published a series of articles on architects such as Le Corbusier, Ludwig Mies van der Rohe and Walter Gropius (see pp.94–7, 92–3 and 88–90) in the journal *Pencil Points*. Along with the recent "International Style" exhibition at New York's Museum of Modern Art, which brought European Modernism to the attention of the American public, Nelson's writing helped to consolidate the influence of the movement in American architecture and design in the 1930s.

An office-chair design, named the "Swag-legged Chair" (below; 1958). As this photograph demonstrates, the chair's highly flexible structure – made possible by the way in which the back and seat components are fixed together – offers the sitter an increased level of mobility.

EARLY WRITING AND ARCHITECTURE

From *Pencil Points*, Nelson moved to *Architectural Forum* – first as an Associate Editor from 1935–43 and then as a Consultant Editor from 1944 to 1949 – and celebrated in his writing the work of Modernist architects and designers. He also remained a practising architect, joining the firm of Fordyce & Hamby in 1937 and later working in partnership with William Hamby on the design of the Fairchild House (1941), one of the few Modernist residences in New York City.

NEW IDEAS OF DOMESTIC DESIGN

When Hamby & Nelson closed in 1942, Nelson dedicated much of his time to writing, and in 1945 published a book – co-written with the designer Henry Wright (who had also worked on *Architectural Forum*) – entitled *Tomorrow's House*. This book focused on the way in which Modernist ideas of design could be practically applied in American homes: for example, through open-plan living.

In the same year Nelson developed one of his most significant design concepts, the "Storagewall", based on the idea that the space wasted within the

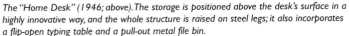

The "Home Desk" (1946; above). The storage is positioned above the desk's surface in a highly innovative way, and the whole structure is raised on steel legs; it also incorporates a flip-open typing table and a pull-out metal file bin.

The "Marshmallow" sofa (1956; right) was one of Nelson's most popular designs. Its simple yet strong form, with its round, multi-coloured cushions – resembling the sweets from which it derives its name – is both functional and evocative of 1950s Modernism.

wall cavities of houses might be used more effectively for storage. This novel idea of combining architectural structure with furniture inspired D. J. De Prée, President of the Herman Miller furniture manufacturing company, to produce the "Storagewall" and to take on Nelson as the company's Design Director (succeeding Gilbert Rohde, who had died in 1944). One of Nelson's first important actions within the company was to persuade De Prée to develop the designs of the young Charles Eames (see pp.148–51) from 1946.

POST-WAR CAREER

Nelson continued to combine his work at Herman Miller with that of a design practitioner. In 1947 he opened his own office in New York, in which was created a series of influential designs, many of them for Herman Miller; these included the "Ball Clock" (1950; above right), the "Bubble Lamp" (1952), the "Marshmallow" sofa (1956; right) and the "Sling" sofa (1963). Through the 1950s and 1960s Nelson and his team from Herman Miller also worked on exhibitions (including the United States Exhibition in Moscow with Charles Eames in 1959, and the Chrysler and Irish pavilions at the New York World's Fair in 1964), interiors (including the Chicago showroom in 1948, the New York showrooms in 1953 and 1956, and the Washington showroom in 1964) and urban planning. His role as a leading representative and spokesman of the American community of modern designers remained unsurpassed until his death.

The Finnish-born Eero Saarinen (1910–61) was a member of the generation of architect/designers that helped to make the United States the centre for modern design following World War II. Along with designers such as Charles Eames (see pp.148–51), George Nelson (see pp.154–5), Harry Bertoia and Isamu Noguchi, he was instrumental in

Eero Saarinen

evolving a new form of Modernism that embraced organic, human-friendly forms rather than the severe rectilinear outlines of traditional Modernism, yet which celebrated industrial manufacture rather than craft processes.

The son of the Finnish National Romantic architect Eliel Saarinen, Eero Saarinen spent his working life in the United States as a significant post-war architect and designer. From his early collaboration with Charles Eames through to his work for Knoll, he created some of the century's most influential furniture pieces.

The "Womb" chair and ottoman (below; 1946–8), manufactured by Knoll. Consisting of an upholstered fibreglass shell with latex-foam cushions mounted on a tubular steel frame, the chair was designed so the sitter could comfortably curl up in its welcoming form.

EARLY LIFE AND CAREER

Although he made his reputation in the "New World", Saarinen had his roots in the "Old World". He lived in Finland with his father, Eliel Saarinen, an architect, and his mother Loja until 1923, when he moved with his family to the United States; his father had been awarded second prize for his skyscraper design for the Chicago Tribune Tower competition (first prize went to Frank Lloyd Wright), and went on to teach architecture at the University of Michigan in Ann Arbor. Eero remained close to his father until the latter's death in 1950, and never considered being anything other than an architect. Yet for Eero architecture was a discipline akin to fine art, and to sculpture in particular. He described himself as a "form-giver", rather than an architect, and everything he designed possessed a strong sculptural quality. Indeed, before he went to Yale University (where he studied architecture from 1930 to 1934), he spent a year in Paris training as a fine artist.

COLLABORATION WITH CHARLES EAMES

Saarinen's first experience of design was in helping his parents to develop wooden furniture for the Kingswood School for Girls outside New York in 1929, while in 1934 he worked briefly on a furniture project with the designer Norman Bel Geddes. He travelled in Europe between 1934 and 1935 and on his return to the United States taught for a brief period at the Cranbrook Academy of Art near Detroit, Michigan. Cranbrook, originally a utopian, craft-oriented institution, was founded by the publisher George C. Booth and Eliel Saarinen in 1927, and Saarinen became Director in 1932. The school's graduates included two figures who would go on to have a great significance in Eliel's career – Charles Eames and Florence Schust (later Knoll).

In 1937 Eliel left teaching to set up an architectural practice in Ann Arbor with his father and in the same year met Charles Eames, who was at Cranbrook at the time. Saarinen and Eames collaborated on various projects,

The classic "Tulip" chair (1955–7; left), designed by Saarinen and manufactured by Knoll. The chair – named for its resemblance to the flower – was an exercise in visual deception. Although it appears to be a single form, its pedestal base is made of aluminium and the shell seat of fibreglass; their shared whiteness helps to create the illusion of unity.

Crowds in the waiting area of the new TWA building (1962; right) at Idlewild (now John F. Kennedy) Airport, New York. Saarinen's design for the building used organically shaped forms to evoke a bird or an aeroplane in flight.

culminating in the range of furniture that won them the first prize at an exhibition, held at the Museum of Modern Art in New York in 1940, entitled "Organic Design in Home Furnishings".

From 1941–7 Saarinen continued to work as an architect in partnership with his father and J. Robert Swanson, and spent the early 1940s experimenting with Eames in the use of moulded plywood for the United States Navy. Although Saarinen and Eames remained close friends, they moved in different directions after 1946. While Eames produced designs for Herman Miller, Saarinen worked for a new company, Knoll Associates, formed by Florence Schust and her husband, Hans Knoll.

CHAIRS FOR KNOLL

Saarinen designed a number of chairs for Knoll that were to become landmarks in the history of 20th-century furniture. The first, designed in 1946, was an upholstered lounge chair called the "Grasshopper", which, although interesting, was less radical than his now famous "Womb" chair (1946–8; opposite), made from a single piece of fibreglass; the chair was

upholstered in latex foam and set on a bent tubular steel frame. Complete with an upholstered footstool, it was conceived as a comforting, enveloping sculptural form that reflected its name.

Between 1948 and 1956 Saarinen created a range of office chairs for Knoll; these had shell seats and pedestal feet, and were intended for the General Motors Technical Center, a building of his own design (left). His second "classic" chair, the "Tulip" (above left), was produced as part of a range of pedestal items for Knoll between 1955 and 1957. Underpinning this design was the search for a "one-piece, one-material" form; the pedestal was developed to avoid what Saarinen described as a "slum of legs". Although the "Tulip" chair was made from fibreglass and aluminium, its all-white plastic coating gave it a deceptively uniform appearance.

The Styling Division building, part of the General Motors Technical Center in Warren, Michigan (1951–7; left). Saarinen's extensive use of glass curtain walls in this building demonstrates his understanding of, and commitment to, the most advanced technology.

With the notable exception of Alvar Aalto the Finnish contribution to modern design was, for the most part, made by individuals working for the applied art industries, glass and ceramics in particular. The dramatic move into a design idiom for the 20th century came in the post-war years. In that context Kaj Franck (1911–1989)

Kaj Franck

Kaj Franck was one of Finland's leading designers in the industrial arts from the late 1940s onwards. He played a leading role in helping Finnish ceramics and glass to find new directions in these years, acquiring an international profile in the process.

Franck's glass vase, created in the 1950s by the Nuutajärvi glassworks (below), exemplifies the designer's ability to evolve simple but dramatic forms. The vase is a unique piece, blown and moulded in clear and smoked glass, and finished by hand; it contrasts with other pieces by Franck from these years, which were created in larger series.

played a key role. Working for both the large ceramics and the glass factories, he had an unprecedented influence on Finnish tableware in the 1950s and 1960s. A modest, self-effacing man who didn't like the idea of the "signed object", he was none the less, along with Tapio Wirkkala and Timo Sarpeneva, at the heart of post-war Finnish Modernism. As he explained, "the aim of design was to make the resulting products serve mankind."

POST-WAR DESIGN IN FINLAND

Following World War II a new energy was apparent in modern design. The austere Modernism that had characterized the work of many architect-designers in the inter-war years was replaced by a softer, more lyrical sensibility that was, none the less, still very much "of its time". The strongly Germanic nature of Modernism's first phase was tempered by other national approaches. Among them those deriving from the Scandinavian countries made an enormous impact on the international marketplace. Finland in particular experienced a new wave of design activity which was quick to penetrate the international consciousness.

TRAINING AND WORK FOR MANUFACTURERS

Trained between 1929 and 1932 as a furniture designer at the Central School of Industrial Arts in Helsinki (where he later taught in the 1960s), Franck spent his early career as a freelance designer of lighting and textiles. Indeed it was as a textile designer of repute that the ceramics company Arabia approached him in 1945, asking him to head their design-planning studio. By 1950 he had become the company's Artistic Director, replacing Kurt Ekholm who had been in post since 1931.

WORK FOR IITTALA

In 1946 Franck was also approached by Iittala which, along with Nuutajärvi and Riihimaki, was one of Finland's most successful glass manufacturers. Franck gained his extensive glass-making experience through working with these companies. With a foot in both applied art camps, therefore, he began to make his contribution to the new Finnish design movement, which reached its peak at the Milan Triennale exhibitions of 1951 and 1954, where it was singled out as one of the most significant manifestations of contemporary design activity. While the face of Finnish design presented by Wirkkala (see pp.164–5) and Sarpaneva in Milan in the early 1950s was expressive and sculptural in nature, Franck's approach was more restrained

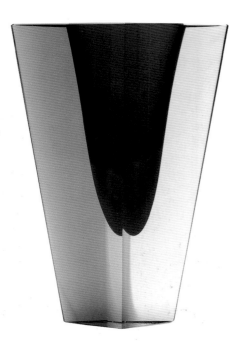

Two pieces from the "Kremlin Bells" series of double carafes designed for the Nuutajärvi glassworks (1958; left). Among his most decorative pieces from the era, they are made of blown and moulded clear and smoked glass, and their colourful forms anticipated developments in Finnish glass in the following decade.

"Flat Fish" (right), a range of decorative glass art objects designed by Franck and made by the Nuutajärvi glassworks in the 1950s. Alongside the simple utility items that he produced, Franck enjoyed creating decorative objects that exploited the expressive possibilities of their materials and that explored abstract forms whose origins lay in the natural world.

and practical. His first major success came with the range of inexpensive ceramic tableware items named "Kilta" on which he began work in 1948 amidst post-war shortages. Aimed at newly-weds, "Kilta" was a "mix-and-match" set of tableware items, made of ovenware faience, some pieces of which were multi-purpose, and which were available in a range of colours – white, black, blue, green and yellow – that could be mixed freely together (below). Franck's aim was to get away from the idea of the fixed table service and to introduce a greater degree of flexibility and informality into dining. His inspiration owed much to Russel Wright's (see pp.128–9) ideas about the links between modern living and modern design, but Franck's designs were much plainer in appearance than Wright's and came in a more sober assortment of colours. So popular was the "Kilta" range that it remained in production until 1974.

LATER WORK

In 1950 Franck left Iittala and joined Nuutajärvi. There he quickly put in a place a design policy in which the evolution of simple, everyday wares of good quality could be produced in large numbers. A number of classic designs emerged in the early decade, several of which were very utilitarian and resembled pieces of laboratory glass. Franck also had a decorative, sculptural side to his creative personality, however, as his small stylized glass sculptures of birds and fish demonstrate (above). Alongside everyday wares he clearly celebrated the role of the ornamental object, as his two piece-bottle "Kremlin Bells" (1958; above, left) makes abundantly clear.

The "Kilta" range of tableware (below) was launched by Arabia in 1952. Made of glazed earthenware, this was a "mix-and-match" service available in a limited range of shapes and colours, which mirrored the informal eating habits of the post-war generation.

Denmark's contribution to modern design (especially furniture) in this century has been considerable, particularly in the context of the applied arts. The pre-war legacy of Kaare Klint (see pp.64–5), in combining traditional values with a strong sense of the needs of the 20th-century, was strongly felt in the years after 1945, and influenced

Hans Wegner

The cabinet-maker and designer Hans Wegner was instrumental in the emergence of the "Danish Modern" furniture movement, which dominated international design discussions and stylish interiors of the 1950s.

Denmark's three leading furniture designers of that period – Børge Mogensen, Finn Juhl and Hans Wegner (b.1914). All three men played a key part in the formation of the "Danish Modern" movement, but Hans Wegner stands out as the designer who created a range of chairs – 500 in all – examples of which have become classics and which have come to stand for a period when craftsmanship, traditional values and modern living could be seen to be working together in harmony.

A tubular steel and rope reclining chair (1950; below). This was one of his more experimental designs, in which he temporarily abandoned wood in favour of more innovative materials.

TRAINING AND EARLY WORK

In 1931 Wegner was apprenticed to a cabinet-maker in Jutland and from him learned the skills that he was to exploit throughout his long career. He went on to train as an architect at the Architectural Academy in Copenhagen (1936–8) and finished off his studies with a period of time spent at Copenhagen's Applied Arts School. From the start, therefore, he combined furniture-making abilities with an understanding of architecture.

Wegner completed his design apprenticeship with a period of five years (1938–43) working as an assistant to the architect Arne Jacobsen (see pp.142–5) and his collaborator Eric Møller, at a time when they were working on Århus Town Hall. Jacobsen's uncompromising Modernism undoubtedly confirmed Wegner's decision to commit himself to this style. In 1943, Wegner opened his own office in Gentofte (now run by his daughter).

WORK FOR HANSEN

The final aspect of Wegner's early career to decide his future was a meeting, around 1940, with the cabinet-making firm of Johannes Hansen, who took on the task of manufacturing his early designs.

During the decade following the end of World War II Wegner went on to produce a number of chairs which earned Denmark an international reputation. In 1951 he was awarded the Lunning Prize – given for Scandinavian achievement, and which he shared with the Finn, Tapio Wirkkala (see pp.164–5) – and went on to win a silver medal at the 1957 Milan Triennale (see pp.166–7).

Wegner designed his first important chair in 1944. Called the "Chinese" chair (opposite, right) it was produced by Johannes Hansen and was characterized by a modern elegance and minimalism while also – through the material used and its structure – recalling

Two of a set of six beech and plywood stacking chairs and a matching circular table (1949; left), designed by Wegner for Fritz Hansen. The curved backrests, tapering legs and biomorphic forms of the chair seats mark them out as clear modern statements, albeit realized in a traditional material.

Wegner's "Chinese" chair (below) – originally produced by PP Møbler in 1944, and then manufactured in 1945 by Fritz Hansen – was a skilful blend of traditional and modern. Its simple, solid-wood form (in beech or teak) recalls vernacular pieces, yet it displays a new sophistication and comfort in the subtlety of its curves and, in this Hansen version, in a leather upholstered seating-pad that replaced the rattan of the older model.

traditional chair types. The quality of the finish of the chair and of its construction, which depended upon cabinet-making skills, was to become a hallmark of Wegner's pieces over the next few decades. His 1947 "Peacock" chair was a dramatic, modern version of a traditional Windsor chair, a furniture type that was popular in Scandinavia (along with the indigenous "stick-back" chair). While rooting himself in tradition, Wegner was, however, also deeply committed to the modern lifestyle for which single items of light

The "Flag line" chair for Fritz Hansen (1950; below). Evoking the traditional form of a deckchair, this highly sculptural solid-wood piece, with its tapered legs, cantilevered arms and lightly padded seat and backrest, is nevertheless modern.

yet comfortable furniture were of more use than the conventional heavy "suites". It was this combination of lightness with comfort that earned his 1949 chair the title of, simply, "The Chair". Wegner was only 35 years old when he designed what is now considered to be one of the classic chairs of this century. With its back subtly combined with the arm rests in a single curve, and its woven cane seat, this chair succeeded in encapsulating the post-war spirit of organic Modernism.

LATER CHAIRS

From 1949 onwards Wegner went from strength to strength, working with a variety of chair forms, most of which employed wood in various guises (although he moved into tubular steel in later years) and which focused on the importance of the frame. Up to the 1970s he worked with a range of companies – including Fritz Hansen, PP Møbler, Carl Hansen and Planmobel – producing pieces such as the "Shell" chair (1949), the "Y" chair (1950), the "Silent Valet" (a folding jacket rest; 1953), an office chair in 1955 and the "Bull" chair in 1960. He also branched out into silverware, lighting and wallpaper. Above all, however, Wegner is remembered for his early chairs, which are still manufactured today.

Ernest Race (1913–64) was a key figure in the emergence of a post-war modern furniture movement in Britain. For a decade following 1945 he was instrumental in formulating the "Contemporary" style – a term used to distinguish this lighter, more organic and playful body of furniture and furnishings from those linked with pre-war

Ernest Race

Modernism, its more austere predecessor. The style was no less rigorous in its emphasis on new materials or in its approach to function, but it simply oriented itself more to the user's needs than to the rationalism of mechanized mass production. It was a democratic style that sought to make modern, high-quality objects available to a wide social sector.

Ernest Race translated the technological breakthroughs of World War II into a new furniture style to suit the contemporary mood; several of his designs have become mid-century classics.

Race designed the "Neptune" lounge chair (below) for the P&O Line shipping company in 1953. The simple plywood frame of the lightly upholstered folding chair was both eminently practical and, with its subtle curves, pleasing to the eye.

TRAINING AND EARLY WORK

Race was one of the strongest innovators in this period, especially in relation to the application of new materials to furniture manufacture. He trained at the Bartlett School of Architecture (part of the University of London) between 1933 and 1935 – but before finding his way into the world of furniture took an interesting diversion for a short period of time. In 1937 he travelled to India to visit a missionary aunt who ran a weaving centre in Madras. He was very taken by the beautiful textiles that he saw there, and on his return to London he opened a shop – Race Fabrics – to sell cloth woven in India. He also undertook a design apprenticeship, working first as a model-maker and then as a draftsman in the lighting company Troughton & Young.

WAR AND POST-WAR YEARS

The war years proved to be crucial for Race, as they were for many other designers of his generation, including the American Charles Eames (see pp. 148–51). Race was employed in the aircraft industry during World War II and became aware of the advances that were being made in materials technology. After the war he joined forces with an engineer called J.W. Noel Jordan to form Race Furniture, an enterprise committed to finding ways of using scrap material from war manufacturing to make furniture in the prevailing climate of shortages.

Wood was in particularly short supply, so Race and Jordan concentrated on using metal – especially aluminium. The result was Race's highly innovative "BA" dining chair (opposite, above), which was made from sand-blasted aluminium scrap and which, with its refined, tapering legs, elegantly curved back and minimal upholstery on the seat and backrest, combined strength with lightness and visual minimalism. The chair starred both at the "Britain Can Make It" exhibition put on in 1946 at the Victoria &

A 1952 interior (above) containing items by Race, including (moving anti-clockwise from centre): his "Ladies'" chair, a wing chair, an easy chair, an occasional table, a settee, and a dining table and set of "BA" dining chairs (seen in the righthand background).

A cross-section showing the fabrication of the late-1940s wing armchair (right). Visible here are the steel rod frame that gave the chair its organic form, and the traditional upholstery techniques used to create the comfortable seat.

Albert Museum in London by the newly formed Council of Industrial Design, and at the 1951 Milan Triennale (see pp.166–7), where it was awarded a gold medal.

SOUTH BANK DESIGNS AND LATER WORK

Race followed up the success of his "BA" chair with two more designs, conceived as outdoor pieces for the Festival of Britain, held on London's South Bank in 1951. "Antelope" (see p.153) and "Springbok" were exercises in the use of steel rod. The ubiquity of the chairs at the 1951 event made them symbols of the occasion in many ways and they certainly entered the public's consciousness in a dramatic manner. The influence of the steel rod legs, capped by ball feet, soon penetrated the popular "Contemporary" environment, enhancing a wide range of obects from coat racks to coffee tables. The atomic symbolism of the ball feet was important, but they were also there, of course, for practical reasons as well ensuring that the steel did not force its way into a carpet or parquet floor.

Race's success was at its height by 1951, but he went on to create more modern icons, among them the "Flamingo" chair (1959) and the "Sheppey" sofa (1963). He remained with Race Furniture (which still produces his designs) up to 1954, subsequently working as a freelance designer up until his death ten years later.

Perhaps more than any other practitioner, Tapio Wirkkala (1915–85) represented internationally the innovative design movement that emerged in Finland after World War II. His very appearance – a craggy face, with wild hair and a beard – symbolized the way in which Finnish design of these years was inspired by nature and the elements in its

Tapio Wirkkala

search for a new, organic Modernism. Indeed, for much of his career Wirkkala spent part of each year in northern Lapland, and his bold, almost abstract designs – whether for glass, furniture, jewellery, cutlery, banknotes or stamps – reflected Lapland's dramatic landscape and the spirit and traditions of Lapp culture.

Tapio Wirkkala was one of the handful of designers who gave Finnish modern design an international reputation after World War II. His sculptural expressiveness and versatility – with glass featuring prominently – transformed a wide range of Finnish artefacts.

The "Kantarelli" vase (below), designed for the Iittala glassworks in 1946 and made from blown crystal with lines cut into its surface. It was one of Wirkkala's first designs for Iittala and won a Grand Prix at the 1951 Milan Triennale.

GLASS DESIGNS

Although he trained in Helsinki as a sculptor from 1933 to 1936, Wirkkala is best known as a glass artist and designer. He came to prominence as the winner of a glass art competition organized in 1946 by the Finnish manufacturer Iittala, and designed objects for the firm from that year until his death. Although Wirkkala attended an intensive course in glass-making, he approached the medium as a fine artist. He himself made the moulds into which the glass was blown or cast and pressed natural objects such as wood and leaves on to the glass to create textures and surface treatments; his irregular, highly textured pieces resembled no others that had come before.

Among Wirkkala's first notable and widely publicized pieces was his range of "Kantarelli" vases (1946; left), the fluid forms of which were modelled on a chanterelle mushroom and etched with fine lines. Although the craftsmen at Iittala initially found his delicately etched designs difficult to reproduce on a mass scale, Wirkkala worked closely with them until the technical problems were overcome. His "Leaf" and "Lichen" bowls (1951) showed how far he exploited traditional glass techniques to achieve new visual solutions; the opaque surface of the "Lichen" bowl was produced by acid-etching. From 1959 to his death, the Italian glass company Venini also manufactured Wirkkala designs.

THE MILAN TRIENNALES

Wirkkala established an international reputation through his work for the 1951 Milan Triennale exhibition (see pp. 166–7).

A vase (right) designed in the early 1960s for Iittala. The combination of the strong geometric form of this piece with its moulded surface pattern and deep colour is characteristic of Wirrkala's simple yet dramatic glassware designs.

With his wife, the graphic artist Rut Bryk, who went on to work in the art department of the Arabia ceramics firm in the 1960s, he designed and organized the Finnish exhibit. This striking display – with a backcloth showing a view of the Finnish landscape – featured a large number of ceramic and glass designs, including 30 of his own pieces (among them the "Kantarelli" vases and "Lichen" bowl). The Finnish contributors were awarded six Grand Prix, three of which went to Wirkkala). He was also responsible for the equally successful Finnish exhibit at the Milan Triennale of 1954, a success that helped the Scandinavian countries to dominate the Triennale events throughout the 1950s.

A simple, asymmetric, cast and polished solid-glass dish (1952; above) designed for Iittala. Wirkkala's skill as a sculptor enabled him to create this organic, minimal form, which is made dramatic by the thick outer edge. The design was included in the 1954 Milan Triennale, and helped to consolidate Finland's international reputation in this medium.

A range of goblets called "Tapio" (left), designed by Wirkkala for the Iittala glassworks (1954–6). The group – which is characterized by the heavy bases and elegantly curved waists of the pieces – is made of blown colourless glass, with a single air bubble in each foot.

OTHER MEDIA

Although glasswares played a large part in Wirkkala's career, he was a versatile and prolific designer in many other media, and in the 1960s moved away from one-off art pieces to industrial design. Between 1956 and 1985 he designed a wide range of ceramics for the German manufacturing company Rosenthal, including a black porcelain teapot (1968) and the commemorative "Century" service (1979). He also created sculptural pieces, including bowls, from layered laminated wood and designed furniture: for example, a table for the Finnish furniture company Asko (1958). One of his most memorable projects was a modern, tapered version of the traditional Finnish "puukko" sheath knife, designed for the metalwork company Hackman in the early 1960s. He also worked on a number of cutlery ranges and designed a metal floor lamp (1960).

LATER CAREER

In the 1970s Wirkkala returned to sculpture, producing bronze figures of birds. In other designs he retained his interest in Finnish traditions, but succeeded in reworking them in a radically modern way; in 1981, for example, he designed three chests of drawers – one was for his wife, one for his son, Sami, and the other for his daughter, Maaria – which were manufactured using traditional techniques and wooden nails.

A laminated birch and metal table designed by Wirkkala in the 1940s (above), expressing his sense of harmony and elegance in a medium other than glass. Wirkkala's sculptural training gave him the versatility to work across a range of media; he also designed wooden tableware and metal cutlery.

Milan Triennales

In the years after World War II the Triennales of Milan were pre-eminent in highlighting and celebrating new developments in modern design. Designers flocked in their droves to that city, eager to see all the innovative work coming out of European countries such as Finland, Sweden, Germany, and indeed Italy, in a single venue. Design journals worldwide published news of the events and reputations were established overnight.

The décor and lighting of the entrance to the Congress Room at the 11th Triennale in 1957 (above) were designed by Achille and Pier Giacomo Castiglioni, who made many significant contributions to the Triennales in the 1950s.

The "Lady" armchair (1951; below) by Marco Zanuso (see pp.196–9) was made by Arflex and pioneered the use of rubber-foam upholstery to achieve a new organic form and comfort; it won a Grand Prix at the 1951 Triennale. Zanuso also won awards at the 1954 and 1957 events.

ORIGINS OF THE TRIENNALES

In 1923 the critic Guido Marangani conceived a biennial exhibition to be held in Monza, and intended to show local artisanal work. By 1930, however, the show had become an "International Triennale of Modern Decorative and Industrial Arts", proving itself a platform for avant-garde activities in Europe.

In 1933, the Triennale was held in Milan for the first time, in the purpose-built Palace of Art, a neo-classical "Novecento" building designed by Giovanni Muzio. The fifth and sixth Triennales, (1936 and 1940) were clearly marked by the presence of the Fascist regime. At the first of these events, Marcello Nizzoli (see pp.172–3) – with the architects Giancarlo Palanti and Edoardo Persico, and the sculptor Lucio Fontana – designed a "Victory Salon", lined with heads of Roman leaders.

POST-WAR TRIENNALES

Following the defeat of Fascism, the Triennale was revived and came to represent the idea of Italian "Reconstruction": an economic, political and cultural "rebirth" that came with the emergence of the new Republic. The eighth event of 1947 was preoccupied with housing the homeless, and many young architect-designers – among them Ettore Sottsass (see pp.216–19) and Vico Magistretti (see pp.216–17 and 198–201) – exhibited furniture items that they had designed with this in mind.

By 1951 the design renaissance that had taken place in many European centres as part of the effort to revive post-war trade and culture was visible at the ninth Milan Triennale. Italy led the way with a stunning display of products entitled "The Form of the Useful", in which progressive Italian companies such as Olivetti and Piaggio showed objects produced by the new industrial designers of the day; these included the Castiglioni brothers (see pp.194–5), Marcello Nizzoli and Gino Valle.

Italy was not the only country to excel at the 1951 event; in that year Tapio Wirkkala (see pp.164–5) designed the Finnish exhibit, which, with its art glass and ceramics, won numerous prizes. Germany also showed the new, rigorous "Neo-Functionalist" direction (which also incorporated a revival of Bauhaus ideas) of its post-war industrial design, making clear that it was a powerful force within the international marketplace.

The 14th Triennale, held in 1968, was closed prematurely because of violent student demonstrations in the park outside the Palace of Art. Shown here (right) is the recreation and refreshment area, designed by Joe Colombo (see pp.208–9), of an exhibition entitled "Italian Expression and Production", with earphones, an ashtray and a glassholder provided for each user.

Achille and Pier Giacomo Castiglioni designed the Congress Room at the 11th Triennale in 1957 (below). The lighting – which included the minimal "Bulb Lamp", based on an industrial 1000-watt bulb, and manufactured by Leuci – was particularly innovative, and formed part of a development of work already undertaken by the brothers for the ninth Triennale in 1951.

The next Triennale, held in 1954, kept up the same level of momentum, as did the 11th Triennale of 1957, at which Hans Wegner (see pp.160–1) was awarded the Grand Prix. By this time it was obvious that the concept of industrial design was firmly rooted in European culture and that the leading countries were all working hard at defining their own versions of it. However, in 1964 there was a re-orientation. The "star system" – which promoted designers as "heroes" and representatives of high culture, dominating the previous decade and reaching its peak towards the end of those years – had begun to pall, so the organizers of the 12th Triennale decided to focus less on designers and more on consumers, choosing "Leisure" as the key theme of the event.

The social upheaval of 1968 led to the decline of the Triennale. That year's event was closed down prematurely by students demonstrating on the street outside. Although subsequent events were held through the 1970s and 1980s, the Triennale never regained the vital role that it had enjoyed in the optimistic decade after World War II.

The Italian architect and designer Gio Ponti was instrumental in establishing the concept of the Triennales in the 1920s and 1930s. He designed this stainless-steel flatware set (right) for Krupp Italia in 1936; it was exhibited at the sixth Triennale in Milan – the second event to be held in the purpose-built Palace of Art.

Robin and Lucienne Day (b.1915 and 1917 respectively) were among Britain's leading designers of the 1950s. Their youth, talent and optimism marked them out as symbols of the new post-war era and – both in collaboration and individually – they designed some outstanding furniture and fabrics that were celebrated internationally and helped to put

Robin & Lucienne Day

their country on the modern design map. For a time the Days became public figures, rather as the American industrial designers had been in the 1930s, with the media treating them as "style leaders". They were presented as glittering examples of the new lifestyle, manifested through the way in which they decorated and furnished their home in Chelsea (the subject of a profile in *House and Garden* magazine in 1952); this served to emphasize their celebrity status, as did their appearance three years later in an advertisement for Smirnoff vodka (shown on the left).

Robin and Lucienne Day played a major role in establishing a contemporary aesthetic for the British interior in the 1950s and 1960s.

A room in the "Homes and Gardens" pavilion at London's Festival of Britain exhibition (1951; below). The shelves, dining table and chairs, and fitted storage furniture were all designed by Robin Day. Their light, open appearance signalled a new sensibility in interior design.

TRAINING AND EARLY WORK

Both Robin and Lucienne Day trained at the Royal College of Art in London: Robin from 1934–8, following earlier training (from 1930–33) in furniture at a local technical school in High Wycombe, Buckinghamshire; and Lucienne from 1937–40, having previously studied at the Croydon School of Art. The couple married in 1942 and worked closely together from that year.

ROBIN DAY

Until 1948 Robin had been making a living as a graphic and exhibition designer, because he had had few opportunities to work on furniture. His breakthrough came in 1949 with a design that he submitted, with furniture designer Clive Latimer, to a competition for low-cost furniture organized by the Museum of Modern Art in New York. The modular storage units in formed plywood with aluminium frames won first prize in the storage section for an innovative design using new materials. The overall competition had attracted 3,000 entries (the prize for seating was won by Charles Eames; see pp. 148–51), so for Day and Latimer this accolade represented a great achievement.

Robin's success came to the attention of Lesley and Rosamund Julius – owners of the British furniture manufacturer Hille – who were on a trip to the United States and were keen to work with living designers. They commissioned Day and Latimer to design furniture for the 1949 British Industry Fair, for which Day produced a dining-room suite made of wood.

From 1950 Day worked as Design Director for Hille, concentrating on its total corporate identity and also, more significantly, designing many chairs and other types of furniture – such as cabinets and desks – for the contract market over the next two decades. His early practical experience in the

Robin Day's contribution to the public sphere is demonstrated by his interior treatment of a BOAC Super VC10 aeroplane (1963; left). Day chose the upholstery, wall-coverings and carpets, and also collaborated on the design of the seating and catering equipment.

The propylene chair for Hille (below), launched in 1963, was one of Robin Day's most influential designs. His earlier experiments with moulded plywood led naturally to this design for a chair consisting of a single-shell seat and back mounted on tubular steel legs, which was cheap and easy to manufacture, light, colourful and stackable. A huge success, it soon became a ubiquitous object in public interior spaces.

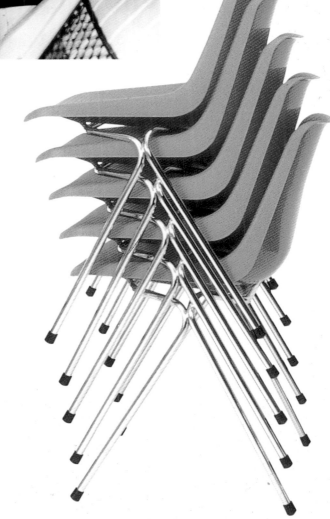

furniture industry was to prove very useful to Hille, because it meant that he could involve himself in the whole process of furniture-making, from design through prototyping to final manufacture.

The year 1950 saw the emergence of the "Hillestak" chair: a small side-chair in pre-formed laminated plywood with a strong modern appearance. In 1951 Day was responsible for furnishing two rooms – including a dining-room (see opposite) – in the Festival of Britain's "Homes and Gardens"

Metal seating (below), designed by Robin Day and manufactured by Hille in 1995. This light, elegant design was created for public waiting areas such as train stations and airports, and has been installed in many places including London Underground stations.

Lucienne Day's discreet but powerfully modern pattern of 1958–9 (left), produced for Rosenthal's "Regent Street" china service. She worked for this German company from 1957–68, providing a wide range of modern patterns for application to their products.

LUCIENNE DAY

In 1947, Lucienne and Robin Day travelled to Scandinavia and, inspired by what they had seen, returned determined to help create a modern design movement in Britain. From that point, Lucienne's textiles were to play a significant part in achieving this ambition. Although she had already undertaken some professional commissions and exhibited work, her first significant commission came in 1948, in a request from Alistair Morton at Edinburgh Weavers to design two chintzes for the company. The striking results brought her to the attention of Heals Wholesale and Export Ltd.

In 1951 Lucienne collaborated with Robin on two installations. She designed "Calyx" – her most successful and best-known design – for the Festival of Britain. It won the First Award of the American Institute of Decorators, and also received a gold medal at the 1951 Milan Triennale, while at the 1954 Triennale four of her textiles – "Graphica", "Tickertape", "Spectators" (opposite, right) and "Linear" – won the prestigious Grand Prix.

Pavilion, as well as furniture for the auditorium, restaurant and foyer at the Festival Hall in London. Also in that year he designed a "Contemporary" interior for the Milan Triennale (see pp.166–7), which included a textile by Lucienne Day; the Days both won gold medals for this work, representing yet another remarkable achievement for British designers.

In 1963 Day and Hille together made a breakthrough with the launch of a low-cost, single-shell chair made of the new plastic polypropylene. The chair was an instant success – not least because of Hille's clever marketing decision to send out 600 free samples to architects, designers and journalists. The *Architect's Journal* correctly prophesied that it would "prove to be the most significant development in British mass-produced design since the war".

Robin also designed appliances – including radios and television sets for the British firm Pye – as well as producing many other items for both public and private interiors. This work ranged from office equipment and carpets to passenger-aircraft interiors for BOAC (see p.169).

"Too Many Cooks" (left), designed by Lucienne Day in the late 1950s for the Belfast linen company Thomas Somerset. The freshness of the light, figurative pattern – which combines a vernacular style with a modern sensibility – earned Lucienne a Design Council award.

Lucienne Day's "Trio" pattern (right), created in 1954 for Heals, shows her ability to adapt fine art-oriented imagery to textiles. Her combination of a graphic striped background with a "hand-drawn" abstract pattern and a strong "Contemporary" feel resulted in an innovative design.

"Flotilla" (1952; above), one of Lucienne's most successful designs for Heals, continued the marine-based imagery that had become popular at the Festival of Britain a year earlier. The textile's appealing abstract forms reflected the style of the day.

"Spectators" (right), designed for Heals in 1954. Its semi-abstract forms and strong yet controlled colours made it a favourite. It featured in numerous interiors conceived in the "Contemporary" style, and won a Gran Premio at the 1954 Milan Triennale.

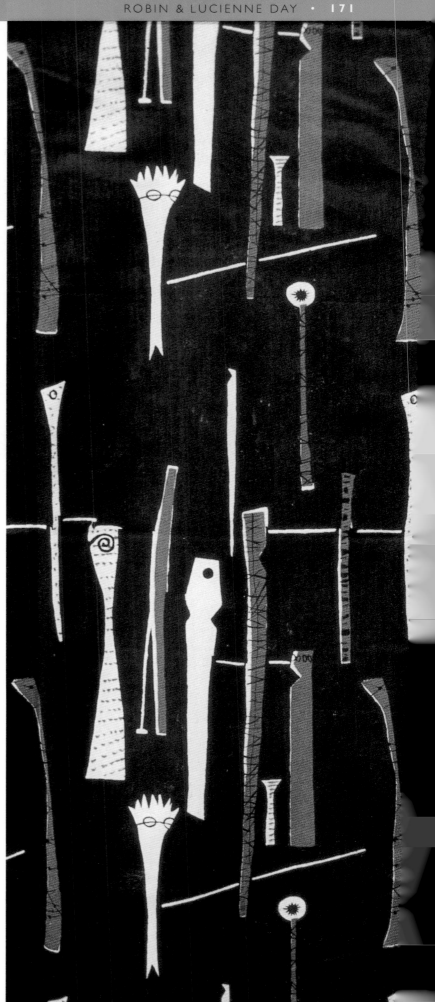

Following the success of "Calyx", Lucienne produced "Flotilla" (above) for Heals, which was inspired by marine imagery and had a smaller repeat; this fabric was used in the People's House at London's Ideal Home Exhibition (1952). Other popular designs, including "Small Hours" and "Strata", followed fast on its heels.

From 1954 until 1974 Lucienne produced about half-a-dozen designs per year for Heals. This work was characterized by originality, freshness and a strong vision of modernity. Her motifs — many derived from plant forms, but highly stylized in interpretation (and sometimes entirely abstract) — combined with a unique sense of colour marked out her designs from others. They depended heavily for their influence upon the abstract art of the period — in particular, the work of the Spanish painter Joan Miró — but in their translation into a new medium they took on a new life and quality.

Through the 1950s and 1960s Lucienne expanded her range into wallpapers, ceramics and carpets, showing the variety that characterized her fabrics in all three of these areas. She produced wallpaper patterns for Crown (1954–64), worked on ceramics for Rosenthal (1957–69; see opposite, above left), and designed carpets for a number of companies.

However, from the mid-1970s Lucienne stopped designing for mass production companies, and began to produce what she called "silk mosaics" — large decorative hangings for use in interiors. A striking example hangs in the John Lewis store in Kingston, Surrey, and another in the foyer of the QE II Conference Centre in London. Her hangings are also owned by museums in Sweden, the United States and Canada, as well as by the Victoria & Albert Museum in London and the Whitworth Art Gallery in Manchester.

The impact of the work of Marcello Nizzoli (1887–1969) on modern Italian and international product design has been highly significant. Nizzoli did not actually begin working in this field until the age of 53, after a long and successful career in textile, graphic and exhibition design, but this substantial and varied background made his contribution to

Marcello Nizzoli

Having established his early career as a successful graphic and exhibition designer, Marcello Nizzoli went on to create Olivetti's ground-breaking office machines of the late 1940s and early 1950s. He subsequently became an industrial designer of note, influencing many who came after him.

Nizzoli's "Lettera 22" portable typewriter (below), designed for Olivetti in 1950, established the company's post-war commitment to modern design. The typewriter's simple metal body-shell and neutral colour marked it out as a piece of functional, modern design, and it quickly became an international best-seller.

the world of product design – when it came – both sophisticated and unique. He is best known for his innovative work for the Olivetti office machinery manufacturing company, for which he designed some classic objects in the 1940s and 1950s.

TRAINING AND EARLY WORK

Having trained in architecture, materials and graphics at the Scuola di Belle Arti, Parma, in 1910, Nizzoli started out with a breadth of skills and interests that he maintained throughout his working life. He was described by his biographer Germano Celant as a "practical man", and certainly the range of his completed work bears witness to a continual commitment to personal discovery through practice. His first work in the 1920s was on textile designs and on illustrations for advertisements and fashion magazines in Milan; with its use of abstract geometry as surface pattern, this output revealed the strong stylistic influence of the decorative work of the Wiener Werkstätte, as well as of the Italian Futurists. Shawls embroidered with Nizzoli's designs were shown at the first Decorative Art exhibition at Monza, Italy (1923), while for the two subsequent events – held in 1925 and 1927 – he provided poster designs that demonstrated his growing interest in the neo-classical "Novecento" movement. In contrast, in 1925–6, he produced two stunning posters for the Campari company, showing, this time, a deep fascination for the work of the Cubist painters.

By 1930 Nizzoli had developed an interest in Italian Rationalism – an architectural and design movement influenced by German and French Modernism – and this brought him into contact with two of the movement's key promoters, Giuseppe Terragni (see pp. 114–15) and Edoardo Persico. In 1934 Nizzoli formed a partnership with Persico, and together they created a number of designs in Milan, including minimalist interiors for two Parker Pen shops (1934 and 1935); a tubular steel display for the Hall of Gold Medals at the Aeronautical Exhibition (1934); and the Victory Salon at the 1936 Milan Triennale (see also pp.166–7).

WORK FOR OLIVETTI

In 1938 Nizzoli was approached by Adriano Olivetti of the office-machinery firm to design a shop in Venice. His first encounter with this progressive industrialist was to prove decisive and, by 1940, Nizzoli had been employed by the company to work on the appearance of its machines. His task was to extend the "corporate image" of the company to the design of its products, and Nizzoli was clearly equal to the challenge.

THE POST-WAR PERIOD

A few results of this work emerged before the start of World War II – for example, with the launch of the "Summa 40" adding machine, complete with a new body-shell – but the real transformation came after 1945 with the appearance of a new typewriter, the "Lexicon 80". This fresh, innovative piece had a simple, organically shaped shell made of two elements.

From the 1950s Nizzoli produced a range of novel designs for Olivetti, among them the "Lettera 22" portable typewriter (1950; opposite) and for the sewing-machine makers Necchi, each of which provided not only a new form but also a new definition of the product itself. Other successes

Nizzoli began his career as a graphic designer. Among his many achievements was this 1930s poster for Campari (right), which makes clear his debt to avant-garde fine art and to Cubism in particular.

In collaboration with the sculptor Lucio Fontana and the architects Giancarlo Palanti and Edoardo Persico, Nizzoli worked on the graphic imagery of the "Victory Salon" (below), for the 1936 Milan Triennale. It was designed to celebrate Italian military achievements.

"CAMPARI,,
l'aperitivo

DAVIDE CAMPARI & C. - MILANO

included the "Supernova" and "Mirella" sewing machines for Necchi (1956; see below). In 1960 he designed a new petrol pump for the AGIP company, showing his versatility as an industrial designer.

Though continuing to work in the new area of product design, Nizzoli also sustained his interests in other media, including exhibition displays and architecture. Indeed, one of his last designs (never realized) was for a whole village – a fitting project for a designer who had exerted such a substantial influence on the mass environment of the 20th century.

Nizzoli's design for Necchi's "Mirella" sewing machine (1956; below) was among Italy's finest industrial design achievements of the 1950s. The machine's unified, streamlined body-shell served as a model of Italy's forward-thinking design approach for many years.

By the 1950s, a second generation of industrial designers was emerging in the United States. Several members of the first generation, including Walter Dorwin Teague and Raymond Loewy, continued to thrive, but some of the new designers took a wholly different approach to working with corporations. The American Eliot Noyes (1910–77),

Eliot Noyes

for example, rejected the concept of "styling" and refused to turn into a "call-girl to industry". Inspired more by the values of European Modernism than by those of American commercial life, he saw himself as "a bridge between large corporations and the artistic sensibility" and, through his work, helped change the image of design in the United States.

The industrial designer Eliot Noyes made a significant impact in the post-war years both through his curatorial work at New York's Museum of Modern Art and through his designs for IBM. He helped to make American design a cultural rather than a merely commercial phenomenon.

A proposal by Noyes – in collaboration with engineers from the General Electric Company – for an "All-Electric House" (1954; below). Special features included glass walls, central air-conditioning, vacuum-cleaning systems and intra-house television circuits, proving Noyes's commitment to the future and to his role as creator of its material culture.

TRAINING AND EARLY WORK

Noyes majored in architecture at Harvard University (from 1928–32), but also studied Classics. This academic training produced a rigorous and rational approach towards everything he did. He went on to study architecture at Harvard's Graduate School of Design from 1932–5 and 1937–8. Here he was taught by the European Modernists Walter Gropius (see pp. 88–9) and Marcel Breuer (see pp.108–11), an experience that set Noyes in the direction he was to pursue for the rest of his career.

On graduating in 1938 Noyes worked for a local architectural practice, but in 1939 was invited to work for Gropius and Breuer in Cambridge, Massachusetts. From there he became the first Curator of Industrial Design at the Museum of Modern Art in New York, a post that he held from 1940–42. The important "International Style" exhibition had been held at the museum in 1932 but, until 1940, no significant steps had been taken to show that design should be regarded as separate from architecture.

One of the first steps that Noyes took was to curate the competition and exhibition – "Organic Design in Home Furnishings" – that gave Charles Eames (see pp. 148–51) and Eero Saarinen (see pp.156–7) their first public platform; it also gave Noyes time to work out what, for him, constituted good design. He was optimistic that such a thing existed and campaigned on its behalf, claiming that "the public would buy good design if it had a chance."

WORK FOR IBM AND OTHERS

In 1946 Noyes was approached by Norman Bel Geddes to become Design Director of his office. The philosophies of the two men were very different, but this move led Noyes to the IBM (International Business Machines) company, where he took over work on the "Model A" electric typewriter – a machine that was much simpler and yet more sophisticated than its American counterparts. In 1947 he opened his own office – Eliot Noyes & Associates – to undertake local architectural projects, as well as pursuing an architectural career from his home town, New Canaan, Connecticut. Noyes also designed many of IBM's corporate office buildings.

The IBM exhibit at the New York World's Fair of 1964 (right). Entitled "IBM Day at the Fair", the enormous dome housed an exhibition on the company's achievements, including Noyes's work on office machinery.

A maquette (below) of the restrained petrol-station forecourt that Noyes designed for Mobil in the mid-1960s. He acted as a consultant for the company, transforming its entire visual image – from its graphics to its petrol pumps and the architecture of its petrol stations.

LATER WORK

From 1960–76 Noyes was employed to give general corporate-design advice to the Westinghouse company; from 1964–77 he also worked as a consultant for Mobil, designing a revolutionary round petrol pump that was adopted worldwide. He advised on general design policy for Pan Am from 1969–72, and for the following five years Noyes was President of the Massachusetts Institute of Technology (MIT).

Noyes was much more than a product designer, combining architecture, industrial design and consultancy. He was praised for his IBM pavilions at the World's Fairs at Brussels and San Antonio in the 1950s, and won a *Progressive Architecture* award for his own house in New Canaan (1954). Other work included writing on design for *Consumer Reports* (1947–54), and Presidency of the annual International Design Conference in Aspen, Colorado.

In 1956 Noyes was asked by IBM to become Design Director – a position he held until his death. His role with IBM was enviable for a young industrial designer; he brought in the American Paul Rand, a Modernist, to do the graphic work, a field in which Rand was already acclaimed; he persuaded the company to commission his friend Charles Eames to design special films and exhibitions; and he designed many machines himself, including electric typewriters. Noyes also advised on IBM's "corporate character", broadly defining this in terms of the company "helping man extend his control over the environment".

Noyes's design method was highly sculptural; he had prototype typewriters carved in wood to present to the board, and depended upon accurate working models. His early machines – including the "Executive" (1959) and "Selectric" (1961; right) – were organic in form; his designs were not simple exercises in styling, but rigorous attempts to remove unnecessary detail. He rejected the commercialism of annual model changes and encouraged a longer-lasting design approach that took into account the role of corporations in society.

The "Selectric" golfball typewriter (right), designed for IBM in 1961. The machine's elegant, undecorated sculptural housing shows Noyes's commitment to the European design method and his aversion to the superficiality of of American streamlining.

Although his life was short, Hans Gugelot (1920–65) was enormously influential in the post-war years in setting down a "neofunctionalist" product design style; this emphasized geometrical simplicity and the removal of unnecessary detail, and by the 1980s, had become internationally established as the status quo in product design.

Hans Gugelot

His tremendous intellectual and practical rigour provided a solid foundation for what amounted to a new movement – based no longer on artistic principles but on scientific rationalism – and which, from the 1960s onwards, produced a new visual minimalism that became a common language for consumer machines.

Hans Gugelot represented Germany's post-war bid for leadership in the arena of systematic design emanating from advanced technology. He was closely involved with the radical educational experiment at Ulm from the early 1950s to the late 1960s, and was responsible for a number of minimal, Neo-Functionalist designs in these years.

Gugelot collaborated with Dieter Rams in the design in 1956 for a combined radio and record player – the "SK4" – for Braun (below). It consisted of a "U"-shaped metal cabinet framed by two wooden sides and, nicknamed "Snow White's Coffin" because of its monochrome minimalism and transparent lid, quickly became an icon of German Neo-Functionalist design.

TRAINING AND EARLY WORK

Although Gugelot achieved all his successes in Germany, he was actually Dutch, born in Indonesia and educated in Switzerland. He trained first at an engineering school in Lausanne (1940–42), following this with an architectural education at the Federal Technical College in Zurich (1942–6). He stayed in Zurich to work in the office of Max Bill, an ex-Bauhaus architect, and it was here that he began to find his own voice. Gugelot was also concentrating on furniture design at this time, and some of his simple wooden chairs were manufactured by the Horgen-Glarius company.

THE HOCHSCHULE FÜR GESTALTUNG AND BRAUN

In the early 1950s, Max Bill was called to Germany to head a new educational institution – the Hochschule für Gestaltung (Design High School) at Ulm (see pp.178–9). Through Bill, Gugelot was invited to become Head of the product-design department at the school, and left for Germany in 1954.

For the next decade, Gugelot dedicated much of his energy to developing a curriculum and teaching in an institution that favoured the scientific/technological model of design, albeit with a strong theoretical underpinning and links with the social sciences.

Gugelot's entrée into product design began through links made through the school with the owners of the Braun electronics company. Having established the company in Frankfurt after World War II, the brothers Erwin and Artur Braun wished to evolve an entirely new approach towards the design of its products and, in 1955, asked Gugelot to work for them as a consultant. Together with Otl Aicher (Head of Visual Communications at Ulm), Gugelot produced a group of radios for Braun that was shown the same year at the Düsseldorf Radio Exhibition. The designs were characterized by a cleanness of line that highlighted the efficient function of the machines rather than disguising or decorating it. Dieter Rams (see pp.184–7) joined the company, also in 1955, and the following year Gugelot collaborated with him in designing the cabinet of a combined radio and record player, the "SK4", which became known as "Snow White's Coffin" (see left).

An electric razor (1962; above), designed for Braun by Hans Gugelot with Dieter Rams and Gerd Alfred Müller. The simple, ergonomic form of this object earned it an international reputation as the pioneer of a new rationalist approach towards designing practical items.

The "M125" office system (1957; below), manufactured by Bofinger. The office furniture that made up this minimal interior could all be assembled from knock-down kits designed on a modular principle, and exemplified Gugelot's highly practical and systematic approach towards design at this time.

A carriage for the Hamburg U-Bahn (above), designed in 1962 by several people linked to the Hochschule at Ulm, including Hans Gugelot, Herbert Lindinger and Helmut Muller-Kuhn. By becoming involved with this and other "live" projects, the designers were able to influence the wider environment with their systematic ideas and minimal style.

LATER WORK FOR BRAUN AND OTHER COMPANIES

Gugelot produced a number of key designs for Braun in the 1960s, including the company's simple display at the 11th Milan Triennale of 1957 (see pp.166–7) and the "Sixtant" electric razor (1961). Other clients also benefited from his vision, and in 1959 he began work, with a number of Ulm students, on the design of the Hamburg U-Bahn underground transport system (see above). The team, headed by Gugelot, provided a complete service that resulted in a unified design – from the train's exterior right down to its small interior details – that was minimal, with no unnecessary detailing. All of Gugelot's design thinking was underpinned by this concept of the "system" – in other words, the idea that nothing exists on its own but is part of a greater entity.

Among Gugelot's longest-standing and most familiar designs was that used for Kodak's "Carousel S" (1963): a radically new concept for holding and showing colour transparencies that has yet to be superseded. Indeed, the universality of many of Gugelot's designs was such that those still surviving look as fresh today as when he first designed them.

Hochschule für Gestaltung Ulm

Of the educational institutions that have exerted great influence upon the progress of modern design through the 20th century, two of the most prominent examples were German. The Bauhaus was opened in Weimar under the leadership of Walter Gropius (see pp.88–91) in 1919, but was closed by the Nazis in 1933 because of its perceived threat to National Socialism. In the post-war years, with democracy restored and reconstruction underway in Germany, this premature end to the programme of progressive design education was strongly felt. Indeed, the concept of modern design was so powerful a symbol of freedom that a woman called Inge Scholl decided that reviving the programme would be a fitting tribute to her brother and sister, Hans and Sophie Scholl, who had been killed by the Nazis.

EARLY DAYS OF THE SCHOOL

From 1947 onwards Inge Scholl initiated an active fund-raising campaign for a new school, and the project was officially launched in 1951. Scholl married a local graphic designer, Otl Aicher, who was involved with the project from an early stage. He was Head of Visual Communications at the school from 1954–66, and among his many legacies were the typographical innovations (very simple, sans-serif typefaces) that he developed and promoted.

The Zurich-based ex-Bauhaus architect, designer and sculptor Max Bill was invited to design the building (1953–1955; see below) for the new school and to lead it as its first Rector. At Bill's invitation Hans Gugelot (see pp.176–7) became head of the product-design department in 1954.

THE SCIENCE OF DESIGN

The Hochschule für Gestaltung (High School for Design) was officially opened in 1955. At the start it set out to continue the Bauhaus programme, but within a few years it became clear that the artistic component of that project was less and less relevant and that, increasingly, a systematic model – deriving from the world of science and technology – was more appropriate. The tension between these two approaches was eventually to divide the school, and was one of the reasons for its closure in 1968. In its

Industrial-design staff who worked at Ulm (below), including Hans Gugelot (seated), with some of their products. The school was successful at bringing many "live" projects into its charge, thereby achieving results that could affect a wider audience.

The Hochschule für Gestaltung (High School for Design; left) was established in post-war Germany to continue the project initiated by the Bauhaus three decades earlier. Its highly rational programme defined design as a systematic process, although differences of opinion emerged during the school's short history.

From 1962–3 staff at Ulm were involved in redesigning the corporate image of the German airline Lufthansa (left). Their brief ranged from graphics to plastic containers for in-flight meals, with the former aspect led by graphic designer Otl Aicher and the product side under the control of Hans Roericht.

A student project of 1967–8, led by Herbert Lindinger and Claude Schnaidt, for a bus station in Hanover (below). The simple forms, combined with clear, graphic information, reflected the rational "problem-solving" approach to design adopted at Ulm.

13 years, however, the school succeeded in radically redefining the meaning of design; it also contributed a number of important "real-life" projects, including the Hamburg U-Bahn and pieces for Braun (see p.177), as well as sets of simple, white, geometric stacking china for Rosenthal. The school educated a generation of product designers, many of whom – such as the Czech Hans von Klier, in charge of corporate identity at Olivetti from 1969; and the German Hans Roericht – went on to become highly influential.

The Argentinian design theoretician Tomas Maldonado was invited to join the project by Max Bill and later took over the Rectorship. From the outset the school valued the relationship between theory and practice, and social-science subjects – including psychology and sociology – were taught there. However, Maldonado and his theory of "scientific operationalism" – in which the design process could be systematized in a purely non-intuitive scientific manner – moved the school's thinking away from Bill's direction.

This shift was keenly felt by the early 1960s, when Bruce Archer – a British pioneer of the "Design Methods" movement (which held that it is possible to develop a systematic and almost entirely rational design process) visited the school, as did other figures, such as Charles Eames (see pp.148–51). The continual debates, combined with the constant problem of funding and the local state authority's unease about the radical nature of the institution, led to the school's closure in October 1968.

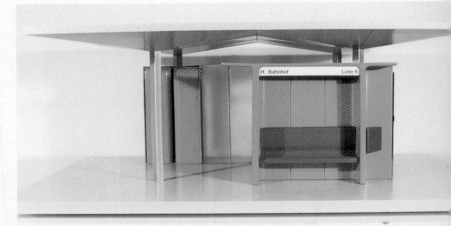

A model of a city bus designed for Hamburg (below), part of a project in city transport undertaken by Herbert Lindinger in collaboration with Michael Conrad and Pio Manzu. The proposal was for a very simple, functional design with no unnecessary details.

Japanese product design played an important international role in the post-war years. However, the contribution of specific individuals is generally difficult to define, since – with the exception of Kenji Ekuan, who established the design consultancy GK Design in 1957 – most product design went on anonymously within the large firms. The SONY

SONY

Corporation – formed in 1946 as the Tokyo Telecommunications Engineering Corporation and renamed in 1958 – was particularly innovative and influential in this respect. In the early days SONY inevitably borrowed its basic design ideas from abroad (from the United States at first, later from Germany) for products new to Japan such as tape recorders and portable radios and televisions, but it went on to create a range of highly novel objects.

Akio Morita, the Chairman and Executive Officer of the Japanese electronics company SONY, which he formed with Masaru Ibuka at the end of World War II. His enthusiasm and expertise have played a significant role in the firm's international success, particularly through his commitment to the concept of "modern design". He was the first Japanese businessman to be featured on the cover of Time *magazine.*

The SONY Watchman "Voyager" pocket television (1982; below). This compact piece of high technology typifies the company's interest, from the late 1950s onwards, in creating miniature objects. Made possible by advances in modern electronics, the concept of miniaturization was also deeply embedded in traditional Japanese material culture.

ORIGINS OF THE COMPANY

In 1946 Masaru Ibuka, who had owned a company called Japan Precision Instruments during the war, joined forces with another businessman, Akio Morita, to form what was to become the SONY Corporation. Venturing initially into the new area of tape recorders – with no thought given to design and an exclusive focus on engineering – they launched the first model on the Japanese market in 1950. However, in 1954 they were given a licence to produce transistors in Japan and, a year later, produced their first transistor radio – the "TR-55" – which bore definite signs of having been created on a drawing-board, with its design clearly deriving from the American concept of styling. When, three years later, the company launched a pocket-sized transistor radio – this time with a lemon yellow plastic body-shell – it was apparent that its designers were still looking firmly in the direction of the United States for their inspiration.

A NEW DESIGN ETHIC

Despite its dependence upon foreign styling, SONY was beginning to define design in a new way: as a meeting between advanced technology and marketing. The company needed an appropriate style to represent that meeting and found it, during the 1960s, in visual and physical minimalism – a combination of Japanese minimalism and German Functionalism. For instance, the highly successful "TV8-301" – one of the first transistor televisions, with a miniature 8-inch (20-cm) screen, produced in 1958 – had a functional appearance with no extraneous features, and a steel case in two tones of grey. From this point SONY let the technology and the performance of its objects dictate their appearance to a considerable extent. Following this requirement the company's designers applied enough visual decision-making to let the products convey a high level of technological virtuosity, efficiency, rationality, beauty, originality and modernity, achieving these qualities by following the rules of aesthetic minimalism and by paying attention to the smallest details.

For Good Living –
and Good Giving!

SONY

TR 610

The pocket-portable

6-transistor radio

that works superbly
even in fringe areas!

So small, you can carry SONY in your pocket or pocketbook. Yet so powerful, you get wonderfully clear reception and superb tone even in fringe areas! Ideal at home, at the office, when you travel ... *anywhere!* AND A GRAND GIFT, TOO! ... because SONY is as handsome as it is efficient!

Illustrated: SONY TR 610—1-inch deep, 2⅝ wide, 4½ high ... with 6 transistors. In red, black or ivory. Hi-impact unbreakable case, complete with battery, earphone (for private listening) and carrying case $39.95

SONY
TR 810

World's slimmest 8-transistor pocket-portable radio (less than 1-inch thin) yet tremendously powerful! Complete with battery, earphone and carrying case $49.95

mfg. by the **SONY CORP.**

"THE PEAK OF ELECTRONIC PERFECTION"

distributed in U.S. by
Delmonico International

Division of Thompson-Starrett Co., Inc.,
42-24 Orchard St., Long Island City 1, N. Y.
In Canada, by General Distributors, Ltd.,
791 Notre Dame Ave., Winnipeg 3, Manitoba
At fine radio stores and department stores, or write Dept. L, for name of nearest store.

The SONY portable transistor radio model "810" was produced in the late 1950s and is promoted in the advertisement (right) as a "lifestyle" product. Visually, its rational geometric form is combined, through an emphasis placed on its chrome-finished dials, with an evocation of a world of advanced technology, as conveyed by the control panels in contemporary automobiles.

An advertisement (left) from the late 1950s for SONY's little transistor radio, the "TR610" (1958). The company transformed an American technological breakthrough into a desirable consumer object through the use of attractive colours and design details, as well as graphics that evoked the dream world of American product styling.

The "Stowaway" personal stereo cassette player (right), the name by which the SONY "Walkman" was first known in Britain. Launched in 1979, it is said that the product was developed in response to Akio Morita's desire to listen to good music while travelling on aeroplanes. It rapidly became a huge international success story.

For Good Living And Good Giving!

SONY — TR 812

The New Portable, All-Transistor, 3-Band
Radio That Brings The World To You!

This is the radio the world has been seeking—SONY TR 812. It's an AM radio, MARINE BAND radio, SHORT-WAVE radio—and it's really portable! In addition, it has an exclusive tuning-and-voltage meter that assures precision tuning in every band, and also indicates condition of batteries! All this with, of course, superb tone and great power! For yourself or as a gift, no finer set could be wanted for indoors, outdoors or travel!

Illustrated: SONY TR 812. The 3-band radio that brings the world to you! Receives Standard Broadcasts and has 2 Short-Wave Bands for World Wide, Marine and Amateur reception. $69.95

SONY TR 810

World's slimmest 8-transistor pocket-portable radio that brings the world to you! Receives Standard Broadcasts and has tremendously powerful! Complete with battery, earphone and carrying case $49.95

mfg. by the **SONY CORP.**

"THE PEAK OF ELECTRONIC PERFECTION"

distributed in U.S. by **Delmonico International**
Division of Thompson-Starrett Co., Inc., 42-24 Orchard Street, Long Island City 1, N.Y.

The way Sony have drawn hi-fi stereo sound from their new pocket sized Stowaway is a brilliant technical achievement.

Even Sony think they've done quite well.

This is Sony's new Stowaway, actual size. To see how small it is put your hand over the picture.

Tiny, isn't it? Yet it plays standard music cassettes and rates as a serious piece of hi-fi equipment.

If you really want to know about its performance in Hz, SPL and watts per channel ask your

Sony dealer or any of the staff at Sony's showrooms, 134 Regent Street, London.

In layman's terms, though, Stowaway's sound is technicolour stereo to dazzle your ears.

Since it is the world's smallest cassette player it comes as no surprise to learn it is equipped with a set of the world's smallest, lightest hi-fi headphones.

They can pick up the tiniest tinkle of a triangle, or rasp the inside of your brain with the deepest bass of a synthesiser. You can plug in a second set of 'phones should you ever want to share your favourite music with a favourite friend.

Sony's little masterpiece runs off batteries, so you can tuck it in a pocket to play your own choice of music on the train, the plane or in a hotel room far from home. Or you can buy an adaptor to run it off the mains.

Listen to Stowaway for yourself. You won't believe it till you hear it, and even then you may find it difficult. **SONY**

The world's smallest stereo cassette player.

Through the 1960s and 1970s SONY continued to apply these principles to a large number of electronic consumer goods that were also technologically innovative; these ranged from the first home video recorder (1964), the Trinitron colour TV (1968) and the hugely successful Walkman personal cassette player (launched in the late 1970s; above), to the Mavica filmless camera of the early 1980s and the Profeel TV of 1987.

INTERNATIONAL IMPACT

In 1978 the company created its "Product Planning Centre": a central design facility that linked the process very closely – and more strategically than before – to "lifestyle" marketing. The Walkman was the first result of this initiative, and its close integration of product innovation, engineering, design and marketing demonstrated SONY's new policy in action. It was a policy that placed design so firmly at the centre of corporate thinking that it became impossible to disentangle the two areas, and represented an achievement from which many Western companies still have much to learn.

SONY's contribution to post-war product design has lain, essentially, in the way in which it exploited new technology to create new product types, with an emphasis (at least in the early years) on miniaturization and portability. The "aesthetic of economy", with its roots in the minimalist Japanese interior, found its way into high-technology consumer goods, and in doing so helped to create a new approach to modern product design.

Douglas Scott (b.1913–90) was one of Britain's first professional industrial designers, but his name was unheard of beyond that sphere despite the ubiquity and longevity of many of his designs, ranging from the Aga stove (1938) to London's "Routemaster" bus (1953) and the British Post Office's STD call-box fittings (early 1960s).

Douglas Scott

The "Mark VII" colour television camera (below), designed for Marconi in 1967. The simple form and functional anonymity of this design were hallmarks of Scott's work.

His designs are not showy – his main concern always rested with a product's ease of manufacture, performance and practicality – but they are visually pleasing. Through the course in industrial design that Scott taught at the Central School of Arts and Crafts in London in 1945, he also educated many subsequently successful designers.

Britain's post-war industrial designers were less openly celebrated than their American counterparts, but the product designer Douglas Scott achieved the same level of success as Raymond Loewy and Walter Dorwin Teague (see pp.116–17). He was responsible for many designs that quickly became familiar objects in post-war Britain.

TRAINING AND EARLY WORK

In the British Arts and Crafts tradition, Scott trained initially as a silversmith at the Central School between 1926 and 1929, and this background remained useful to him throughout his career. His early employment, from 1929–36, was with two firms of lighting designers, the first in Birmingham and the second in London.

In 1936 Scott's life changed dramatically. He applied for a job in the London office of the American "super-star" designer Raymond Loewy (pp.120–123) and was accepted; suddenly he was introduced to an entirely different world of design – one that was linked with modern living and style. The three years spent in Loewy's office brought Scott into contact with a wide range of companies involved in the manufacture of consumer goods and machines, among them GEC and Electrolux; he even experimented with car design, producing proposals (which were influential, but not used directly) for the Sunbeam Talbot and the Hillman Minx.

NEW DIRECTIONS

When Loewy's office closed with the onset of World War II, Scott changed direction once again and gained employment in the De Havilland engineering works, where he acquired a totally different, but equally useful, kind of knowledge. At the end of the war he moved in two directions that were to dominate the rest of his working life. On the one hand he went into design education, initially teaching evening classes on a casual basis in 1945 and progressing to regular employment at London's Central School of Art and Design in 1946; and at the same time he set up his own freelance office as an industrial designer.

In 1946 the "Britain Can Make It" exhibition – organized by the newly formed Council of Industrial Design (later the Design Council) – was held at London's Victoria & Albert Museum. Scott was represented at the exhibition – his refrigerator for Electrolux, which had been fitted in prefabricated housing, was on display – and he became part of the new optimism that characterized this area in the otherwise grey early post-war years.

In 1967 Scott designed a new earth-digger – the "HY-MAC" excavator – for Peter Hamilton Engineering Ltd (right). The digger became one of Britain's most successful exports and a symbol of what the country could achieve; it won a Design Council award in the year of its manufacture. The design has such a strong personality that for many people it is now accepted as a familiar part of the everyday landscape.

LONDON TRANSPORT AND LATE WORK

Scott first collaborated with London Transport in 1948 on the RTC Green Line coach and on the RF coach. He approached this new challenge enthusiastically, combining practicality with minimum styling. The double-decker "Routemaster" bus (left and below) was his greatest achievement: more than just a practical piece of designing, it is still in use and has become one of London's most familiar sights.

Through the 1960s and 1970s Scott continued to teach and to design – including classics such as Ideal Standard's "Roma" wash-basin – while maintaining his anonymity. In the mid-1970s he set up a design course at the College of Art and Design in Mexico City, but returned to England in 1979.

The upper deck interior of London Transport's "Routemaster" bus (above), launched in 1959 and widely used by the early 1960s. This was a reworked version of the pre-war design developed by the company's in-house team, but the restrained tartan moquette and the colour scheme – "burgundy red, Chinese green and Sung yellow" – were the result of Scott's initiative.

The exterior of the "Routemaster" bus (right), designed by Scott in conjunction with the company's in-house designers and engineers. Their brief was to create a new, light bus that would carry a greater number of passengers more comfortably than ever before. Scott was responsible for the body-styling, which involved softening the curves at the corners and emphasizing the vehicle's horizontality.

In the 1950s and 1960s Germany had led the way in developing a product design philosophy and a style that had their roots in the rational Bauhaus approach of the years preceding World War II. Instead of working with decorative items such as teapots and wall-hangings, the product designers of the 1950s who were linked with the

Dieter Rams

"Neo-Functionalist" movement (whose ethos was geometrical simplicity and a minimum of decoration) in post-war Germany took products that had hitherto been the territory of the engineer and turned them into visual symbols of the "second machine age". What evolved in Germany during these years in turn inspired a much larger, international product design movement which, by the 1970s and 1980s, had reached as far afield as Japan and Singapore, and become *the* late 20th-century product aesthetic.

Of all the designers working in the decade following 1945, Dieter Rams employed the most rational aesthetic in his high-technology products. Working for the Braun electronics company and the Vitsoe furniture firm, he produced designs that have epitomized German Neo-Functionalism at its most rigorous.

The "Transistor 1" (1956) pictured below was one of Rams's first designs for audio equipment for the Braun company. The usual wooden shell was replaced by plastic and the form of the object exhibited a geometric minimalism that had never been seen before in a product of this nature.

COMMITMENT TO TECHNOLOGY

Through his collaboration with the Braun electronics company, Dieter Rams (b.1932) had an enormous part to play in what in the 1950s was a uniquely German phenomenon. While American designers favoured "Detroit" styling, with copious quantities of chrome and extra detailing embellishing their consumer machines, and the Italians looked to abstract organic sculpture to provide inspiration for their new typewriters and vacuum-cleaners, Germany adopted a much more purist approach. This was undoubtedly linked to the cutting short of the Bauhaus project by the Nazi regime (see pp.90–91) and the feeling that there was unfinished business still to be done; it also reflected the German nation's strong image of technological sophistication, and indicated its desire to present this image to the world market in the years following World War II.

Through his designs, Rams played a significant role in translating this broad influence into a product philosophy with universal appeal. Much of this was also to do with his individual character. Many of his colleagues have described Rams as a man with an acute sensitivity to order and chaos – one in particular likening him to "someone who has a very keen sense of hearing, but who is forced to live in a world of shrill dissonance". His clearly enhanced sensibilities and innate "will to order" compelled him to see the design process as one of cleaning up, simplifying and reducing chaos, and in this capacity he stood for a society trying to deal with a confusing world in which material goods and mass communications systems were making life increasingly complex.

PHILOSOPHY OF DESIGN

Rams's product philosophy was also highly developed. For him the role of machines in the domestic environment were to be that of "silent butlers": invisible and subservient, and there simply to make living easier and more

The Braun "TP1" record player (1959; above) for 17-centimetre (7-inch) records, is shown here attached to the "T3" pocket receiver, both designed by Rams. They display his characteristic use of unornamented geometric forms and are cased in functional grey plastic body-shells.

The "Atelier 1" receiver with front controls (1957; below) positioned on top of the "L1" loudspeaker of the same year, both manufactured by Braun. Used in combination with each other, these simple, geometric hi-fi units display a minimum amount of visual details. The control knobs, for example, were left unadorned and no chrome is in evidence.

comfortable. They were to be as self-effacing as possible and leave room for the role of beauty to be played by, say, a vase of flowers (in Rams's case, the white tulips that he frequently chose to accompany his otherwise austere environments). It was not, therefore, that the aesthetic dimension of life was unimportant, but simply that – in his view – it was not the task of domestic machines to provide that dimension. In this sense Rams allied himself – in theory, at least – with the engineer, although in reality he far exceeded that role.

TRAINING AND EARLY WORK

Rams was born in Wiesbaden and, during a great deal of time spent as a child in his grandfather's carpentry shop, came into contact with materials and the process of manufacture. In 1947 he attended the School of Art in his home town to study architecture and interior decorating, interrupted his studies between 1948 and 1951 to complete an apprenticeship as a carpenter, and finally graduated from the School of Art in 1953. He spent the next two years in the architectural office of Otto Apel in Frankfurt, where he came into contact with the American practice Skidmore, Owings & Merrill, whose architects were working on American Consulate buildings in West Germany. Through their work Rams undoubtedly witnessed at first hand the purism inherited from Ludwig Mies van der Rohe (see pp.92–3), which he was later to apply to his own product design.

WORK FOR BRAUN

The major turning point for Rams came in 1955, the year he joined Braun. The company had been formed in Frankfurt in 1951 and was owned by the brothers Erwin and Artur, who were searching for a new way of marketing their electronic goods and of projecting the right image on to the marketplace. To assist with this new approach, they chose two designers – Otl Aicher and Hans Gugelot, who were teaching at the Hochschule für Gestaltung at Ulm (see pp.176–9) – with whom they had worked on an exhibition presentation in Düsseldorf. Both men were to continue working with Braun in the capacity of consultants, but the designer whom they employed on a full-time basis was Dieter Rams. In his interview for the job,

The Braun "Aromaster" coffee-maker, model KF 20 (1972; above). In the late 1960s and early 1970s, designs emerging from Rams's office began to exhibit strong colours, a shift away from the early grey housings for his products, and a sign that Pop culture had an impact on even this most Functionalist of designers.

he was asked to rearrange one of the company's rooms to reflect Braun's concept of "good design", and his approach of minimal intervention was enough to persuade Erwin and Artur that he was the right person for them.

Before long, Rams was working on products for the company, and in 1956, together with Hans Gugelot, he produced the "SK4" combined radio and record player, which represented a radical departure in product design. Its pure white metal body-shell, clean lines, undisguised function and clear control mechanisms combined to create a completely different image for the product from that of its pre-war predecessor (for illustration, see p.176). The latter had been housed in a curved wooden box and was much closer to being perceived as a piece of furniture, whereas the new design shed this image and was clearly a piece of functional domestic equipment.

NEW APPLIANCES

Rams's career was taking off. Through the 1950s and 1960s he designed numerous pieces of audio equipment for Braun – innovating every step of the way – from his "Atelier 1" hi-fi system (see p.185, bottom), to diminutive transistor radios with neatly punched loudspeaker grills, to portable televisions. He worked simultaneously on a wide range of photographic equipment, home appliances and, from the mid-1960s, personal-care items including small hair dryers.

Rams's first home-appliance design was the "kitchen machine" food-mixer (1957). Once again its form was radically new and its simple body-shell, parallel seamlines and rigorously researched curves made a dramatic contrast to the exaggerated, bulbous forms of earlier American streamlined models. Other home appliances produced by Rams were also far ahead of their time. They included his cylindrical desk fan, the "HL1" (1961), and his rectangular toaster, the "HT2" (1963), both of which were emblematic of the new, rational forms that he was creating for items with old functions. The British artist Richard Hamilton was so entranced by the novelty of Rams's objects that in the mid-1960s he integrated some of them into a series of paintings, echoing the way in which the French artist Marcel Duchamp had exhibited a ready-made commercial urinal in an art exhibition back in 1913.

LATER WORK

Rams's later designs include countless highly familiar objects in today's environment, among them Braun's small, square, black alarm clock (see opposite, centre) and a range of electric razors (for example, see below). They have become familiar appendages of the late 20th-century environment, their simple, functional forms being both unobtrusive and pleasant to live with. Although the technological ethos always dominates Rams's work, his innate sense of balance and proportion is such that his objects never offend or jar the senses in any way. Although Braun employed Rams, a special arrangement was made for him to design furniture items – seating and storage in particular – for another company that began life as Otto Zapf but later became known as Vitsoë, and which was based in

Dieter Rams started designing electric razors for the Braun company in the mid-1950s. This model from the late 1970s – the "Micron Plus" (left), designed in collaboration with Roland Ullmann – has a curved form, shaped and textured for easy handling, and a shiny metal top. These features were incorporated into nearly all Rams's designs for razors.

Eschborn. Equal rigour and attention to detail characterize all the work Rams has carried out there, which consist of simple, geometric pieces made of wood and metal, intended for mass manufacture; Rams has worked for the company from 1957 onwards. The pieces he has designed for Vitsoë are all minimal in appearance and make extensive use of metal and black leather. His shelving systems, the shelves of which are made of wood, look equally good in an office or in a domestic interior and succeed in blurring the boundaries between the two environments. Once again Rams's designs have a kind of neutrality that allows them to be influenced by the context into which they are placed. Thus his furniture pieces look right in an office if surrounded by filing systems and telephones, but look equally well in a living room surrounded by domestic objects in a softer, decorative setting.

Interestingly, therefore, it can be seen that Rams, in his work on furniture, has taken the approach that he evolved in the area of consumer machines, not vice versa as is the usual pattern. Above all his pieces exude quality, their simplicity and minimalism demanding that every detail is carefully thought through in the design process because a single flaw would be visible immediately.

A Braun calculator (left), designed in the late 1970s. Although still relatively austere in its use of a basic black plastic body-shell, this object also employed colour inventively both in order to differentiate the functions of its buttons but also to inject an almost unprecedented level of expressiveness into the design. This tendency was visible in much of Rams's work in this decade.

Rams has always worked very closely as a member of a team, claiming that anonymity and collaboration are inherent characteristics of the design process. While not actively seeking fame, he has none the less become – through the integrity and continuity of his work – a key spokesperson for German design since World War II. He carefully underplays this role, however, continuing to see design as a collaborative process in essence. Although his name is used in company publicity to some extent, he still believes in the concept of anonymity that, for him, is a fundamental characteristic of designed objects.

Rams represents the generation of designers for whom the future is unreservedly based on an optimism born of growing up in post-war Germany with the belief that faith in technology would put the world back on its feet. His designs remain symbols of that confidence and even in the much more ambivalent climate of the 1990s, they are strong enough to carry that message forward into the next century.

A pair of "Phase 4" alarm clocks (1979; above), designed for Braun in collaboration with Dietrich Lubs. These unassuming timepieces, with their clear faces and easy alarm mechanisms, were available in simple black or white. They became ubiquitous objects in the 1980s, showing that German Neo-Functionalist design had achieved a universal appeal by that decade.

The "Phase 1" digital alarm clock (1971; right), also designed in collaboration with Dietrich Lubs. This simple black and white design with its clear numbering was one of the first of its kind to meet with widespread public approval. Its simple fascia contrasted dramatically with the tendency within Japanese electronic product design in the 1970s, which was to make items look as complex as possible as a sign of technical virtuosity.

Modern product design came late to Britain, in comparison with the United States, Germany and Italy. With the exception of the progressive work of Wells Coates (see pp.124–7), the Russian architect and designer Serge Chermayeff and a handful of others in the inter-war years, the modern influence emerged only gradually through the

Kenneth Grange

In his work with companies such as Kenwood, Kodak and British Rail, Kenneth Grange has consistently aimed to improve the design standard of goods that make up the everyday environment.

1940s and 1950s, and in a predominantly anonymous manner. Kenneth Grange (b.1929) witnessed this early development from the sidelines initially – being younger than some of the key pioneers – but, by the end of the 1950s, he had helped to consolidate a new profession. This was to expand in later years although, in contrast to the situation in Germany and Italy, British product design never adopted a self-conscious image with celebrity designers. It remained, rather, a relatively behind-the-scenes activity.

The Kodak Instamatic Camera series "33", "133" and "233" (below), was launched in 1968. Grange's task was to create a camera for the European market that could use Kodak's new cassette film; the result was simple and compact, and over 20 million were sold.

TRAINING AND EARLY WORK

As was typically the case in Britain in the 1940s, Grange was educated not as an industrial designer but as a fine artist/illustrator who saw his future in the world of what was then termed "commercial art". At the Willesden School of Art, where he studied from 1944–7, he learned to draw – a skill that has remained invaluable throughout his career. Grange's early work experience was as an architectural assistant, first with a company called Arcon in 1948 and, following his military service in the Royal Engineers – during which he also took a job as a technical illustrator, and came to love machines for the first time – with Bronek Katz from 1949–50. For the latter, where he was also employed as an architectural assistant, he became heavily involved with commercial (trade) exhibition work – a fruitful area for designers at that time. After leaving Katz, Grange moved on to work for the architect Gordon Bowyer (1950–52) and then took a job (1952–8) in the office of Jack Howe – originally a partner in Arcon where Grange had started out. Howe had designed the memorable street furniture used for the Festival of Britain held on the South Bank of the River Thames in 1951, and was himself an important pioneer of industrial design in Britain.

During his six years with Jack Howe, Grange began to receive his own commissions for exhibition work, and in 1958 Howe asked him to collaborate on a pavilion for the Kodak company at the World's Fair in Brussels. This project led to Grange being asked to redesign Kodak's old-fashioned box camera – his first product-design commission. The result – the model "44a" – quickly became an enormous success.

DESIGN PHILOSOPHY

Grange based his designs on the concept of simplification, much as his contemporaries in Germany were doing. He sought clarity and concision, and has succeeded in achieving these qualities in his many designs for the

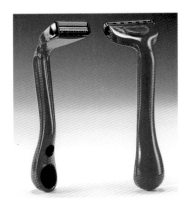

A sewing machine in the "800" range (left) designed for Maruzen in the mid-1960s. Grange made several improvements to the existing model – such as increasing the space in front of the needle – and gave it a stylish body-shell to appeal to the European market.

The "Protector Razor" (right), designed by Grange for Wilkinson Sword and launched in 1992. The base construction and soft pads make the razor safer than previous models, while the bright colour enhances its robust design.

myriad companies in Britain and Japan for which he has worked since 1959. Grange's philosophy of design focuses on the concept being completely integrated into the production process, although he is committed to "good design" as a prerequisite for modern living and also as a vital strategy for industrial survival.

Like many other designers, Grange bemoans the short-term thinking that he feels is characteristic of many British companies. However, he has still managed to find enough good British companies with which to work throughout his career. He designed products for, among others, the Venner parking-meter company, Kenwood (probably Grange's strongest supporter through the 1960s), Wilkinson Sword (designs include the "Protector Razor", above, right), Milward Courier, British Rail (designs include the "125" train; below) and Morphy Richards. Many of his designs – from parking meters to razors, irons and the famous Kenwood "Chef" food-mixer – are still in production, proving their ability to withstand the test of time.

PENTAGRAM

In 1972 Grange joined forces with an existing group of architects and graphic designers – Theo Crosby, Alan Fletcher, Colin Forbes and Mervyn Kurlansky – to form Pentagram, Britain's leading design consultancy, which has worked with Penguin Books, Olivetti and IBM, among others. Since the 1970s Grange has had a number of Japanese clients, including Maruzen, for whom he designed sewing machines (under the trade name of Frister Rossman; see above, left); Shiseido, for whom he creates containers for men's toiletries; and Inax, which manufactures bathroom fittings. He has become very popular among manufacturers in Japan, demonstrating that British design and designers are desirable commodities abroad.

Grange's work on the exterior of British Rail's "125 High Speed Train" (below), which has been in service since 1976, provided the company with a powerful modern image. Grange used wind-tunnel testing to justify the form created for the front of the train; its futuristic, streamlined shape is enhanced by the absence of buffers.

Action and Reaction

Action and Reaction

By 1960 the early Modernists' democratic desire to use mass production to make material goods available to all had been superceded by a recognition that design was an important symbol of modernity and, in social terms, a mark of sophistication and cultural awareness. As a consequence designers had a greater responsibility to meet those symbolic requirements adequately and to create the goods that could perform that role.

Nowhere was this more evident than in Italy in the 1960s. The developments of the previous decade that led to a modern Italian design movement aimed at a sophisticated international market were continued. In the hands of men such as the Castiglioni brothers, Vico Magistretti, Marco Zanuso, Joe Colombo (see pp.194–201 and 208–9) and others even such mundane materials as plastics took on a new importance. Their elegant neo-modern designs for furniture, lighting objects, office machinery and electrical products became symbols both of a new Italy and of a new international aspiration towards a better quality of life. The evidence of this new renaissance was visible at the Milan Triennales of 1957 and 1964. The Italian design magazines – *Domus*, *Abitare*, *Stile Industria* and *Casa Vogue* among them – spread Italy's remarkable achievement around the world and its designed objects stood for a new cosmopolitanism.

Finland's design culture also reached new levels at this time and it could boast a small number of progressive designers who were influential on an international scale. Like the Italians, several used new materials, especially plastics, and the work of men such as Esko Pajamies, Eero Aarnio and Yryo Kukkapuro was quickly picked up by the international design press. Their brightly coloured products were the mark of a new confidence, affluence and optimism in that small country. In France the same trend was visible, with Pierre Paulin, Olivier Mourgue and others creating innovative furniture objects. So original were Mourgue's designs that the director Stanley Kubrick used his furniture to evoke a futuristic environment in his film *2001*.

The optimism that these and other countries displayed through their design production in the 1960s reflected the peak of the post-war consumer boom. Design ideals established before World War II were re-energized and reformulated to meet the changing social and psychological needs of a new audience that saw modern design as a means of identifying itself with the present and, more importantly, with the future.

It is unlikely, however, that the early Modernists, with their strong ideological commitments, would have identified with the slickness and exclusiveness of many designs of the 1960s. Increasingly these came to stand for the high level of conspicuous consumption that characterized those years. While many designers took on the task of creating the visually innovative goods that filled the magazines, others began to feel that a kind of betrayal had taken place.

The shift that came quite suddenly in the mid 1960s was stimulated by a number of converging elements. The emergence of a youth consumer market, and accompanying emphasis on fun and expendability played a key role in helping to undermine the value system, based on the ideas of rationality and universality, that had underpinned the Modern Movement in architecture and design. The new "Pop" aesthetic prioritized the throw-away and the temporary and outlawed the permanent. This shift in consumption values had an enormous impact on prevailing ideas about design and in the mid 1960s a new radicalism emerged in the work of people like Peter Murdoch and the Archigram architectural group in Great Britain (see pp.220–23), and of Ettore Sottsass (see pp.216–19) in Italy.

Now design openly took its lead from popular culture. This was not the first time this had happened, but it represented a real challenge to the values of Modernism that had dominated design ideals through the century. The work of the American consultant designers for industry in the 1930s had rehearsed the idea of basing design on popular dreams and aspirations, and the aesthetic of streamlining had had little in common with high culture. This had led naturally on to the work of the American automotive designers of the early post-war years who had based their visualizations entirely on the popular imagination and the desires of the mass market. Harley Earl (see pp.214–15) at General Motors, and his counterparts at Chrysler and Ford, had had little interest in the high-minded values of Modernism when they created their "dream machines".

In the 1960s, therefore, a fundamental divide, which had been in existence since the early century when the machinery of mass production turned the ideals of the Modern Movement heroes into consumer stylistic choices, became apparent, with designers openly challenging the relevance of Modernism in a mass marketplace. By the middle of the decade the design world openly acknowledged the fact that Modernism was in crisis. Advances in technology added fuel to the fire: developments in electronics made the components of products so small that it was no longer necessary for their housings to reflect their inner workings. In the hands of designers, products increasingly became lifestyle accompaniments, objects of fashion rather than of utility, and the tried-and-tested theory of Functionalism became redundant as a consequence.

Not many designers responded to this shift overnight, however. Most had been, and indeed continued to be, educated within the Modernist tradition and were reluctant to abandon its persuasive and comforting beliefs. A commitment to value, quality and the rule of function made it difficult, and indeed for many undesirable, to join what was beginning to look like a new era of "Postmodernism" in design.

Only a few were able and willing to reflect the new impulse in a self-conscious way. While Sottsass had already been committed to a symbolic approach to design since the 1950s, in the second half of the 1960s he was joined by a younger generation of architects and designers who sought an alternative to what they saw as the pretentiousness of Italian post-war design. Their work was theoretical for the most part, but it was clear to Superstudio, Archizoom, Gruppo NNN and to individuals such as Gaetano Pesce (see pp.224–5) and Ugo La Pietra that the idea that a single set of values, attitudes and beliefs could support all of design was gone for ever.

An interior created by the Danish
architect-designer Verner Panton in
the late 1960s. It contains furniture
and dramatic hanging lights that
characterized the expressive,
"space-age" neomodern style
of that decade.

The Castiglioni brothers were a powerful force behind the modern Italian design movement that emerged after World War II. The almost mythical status that they enjoy today is the result of their uncompromising approach towards design, which involved rethinking the function, the form and the means of manufacture of every project

Pier Giacomo
& Achille Castiglioni

they worked on. Meticulous design details, elegant styling and superb quality characterize their products, which range from furniture and lighting to domestic wares. They have also made a significant contribution to Italian design through their involvement with the Milan Triennales and the formation of the ADI (Associazione per il Disegno Industriale) in 1954.

Pier Giacomo and Achille Castiglione were senior figures in post-war Italian design. Their originality in the areas of concept and visualization earned them an enormous following, and their work was been instrumental in highlighting design's importance within human culture.

The tractor-seat stool, "Mezzadro" (right), was designed as early as 1957, although production by the Zanotta company was delayed until 1971. One of the brothers' best-known pieces, it demonstrates their interest in using the ready-made utility object as a source for redesign.

TRAINING AND EARLY WORK

In 1938 Livio Castiglioni (1911–79) and Pier Giacomo Castiglioni (1913–68), who had graduated in architecture from the Polytechnic of Milan in 1936 and 1937 respectively, opened a design studio in Milan with Luigi Caccia Dominioni. Their first successful project was the "Model 547" radio, designed for the Phonola company. Shown at the Milan Triennale in 1940, it was a pioneering piece of industrial design which created a new form for a new product. The radio was given a totally new image by being clad in a Bakelite shell that emulated the shape of the more familiar telephone. Livio and Pier Giacomo closed their studio in 1940, reopening it in 1944 when they were joined by their younger brother Achille (b.1918), who had just graduated – as they had done – in architecture from the Polytechnic of Milan.

The three brothers concentrated on exhibition design and lighting, and together created a number of radical lighting designs, one of which – the "Tubino" – was literally a piece of bent tubing with a minimal shade. It was exhibited at the Milan Triennale of 1951, and its simplicity and versatility were to be characteristic of their many subsequent lighting experiments.

THE 1950S

In 1952 Livio left to work independently; Pier Giacomo and Achille continued to work together on a range of projects that reflected their highly original aesthetic and functional solutions to design problems. Their illumination system for the industrial design section of the tenth Milan Triennale in 1954, for example, combined sculptural form with utility. So too did the "Spalter" vacuum-cleaner (1956), manufactured by Rem and made of bright red plastic. The evocative curves of the cleaner were both visually pleasing and practical, allowing it to hang close to its user's body on a leather strap. Other original designs for seating and lighting followed: the "Luminator"

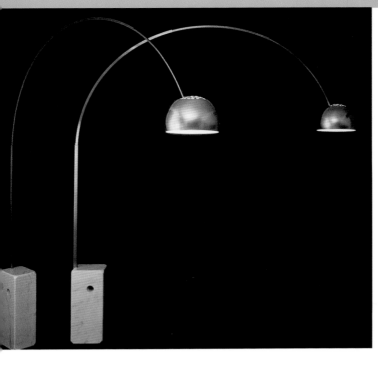

The "Arco" lamp (left), designed by the brothers and manufactured by Flos in 1962, is a seminal piece of late Modernism. With its marble base and dramatic steel arch it dominated many chic 1960s interiors, illuminating their contents without the need for any attachment to walls or ceilings.

The elegant "Snoopy" table lamp (right) was manufactured by Flos in 1967. Made of metal, glass and marble – a typically Castiglioni combination of materials – it was inspired by the cartoon dog of the same name. The marble lends the lamp a stability that is unexpected in such a top-heavy form.

lamp (1955) and "Bulb" lamp (shown at the 1957 Milan Triennale; see pp.166–7), both of which had exposed bulbs, and two experimental seats for Zanotta – the "Mezzadro" and the "Sella" (both 1957) – based on a tractor seat and bicycle saddle respectively. Such designs demonstrated the influence of Marcel Duchamp's "ready-mades" – the appropriation of the unadulterated utility object whose form is determined by use alone. The Castiglionis paid homage to this policy of minimal interference in many designs; the "Mezzadro" stool, for example, was simply a brightly coloured metal tractor seat screwed on to a cantilevered steel support (opposite).

THE 1960S ONWARDS

During the 1960s Pier Giacomo and Achille continued to produce a number of interiors and designs. These included the Montecatini Pavilion at the Milan Fair of 1962, which they lit dramatically with cone-shaped lights suspended from wires; the latter were the "Taccia" and "Toio" lights (both 1962 and manufactured by Flos), the second of which used an off-the-shelf car headlight. Also at Milan were the "Arco" lamp (1962; above) for Flos, which was a typical Castiglioni combination of high-quality traditional materials (a marble base) and modern technology (a thin arc of pressed aluminium and a spun aluminium reflector); and a hi-fi set for Brionvega

that could be moved around on castors. After Pier Giacomo's death in 1968, Achille continued to produce radical and innovative designs for companies such as Flos, Ideal Standard, Zanotta and Alessi. These included lights ("Gibigiana", 1980), cutlery, drinking glasses ("Par", 1983), chairs ("Rosacamuna", 1983) and tables (the "Cumano" metal garden table, produced by Zanotta from 1979, that folded flat for storage).

The Castiglionis' domination of Italian design is the direct result of the rigour and originality of their work, which has earned the respect of the international design community.

The "Sanluca" armchair (1960; below), designed by Achille and made by Gavina. Its form was inspired by the organic curves of the "Neo-Liberty" architectural movement; it consists of a moulded plywood shell covered with a thin layer of upholstery.

M arco Zanuso (b.1916) is one of the elder statesmen of modern Italian post-war design. A serious and highly intelligent man, he has created many timeless classics during a long and distinguished career. He has also played an important part in the infrastructure of Italian design. He was Professor of Architecture, Design and Town

Marco Zanuso

Planning at the Polytechnic of Milan (1945–86), contributed to the debate about modern design in periodicals such as *Domus* and *Casabella*, played a role in the formation of the ADI (Associazione per il Disegno Industriale) in Milan in 1954 and helped to organize the early post-war Triennale exhibitions in Milan.

Marco Zanuso was instrumental in the evolution of a neo-modern design movement in Italy after 1945. Through his work with leading product manufacturers – including Arflex, Brionvega and Kartell – he contributed important objects in the 1950s and 1960s; he was also a vital educational and organizational force behind the growing international awareness of contemporary Italian design.

EARLY TRAINING AND WORK

Born in Milan, Zanuso trained as an architect at the city's Polytechnic (1935–9). After serving in the Italian army, he set up his own practice in Milan in 1945. In 1948 he entered the Low-Cost Furniture competition at the Museum of Modern Art, New York, with a design for a bent metal-framed chair that incorporated a new mechanism for joining the frame to the fabric seat. Similar technological innovations featured in his second success – the much publicized "Lady" armchair (1951), manufactured by Arflex – one of the first pieces to use foam-rubber upholstery. The curves

The "Maggiolina" chair (1949; right) was the result of intensive research into furniture manufacture that would combine minimum structure with maximum comfort; in this case, steel tubes were used for support with the seat hanging from the frame. The design was awarded a prize at the ninth Milan Triennale of 1951, and was reproduced by the Zanotta company in the 1970s.

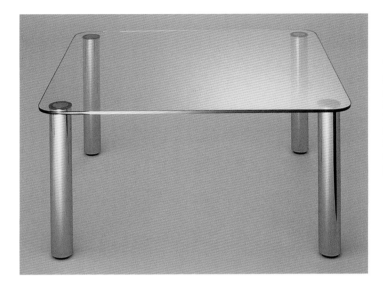

The "Marcuso" table (1960s; left). The simplicity of this coffee-table — achieved by the combination of its sturdy chromed legs and the glass top — produces an unambiguous image of modernity. In the context of modern Italian design at the time, this was an image of luxury rather than reflecting the earlier 20th-century preoccupation with democracy.

The "Celestina" chair (1978; right), manufactured by Zanotta, was a reworking of the traditional wood and metal garden chair. Zanuso's version has the added luxury of leather applied to the wooden slats.

of this highly original chair, which characterize much of Zanuso's work, were created largely by the technical manufacturing constraints of the plastics that he loved to use. His sofabed (1955), also for Arflex, was designed with a new mechanism that enabled it to convert from sofa to bed.

COLLABORATION WITH RICHARD SAPPER

Zanuso enjoyed a long and fruitful collaboration with the German designer Richard Sapper (see pp.230–33), working on a range of products that established them as among the most gifted of post-war industrial designers. Their first joint project — a child's stacking chair for Kartell (see p.231) — was a pioneering example of the use of injection-moulded polyethylene and was not produced until 1964, although research for the design had begun in 1954. From 1959 the duo were retained as consultants by Brionvega, a leading Italian manufacturer of electronic goods which was committed not only to pushing back technological barriers but also to creating stylish products that outstripped their Japanese and German competitors in terms of visual appeal.

With Sapper, Zanuso worked on a series of remarkable radio and television sets for Brionvega through the 1950s and 1960s, demonstrating his dual interests in technology and form. "Doney 14" (1962) was the first completely transistorized Italian radio; the "LS 502" (1964) was a battery-powered portable radio that folded into a small box for easy transportation. The challenge for Zanuso was to arrange the inner components in such a way that they could be fitted into a neat, sculptural body-shell. The same priorities were reflected in designs for the "Sirius", "Virgo" and "Algol" televisions (all 1964), culminating in the dramatic, minimal, cube-shaped "Black 201" (1969) set — the ultimate black box which, until it was switched on, gave no indication of its function.

DESIGN STYLE

Rigour and originality remained Zanuso's hallmarks throughout the 1960s and were revealed in numerous products, notably the kitchen-scales for Teraillon (1968); the yellow-cased knife sharpener for Necchi (1966);

and the compact (16cm/6¼in) folding "Grillo" telephone made of ABS plastic (1966; for Siemens). Whether working on furniture, products or architectural projects (he created a series of buildings for Olivetti, including headquarters in São Paulo, Brazil, between 1956 and 1958, consisting of a honeycomb of cells with a thin vault roof), Zanuso consistently defines the design process as a series of simple problems that may be elegantly resolved through reason and imagination — an approach that he promotes frequently in his teaching, lectures and speeches. These contributions to post-war international design have made him one of the most widely respected members of his profession.

The "Martindale" chair (below) was designed for Arflex (an offshoot of Pirelli) in the 1950s. The chair's body consists of a metal frame with rubber webbing attached, and is upholstered in foam rubber. The resulting organic form is typical of 1950s' designs.

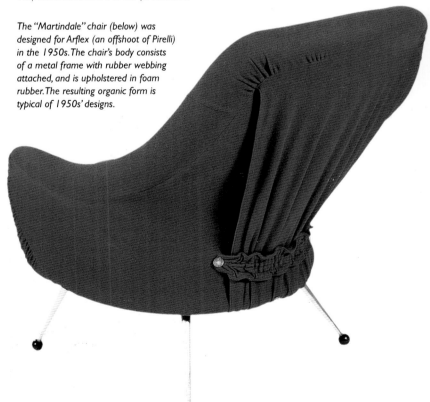

Vico Magistretti was born in 1920 in Milan, where he still works as an architect and furniture designer, operating out of a small studio with the assistance only of a draughtsman. For the past 50 years he has represented the rational face of post-war Italian design, which seeks timeless solutions to technical and formal problems; yet in conducting

Vico Magistretti

this search he has consistently produced startling, original designs that have helped to create the international identity of the modern Italian design movement. Magistretti states clearly the importance of collaboration between industry and designers: "Design in Italy is born halfway between designers and manufacturers." This approach has enabled him to work with various companies on over 120 designs, of which some 80 are still produced.

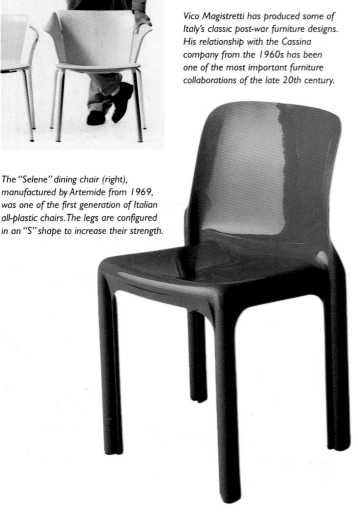

Vico Magistretti has produced some of Italy's classic post-war furniture designs. His relationship with the Cassina company from the 1960s has been one of the most important furniture collaborations of the late 20th century.

The "Selene" dining chair (right), manufactured by Artemide from 1969, was one of the first generation of Italian all-plastic chairs. The legs are configured in an "S" shape to increase their strength.

TRAINING AND EARLY WORK

Like his father, who was also a Milanese architect, Magistretti was educated in a climate of architectural Rationalism. Unlike his father, however, he was taught by Ernesto Rogers, a Communist who argued in favour of pre-fabrication and architectural solutions to social problems, and who became the influential Editor of *Domus* magazine for two years at the end of World War II. This experience, combined with the era of post-war reconstruction and industrialization in which Magistretti came of age, led him towards industrial design rather than towards one-off architectural projects.

When he graduated from the Polytechnic of Milan in 1945, Magistretti joined his father's studio. He spent the next few years designing low-cost furniture for the inexpensive housing that was being built for people made homeless during World War II. For this purpose he designed a removable bookcase consisting of two free-standing adjustable tubular-steel side supports fixed between floor and ceiling, and a folding, portable armchair, with striped fabric, modelled on the deck-chair, which were exhibited in 1946 by the Riunione Italiana Mostre Arredamento (RIMA, the Italian Association for Exhibitions of Furnishings) in Milan (opposite, right). Magistretti responded eagerly to this challenge and produced designs that were simple, rational and, above all, elegant solutions to the problems. The emphasis was on lightness and practicality, qualities also found in his small stackable wooden table produced by a new manufacturing company, Azucena, in 1949.

THE 1950S

Much of Italian design and architecture in the 1950s straddled a middle path between tradition and modernity, acknowledging the need to modify rigid pre-war Modernist principles in the post-war climate. During this decade Magistretti devoted more time to architecture and to creating the institutional framework for Italian design – for example, by helping to plan the Milan Triennale exhibitions, where he won a gold medal in 1951 and

The "Demetrio" table (left) was designed in 1964 and manufactured by Artemide in 1966, part of a series of plastic furniture items on which Magistretti worked. Its shiny (glass-reinforced resin) surface and strong colours – apple green, red, black and white – helped lend a new luxury image to plastic products.

A removable bookcase and folding chair (right) on exhibition at the RIMA show in Milan (1946). The chair is based on the traditional deck-chair, while the shelf has extendable fittings at either end to make it easy to fit into different spaces. Both pieces were designed specifically for the new apartments built to house the homeless after World War II.

first prize in 1954 (see pp.166–7). His buildings included the high-rise Torre Parco (Park Tower, 1956) and an office block in Corsa Europa, a street in Milan. In 1959 Magistretti was commissioned to design furnishings for the Carimate golf clubhouse and pool and, as part of this project, he developed a chair that was to change the direction of his career dramatically. The "Carimate" chair, as it became known, was a hybrid (see p.201). It combined a traditional rural design – it was made of wood with a rush seat – that was reminiscent of chairs by the Danish designers Kaare Klint (see pp.64–5) and Finn Juhl, with bold red paintwork that clearly made it a product of its time.

THE 1960S ONWARDS

The "Carimate" chair became an icon of the early to mid-1960s, visible in restaurants and public interiors – as well as in domestic settings – around the world. Wherever it was presented it brought with it a feeling of the new lifestyle being enjoyed by young, affluent consumers during this period; in London, New York and Tokyo, however, it also generated an atmosphere of traditional Italy and of exotic Mediterranean culture. This international success was the result of a collaboration with the furniture manufacturer Cassina (see pp.212–13), whose owner/director, Cesare Cassina, had approached Magistretti in 1960 and asked if he could mass-produce the chair, thus initiating a highly fruitful and long-lived relationship.

From the early 1960s onwards Magistretti was preoccupied with designs for furniture and lighting for companies such as Cassina, Artemide and O-Luce. Notable designs include the upholstered "Maralunga" sofa (1973), with movable headrest and arms; the "Broomstick" pieces (1979); and the "Sindbad" sofa (1981, see p.200), a design inspired by the horse blankets that Magistretti bought on one of his frequent visits to London to use as throws. The chair's resulting "blanket" cover was attached to the simple wooden base using clips at the back and could therefore be easily removed and changed. The chair is a typical Magistretti design in that it combines informality and a sense of fun with functional simplicity.

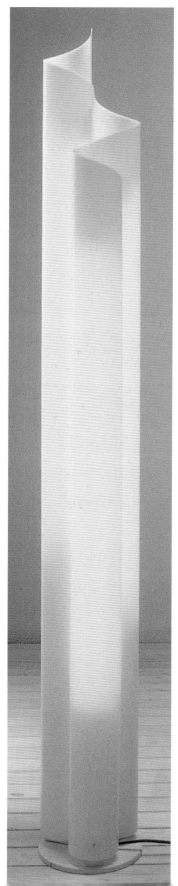

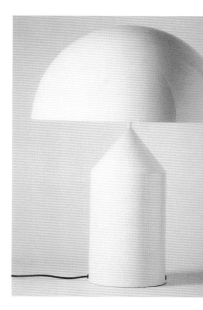

The "Chimera" light (1966; left), manufactured by Artemide. The serpentine plastic body of this sculptural piece gives the object added support because of the increased amount of material used.

Although he was a prolific product designer during this period, Magistretti did not abandon his architectural work, and he went on to design a number of showrooms, houses and other buildings. These included a primary school in Meda, outside Milan (1969, in collaboration with Gae Aulenti), and the biology-department building of the State University of Milan (1978, with F. Soro).

EXPERIMENTS WITH PLASTIC

It was Italian designers who transformed the perception of plastic from a cheap material to a stylish, sophisticated one. As with Marco Zanuso (see pp.196–7), who produced the first injection-moulded polyethylene chair, and Joe Colombo (see pp.208–9), whose "Elda" design was the first large armchair with a fibreglass shell, it was a series of experiments with plastic furniture that helped to establish Magistretti's reputation.

In 1964 he designed, for Artemide, the "Demetrio" table (see p.199); this was in many ways a reinforced injection-moulded resin version of the wooden stacking table of 1949 and was inspired, Magistretti claims, by photographers' plastic developing trays. The "Stadio" table, which he designed in 1966, was larger in size, with an "S"-shaped curve in the legs that was used to strengthen them. Most successful of all was the "Selene" chair (1969; see p.198), a simple design in ABS plastic with the same leg-strengthening detail as the "Stadio" table. Produced in green, red, white and black, this chair rapidly enjoyed international success and is still produced by Artemide.

As was the case with the designs of Marco Zanuso and Joe Colombo in plastic, Magistretti succeeded in giving the material a neo-modern "chic" that appealed to a sophisticated international market. The combination of bold, bright colours, shiny surfaces and sleekness of form managed to eradicate all the connotations of "cheap and nasty" that plastic products had carried with them in earlier decades, and transformed them into highly collectable items.

The lacquered metal "Atollo" light (1977; above) was produced by O-Luce. The simple geometric composition depends on elegant proportions for its visual impact. The diffusor – positioned so as to create an interesting play of shadows – appears to be floating unsupported in mid-air.

The "Sindbad" chair and sofa (below), designed in 1981 and manufactured by Cassina, demonstrated Magistretti's continuing ability to create something entirely new. Inspired by horse blankets purchased on his visits to Britain, the designer created a novel concept for seating that was simple and colourful, comfortable and informal.

A Milan restaurant in the early 1960s, equipped with Magistretti's "Carimate" chairs (above), designed in 1963 and manufactured by Cassina. With their red-painted wood frames and sense of rural informality, the chairs were a familiar sight in public spaces.

LIGHTING

Magistretti also shared the Italian preoccupation with lighting during the 1950s and 1960s. Among his experiments was the "Eclisse" light, designed in 1966 for Artemide, which won a gold medal at the 1967 Milan Triennale. Available in bright red or white, the simple metal form was designed to be free-standing or wall-mounted; the brightness could be modified by turning one half-sphere inside another to provide a partial or even total "eclisse" (eclipse). By contrast, the "Chimera" (1966; left) was a highly sculptural floor lamp with a sensual, folded-linen-like form. The "Attolo" table lamp (1977; right), one of Magistretti's best-known designs and winner of the 1979 Compasso d'Oro prize for product design, provided yet another original answer to the question of illumination; it is an exercise in the harmony of geometric forms, enhanced by the play of the shadows that it creates.

DESIGN STYLE AND REPUTATION

The timeless nature of Magistretti's designs is the result of a search not for a style but for the rational realization of particular ideas. His objects are typically simple concepts that provide elegant solutions to design problems; they stem from an initial idea that is followed through to its logical conclusion and then realized in the light of technological, economic and other practical constraints. He is, above all, a pragmatic designer, for whom what is imaginable must be continually reassessed in the light of what is or is not possible.

However, Magistretti's valuable contribution to post-war Italian design goes beyond his designs alone. His lively, enthusiastic presence has inspired the many students he has taught in a number of institutions both in Italy and elsewhere, including the Domus Academy in Milan, the Royal College of Art in London, and the School of Architecture in Tokyo. He has been a strong and influential ambassador for modern design, and an example of consistency and self-effacement.

Plastics

In the 20th century, plastics have had a greater impact on the public and private environment than any other material. Since their discovery in the late 19th century they have become one of the most widely used materials, revolutionizing mass production and presenting designers with an unprecedented aesthetic and ecological challenge.

Daniel Weil's "radio-in-a-bag" (right) was designed in 1981 and produced on a batch basis by Parenthesis Ltd; in 1983 it was also manufactured by Apex in Japan. Weil used transparent vinyl to contain the mechanical components of the radio while allowing them to remain visible.

The "Universale" chair, model 4857 (below), was designed by Joe Colombo (see pp.208–9) and manufactured by Kartell in 1965. The design was the result of an attempt to make a plastic injection-moulded chair in a single piece. To achieve the shiny surface Colombo used ABS plastic, which was replaced by polypropylene from 1976.

EARLY PLASTICS

The first natural and semi-synthetic plastics were discovered in the mid-19th century, including Parkesine in 1855 and celluloid, which was patented in 1870. These early plastics were used as inexpensive substitutes for materials such as jet, amber and ivory. Bakelite was the first totally synthetic early plastic, and also the most successful. Its discovery by the Belgian-born inventor Leo Baeckeland in 1907 coincided with the growth of the electrical industry, where it was rapidly used as an alternative to rubber for insulation in fittings such as plugs and switches. Bakelite thus had from the outset a modern identity that designers of the 1920s and 1930s used to update the appearance of the new electrical goods – such as refrigerators, radios and telephones. Bakelite forms were made using moulds into which the raw liquid material was poured; the resulting smooth, curved shapes were both easier to remove and part of the fashionable "streamlined" style of the 1930s.

Plastics were ideally suited to mass production. The expensive initial tooling costs were offset by the small unit cost, and huge numbers of plastic goods rolled off the production lines. From around 1927 petrochemical plastics – including vinyl, acrylic, nylon, polyester and cellulose acetate – were being developed, but were not widely used until after World War II.

AFTER 1945

Technological breakthroughs associated with the war effort increased the range of plastics available for manufacturing consumer goods, and foamed plastics, polyurethane and glass-reinforced plastics joined the ever-expanding options open to designers. Ironically, however, plastics also started to be seen as cheap and were often perceived as inferior to natural materials.

The challenge to post-war designers was to re-establish plastics as materials in their own right and to exploit the unique combination of properties they offered: lightness, colour, malleability, cheapness, hygiene, robustness and imperviousness to water. In the 1950s many designers worked hard to achieve this. The plastic chair designs of Charles Eames (see pp.148–51) and Eero Saarinen (see pp.156–7), for example, inspired Marco Zanuso to design the first injection-moulded polyethylene chair (see pp.196–7). The Danish designer Verner Panton (see pp.204–5) developed the first one-piece plastic cantilevered chair in the 1960s, and the full

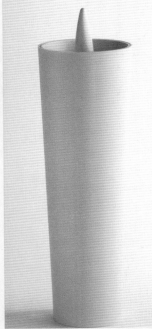

A toilet brush designed by Philippe Starck (above), one of a range of plastic household objects that this French designer created in the 1990s. Its simple elegance is a mark of the way in which Starck considers plastic to be a legitimate modern material to be used alongside others such as wood and metal.

potential of mass-produced office furniture was seen three years later, when British designer Robin Day (see pp.168–71) produced the "Polyprop" chair for Hille & Co. Ltd that went on to sell over 14 million copies worldwide.

THE PRESENT AND BEYOND

Plastics are highly versatile materials. Pop designers of the 1960s used soft plastics such as vinyl and polyurethane foam to make flexible, inflatable and, in theory, disposable furniture. Among the best-known examples were the transparent "Blow" chair (1967) designed by De Pas, D'Urbino and Lomazzi. In the 1970s, however, the oil crisis and awareness of environmental issues such as biodegradability led to a decline in the popularity of plastics, but by the 1980s and 1990s a more balanced use of this material had emerged.

Designers such as Philippe Starck (see pp.246–9) have made extensive use of plastics, while tempering this with environmental concern. Starck's "Louis 20" chair, for example, combines a polypropylene moulded body with aluminium rear legs which can be removed and recycled. The unique combination of properties that has made plastics such widely used materials in the 20th century will almost certainly guarantee their place in the 21st. The challenge for the next generation of designers, however, will be to balance their advantages with long-term environmental concerns.

The frontispiece from a 1947 publication entitled Plastics in the Home (above), showing a range of many different types of plastic material encountered in daily use at that time. These included Bakelite (used for the round body-shell of the radio), melamine (used for crockery) and vinyl (used to make the curtains and the raincoat).

A range of sealed plastic food containers (right) manufactured in the United States by the Tupperware company from 1949. Made of polyolefin, which was flexible and opaque, the containers were available in a number of fashionable colours. They were very popular in the 1950s, and sold in enormous numbers through Tupperware parties held by housewives for their neighbours.

The Danish architect and designer Verner Panton (b.1926) has lived and worked in Switzerland since the mid-1950s. One result of his self-imposed exile is that his prolific and original design work has no national characteristics. There is no evidence of the craft traditions beloved of the Danes, nor of the rigorous rationalism associated with

Verner Panton

the Swiss. His affiliations – if any – are with the United States and Italy, whose post-war designers sought to create a sophisticated, modern design movement responsive to new materials and new forms. In the 1960s he was part of an international attempt to promote the redemptive powers of new technology and synthetic materials.

The Danish designer Verner Panton has worked since the mid-1950s on innovative design proposals combining visual and technological breakthroughs. Based in Switzerland, he adheres to no single national movement, belonging instead to the international design community.

Panton's most outstanding contribution has been the stacking chair (1960; below), manufactured from 1967 by Vitra for Herman Miller. This was the first one-piece, cantilevered, all-injection-moulded plastic chair to be designed and made.

The "Panthella" lamp (1970; right), by Louis Poulsen, consists of a hemispherical acrylic shade mounted on a flared stem. Panton intended the lamp to look as though it were a single "space-age" form, emitting a light with no obvious source.

EARLY WORK AND EXPERIMENTS IN SEATING

Panton was educated at the Technical School in Odense and graduated from the Academy in Copenhagen in 1951. From 1950–52 he also worked on experimental furniture in the studio of Arne Jacobsen (see pp.142–5), who in turn was inspired by the work of Charles Eames (see pp.148–51) and Eero Saarinen (see pp.156–7). Panton set up his own studio in Binningen, Switzerland, in 1955. By the end of the decade he was internationally known for his futuristic chair designs. These were produced by the Danish company, Fritz Hansen, which retained strong links with Panton. The "Cone" chair (1958) was made of sheet metal bent into a cone shape, with fabric-covered foam upholstery and a drop-in seat. The "Heart" series (1959; opposite, below) also combined metal frames and stretch-knit upholstery.

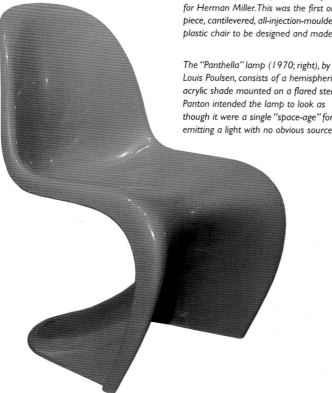

Panton created a number of highly innovative lights for the Luber company in the 1960s and 1970s. The "Hanging Chandelier" (c. 1970) — variations of which appear in this interior (left) — comprises shell disks suspended from a circular metal ceiling plate derived from atomic structures.

The "Heart" chair (below) was designed in 1959 for the Danish furniture manufacturer Fritz Hansen. The extraordinary — and for its time highly futuristic — form was achieved through the use of bent sheet metal covered with foam and stretch-fabric upholstery.

The "Stacking" chair (1960; opposite, left), however, was the most innovative. With its curving, cantilevered design, it was the first one-piece moulded plastic chair. Made originally of GRP (glass-reinforced polyester), it was manufactured by Hansen until 1968, when the American company Herman Miller took over the design and began mass production. The concept of organic seating designed to fit the human form has continued to preoccupy Panton. His range of designs includes the "S" chair (1965), made from a single sheet of plywood; a flowing system of steel-wire seating, in which the seats formed a sinuous, curved row (1972); and, in the late 1980s, a series of bizarre "Post-modern" organically shaped plastic chairs.

THE DOMESTIC LANDSCAPE

From the mid-1960s Panton designed a range of lights that, like his seating, exploited new technologies and "space-age" forms; these included the "Hanging Chandelier" (above) and the "Panthella" (opposite, right). From the late 1960s Panton also began designing floor coverings and textiles. He produced a large range of fabrics for the Swiss company Mira-X, notably "Spectrum" (1969), with an abstract Op Art design; and the chintz fabrics that made up the "Diamond" (1984) and "Cubus" (1987) lines.

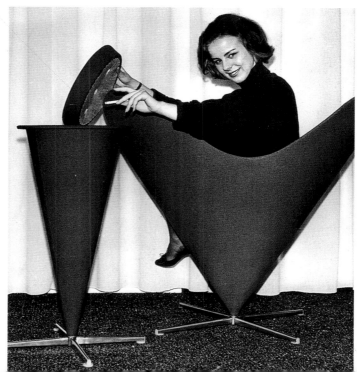

Antti Nurmesniemi (b.1927) and his wife Vuokko Eskolin-Nurmesniemi (b.1930) have played a leading role within Finnish design since the 1960s. Their contributions to interior, industrial and furniture design, and to textiles and fashion respectively, have helped to establish Finland's post-war international reputation for innovative design. Together, for

Antti & Vuokko Nurmesniemi

example, they created the Finnish exhibition at the Milan Triennale of 1960; and in 1976 they designed the striking "004" chair (only produced as a prototype), which combined Antti's sense of structure and form with Vuokko's black-and-white fabric upholstery – the latter a tribute to her eye for simple surface pattern.

TRAINING AND EARLY WORK

Both Antti and Vuokko trained at the Institute of Industrial Art in Helsinki, Antti as an interior designer and Vuokko as a ceramicist. On his graduation in 1950, Antti was employed as a furniture designer for the Stockman department store in Helsinki. From 1951 he worked in the architectural studio of Viljo Revell in Helsinki and subsequently for Giovanni Romano in Milan, before opening his own interior-design studio in Helsinki in 1956. After Vuokko's graduation from the Institute in 1952 she went to work for the textile company Marimekko, where she was one of the company's leading designers from 1953 until 1964, the year in which she formed her

The sauna stool shown below was designed by Antti in 1952 for the Palace Hotel in Helsinki. Made of laminated birch veneer with teak legs, it was in production for several years and has became a classic of post-war Finnish design. The stool was awarded a prize at the 1964 Milan Triennale.

Antti Nurmesniemi and Vuokko Eskolin-Nurmesniemi are two of Finland's most successful and well-known designers. While Antti has pioneered modern product design in that country, Vuokko has helped earn it a reputation as a home of progressive textile printing.

Antti's design for the "Antti Slim" telephone (below) was produced by the Japanese company Fujitsu in 1984. Because the inner components are so small, the size of the telephone was determined solely by the distance between the ear and the mouth.

The couple's influence was not restricted to product design, however. In 1967, with the painter Ahti Lavonen and the sculptor Veikko Eskolin, Antti and Vuokko designed an exhibition in Helsinki that they called "Bubble on the Shore" – a translucent tent-like structure near the seashore in which Antti exhibited his "001" chair. In 1971 they worked on another concept – "The Living Table" – a kind of platform on which they placed what they called the "necessary tools for living", some of them designed by Antti, including a glass vase, microwave oven and magazine rack.

Through the 1970s and 1980s the couple continued to represent Finnish design abroad and to work on their individual projects at home. Antti concentrated on furniture, while Vuokko expanded her range to include utility items – such as washbags and purses – all made from her own textiles. In 1988 Vuokko introduced a more overtly elegant element into her clothing designs but remained committed to natural materials. The couple's own lifestyle symbolizes their achievements in post-war Finnish design, combining sophistication with comfort, simplicity with beauty, and stressing the importance of colour, texture and ecologically sound materials.

A cotton fabric designed by Vuokko and entitled "Auranko" (above). This fabric was produced in 1964, and its bold surface image is characteristic of the prints that she created during this decade.

Vuokko designed the cotton shift "Helle" (right) in 1964 from a black-and-white patterned fabric that she also designed, called "Pyorre". The pattern was also used on furniture pieces designed by Antti, with a very different effect. This demonstrates the versatility of Vuokko's boldly graphic designs.

own firm. She designed simple patterns, which were printed on natural fabrics and made up into clothing that emphasized the qualities of freedom and utility rather than fashion.

In 1957, the year after he had set up his studio, Antti designed the cast-iron "Finel" coffee pot (available in black, white and red) and a range of cooking pots for the cast-iron company Wärtsila. The coffee pot had a cylindrical metal body that tapered towards the top and a black plastic handle. The pots were produced in bright colours – red, white, yellow and brown – and before long they could be found in most Finnish middle-class kitchens. In the late 1950s Antti also designed chairs in polished steel and leather, and their "chic" modern appearance helped him to win the Lunning Prize for design in 1959. In 1964 he won a prize at the Milan Triennale for another chair design, the sauna stool. Throughout the 1960s he worked on many interiors for banks, restaurants and offices, introducing a sophistication previously seen in Finland only in the work of Alvar Aalto (see pp.74–7).

INFLUENCE ON FINNISH DESIGN

Antti Nurmesniemi helped to change Finland's reputation from that of a source of high-quality indigenous decorative-art products to that of a producer of international industrial design. Together with Eero Aarnio, among others, he introduced a new sophistication into Finnish design that acknowledged indigenous traditions but which also brought Finland into the international marketplace. This was particularly evident in such designs as the little horseshoe-shaped wooden sauna stool (originally designed in 1952 for the Palace Hotel, Helsinki; see opposite, right).

Although he only lived to the age of 41, Joe Colombo (1930–71) was a key figure of modern Italian design in the 1950s and 1960s. During a short career he worked on countless products and systems that combined technological innovation with new ways of thinking about how they fulfilled their functions. He saw the role of the designer as much

Joe Colombo

more than just a creator of products, but rather as a shaper of the environment in which we live. It has been said of him that he "lived life as if it were a race", and he certainly achieved a great deal in a very short time, combining designing with a love of physical activities, especially skiing and driving fast cars.

Joe Colombo was one of the most far-sighted Italian designers of his generation, and carried out extensive research into the concept of the ultimate human habitat. He was a familiar sight in Milanese design circles, recognizable by his size, his beard and his pipe.

The highly original "Tube-chair" (1969; below) consists of a series of semi-rigid plastic tubes covered with plastic foam and fabric that could be linked in various ways to create a range of sitting objects.

TRAINING AND EARLY WORK

Colombo trained as a painter at the Brera Academy of Fine Art in Milan, graduating in 1949, and, in the early 1950s, became a member of the "Movimento Nucleare" (the Nuclear Movement), an avant-garde Italian fine art movement led by Enrico Baj. In 1953 he was commissioned to paint the ceiling of the Santa Tecla night club in Milan, and in 1954 he was put in charge of the display of ceramics from Albisola at the Milan Triennale. In that year he also enrolled as an architectural student at the Polytechnic of Milan.

DESIGN CAREER

Colombo's father died in 1959, leaving him in charge of his electrical equipment manufacturing firm. In 1962, Colombo established his own studio in Milan and concentrated on interior design and furniture. From the outset his approach emphasized the interior as a kind of system – a sum of its component parts in which furniture was an important element. Early interiors included the Continental Hotel in Sardinia (1964) and the Leka Sport store in Milan. At the same time Colombo pursued his other two main interests: the idea of the "living system" and the use of new materials and forms in mass-produced furniture. His "Mini-kitchen" (1963) showed his interest in self-contained units, a concept that led to the idea of the "mobile living-unit", inspired by developments related to space travel. Colombo's final contribution to the concept was the experimental "Total Furnishing Unit" (opposite, left) shown, after his death, at the exhibition "Italy: The New Domestic Landscape", held at the Museum of Modern Art, New York, in 1972.

The design of the "Linea 72" in-flight service for Alitalia (1970; above) was the result of Colombo's research into ways of securing objects during movement. The brief had tight constraints governing size, weight and production cost.

Colombo aimed to fulfil the basic living requirements in the "Total Furnishing Unit" (1971; below). The four sections – Kitchen, Cupboard, Bed and Bathroom – showed that domestic behaviour could be reduced to a simple set of functions.

The "Rotoliving" unit set up for dining, with the "Cabriolet-Bed" in the background (1969; above). The objects in this futuristic interior, which were intended for use in a contemporary habitat, put Colombo's research on living patterns into practice.

COLOMBO AND MODERNITY

Colombo made futuristic forays into furniture design, seeking new formal solutions to the problem of the chair. The "Elda" armchair (1963) had a fibreglass shell; in 1964 he produced a curved plywood chair; and the "Universale" chair (1965; see p.202), for Kartell, was the first single-piece chair (excepting the legs) with a moulded plastic back and seat. Thus, together with Vico Magistretti (see pp.198–201) and Marco Zanuso (see pp.196–7), Colombo was responsible for validating plastic as an appropriate material for modern furniture. He repeated this commitment in his design for the plastic "Boby" trolley (1970), available in red, yellow, black and white.

Colombo's lights were as radical as his chairs. His intention was to create new forms and ingenious new ways of directing light, using sophisticated technology such as the halogen lamp. As with all his designs, Colombo started by defining the problem and then looked for new ways of solving it. His solutions with lamps were imaginative – for example, the "Acrilica" (1962), consisting of a "C"-shaped Perspex convector with a metal base and fluorescent tube; "Spider" (1965), a bulb with a pressed-metal shade that could be attached to a table-lamp base or to wall or ceiling fixtures; and "Ciclope" (1970), a hanging lamp designed to slide vertically along two parallel cables. The same approach resulted in other memorable products, including two sets of drinking glasses (1964), "Smoke" and "Assimetrico", the "Optic" alarm clock (1970) and an air conditioner for Candy (1970).

Although a generation younger than Marco Zanuso (see pp.196–7) and Vico Magistretti (see pp.198–201), the Italian architect and designer Mario Bellini (b.1935) has, none the less, earned himself a reputation alongside them as a key post-war industrial designer. From the 1960s onwards he has spanned architecture, furniture and product design,

Mario Bellini

applying to each area the same commitment to function and elegant styling. His work for the Italian manufacturers Olivetti and Cassina, in particular, represented the high point of Italian chic from the 1960s to the 1980s.

Mario Bellini's office machines created for Olivetti from the 1960s – as well as his numerous products for other companies based in Italy and elsewhere – are among the most sophisticated of their kind. His grasp of advanced technology, and understanding of its link to human behaviour and needs, is outstanding.

The "ETP55" portable electronic typewriter (1987; below) has been among Bellini's most expressive designs for Olivetti. Based on a simple wedge shape (which the designer had developed over the previous decade), this model uses colour to create its own identity and set it clearly apart from its competitors.

TRAINING AND EARLY WORK

Bellini trained as an architect, graduating from the Polytechnic of Milan in 1959. He spent the next three years as an apprentice in the design department of the city's La Rinascente store, and from 1962 onwards he worked in his own studio in Milan as well as teaching in the Higher Institute of Industrial Design in Venice (1962–9). During the 1960s his strong commitment to product design emerged. Industrial design was expanding apace in Italy at that time, as Italian designers formulated a sophisticated style in order to compete with German products (which concentrated on advanced technology) and with Japanese goods (which emphasized low cost to the consumer).

Extending the pioneering work of Zanuso and Marcello Nizzoli (see pp.172–3), Bellini devoted much of his energy to creating an Italian idiom that acknowledged the supremacy of function but also respected the importance of form. His product-design career opportunity came in 1963, when he joined Olivetti as a consultant. The patronage of this forward-thinking company gave him a chance to put into reality ideas which might otherwise have remained on the drawing-board. By the 1970s Bellini had a number of electronic successes to his name, among them the "Divisumma 18" calculator (1972), made of brightly coloured plastic with a rounded, form and covered with a thin rubber membrane; the "Lettera 10" portable typewriter (1976–7); and the "Logos 80" printing calculator (1978).

DESIGN STYLE

Less flamboyant a personality than some of his contemporaries, Bellini is a reserved and sensitive man who lets his work speak for him much of the time. His approach to design is based more on instinct than on philosophical ideas, and he was less overtly radical than his fellow-consultant at Olivetti, Ettore Sottsass (see pp.216–19). However, Bellini's highly original forms have touched an international nerve, and his designs are known worldwide for their elegance and sophistication.

His architectural background enabled him to experiment in a number of design areas. He was particularly interested in furniture, and his relationship with a range of companies – Cassina and C&B (later B&B) Italia among

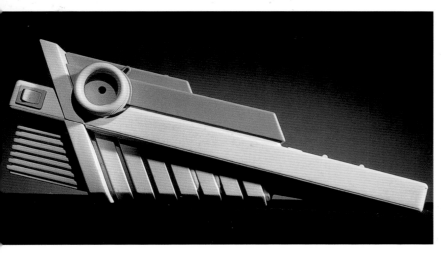

them – resulted in such classic designs as the monumental "Il Colonnato" table (1977), comprising three marble columns and a marble top; and the simple, yet highly original, leather-clothed "Cab" chair (1976), which zipped up at the side like a boot (both designed for Cassina). Sumptuous form, luxurious materials and a high level of finish were the hallmarks of many of his furniture designs.

Although an individual sensibility clearly informs Bellini's work, stylistically it is highly eclectic, as seen in the contrast between, for example, the "Area" hanging light (1974; left), based on the concept of a piece of translucent cloth frozen in space; and the accordion-shaped polyurethane "Teneride" office chair (1970). His inventive approach to material, function and form can be seen in such other notable designs as the "TC 800D" stereo-cassette deck for Yamaha (1974), a car interior for Lancia (1977–8), and the "Persona" office chair for Vitra (1979–84).

A water tap (below) designed in 1978 in collaboration with Dario Bellini for Ideal Standard in Italy. This chromed brass tap is among the most overtly sensual of Bellini's designs, and its organic form was clearly influenced by modern sculpture.

OTHER ACTIVITIES

Like so many of his Italian contemporaries, Bellini has also acted as a spokesman for modern Italian design through many varied activities. He has taught and lectured at numerous international educational and cultural centres; he has designed and curated notable exhibitions, among them "The Domestic Project" (1986), which formed part of the 17th Milan Triennale; and from 1986 to 1991 he was Editor of *Domus*, the internationally renowned Milanese architecture and design magazine.

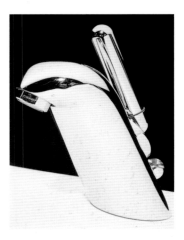

The "Area" lamp (above) – manufactured by Artemide in 1974 – was one of a series of floor and ceiling lamps. Bellini developed this light following his experiments into the production of organic forms created by stretched membranes. The handkerchief-like shades were made from light-diffusing polyester.

The "Figura" office chair (right) was developed between 1979 and 1984 by Bellini with Daniel Thiel, and produced by Vitra. Based on an existing chair, this later version was "dressed" with a cloth that was then "belted" around the middle – as if it were a waist. The idea was to make a highly technological design relate more directly to the human body.

Cassina

The furniture manufacturing firm, Cassina, has played a significant part in modern Italian design. Under the directorship of Cesare Cassina (1909–79) and since, it has worked with many leading contemporary designers to create an identity both for itself and for post-war Italian furniture design in the international marketplace. Through sympathetic and constructive relationships with many distinguished designers, this relatively small family firm with its artisanal origins has developed a range of furniture that was found in the living rooms of sophisticated, cosmopolitan consumers across the globe.

Gaetano Pesce's felt chairs – named "Feltri" (below) – were produced by Cassina in 1987. The company had worked with this innovative designer for over 20 years, manufacturing a number of his furniture objects. These throne-like armchairs sustained that tradition of experimentalism, their soft fabric impregnated with resin to ensure rigidity.

ORIGINS AND DEVELOPMENT

The company's roots go back to the 18th century. Based in Meda, north of Milan, the Cassina family's furniture workshop provided wooden furniture in traditional styles for the local community, but by the early 20th century its team of joiners was concentrating on the manufacture of small, custom-designed work tables. Cesare Cassina, who, with his elder brother Umberto (d.1991), took over the running of the firm in 1927, trained as an upholsterer in Milan and, as a result, the workshop began to make armchairs and other upholstered items. In the 1920s and 1930s Cassina focused on drawing-room suites in conservative styles, and design was undertaken in-house, much of it by Umberto himself.

The major shift in Cassina's approach towards furniture manufacturing and design came after 1945. The firm had expanded to employ 30 upholsterers and joiners; by 1955 the number had risen to 40. This increase of employees was, however, less significant than the shifts in the process and scale of manufacture. There was a move to produce furniture in larger numbers and, in order to penetrate the international marketplace, to produce pieces that were more obviously "of their time". Between 1947 and 1952 production increased rapidly, due both to demand from department stores for furniture in the modern style, and to a commission from the Italian Government to supply furniture for ships.

COLLABORATION WITH DESIGNERS

The company's associations with Modernist designers began tentatively. The results of their work with Gio Ponti (see pp.138–41), who met Cesare Cassina in 1950 in connection with the ship furniture contract, were the first really positive examples. Their collaboration engendered the "Superleggera" chair, which consolidated Cassina's new post-war direction. The chair had a long gestation period – 1950–56 – during which employees

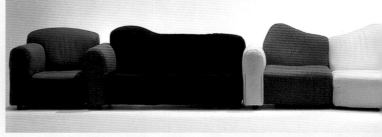

The husband-and-wife design team Afra and Tobia Scarpa worked with Cassina from 1963. "Soriana" (1970; left), an informal piece of seating with a plywood base, chromium-plated steel frame and a polyurethane foam filling, was available upholstered with either fabric or leather.

The "Rotonda" table (1976; right), by Mario Bellini, has a stocky wooden base, and was made in ash or walnut, with a wooden or glass top. The simple form is characteristic of Bellini's designs.

Vico Magistretti has worked with Cassina since 1960, and is their longest serving collaborator. His "Nuvola Rossa" shelving system (right) was launched in 1977. Available in beech or black-lacquered finish, the four central shelves are removable.

at Cassina discovered how to mass-produce a designer's proposal. The whole process – from prototype to final manufacture and marketing – had to be learned from scratch, but, once perfected, it provided the basis for the successes enjoyed by the firm through its collaborations with a number of contemporary designers. They included, in the 1950s, Carlo di Carli (simple wooden-framed dining chairs), Ico Parisi (padded shell sofa and chairs) and Gianfranco Frattini (including the "831" armchair). In the 1960s, 1970s and 1980s, designs were produced by Vico Magistretti (from 1960; see pp.198–201); Mario Bellini (from 1962; see pp.210–11); Tobia and Afra Scarpa (from 1963); Gaetano Pesce (from 1964; see pp.224–5); and Paolo Deganello (from the early 1970s).

As well as producing important new designs, Cassina manufactured, from the mid-1960s, a series of early 20th-century chairs, called "I Maestri" (The Masters). These included pieces by Charles Rennie Mackintosh (for example, the "Hill House", "Argyle" and "Willow" chairs); Le Corbusier, Pierre Jeanneret and Charlotte Perriand (for example, the "LC4" chaise-longue and the "LC2" or "Grand Confort" sofa and chair); and Gerrit Rietveld (the "Red/Blue" and "Zig-Zag" chairs). This series was another imaginative and practical way of demonstrating Cassina's continuing belief in the part that design can play in shaping contemporary culture.

Pesce's series of upholstered chairs, sofas and ottomans (left) – named "Cannareggio" and produced by Cassina in 1987 – could be used individually or linked together. Based on plywood frames with polyurethane padding, the pieces had an in-built versatility described by Pesce as "a diversity that may or may not be formal".

arley Earl (1893–1969) was almost singlehandedly responsible for creating the concept of consumer styling. Standing outside the canon of "good design", as defined in Europe in the 1920s and adopted by many American designers in the 1950s, his approach to the design of automobiles sought to please and, in doing so, to increase

Harley Earl

sales. As Head of General Motors' Styling Section, his contribution to car design was a singularly American one, in which an ideal of glamour and luxury could be bought. Earl thus helped automobiles to make the transition from machines to desirable objects, and, probably unconsciously, played a role in moving design away from its purist Modernist phase towards a preoccupation with consumer appeal and with style for its own sake.

Harley Earl was significant in establishing a design approach that rejected the timelessness of Modernism and allied itself, instead, to the stylistic vagaries of fashion. He is shown here with a model of the Buick "Y-Job".

The interior of the 1954 Cadillac (below), a show car designed by Earl for General Motors and exhibited that year in Miami. The steering wheel and instrument panel refer visually to aeroplane styling.

EARLY TRAINING AND WORK

Earl was born, appropriately, in Hollywood, where his father was a carriage-maker and Earl became his apprentice. After World War I he studied engineering at Stanford University, while at the same time earning a living by creating flamboyant, colourful and individualistic custom-made automobiles for Hollywood stars. In 1919 his father's company was bought up and, as a result, he was summoned to Detroit by the General Motors Company to work on a model for its newly formed Cadillac division.

For the next 32 years Earl was ultimately responsible for the design of all of General Motors' automobiles. He was in many ways ideal for the job. His philosophy – which was instinctive rather than rational – was based on the belief that cars should be individual and visually appealing, and replaced by new models as soon as that appeal wore off – an approach ideally suited to the economics of mid-century mass production in the United States.

CLASSIC DESIGNS FOR GENERAL MOTORS

Earl's first design – the "La Salle" (1927; opposite, above left) – proved a great success. As a result, Alfred J. Sloan, the Managing Director of General Motors, invited Earl to work for the company under contract and, in 1927, the Art and Color Section was established with Earl in charge. The 1934 "La Salle" was his second major success. In 1937 the Art and Color Section became the Styling Section, and Earl initiated the concept of the "dream car": a futuristic automobile that, although ahead of its time, incorporated features that could easily become standard in the car of the near future.

Earl used clay to experiment with new, exciting, space-age forms. The Buick "Y-Job" (above left), for example, although designed in 1937, had many features that anticipated post-war models: visual unity, a long, low profile, and lavish use of chrome. His post-war designs developed these features further, adding two-tone paintwork, wraparound windscreens and, most distinctive of all, tailfins. The fins were inspired by military aeroplanes, and, after the launch of the first finned Cadillac in 1948, were widely copied.

Earl driving his General Motors Cadillac "La Salle" (above) in 1927, the year of its launch. The design was remarkable for its use of soft curves, harmonious form and long, low profile; it represented a new-found elegance in American automobile design.

CHEVROLET

As fine a car as anyone (including wealthy people) could want

Between 1948 and 1958 General Motors produced some of its most dramatic models, all masterminded by Earl. Cars became longer, lower and more jet-like, with exaggerated curves. In 1952 Earl introduced "Motorama", an annual event at which new models were launched.

Earl retired in 1959, the year in which the pink Cadillac "Eldorado" convertible was launched. Three years later Ralph Nader, in *Unsafe at any Speed*, claimed that General Motors' Chevrolet "Corsair" was "one of the greatest acts of industrial irresponsibility in the present century". The tide had turned and Earl's ideas went out of favour, but his influence lives on wherever pleasure, style and fantasy take precedence over "good design".

This two-door Chevrolet Impala sport coupe was released soon after Earl's retirement from General Motors in 1959, but it illustrates the way in which his leadership of the General Motors styling department influenced all the models produced by the company. The Chevrolet Impala, lower-priced than the Cadillac, was nevertheless given the same streamlining treatment, complete with chrome detailing and fins. The contemporary advertisment shown above demonstrates how the American car industry sold their products as appendages of an affluent lifestyle, rather than a functional necessity.

The "Firebird 11" (1956), an experimental Pontiac show car designed by Earl. The dramatically futuristic curves and detailing – of the tailfin, in particular – like the 1954 Cadillac, owe much to contemporary jet styling. Every detail is suggestive of high speed, with the car's real image far removed from that of the family vehicle presented here.

The long career of the Italian architect and designer Ettore Sottsass (b.1917) has been distinguished by intellectual and philosophical integrity, as well as by the originality of his many designs. A child of Modernism, he became one of its first and most articulate critics, developing a wide range of intellectual and aesthetic alternatives to demonstrate

Ettore Sottsass

its shortcomings. He has been associated with a number of important Italian design groups, including Studio Alchimia and Memphis. In this way he has been an instrumental part of the major shift in international design in the 20th century, and has inspired several generations of young designers throughout his own journey of self-discovery.

Ettore Sottsass is among the most prolific and consistently radical of 20th-century designers. Based in Milan since 1945, he has dominated the second half of the century both through his work with Olivetti and others, and through his own research in which he has regularly challenged the limitations of traditional Modernism and found rich alternatives.

The "Valentine" typewriter (1969; below), designed for Olivetti. With its bright red ABS plastic body and an easily removable case, the typewriter was portable and influenced by the ethos of the cheap, versatile ballpoint pen.

TRAINING AND EARLY WORK

Sottsass was born in Innsbruck, Austria. His father, Ettore Sot-Sas, studied under leading architects in Vienna and in 1928 moved with his family to Turin, where he became one of Italy's leading Modernist architects of the inter-war years. Sottsass Jnr trained as an architect at the Polytechnic of Turin, graduating in 1939. After three years in the Italian army (from 1942–5), he set up his own design studio in Milan. He began his career designing interiors and furniture for the new post-war housing in the city, a project in which he worked alongside contemporaries such as Marco Zanuso (see pp.196–7) and Vico Magistretti (see pp.198–201), who were also involved in designing furniture items for small spaces in the new apartment blocks around the city. At the same time Sottsass was closely involved with contemporary movements in the fine and applied arts, and worked on a number of abstract sculptural projects in the privacy of his studio. This need to work simultaneously on a professional and personal front has remained constant throughout his career.

Sottsass' first big professional opportunity came in an invitation from Olivetti in Ivrea for him to join the company as a consultant industrial designer. This was an imaginative move on Olivetti's part, given Sottsass' hitherto strongly architectural, fine art and interior design orientation. In 1958 Roberto Olivetti asked Sottsass to redesign the company's first computer, the room-sized "Elea 9003", and throughout the 1960s Sottsass went on to create a highly successful range of typewriters, including "Praxis" (1963) and "Tekne" (1964), which were strikingly simple, modern machines. In these pieces Sottsass rejected the streamlined forms of his predecessor Marcello Nizzoli (see pp.172–3), favouring instead a less overtly expressive aesthetic.

DEVELOPMENT OF PERSONAL STYLE

With his own design practice well established in Milan on the strength of the contract with Olivetti, in the early 1960s Sottsass was able to develop a personal design language. He was strongly inspired by trips both to the West (he visited the United States in 1956 and again in the early 1960s), where he first encountered Pop Art and pop culture, and worked with the visionary designer George Nelson (see pp.154–5) in New York; and to the East (he visited India in 1961), where he came into contact with Tantric art.

Both of these visits gave Sottsass a chance to distance himself from from what he termed "European anxiety", and to think about design from new and different perspectives. They reinforced his deep suspicions about the rationalism of pre-war Modernism, and he began to explore design primarily as an arena for sensuousness and communication. The Modernist tenet that design could determine behaviour, dictate lifestyles and reinforce ideologies was abhorrent to him, and he set out to express these concerns in a range of personal projects. These included Pop-inspired shelves, desks and wardrobes exhibited in Milan in 1965 and 1966; the "Grey" furniture (1970), produced only as prototypes by Poltronova; and a range of ceramic objects inspired by Indian mysticism: "Ceramics of Darkness" (1963), "Ceramics to Shiva" (1964), the monolithic, sculptural ceramics of 1967, and the "Tantra" (1969) and "Yantra" (1970) series.

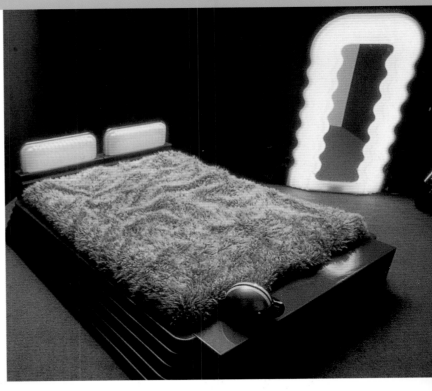

The "Ultrafragola" mirror (1970; above), with its wavy fibreglass frame, was made by the Poltronova company; it was one of a set that included wavy standard lamps, cabinets, a table and a fur-covered bed. These pieces were part of a project to rid furniture design of the legacy of good craftsmanship and to ally it instead with the world of the image.

The "TC 800" (left), designed for Olivetti in 1974, was an intelligent office terminal system. It demonstrated the designer's continued interest in producing pieces of high-technology machinery at a time when his research seemed to be taking him further from the object and towards a more conceptual approach.

The "Elea 9003" computer (below) – designed in the late 1950s when computers took up whole rooms – was Sottsass' first collaborative project with Olivetti. In this case he restricted his intervention to lowering the height of the cabinets so that operators could see one another, and colour-coding the control panel.

A pearwood and laminate kitchen storage unit (above), shown at "Ruins", an exhibition of Sottsass's work that was held at the Design Gallery in Milan in 1993. In the sixth decade of his design career, Sottsass's work still shows an originality and freshness.

Through his encounters with Pop Art, pop culture and Indian mysticism, Sottsass therefore found a way of sidestepping contemporary mainstream Italian Modernism. His range of radical designs for furniture, ceramics and jewellery set out to liberate rather than to constrain – representing a shift in perspective that offered important new directions for the world of design. While this was recognized inside Italy, at the time Sottsass was less well known internationally, although his large ceramics of 1967 were exhibited in Stockholm.

At this time, in fact, Sottsass was visible within the design world as a kind of irritant. His radical personal experiments were incomprehensible to those in the mainstream, who perceived him merely as part of an "alternative culture". His successes with Olivetti, however, confounded the sceptics, who were forced to acknowledge that he was a designer of enormous talent and foresight. Increasingly, in the late 1960s, Sottsass acquired a following among Italian and foreign designers who saw in his work the possibility of a real modern alternative to what was becoming, for many, the limitations of later Modernism with its glossy objects and status-conscious designs.

STUDIO ALCHIMIA

Sottsass' contribution to the exhibition entitled "Italy: The New Domestic Landscape", held at the Museum of Modern Art, New York, in 1972, was an interior consisting of a number of movable linked living units. In 1976 a solo touring exhibition of his work opened at the International Design Centre, Berlin, and in 1977 he had a solo exhibition at the Pompidou Centre, Paris. Despite this increased international exposure, the 1970s were difficult years for Sottsass, both personally and professionally. Disillusioned with the possibilities of design, he moved towards the abstract concept, concentrating for most of the time on drawings, prints and photographs. By the late 1970s, however, he had entered what would turn out to be the most influential phase of his creative activity.

Sottsass' renewed involvement with design was made possible by the formation in 1976 in Milan of Studio Alchimia, a loose grouping of designers associated with the radical design movement that included Alessandro Mendini and Andrea Branzi. The group rejected the Bauhaus tenets of good design in favour of witty, anarchic pieces of furniture, which they showed at the therefore ironically named

Glassware (right) designed for Venini in 1995. Sottsass added designs for glass to his repertoire in the early 1970s. However, he was less interested in the crafts aspect than in creating new kinds of images from this rich material which, although rooted in the past, could be manipulated to express the present.

These projects, which were workshop-produced, represented Sottsass' personal work. In them he developed a new approach to design which prioritized "meaning" over function and concentrated on the response of the audience to the object in question, rather than on the nature of the design process. Sottsass was increasingly interested in the different ways in which people interacted with objects, and in the power of objects upon those who interacted with them; style and taste did not concern him.

This work inspired the generation of architects and designers who, from 1966 to the early 1970s, identified with the "Anti-design" movement that included such groups as Superstudio, Archizoom and Gruppo Strum (see pp.222–3). They found in Sottsass a natural leader, for even his commercial products for Olivetti had been inspired by a desire to find a new creative starting point for design, prime examples being the bright red, moulded-plastic "Valentine" portable typewriter (1969; opposite) and a secretary's chair in bright yellow plastic and lacquered aluminium with "Mickey Mouse" feet (1969).

The "Medici" dinnerware service (above) was designed for the American company Swid Powell in 1985. The desire for decorative surfaces – which in the mid-1980s was seen as one way of escaping the limitations of high Modernism – is met here by Sottsass in his use of graphic and semi-figurative designs on the surfaces of the pieces.

"Bau.Haus" exhibitions. Sottsass designed a new range of furniture for Alchimia – including tables, bookshelves and lights – that he covered with plastic laminate embellished with patterns derived from suburban "non-culture", such as the marbled flooring of 1950s' coffee-bars. Once again Sottsass used design as a form of cultural criticism – an approach that he had refined over the years.

THE MEMPHIS GROUP

In 1980 he formed Sottsass Associati together with Marco Zanini, Matteo Thun and Aldo Cibic, and in 1981 he broke away from Studio Alchimia to form his own "studio" in Milan with a group of young friends and colleagues – among them Michele de Lucchi (see pp.252–3), George Sowden, Nathalie du Pasquier, Marco Zanini and Aldo Cibic.

The Memphis group, as it was known, hit the international design-press headlines within hours of its furniture appearing alongside the Milan Furniture Fair in 1981, and became the most important design phenomenon of the decade. Its playful Post-modern designs drew from sources as diverse as Classical architecture and 1950s' kitsch, incorporating a range of bold, bright colours, decorated plastic laminate and unconventional forms.

Sottsass' well-known contributions include the "Casablanca" sideboard and the "Carlton" sideboard – the latter being a tall storage unit that also acted as a room divider. Memphis, whose co-exhibitors included a number of influential designers from beyond Italy's borders – among them Javier Mariscal (see pp.250–51), Shiro Kuramata (see pp.240–41), Hans Hollein, Arata Isozaki and Michael Graves (see pp.236–7) – marked a turning point in modern design, offering an open and international challenge to the precepts of Modernism.

LATER CAREER AND IMPACT ON YOUNGER DESIGNERS

Memphis also marked a turning point in Sottsass' career; at the age of 64 it was a clear statement of his mature philosophy, and his reputation was enhanced as a result. Throughout the 1980s and early 1990s Sottsass went from strength to strength, working for many international clients including Knoll, Cleto Munari and Artemide, and finding a new freedom to work in a personal way, both in his designs for clients and in private experiments.

He made designs for glass, working with craftsmen in the workshops of Murano; for the first time in years he was also involved in architecture, designing (among other projects) the Wall House for a client in Colorado (1986–90). Many young designers travelled to Milan to work with him, and he continued to find inspiration in his own visits to ever more exotic and distant places. In 1994 a large exhibition of Sottsass' work at the Pompidou Centre, Paris confirmed his role as a key designer of the 20th century.

Sottsass designed the "Casablanca" sideboard (below) for the first Memphis show in 1981; it is one of the best known of all his pieces, and an icon of Post-modern design. The sideboard's powerful silhouette suggests some kind of space-age robot; the surface is covered with an Abet-Print plastic laminate printed with Sottsass' "Bacterio" pattern.

Modernism in crisis

In the 1960s several factors combined to lead to a dramatic shift in cultural values and a challenge to Modernism. The advent of mass consumerism, the emergence of a youth market, and a general sense of economic and technological optimism developed into what was known as the "Pop Revolution". Its aspirations – fun, change, variety, irreverence, wit and disposability – were reflected most clearly in new forms of popular music, as well as in fashion. This change was also reflected within the design community. Both focused on renouncing the values of the previous generation, which, in the context of design, were represented by Modernism. New designers sought a more expressive approach that could accommodate the more democratic values of the new age: a design movement that, as the British graphic designer Michael Wolff put it, would "swing like the Supremes".

British fashion designer Mary Quant, at the 1967 launch of her "Quant Afoot" collection of boots (left). Quant was a pioneer in providing the newly affluent female youth market of the early 1960s with clothes that suited the values associated with fun and expendability.

Biba sold clothes imbued with 19th-century nostalgia. The shop's interior (right) evoked Art Nouveau, one of the first period styles to be brought back in the wave of revivalism that came as a result of disillusionment with Modernism.

The logo of the Biba shop (below), designed by John McConnell in 1968. The soft forms of the letters, and the Celtic/Art Nouveau-style graphics, clearly located Biba in the era of 1960s Pop revivalism.

BRITAIN

In Britain, Pop influenced fashion, graphics, furniture and interior design. Mary Quant (above) dominated the first of these categories; in 1955 she opened her shop Bazaar in the King's Road, London, which soon became a Mecca for Pop fashions. In 1963 she launched the Ginger Group, a mass-production clothing company that "brought Quant styling into the price range of every typist and shop-girl"; she also ventured into interior design.

Retail design also reflected the new, irreverent, fun mood. For the shoe shop Mr Freedom, in Kensington, Jon Wealleans created a radically different interior that looked like a brightly coloured children's play area; while the Granny Takes a Trip boutique in the King's Road (opposite, below right) featured the front half of an American automobile thrusting itself out of the shop window, to the surprise of passers-by. Other interior designers – among them Max Clendenning – provided Pop-inspired public and private spaces, and boutiques sprang up across London with their interiors and painted façades proving that shopping could be fun.

The "Spotty" child's chair (1963; above) was made of polyethylene-coated laminated paperboard. It came in a flat pack ready for construction at home, and was an icon of throwaway Pop design. The chair was created by the British furniture designer Peter Murdoch while he was still a student at the Royal College of Art in London.

Furniture designs of the era abandoned security and status in favour of the throwaway ethic. The "Spotty" child's chair, designed in 1963 by Peter Murdoch, was made of paperboard covered with an Op Art polka-dot pattern, and came in a flat pack for home construction (above, right). Although in theory the ultimate throwaway object, it was coated with plastic laminate and, ironically, lasted for a considerable amount of time. Roger Dean designed a fun-fur-covered inflatable pouffe for Hille which, although not literally expendable, could at least be deflated. British Pop design even found its own critic and apologist in the architectural historian Peter Reyner Banham, who sang its praises in *New Society*; the movement's contribution to architecture was provided — if only in theoretical, utopian schemes — by the Archigram team of architects and designers, founded in 1963, which included Peter Cook and Warren Chalk (see p.223).

The façade of the boutique Granny Takes a Trip (right) in London. The car was visible bursting out of the shop window for several weeks before being replaced by another spectacle, proving that the impact of Pop lay in its expendability and ephemerality.

GRANNY TAKES A TRIP

ITALIAN AND INTERNATIONAL ANTI-MODERNISM

In Italy the Pop movement was less an answer to the demands of a new consumer market than an ideological response to the prominent Italian neo-modern design movement. After 1966 a new generation of architect-designers attempted to sever their links with mainstream industrial manufacture and to use design as a political tool. Groups of designers – among them Superstudio (formed in Florence in 1966, with Adolfo Natalini, Cristiano Toraldo di Francia, Gian Pietro Frassinelli, Alessandro Magris, Roberto Magris and Alessandro Poli), Archizoom (Florence, 1966, with Andrea Branzi, Gilberto Corretti, Paolo Deganello, Massimo Morozzi, Dario Bartolini and Lucia Bartolini), Gruppo Strum (Turin, 1966) and Gruppo 9999 (Florence, 1968) – chose to work as collectives and began to create visionary environments and furniture conveying their radical ideas.

Such groups were all inspired by the work of Ettore Sottsass (see pp.216–19). Exhibitions in Milan of his furniture and ceramic pieces inspired by Pop culture and Indian mysticism were beacons for a new generation that sought to undermine establishment values. The movement in general came to be known as "Anti-design", and it actively employed all the design values negated by Modernism, including ephemerality, irony and kitsch. A handful of manufacturers ventured into production. Zanotta, for example, produced the transparent, inflatable "Blow" chair – designed by De Pas,

The cover of the magazine Archigram (issue 4, 1967; above) published by the London Pop architectural group of the same name (formed 1963). Its members included Peter Cook and Warren Chalk, who were fascinated by the aesthetics of Pop – especially those derived from comic books and science-fiction imagery. They created a number of fantasy architectural schemes (as drawings only) focusing on these visual themes.

These "Up 2" armchairs (1969; left), designed as part of a series of six by Gaetano Pesce and produced by C&B Italia (later to become B&B Italia), expanded on release from their flat PVC packaging. This piece was inspired by a woman's body, and was named "Donna"; it was the partner of the "Up 6", a round hassock envisaged as a ball and attached to the woman's feet.

D'Urbino and Lomazzi – in 1967; and the "Sacco" seat – a soft-skinned leather or vinyl bag filled with polystyrene pellets that shaped itself to the sitter's body, designed by Piero Gatti , Cesare Paolini and Franco Teodoro – in 1968. Other icons of Italian Pop design were Gaetano Pesce's "Up" series of inflatable chairs (see pp.224–5 and left); and Piero Gilardi's "I Sassi" (The Rocks), a set of seats manufactured by Gufram in 1967 that looked hard but were made of soft polyurethane foam and sank under the sitter's weight. Giorgio Ceretti, Piero Derossi and Riccardo Rossi used the same strategy in their "Tornerai" (You'll Come Back) armchair (1969), also made by Gufram, as did Archizoom in the somewhat sacrilegious "Mies" armchair (1969), made by Poltronova, which uniquely combined geometry and softness; this had a hard, metal frame and a flat rubber seat that "gave" under the sitter's weight.

By the end of the 1960s antimodernism had become an international concept. In Germany, for example, in the mid-1960s, the graphic designer Ingo Maurer produced a number of witty Anti-design lights. In 1980 he produced "Bulb Bulb", a giant light bulb inspired – as were so many designs in these years – by the American Pop sculptor Claes Oldenburg. In Finland, Eero Arnio designed a bright yellow "Ball" chair (1965, produced by Asko). In the United States the architect Robert Venturi criticized the rigid formalism of Modernism in his book *Complexity and Contradiction in Architecture* (1966), and thus provided the movement with a manifesto.

THE SIGNIFICANCE OF POP

By the end of the 1970s the concept of Postmodernism (see pp.238–9) was fully fledged. Although by its very nature Pop design lacked the gravitas of Modernism and provided only a handful of enduring icons and ideas, it was a significant and influential movement. In essence, it provided a means of transcending a stifling conservatism that – although originally based within a truly revolutionary movement – had come to exclude innovative, stimulating mass-produced design. Pop redressed that situation and injected a new vitality and ideology into post-war design.

This bed (below) – designed by the Italian "Anti-design" group Archizoom in 1967 – was one of a set of miniature models that was never produced. The pieces utilized a number of kitsch strategies – including Hollywood styling and references to Pop culture – to undermine the "good taste" of Modernism.

The "Blow" chair – an unprecedented completely inflatable plastic chair – was designed by the Italian firm of De Pas, D'Urbino and Lomazzi in 1967, and made by Zanotta. The immediate popularity of this fun, collapsible furniture inspired numerous versions by other makers, such as the example shown above.

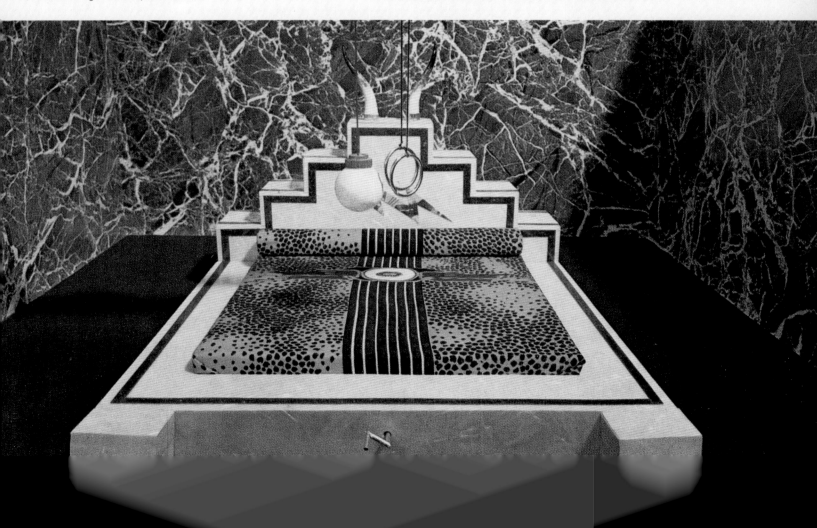

Gaetano Pesce (b.1939) has been one of the most enigmatic designers of the 20th century and, since the mid-1960s, one of the most consistently radical. Working on the borders of fine art, architecture and design, he has been an irritant to mainstream practice, inspiring several generations of young designers to question establishment values.

Gaetano Pesce

Pesce has achieved this less through deliberate provocation than through his creative and intellectual forays into uncharted areas. His originality derives from a liking for soft objects and environments, and from an organic approach that uses new materials to explore decorative and tactile possibilities rather than to create a monolithic view of the future.

The Italian Gaetano Pesce has been one of the most fascinating and consistently radical designers of the second half of the 20th century. Since the 1960s he has regularly challenged the assumptions underpinning modern design, producing many stimulating and highly idiosyncratic objects in the process.

The "Up 5" chair (below) was part of series of six pieces produced by C&B Italia in 1969. Pesce explored the creation of voluptuous shapes through the use of polyurethane moulded foam covered in tightly stretched nylon jersey.

EARLY TRAINING

Pesce was born in La Spezia, Italy, in 1939. He studied graphic design in Padua, and architecture and design in Venice (1959–65), where he spent the early years of his career. In 1959 he was a founder member of Gruppo N, a team of fine artists based in Padua who espoused the idea of programmed art that derived from rational principles outlined at the Bauhaus in the 1920s. He participated in a number of artistic activities with a range of similar groups in Germany (Gruppo Zero) and Paris (Motus) in the early 1960s, but by the mid-1960s he had become disillusioned with the role of fine art in contemporary society and turned towards design as a means of expressing his radical ideas. This change of direction coincided with the work of the Italian "anti-designers" based in Venice and elsewhere (see pp.222–3), and Pesce worked closely with Gruppo Strum, Ugo La Pietra and others participating in happenings and performances.

DESIGN CAREER

Pesce's design career began in the mid-1960s, and in 1969 C&B (later B&B) Italia manufactured the six designs that comprised his "Up" series. One of the most successful was his "Up 5 Donna" armchair, based on the shape of the female body, and his "Up 6" hassock, which was connected to the armchair by a chain (left). Both were made of high-density polyurethane foam covered in bright red stretch nylon, and came as a compressed flat pack which inflated and sprang into shape when the PVC wrapper was opened. The design worked on a number of levels; it was both a political comment on the status of women (the round hassock represented a ball and chain) and a Pop statement about disposability.

Pesce has subsequently continued to use designed objects as a means of personal expression. The "Moloch" floor lamp (1970) – a surreal enlargement of the familiar Anglepoise desk lamp – was followed by a range of other designs, many of them manufactured by Cassina (see pp.212–13). These included the "Carenza" bookcase (1972; opposite, above left); the fibreglass "Golgotha" tables and chairs (1973); the quilt-covered

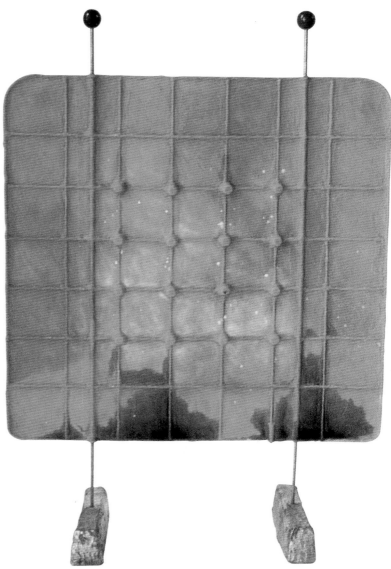

The "Carenza" bookshelf (1972; above). With its craggy unfinished edges it shows that Pesce's vision was far removed from the clean machine-inspired forms of the early Modernists. It was displayed at the Italian design exhibition at the Museum of Modern Art in New York in 1972, and again in 1975 at the Musée des Arts Décoratifs in Paris.

Made of flexible urethane, the "Square" lamp (1986; right) has 16 small bulbs arranged in spreading rectangles within the square, so that the whole plane is illuminated.

The "Seaweed" rag armchair (1992; below). The appearance of this voluptuous sitting-object incorporating "found" waste materials challenges the sleek forms of Modernism.

"Sit-down" armchairs (1975), which were made of Dacron-filled upholstery over polyurethane foam, and resembled padded covers thrown freely over armchairs; the "Sansone" tables and "Dalila" chairs (1980); the "Tramonto a New York" (New York Sunset) sofa (1980), which consists of a bright red vinyl-covered sun setting over cube-shaped cushions that imitate the Manhattan skyline; the thermo-formed Vittel mineral water bottle (1986); felt furniture (1987); experiments in glass (1990; above right); and an enormous range of designs in coloured resin (early 1990s). All of these pieces are clearly informed by a particular vision and sensibility, and all explore the problem of individuality within mass production.

Pesce has a highly international profile. He was based in Paris for a number of years but now works from an office in New York, where he participated in the exhibition entitled "Italy: The New Domestic Landscape", held at the Museum of Modern Art in 1972. Although design is only one of his many activities – he has been involved in architecture, audio-visual presentations, teaching (in Strasbourg, New York and elsewhere) and a number of other creative arenas – it has become his most successful. From his intellectual and creative roots in the Italian rejection of Modernism in the mid-1960s, Pesce has become one of the key post-war designers.

Towards the Millennium

Towards the Millennium

With the 1970s came an end to the domination of a single international design movement. While on the one hand Modernism continued to come under attack and to be widely discredited, on the other hand latter-day Modernists set out to prove the validity of this movement and to persuade us that, even with changing economic, social and cultural conditions, the impulse of technological progress would lead us into a bright future.

As with early Modernism the hottest debate took place within the world of architecture, with design following. The discussion about Postmodernism and its relation to material culture was stimulated by the work of American architects such as Robert Venturi and Michael Graves (see pp.236–7), who made cases for influences from pop culture and for stylistic revivalism, whether of the classical past or of Art Deco motifs. What was clear from the debates that accompanied critiques of their work was that, stylistically at least, alternatives to Modernism were in place and that the most important theme of the last three decades of the century was going to be pluralism – the fact that no one single architectural or design theory or approach was going to be pre-eminent any longer. This open-endedness echoed the fragmentation of western society and the emergence of what came to be called "niche markets". Postmodern architecture reflected this diversity. In Great Britain it adopted a conservative approach in the nostalgic neoclassicism of Quinlan Terry and Terry Farrell, whereas in France and Spain it was more forward-looking.

While architects discussed the valid style of the day, rather like their 19th-century predecessors, designers in the 1970s also had other things to consider. These included the effect of the oil crisis on the cost of plastics and society's growing interest in ecological issues such as recycling. These took the emphasis away from the debate about style and suggested a more serious social role for designers in terms of their relationship with the manufacturing industry. The general sense of a developing disillusionment with technology and all that it had promised also threatened to undermine the very premise on which modern design had been established.

All these fears and anxieties were temporarily forgotten, however, when in the early 1980s design showed that it was as capable as architecture of raising its cultural profile and becoming a central focus of discussion. The catalyst for the new popular awareness of design emanated, not surprisingly, from Italy. The Memphis exhibition, held in Milan in 1981 to coincide with the city's annual furniture fair, was a turning point. With the help of his young colleagues, and with support from sympathetic non-Italians as well, Ettore Sottsass (see pp.216–9) blasted the international design establishment with a show of objects that turned all the familiar values upside down. The Memphis designs for furniture and related items were brightly coloured, decorated and eccentrically shaped with countless visual references to past styles. For the first time design, without the crutch of architecture, was proclaiming itself to be free from the restraints of Modernism and in tune with the post-industrial age. The impact was felt internationally and such was the liberating effect of this event that

individuals in many other countries – including France, Spain, Germany, Holland, Great Britain, Czechoslovakia and Japan – aligned themselves to what Sottsass himself dubbed "the New Design".

Called "the designer decade", the 1980s enjoyed another worldwide consumer boom and the now fully democratic concept of design took on a new meaning in the context of this affluence. The word "designer" was tagged to any commodity that promoted itself as special, from hairdressers to jeans. In the mass-market context of the late 20th century the term "designer" implied a level of individualism and taste that was reassuring to people who wanted to be different. While this may have been just a new marketing strategy, one side effect was the popularization of the concept of design and of designers. Designers became celebrities along the lines of the American industrial designers of the 1930s. Not only Europe, but also Japan and increasingly Korea, Singapore and Taiwan were learning the benefits of having an advanced design culture. In this diverse climate many different styles were on offer, from the radical post-Memphis experiments, to the more serious High-Tech style, which encouraged the use of industrial materials in a non-industrial context. Some companies, such as the Italian metalware firm Alessi, prioritized design over all else, commissioning celebrity designers to create objects for them that rapidly achieved cult status. Design culture spread, and institutions such as the Design Museum in London, which opened in the mid-1980s, provided its public face.

While these developments succeeded in giving the designer a higher profile, granting him or her a place in the cultural hierarchy alongside fine artists and architects, it also had the effect of aligning the concept of design very closely with advertising and marketing. The effect of this was to underplay its more fundamental role as an element within the production process and as part of the everyday material environment. When the bubble finally burst and designer culture, along with the economy, took a downward turn at the beginning of the 1990s, designers had to think of ways of overcoming the superficiality that had characterized the 1980s.

The liberating effects of the early 1980s were still felt and it was possible for designers to work outside Modernism, now with a more mature set of alternative models at their disposal. Equally, however, the values inherited from the early century came back into focus as some designers recognized the continuing significance of these early ideals. Now there were no contradictions, because, with no dominant design theory to react against, each approach could be judged on its own merits. Some designers still wanted a level of celebrity, some preferred a more behind-the-scenes approach. Most understood ecological imperatives and incorporated them into their visions. Above all the design world at the end of the 20th century became global, with an awareness that it was no longer possible to think just in terms of local or national identities. From modest beginnings in the hands of a few individuals who sought to create an improved material world that reflected the modern age, design had blossomed into a force affecting nearly every aspect of modern life.

The American Bar in the Felix
Discotheque at the Peninsula Hotel,
Hong Kong. The bar and the discotheque
were designed by Philippe Starck in
1993. The expressive, dramatic and
almost fantastical forms of the interior
fittings characterize Starck's work,
and mark him out as a leading figure
in a decade that has adopted a
number of quite different strategies
and approaches to design.

Of the generation of "super-designers" who made such a dramatic impact in the design-conscious 1980s, the German Richard Sapper (b.1932) is among the most respected by his fellow designers and other members of the extended design community across the globe. His ability to work beyond geographical frontiers – combining the best

Richard Sapper

of German rational practice with Italian confidence and experience – has marked him out as a significant figure in the last decades of the 20th century, and the way in which he combines consistent rigour, originality and flair with a confident handling of new and complex technologies has earned him an enviable reputation.

Richard Sapper has provided a model for product design that combines the rational approach of his homeland with Italian flair and originality. His work with companies as diverse as IBM and Alessi has shown his ability to create objects ranging from computers to cooking pots with equal commitment and integrity.

The "Tizio" low-voltage light (1972; below) is technically innovative – it can be repositioned with a slight hand pressure – and sophisticated – its simple matt-black sculptural form gives it a presence that exceeds its physical components.

TRAINING AND EARLY WORK

Sapper studied philosophy, anatomy, graphic art, mechanical engineering and finally economics at the university in his native city of Munich (1952–6). In 1956 he began work in the styling office of Daimler Benz in Stuttgart, thereby entering into a world in which engineering and aesthetics were of paramount importance. His life-changing move to Italy came in 1958 when he began work for the Ponti-Rosselli architectural practice in Milan, which involved him in important projects in that city. (These had included the Pirelli office tower, completed two years before his arrival.) Sapper was influenced here by his experience working alongside Gio Ponti (see pp.138–41). In 1959 he left Ponti-Rosselli to work in the design department of Milan's Rinascente department store, where he designed a number of household items, including a hair dryer.

WORK WITH ZANUSO

It was in the crucial year 1959 that Sapper met Marco Zanuso (see pp.196–7), marking the start of a collaboration that would produce many icons of Italian modernity through the 1960s and 1970s. The lessons learned from his time with Zanuso have stayed with and benefited Sapper throughout his working life. The two designers worked on some remarkable high-technology products, including an all-plastic child's chair for the plastics manufacturer Kartell (designed from the late 1950s onwards but not produced until 1964), which doubled as a construction toy (opposite, below); a wide range of highly styled electronic goods for Brionvega (makers of audio-visual equipment), including the "Doney" television set (1962), the "TS502" portable radio (1969; see p.232, above) and the "Black" television set (1970); a sewing machine and a knife sharpener for Necchi (1962 and 1975 respectively); and the compact Grillo telephone (1967).

As well as being "state of the art" in technological terms, it was their sophisticated housings, their well-conceived and attractive control panels, and their strong visual emphasis on function that gave these products an edge over their competitors in the international marketplace.

The "Rocket" digital clock (left) has been manufactured by Ritz Italora since 1971. The simplicity of this product – which has become a familiar object in many different environments in Italy and elsewhere – is characteristic of the designer's work.

The all-plastic child's stacking chair (below), on which Sapper worked with Marco Zanuso from the late 1950s, and which finally went into production by Kartell in the mid-1960s. The chair was one of a generation of plastic objects manufactured in Italy at that time that helped to earn this modern material a new level of "authenticity".

INCREASING SUCCESS

Sapper returned to Germany in 1972 and opened his own studio in Munich. The next stage of his career was ushered in by his design of a low-voltage lamp for the Italian company Artemide. Matt-black, minimal in form and incorporating not only a new look but also a new mode of operation – the subtle balancing mechanism within the lamp allowed its position to be altered by the merest touch of the hand – "Tizio" quickly became a widely publicized cult object, making an appearance in advertisements and representations of interiors whenever an image of modernity and sophistication was required (see p.230). Its elegant and dramatic profile, and visual appropriateness in the minimal interiors of both modern domestic and office environments, made it the perfect neo-modern object. In recognition of this success, the lamp received numerous international design awards, including the Compasso d'Oro design prize in 1979.

Sapper followed up this highly successful design with work in collaboration with the Italian architect Gae Aulenti on new systems of transportation, and on experimental designs for a new car for Fiat, the "Softmore 126X". However, it was with his work for the progressive metal-manufacturing company, Alessi, that Sapper finally entered the realm of the "super-designer".

The "TS502" (1969; above), designed by Sapper and Zanuso for Brionvega, is a compact radio that closes up to conceal its control mechanisms and resembles a small geometric cube with soft corners. Only the handle – which also retracts into the body – remains visible. Though simple in form, the radio was produced in several bright colours.

ALESSI: BEYOND MODERNISM

Sapper's first design for Alessi was the elegant "Cafetière 9090" (1978). Taking as his basis the workings of the company's older "Moka" espresso coffee-maker, he created a new sculptural housing for the product that transformed it almost beyond recognition. It was not only visually appealing but highly practical, with the machine's heavy base and solid metal shape giving what had been a rather dangerous design a new level of safety as it came to the boil on the hob.

The coffee-maker's popular impact – although strong – was subsequently surpassed by another of Sapper's creations for Alessi: the "Bollitore" kettle. Designed in 1983, at the high point of what has been described as the "designer decade", this product was an unprecedented triumph and succeeded in bringing the concept of design within the reach of a larger audience than ever before. Bought more, perhaps, to adorn shelves than to be used for boiling water, this highly original object – with its shiny domed body, "cox-comb" handle and high-pitched whistle – passed way beyond the limits imposed by the rules of rational Modernism. Imbued with cultural resonance and artistic significance, the kettle succeeded in evoking the spirit of the 1980s concept of design. It quickly became a model for other designers searching for a strategy that would extend the relatively simple formula of "utility plus beauty" into a new postmodern arena by transforming the designed object into a subject for the mass media and for

The "Sapperchair" (left), designed for Knoll in 1979, was a characteristically minimal solution to the problem of office seating. It rejected the complex mechanisms and "body-sculpting" of many of its contemporaries, instead combining comfortable yet light upholstery with only the most essential means of adjustment (for example, height).

design-conscious retail outlets in a way not seen before. As one critic commented, it seemed as though design had become the "art of the late twentieth century" – at least in the hands of Sapper.

The collaboration between Sapper and Alessi developed into a long relationship, and the result was a range of other highly successful products emerging through the 1980s and 1990s. These included cooking pots (1986), a teapot (1995), trays (1995) and a set of cutlery (1995). The last of these was the final realization of a project that Alberto Alessi had asked Sapper to undertake on first meeting him in 1977; the long development period was characteristic of the company's determination to get a design right in every detail before it went into manufacture.

Sapper's wooden desk for Unifor (right), which closes into itself when the flap is lifted, was produced in 1988. It serves as an example of the designer's work at the low-technology end of the spectrum and shows how, even in this traditional area, he was still interested in creating simple geometrical forms and producing objects whose appearance was determined by their function.

A design by Richard Sapper for a spaghetti fork (left; 1994), one of a series that he produced for a set of flatware for Alessi. These and other pieces of his work from the 1990s showed the influence of postmodern ideas, which emphasized the expressive and symbolic roles of an object as much as its practical role.

The "Leapfrog" computer (1992; below), designed for IBM by Sapper in collaboration with Samuel Lucente. Sapper has worked as an industrial design consultant to IBM from 1981, participating in the decision-making relating to all its products. As a result the company has consistently produced elegant, minimal objects designed to be as visually unobtrusive as possible.

LATER WORK

As well as collaborating closely with Alessi, Sapper worked with other companies; in 1981 he became an industrial-design consultant to IBM, providing the firm with a number of important products including a portable computer (1986), a personal computer (1991) and the "Leapfrog" computer (1992; left). Each of these products was highly minimal, and characterized by unobtrusiveness and simple elegance. In this respect they retained obvious stylistic links with the work of the early Modernists, but were not constrained by their strict Functionalism.

By the 1990s Sapper had become a giant among industrial designers worldwide, and continued to work for a number of long-standing clients such as Artemide and Alessi. In doing so he has shown that his versatility marked him out as one of the century's most wide-ranging and impressive designers who could not only understand and provide a lasting visual image for the world of advanced electronic technology but who, at the same time, could still respond to the seemingly much simpler challenge of designing everyday objects from teapots to sets of cutlery.

Bořek Šípek (b.1949) is one of the key disseminators of a new sensuousness in design that emerged in the late 1980s and the 1990s. Unconstrained by the order, the geometry and the all-pervading rationalism and purity of earlier Modernism, Šípek has displayed an unreserved openness to the possibilities of decoration, symbolism,

Bořek Šípek

poetry, and personal and collective expression in his design of the "applied art" objects that make up the environment of the late 20th century — whether they be furniture pieces or ceramic, glass or metal items. Everyday objects are transformed by his unique eye, his exuberance and his seemingly limitless imagination.

Bořek Šípek is one of the most overtly decorative designers working in the 1990s. While clearly belonging in the late 20th century, his work also recalls Baroque and Rococo styles.

Šípek's "Sedlak" office desk (below), made of solid wood, laminated wood and steel, was manufactured by Vitra in 1992. The curved form, jagged edges, turned legs and conical waste-bin look eccentric, but the desk is in fact a highly ergonomic design that wraps around its user, with everything in easy reach.

TRAINING AND EARLY WORK

Bořek Šípek (b.1949) is a product of the "new Europe". He was born in Prague but – especially following the opening up of Eastern Europe in the late 1980s – his life has been characterized by movement. He studied at the School of Applied Arts in Prague in 1969, and continued his education over the next ten years, studying architecture at the High School of Fine Arts in Hamburg; philosophy in Stuttgart; and architecture again in Delft. Between 1979 and 1983 he taught design theory at the University of Essen.

EXTRAVAGANCE AND NOVELTY

Since 1983 he has lived and worked in Amsterdam. In 1984, with designer David Palterer, Šípek founded the Amsterdam-based company Alterego, which subsequently put many of his extravagant designs into production. From the mid-1980s Šípek has devoted much energy to working on glass objects, many made by hand in Nový Bor in the Czech Republic, or in Murano in Venice. He has evolved a new expressive language of form and colour, using mythological imagery, that goes beyond the world of the everyday into that of myth and magic. The ideas of ceremony and ritual (for example, an emphasis on eating) pervade his pieces. Šípek has explained that he sees his wild, fantastic forms as a kind of "trace" of a new feeling for design, one that is about emotions and behaviour rather than mere utility.

The "Sedlak" chair (below), designed for Vitra in 1992. The chair's expressive form is a recognizable part of Šípek's personal language of design. For recycling purposes, the elements of the chair can be dismantled and its parts exchanged, a feature that is appearing increasingly in late 20th-century product designs.

Furniture underwent a similar transformation in Šípek's hands. Pieces for Driade in Italy, Vitra in Germany, Gallery Néotu in France and Leitner in Austria were created from a wide range of materials – including rattan, leather, patterned woods and brass – in the designer's relentless search for novelty of form and imagery. While some pieces, such as his rattan chairs for Driade, were voluptuous and anthropomorphic in nature – Šípek even named one chair "Helena" to make overt its links with the female body – others were more medieval in inspiration, such as a little chair named "Ernst and Guduld", made by Néotu in the late 1980s in ebony, padouk and maple, which evoked a jester's hat.

Neither did interiors escape Šípek's influence; he was responsible for transforming Amsterdam's Daybreak coffee shop in 1989, and the Shoebaloo shoe store (above) in the same city two years later. However, it is perhaps as a designer of table-top items that he has really given his imagination free rein. His drinking glasses resemble objects from outer space, his cutlery exhibits forms never before imagined for the purpose of eating food (right), and his bowls and plates are equally unexpected.

Despite the characteristic extravagance and novelty of Šípek's designs, a sense of practicality is not entirely absent from his work, especially in the area of recycling. For example, he designed his cast-aluminium and stained-beech "Sedlak" chair (1992; left) so that it could be dismantled for recycling purposes. Šípek's hallmarks, however, are his originality and freedom of expression, and he has played a vital role as a catalyst enabling design to escape from the straitjacket of the High-Tech style (using industrial materials such as metal and glass in the domestic setting). In 1990, in recognition of his contribution to European design, he was made Professor of Architecture at the Academy of Arts in Prague, a return to his roots.

The Shoebaloo shop in Amsterdam (1991; above). Šípek added to the shop's basic function by including quirky mirror-frames and furniture items with his own idiosyncratic forms; he also exploited the light passing through the wall of small windows in order to create expressive effects on the ceiling.

"Argentomania" (below), a silver dessert cutlery service (signed and numbered ed.3), was designed for the Dutch company Steltman in 1995. Šípek has exaggerated familiar forms to include unusual pointed handles and noticeable ridges where the handles join the implement part of each piece.

A few late 20th-century architects and designers deliberately associated themselves with the Postmodern movement, including the American architect and designer Michael Graves (b.1934). Like the architect Robert Venturi, Graves publicly declared the necessity for design to move beyond Modernism. He saw this as essential, owing to the

Michael Graves

failure of Modernism to cater to the consumer's requirement for designed objects to express — through means such as colour, form, texture and pattern — the cultural values that surround them and give them meaning.

A leading member of the group of American Postmodern architects who came to public attention in the 1970s, Michael Graves is also known for his designs for objects, through which he expressed ideas about the meaning of contemporary material culture. His contribution to the Italian Memphis movement in the 1980s, for instance, and his ceramics for Swid Powell have made him a potent design force.

"Corinth" (below), a ceramic place setting designed for Swid Powell in 1984. The references to the Classical past — both in the product name and in the light, elegant surface patterns — illustrate Graves' Postmodern vision, which incorporated a high level of Neo-Classicism.

ARCHITECTURAL BACKGROUND AND FIRST DESIGNS

Graves was born in Minneapolis and studied architecture at the University of Cincinnati, graduating in 1959. After a year's postgraduate work in the Graduate School of Design at Harvard University, he studied at the American Academy in Rome (1960–62), and taught architecture at Princeton University, New Jersey, from 1962. Two years later he set up his own architectural practice. His early work was inspired by art-historical models — Classicism and Cubism in particular — the understanding of which enabled him to master the use of form and colour.

In the early 1970s Graves was a member of the "New York Five" group of Postmodern architects that also included Richard Meier, John Hejduk, Peter Eisenman and Charles Gwathmay. Graves's early reputation was based on drawings, and it was not until 1982, with the completion of his openly Postmodernist Public Services Building in Portland, Oregon, that he expressed his ideas in three-dimensional architectural form. Prior to this, he had made forays into furniture design with a collection, in 1977, for the progressive American company Sunar Hauserman. In 1981 he contributed a design for a Hollywood Deco-inspired dressing-table, named "Plaza", to Ettore Sottsass' Memphis project (see pp.216–19), thereby helping to add an international flavour to the "New Design" that was presented in Milan.

WORK WITH ALESSI

In 1985 Graves began his collaboration with the Italian company Alessi, which had already ventured into Postmodernism with Richard Sapper's (see pp.230–33) "Bollitore" kettle two years earlier. Graves' design was even more whimsical and oriented towards culture rather than utility. A small plastic bird sat on the spout, which whistled when water came to the boil. It was at once a playful and radical design in that it introduced the concepts of narrative and metaphor into a mass-produced object. More than 500,000 were sold and the kettle became a Postmodern design classic.

Graves went on to design more pieces for Alessi, including a salt-and-pepper set (mid-1980s), a set of trays (1990–91), and a cruet set (1994). He and ten other architect-designers each produced a tea-service for Alessi's 1983 "Tea and Coffee Piazza" project, which was aimed at cultural

institutions such as museums rather than at the buying public. This clever marketing strategy was intended to inject a level of "added value" into Alessi's products. Many of the 1980s "super-designers" – including Robert Venturi, Aldo Rossi and Charles Jencks – worked on the project.

Graves' output was prolific in the 1980s, including ceramics for the American firm Swid Powell (1984), furniture for Sawaya & Moroni (1985), a watch for Cleto Munari in Italy (1987) and carpet designs for the German company Vorwerke's "Dialog" collection (1988). He was so successful that he opened his own retail outlet in Princeton in 1993, the year in which he acknowledged his debt to popular culture with the "Mickey Mouse" teapot. He also worked on architectural projects, including the Swan Hotel in Orlando, Florida (1990), and an addition to the Whitney Museum of American Art in New York (1989–90). His range spanned high culture to popular culture, and he has influenced many of the younger generation of Postmodernist designers.

One of the "V'soske" range of rugs (1979–80; left). Inspired by Art Deco textiles, this design bears witness to Graves' interest in colour; the light terracotta has exactly the same tonal quality as the bird's-egg blue used to offset it. This interest marks yet another of the ways in which Graves moved beyond the restrictions imposed by Modernism.

The geometric form and restrained pattern of the "Big Dripper" sugar bowl and creamer (above; 1986), designed for Swid Powell, is reminiscent of American Art Deco as well as Wiener Werkstätte and Bauhaus designs. This deliberate stylistic revivalism – modified to suit the late 20th century – and the pun in the title are both aspects of the eclecticism and love of irony characteristic of Graves and his Postmodern contemporaries.

The living room – complete with mural – of the Hanselmann House in Fort Wayne, Indiana (1968–70; right). It was not until the early 1970s that Graves began to abandon his Modernist roots, and chairs in this interior – with their tubular steel frames and black leather upholstery – show his dependence on ideas developed at the Bauhaus 40 years earlier.

Postmodernism

The dominant international design movement of the 1970s and 1980s was known as "Postmodernism", describing a style that went against the idea that "form follows function" and emphasized the symbolic roles of an object as well as its practical purpose. The term had been used in architectural theory since the 1970s, but Charles Jencks' *The Language of Postmodern Architecture* (1980) brought it to a wider public for the first time.

THE BEGINNINGS OF POSTMODERNISM

The roots of Postmodernism in fact went back to the 1960s, when the first doubts about the continuing viability of Modernism (see pp.220–23) were becoming apparent. The values associated with the youth-oriented Pop revolution – fun, expendability and individual expression – ran counter to the high-minded, high-cultural ideals of the early part of the century. In 1966 the American architect Robert Venturi's seminal text *Complexity and Contradiction in Architecture* (1966) pointed out the inadequacies of Modernism in the new, multi-faceted culture. Debates raged in the 1970s and 1980s as to whether Postmodernism was an evolution of Modernism, or a wholesale attack on its very essence.

In Italy, for example, the work of the Milan-based design groups Studio Alchimia from the mid-1970s and Memphis from the early 1980s showed all the signs of being Postmodern, in that it embraced historical references, adopted a popular cultural baseline, was openly eclectic, acknowledged the importance of consumer aspirations, and, above all, used the language of form, colour, pattern and texture. Ever-optimistic and forward-looking (rather than "retro" or nostalgic) in essence, Memphis avoided the epithet "Postmodern", preferring the term "New International Style".

POSTMODERNISM ACROSS THE WORLD

By the 1980s, whether or not the term "Postmodernism" was explicitly used, an international movement in design based on its concepts was very much in evidence. In Finland, for example, the former modernist Yryo Kukkapuro abandoned his cool chrome and steel in favour of brightly coloured expressive forms in a range of furniture pieces designed in the

A maquette for an electric fire (below), which was one of a series of models for "elettrodomestici" (household electrical goods) produced for Girmi by the Italian architect-designer Michele De Lucchi (see pp.252–3) in the early 1980s. The intention of the project was to undermine the aggressive black-and-chrome forms of product Modernism and to replace them with softer shapes and expressive colours.

Experimental chairs (below), designed by the Finn Yryo Kukkapuro for Avarte in the early 1980s. His earlier work had been characterized by a late-modern slickness and use of materials such as black leather and tubular steel, but he changed direction to explore the possibilities of colour and expressive form that were in sympathy with the new Postmodern style.

James Dyson's pink "Cyclone" vacuum-cleaner (left), designed in the early 1980s (but not put fully into production until several years later), was clearly a reaction to streamlined, black-and-chrome earlier models that had been produced within the context of "popular Modernism". The complex shape and pastel shades of this cleaner were clearly signalling a new direction in design, although they were accompanied by a progressive attitude towards technology that could be interpreted as more modern than Postmodern.

early 1980s (opposite, right); in Spain Javier Mariscal (see pp.250–51) deliberately worked outside the Modernist canon; and in Britain Daniel Weil's transparent radio of 1981 (see p.202), with its exposed electronic circuitry, readdressed the old adage that "form follows function".

Japan, the home of the electronic consumer product, moved into the field of "consumer" design with enormous energy, producing a wide range of objects that embraced the Pop ideals of fun and expression. From Sharp's "QT50" 1950s-revival radio cassette player (right) to National Panasonic's expressive television sets and Sony's colourful Walkman (see pp.180–81), the Japanese enthusiastically took to Postmodernism, entering into it less on a theoretical than on an overtly commercial level.

A wave of consumer-oriented products swamped the marketplace in the 1980s. A design movement that had begun, theoretically, to embrace the concept of commercial culture had, inevitably, become an inextricable part of that culture. In many ways Postmodernism was a reaction to the perceived inadequacies of what had preceded it. At the same time, by challenging what had gone before, it made way for a new set of possibilities, such as the idea of design as a form of consumer expression. Without the Postmodern movement, the search at the end of the 20th century for a design that is varied but meaningful – with a new simplicity and sensuousness, and an ecological ethos – would not have been possible.

An interior in the "Thematic House" (1982–5; above), the London residence of Charles Jencks. Although better known as a writer and advocate of Postmodernism, Jencks oversaw the decoration of his house himself. Its "Postmodern" qualities lie in its stylistic eclecticism, rich use of colour and strong elements of symbolism.

The Sharp "QT50" portable radio cassette player (1986; below). The machine – whose rounded edges and pastel colours were intended to create a 1950s "retro" appearance – was one of the first Japanese "lifestyle" goods to enter the Western marketplace.

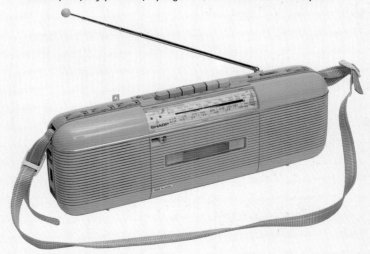

Japan showed at least two faces of modern design to the world in the 1980s. On the one hand, the highly styled electronic goods of the large-scale manufacturers – Sharp, Sony, National Panasonic and others – flooded the marketplace, showing Japan to be the clear style-leader in this field; on the other, a relatively small group of architect-designers

Shiro Kuramata

sought worldwide attention in an effort to show what Japan could offer the international avant-garde in the fields of interior and furniture design. Kiro Kurakawa, Masanori Umeda, Arata Isozaki, Shigeru Uchida, Shiro Kuramata and others bridged the gap between Japan and the West with their progressive designs for buildings, interiors and furniture. By designing boutiques they became linked to the success of the Japanese fashion designers Issey Miyake, Rei Kawakubo (of Comme des Garçons) and Yoshio Yamamoto. Stylistically a range of possibilities opened up, as the contradictions between Modernism and Postmodernism were eroded in the work of these talented designers.

Shiro Kuramata's eloquent and radical furniture designs brought to the world's attention the very important role that Japan had played and continues to play in forming the Modernist and Postmodernist design movements.

Although the minimal, elegant "Apple Honey" chair (1985; below) reflects the familiar forms of Modernism, the hint of colour on the upper section of the tubular steel, and the chair's title suggest that the design was the result of a new sensibility.

APPRENTICESHIP IN INTERIORS

Shiro Kuramata (1934–91) was among the first of these designers to establish himself in the West. He was also by far the most prolific. Trained in woodworking at the Technical High School in Tokyo until 1953, he went on to three years' study in the Department of Living Design at the Kuwazawa Institute of Design in that city. In 1953 he also joined the Teikoku Kizai furniture factory, and over the next decade he worked in the interior design sections of a number of Tokyo department stores, including, in 1957, the famous Matsuya retail outlet. In 1965 he opened his own design office in Tokyo, and he devoted the next decade or so to designing the interiors of more than 300 of Japan's new boutiques and restaurants. This period marked the peak of Japan's post-war economic boom and Kuramata's contribution was an integral part of the process of physically reconstructing the country's identity.

DESIGN CHARACTERISTICS

In essence Kuramata was a minimalist – a great respecter and emulator of traditional Japanese interior design. At the same time he had an intuitively subversive approach towards design. The result was a combination, in his work, of immaculately worked detail and a sense of compositional harmony, with an added element of the unexpected and the idiosyncratic. His famous "wavy" chests of drawers in the "Furniture in Irregular Forms" series (1970; opposite, right), which first brought him international recognition were a brilliant combination of his two tendencies. These beautifully made and detailed multi-drawered pieces were made unusual by their elegantly undulating contours.

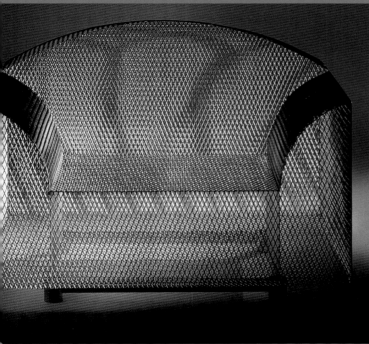

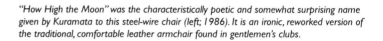

"How High the Moon" was the characteristically poetic and somewhat surprising name given by Kuramata to this steel-wire chair (left; 1986). It is an ironic, reworked version of the traditional, comfortable leather armchair found in gentlemen's clubs.

One of Kuramata's pieces of "Furniture in Irregular Forms" (below), designed in 1970 and now manufactured by the Italian firm Cappellini. With its numerous small compartments and harmonious proportions this recalled traditional Japanese pieces; its dramatic sense of movement also made a great impact in the Western context, suggesting a new, expressive approach towards furniture design.

TRADITION AND INNOVATION

In 1981, with a range of his pieces already on show in the London shop of Zeev Aram (a highly influential furniture retailer), Kuramata was invited to participate in the first Memphis show in Milan (see pp.216–19), for which he produced "Imperial", a three-part cabinet. This was followed in 1983 by "Kyoto" (below), a concrete side-table in which pieces of broken coloured glass were embedded, creating a decorative, expressive piece of furniture that perfectly suited the mood of the day. Over the next few years he went on to create a series of chairs. Their titles, sometimes taken from popular songs, revealed their poetic content. From "Begin the Beguine" (1985), a homage to Josef Hoffmann (see pp.34–7), to "How High the Moon" (1986; above), a metal mesh armchair, and "Miss Blanche" (1989), a plexiglass seat embedded with red roses, Kuramata explored the chair's material and metaphorical possibilities while keeping a Modernist-inspired simplicity.

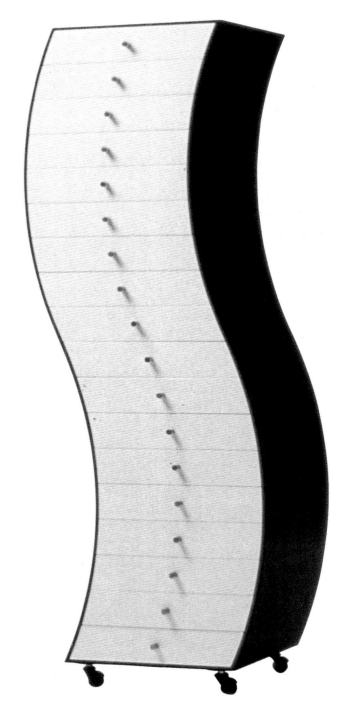

Kuramata also took an interest in designing domestic objects – for example, minimal wood and metal fruit-bowls (1989) made by Central Market of Japan, and a transparent washbasin (1990), enigmatically named "Coup de Foudre" ("love at first sight"). Simple imaginative statements such as these were marks of his ability to create arresting, novel forms from minimal materials, and it was in this ability that Kuramata's originality lay.

Kuramata participated in the Italian Memphis project in the early 1980s, and the suggestively named "Kyoto" table (left; 1983) was exhibited in the third show of that year. Made of concrete and pieces of coloured glass, it fitted in well with the work around it, much of which was playing with ideas relating to surface decoration.

Eva Jiricna (b.1939) played a vital part in the highly visible "High-Tech" style of architecture and design that emerged in Britain in the 1980s, characterized by its use of industrial materials (such as glass and metal) in the domestic context. Unlike many of her contemporaries, however, her embrace of the style was rooted in a set of beliefs

Eva Jiricna

that were both deep and durable. Jiricna's personal approach to design was determined more than anything else by her background as an architect trained in her native Czechoslovakia's powerful modern tradition, which was dominated by the work of such men as Pavel Janak and Ladislav Zak. She is committed to the principles of Functionalism — the idea that nothing is included in a design that does not enhance the object's purpose.

Eva Jiricna, the designer of interiors for many of London's most stylish retail outlets and restaurants, has adapted Modernism to the requirements of the late 20th century while remaining faithful to its basic ideals.

Jiricna's brief for designing this folding table and stool (right) for Formica Ltd. was to use the company's new plastic laminate "Colorcore". Jiricna's geometric surface patterns exploited the decorative potential of this product to the full.

The interior of the Joseph pour la Ville shop in London (1986; below). The dramatic central stairwell with its chromed steel balustrades was one of the designer's favourite features, which she repeated in a number of other interiors from the same decade; the restrained use of colour is also a common theme.

TRAINING AND EARLY EXPERIENCE

Eva Jiricna, the daughter of an architect, received a training in architecture (which in the Czech tradition laid a strong emphasis on science and engineering) in Prague between 1956 and 1962. During her early years in practice she worked at a cement factory and in the State Architect's bureau — places in which the life of a female architect was not always easy. Frustrated by the lack of creative opportunities under Communist rule she increasingly felt the need to leave Czechoslovakia, and in 1968 went to Britain, only returning to her homeland for a visit in 1990.

Her first work in Britain was in the Schools Division of the Greater London Council. She then worked for nine years in the office of the architect Louis de Soissons, where she was involved with the Brighton Marina project, a vast engineering endeavour to reclaim land and build a harbour. In this she benefited from her background in engineering, while the project also served to enhance her expertise in the area of materials and to help her acquire a first-hand knowledge of nautical details. Later she applied the knowledge gained here in a highly personal and imaginative way in the shop interiors that she created for Joseph Ettedgui in the early 1980s.

TRANSFORMING LONDON

In 1976 Jiricna became a British citizen. Over the next decade she expanded her breadth of experience, working with a fellow Czech, Jan Kaplicky, with the architect David Hodges on a number of interior projects, and, for a short time, in the office of the architect Richard Rogers. During this time she became the leading figure in the creation of a sophisticated interior-design style formed to meet the requirements of the chic new retail outlets that were transforming the smarter streets of London. Britain's new retail movement — highly dependent on the designers of the new interiors, among them Fitch & Company and Din Associates — was at the vanguard of an international trend that stressed the role of "lifestyle" in shopping. Jiricna's work in this field was highly respected and extremely influential.

Joe's Café in London (1986; above). The use of tension wires, visible along the side of the space, was a theme that Jiricna borrowed from her experience while working on Brighton's new marina a few years previously.

This chromed steel stairwell (right), with its glass treads, takes pride of place in the interior designed by Jiricna in collaboration with architect Michael Hopkins for the City of London offices of Jardine Insurance (1989). The overall effect is one of cool sophistication.

Together with Kaplicky, she helped to create Joseph Ettedgui's shop (1980) in London's South Molton Street. Her first solo project for the retailer however, was the redesign of his apartment. Using white tiles, glass shelving and sliding doors, she experimented with the idea of introducing industrial materials and techniques into the domestic context.

This style quickly became Jiricna's hallmark, and her subsequent London shops and restaurants – including Le Caprice (1980), Kenzo in Sloane Street (1982), Joseph pour la Ville (1986; opposite, below), Joe's Café (1986; above), and Joseph in the Fulham Road (1988) – were all developments of the theme. Steel, glass, tension wires, complex open-structured staircases and neutral colours were the vocabulary in her language of the interior. Her great skill was to manipulate a space to maximize its light and its drama.

MOVING FORWARD

Following a short period in business with a partner, Kathy Kerr, Jiricna set up her own design office in London – Eva Jiricna Associates – in 1986. By this date her interiors had received worldwide attention through their appearance in magazines, which brought her a number of international projects including a Joan & David shoe shop in Los Angeles and a Vidal Sassoon salon in Frankfurt. The commitment to Functionalism that underpinned Jiricna's approach enabled her to move easily from the style-conscious 1980s to the more serious 1990s. She continued to work through this decade, developing her personal language of design using by now familiar materials and details – such as her dramatic staircases and "marine" imagery – and applying it increasingly widely.

frogdesign

When the young German designer Hartmut Esslinger formed frogdesign in 1969, he set out to create a new language of industrial design. This language stemmed from the marriage of traditional German Functionalism – pioneered by the electrical company Braun in the 1950s and 1960s – with the stylistic eclecticism perpetuated in

frogdesign

the early 1980s by Ettore Sottsass and the Memphis experiment in Milan. With this blend of ideas, Esslinger and the frogdesign team confronted head-on the challenge presented by design in the 1980s – the opposition between the simplicity of Functionalism and the whimsicality of Postmodernism. Frogdesign has been highly successful in this project, applying its own approach not only to traditional objects, such as furniture and ceramics, but also, more significantly, to a range of electronic products, especially computers.

Car telephones, named "CD900" and "Telecar 9" (above), were designed in 1982 for AEG Telefunken, Germany. They show the stylistic softening of forms that typified frogdesign's work of that period.

FOUNDATION OF THE FIRM

Hartmut Esslinger founded the first frogdesign office in Altensteig, Germany, and took the group's name from an acronym of Federal Republic of Germany. Trained first as an electronic engineer at the University of Stuttgart and subsequently as an industrial designer at the College of Design, Swabisch Gmund, in the 1960s, Esslinger was ideally placed to combine the technical with the aesthetic. The frogdesign team has consistently done this in its work for a wide range of clients, including Wega Radio, König & Neurath, Villeroy & Boch, Rosenthal, AEG, Erco and, after an office was set up in Campbell, California, in 1982, Apple Computers, NeXT Computers, Olympus and AT&T. By 1986 frogdesign was also active in the Far East and had opened a Tokyo office.

The early work on colour television sets and stereos for Wega was fundamental to the

Since the 1970s frogdesign has created an exuberant range of goods for the German manufacturer, Hansgrohe. The "Uno" series of showerheads and taps (below) were designed in 1985 with the help of a computer system.

The "frollerskates" (1979; right) count among the more whimsical of Esslinger's projects. Manufactured by Indusco, the skates evoke the sense of speed and pleasure that characterized the team's approach to many of its design challenges.

Frogdesign's range of office furniture for the German company König & Neurath were among the more traditional objects dealt with by the team. While based on the idea of the classic pedestal desk, these units use modern materials such as plastic, and unorthodox pastel colours. The design follows the pared-down principles of Functionalism in its clean lines and lack of unnecessary detail, thus responding to the high-tech demands of the office of the 1980s, as demonstrated by the "King Alpha" model (left).

group's later success. It brought the team in contact with a range of high-technology objects that could be designed according to Functionalist principles, yet with flair and individuality. A minimal aesthetic was applied to the television sets, making them appear strikingly modern with their softly contoured, all-plastic shells and subtle detailing. When Sony bought Wega, frogdesign continued to work for the company and thus came into contact with Japanese notions of marketing, with the emphasis on making electronic goods stylish, well-designed accessories for the mass market. These ideas influenced the design group's approach enormously.

"USER-FRIENDLY" DESIGN

The relationship between the machine and its user has preoccupied frogdesign in its work for high-technology companies. For Apple the brief was to design a "user-friendly" computer. This was achieved through a combination of simple form, the use of gentle colour (in this case, off-white), and a simplification of the control mechanisms. In many ways frogdesign was responsible for domesticating the computer and for transforming it from a master into a servant. In 1984 the Apple "IIc" (right) appeared on the cover of *Time* magazine as "design of the year".

Much of frogdesign's work, with its sense of fun and playfulness, reflects Esslinger's experience of growing up in the 1960s. This is evident in a wide range of designs – from the "frollerskates" for Indusco (opposite, right) to the red "Uno" showerhead system for Hansgrohe (opposite, below left) – that echo the company motto "form follows emotion!"

A GLOBAL PHILOSOPHY

"The purpose of design is to make an artificial environment more human. My goal is and always was to design mainstream products as art," said Esslinger in 1987. He and the frogdesign team have brought the profession of industrial design to prominence in many ways. With the team's ability to confront any design challenge put in front of them, and to apply its broad philosophy to a range of diverse projects, it has demonstrated that the industrial designer is an essential contributor to the world of manufacturing and to contemporary cultural life. Esslinger himself is both a generalist and a specialist who can deal with the specific problem of the radius of a television control knob or the demands of a global market in the late 20th century with equal confidence and expertise.

More than any other industrial design group operating today, the frogdesign team's experience has enabled its members to see and to predict trends. While its work is still concerned with colour and form, it also has to anticipate new technologies as well as new social and commercial trends. In so doing, the frogdesign team (now comprising over 100 designers from around the world) has redefined the meaning of industrial design in the late 20th century.

The "IIc" computer (right) was designed for Apple and launched on to the market in 1984. With its simple, streamlined appearance, this was a highly innovatory design, establishing the computer as a user-friendly object rather than an alien piece of high-tech office machinery.

The French designer Philippe Starck (b.1949) is without doubt the "super-designer" of the late 20th century. His much-publicized image as a creative artist applying his skills to the mundane objects of everyday life evokes a tradition – dating back to Norman Bel Geddes and Raymond Loewy (see pp.120–23) in the United States in the 1920s and

Philippe Starck

1930s – of naming the designer of a product to assist in its sales. By the 1980s, however, with the expansion of the mass media, what had earlier been an essentially national phenomenon had reached international proportions, and Starck's reputation as a magician capable of transforming the everyday environment in front of our eyes is one that crosses geographical boundaries. He is as well known for his hotel interiors, furniture and domestic products in Tokyo as he is in New York, Paris or London, and his talents are sought after in all these cosmopolitan centres.

Starck designed the "Miss Sissi" light (right) in 1990 for Kartell. The small table light is made entirely of plastic and available in a range of colours, and demonstrates that Starck – while always original – is also capable of a simplicity that gives many of his designs a timeless quality.

Philippe Starck, shown here with the "Rosy Angelis" light, produced by Flos in Milan, is arguably the best-known designer of the 1990s. His enigmatic personality and the enormous range of his designs have earned him a place in the popular imagination.

IDEAS AND APPROACH TO DESIGN

True to the "super-designer" tradition, Philippe Starck is both an extrovert and an individualist, with a talent for self-promotion. He talks frequently and fluently about design and about his personal approach to the field. In line with the emphasis on creativity that accompanies all discussions about his work, Starck stresses the role of intuition and the emotions over reason. He feels that his own role is closer to that of the fine artist than to the engineer yet, despite the almost mythical image that he has constructed around himself, his work extends far beyond the bounds of fine art practice. If it is with the world of fine art that he identifies, then it is with the one that existed in 16th-century Italy – the time of the Renaissance, when artists eschewed the differences between the beautiful and the useful – rather than with the contemporary art world which focuses more narrowly on painting and sculpture and ignores, for the most part, the role of utility.

Starck is unique in many ways, but he can also be seen to represent a whole generation of French designers (mainly of furniture), including Jean-Michel Wilmotte, the team of Elizabeth Garouste and Mattia Bonetti, Marie-Christine Dorner and others who emerged in the 1980s. Their success was due to various factors – principally the support of a government-formed organization called VIA (Valorisation de l'Innovation dans l'Ameublement). They also gained the backing of President Mitterrand, who saw in the new design and architecture a way of making France visible once again as a nation committed to high style, and who in 1983 commissioned five leading designers, including Starck, to create a set of interiors for the Elysée Palace.

Starck's work hovers around a number of central themes: lightness, the blurring of the boundaries between technology and art, and, most recently, zoological forms and the human body, and he has favoured certain shapes

A high-sided sofa (left) in the lobby of the Delano Hotel in Miami, the interior of which was designed by Starck in 1995. The dramatic form of this piece of furniture serves as a visual punctuation mark in the space around it.

over others – those of wings and the horn, for example – and returned to them again and again in a number of different contexts. He also comes back to the same materials, with wood and aluminium most recently being joined by plastics.

Above all, Starck's work is enthusiastically modern. While references to the past may occur – for instance, in references to traditional chair types, such as folding seats – the application is always for the present and for the future. Many of the enigmatic names of his pieces derive from the pages of science-fiction writer Philip K. Dick, and it is to the world of sci-fi that many of Starck's designs allude and from which they take their inspiration.

TRAINING AND EARLY WORK

Starck was registered as a student of furniture and interior design at the Camondo School in Paris in 1968 but, it seems, was seldom present at classes. However, he produced his first chair – the folding wooden "Francesca Spanish" chair – at about this time. In 1969 he was appointed Artistic Director at Pierre Cardin, but it was not until the mid-1970s that he began to be noticed – principally for the interior design of two Parisian nightclubs, La Main Bleue and Les Bains-Douches. In 1982 he was awarded a prize from VIA for his "Miss Dorn" chair, a very simple composition in

Bar stools (right) in the interior designed for New York's Royalton Hotel in 1988. Starck was responsible for every detail in the space – from the flooring to the lighting and furniture. The stools' wavy legs betray the humour that is present in much of his work.

A chaise-longue (below) in the Royalton Hotel. The curved back of the chair is a form much loved and used by Philippe Starck, while the use of tubular steel and black leather shows his continued reverence for early 20th-century Modernism.

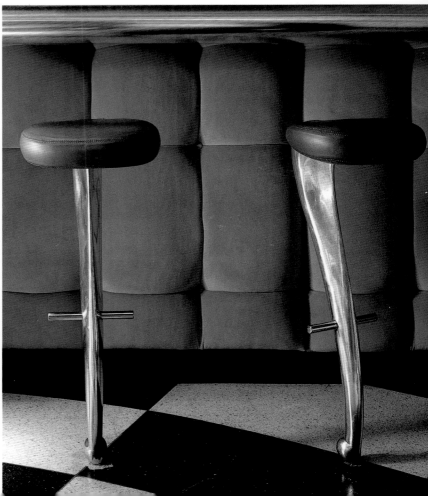

The bar in the Felix Discotheque (above) – on the 29th floor of the Peninsula Hotel in Hong Kong – was designed by Starck in 1993. The padded walls and dramatically illuminated tables create an extraordinary space-age ambience.

The "M5107" television set (below), designed for Saba in 1994. This is one of the relatively rare examples of the designer's work on electronic goods and, although incorporating his well-known curved forms, is among his most restrained designs.

tubular steel with an upholstered cushion; unlike the "Francesca Spanish" chair, this was commercially produced. In 1984, on seeing a piece by Starck exhibited in the VIA gallery in Paris, the owner of the Café Costes – located in the new development around the Beaubourg Centre – commissioned him to design its interior.

Starck's work for the Café Costes – in which he created a dramatic interior space with a central staircase and a giant clock – brought him overnight fame. The uncompromisingly modern and stylish appearance of the interior struck a chord in the consciousness of the international design community and the public alike, and it was featured in magazines across the globe. The simple chairs with curved plywood backs that he designed to fill the space also became commercially successful, and were widely imitated through the subsequent decade.

FURTHER DESIGNS

In the 1980s Starck produced a sequence of chair designs. From "Mr Bliss" (1982) to the expansive "Dr Sonderbar", named after a dirigible pilot (1983); from the witty "Richard III", a bulky bourgeois armchair at the front tapering to a skeletal Modernist structure at the back (1984), to the evocatively curved, metal-formed "Mrs Frick" (1985); through "Lola Mundo" (1986) and on to the plastic and tubular steel minimalism of "Dr Glob" (1988), Starck collaborated with manufacturers — including Driade, Idee, Baleri, Disform and Kartell — in France, Italy, Japan and elsewhere. All the designs were striking in their originality, and all utilized energy and materials in as light and economical a way as possible.

Through the 1980s and 1990s Starck was also preoccupied with architecture and interior design, with his work appearing in urban centres around the world. In Tokyo, for example, his Nani Nani café and Asahi brasserie buildings — created in concrete and glass, and built in the shapes that typified his product designs — were like giant sculptures exploding on to the skyline; it was as if he had simply extended his scale of operation while maintaining his commitment to the same language of form and iconography used in other pieces of work. In New York, Starck designed two remarkable hotel interiors — the Royalton (see p.247) and the Paramount — in 1988 and 1990 respectively. Both were completely controlled by his eye and hand, and he worked on every detail himself, down to the bathroom taps.

PRODUCT DESIGN

Starck has devoted much of his energy in the 1990s to product design, and his desire to make his mark on the most mundane aspects of everyday living made the design of ordinary artefacts — such as door-handles and toothbrushes — especially appealing to him. In 1989 he had produced an example of the latter for Fluocaril, thereby creating the first "designer toothbrush", while in the 1990s he developed — as had so many other seminal designers before him, among them his personal hero Achille Castiglioni (see pp.194–5) — a strong relationship with the Italian metal manufacturing company, Alessi. This close collaboration resulted in what

Typically, when Starck works on projects for hotel interiors, he takes control of every detail, right down to the smallest fittings. These serpentine bathroom taps (above) in the Peninsula Hotel in Hong Kong (1993) reflect the designer's interest in animal forms.

The "Ara" light (left; 1988). The organic horned form at the top of this chromed-steel object is one to which Starck returns frequently in his work, and is the only element that prevents this object from being entirely based on familiar Modernist principles.

quickly took their place as modern design classics, including the "Juicy Salif" fruit juicer (1990), which resembles a space-age creature on spindly legs, and the "Hot Bertaa" kettle (1990–91).

Product design provided Starck with the vast audience that he had always wanted and an opportunity, therefore, to expose his ideas as widely as possible. The production of a plastic water bottle for Vittel in 1990 confirmed his desire to infiltrate fully the world of the banal. In the mid-1990s he focused on this area, ironically becoming closer and closer in his designs to the intimacy of the human body as he moved into the area of mechanized mass production; his zoomorphic and organic forms were mirrors of the shifts in technological thinking at the time, as the machine-styling of early Modernism became increasingly redundant. Starck continues to use design — and the powerful role as a designer that he has done so much to create — to translate the "spirit of the age" into material form, thereby ensuring that none of us, as a consumer, is immune to it.

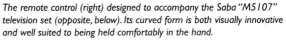

The remote control (right) designed to accompany the Saba "M5107" television set (opposite, below). Its curved form is both visually innovative and well suited to being held comfortably in the hand.

Until the 1970s Spain did not play a prominent role in the story of 20th-century design. However, with the death of the Fascist leader General Franco in 1975 the new freedom engendered, among other things, a new Spanish design movement. This was particularly evident in the Catalonian city of Barcelona which, in search of a regional

Javier Mariscal

identity that would be recognized internationally, saw in modern design a means of regenerating itself. Making frequent references to the turn-of-the-century "Modernismo" style of Antoní Gaudí and others, as well as to the avant-garde heritage of Joan Miró and his contemporaries, a number of architects and designers, including Oscar Tusquets, Josep Llusca and Javier Mariscal, created a movement which made an international impact.

Javier Mariscal is Spain's best-known living designer. His involvement with the 1992 Barcelona Olympics earned him an international profile, while his work across a range of media has been widely reproduced in magazine articles.

TRAINING AND EARLY WORK

Javier Mariscal (b.1950) played a crucial role in the rapid emergence of the modern design activity that engulfed Barcelona in the early 1980s. He was born in Valencia but went to Barcelona to study at the Elisava School of Graphics, from which he graduated in 1971.

Mariscal's first tentative forays into design in three dimensions came in the 1970s. In 1977 he put on an exhibition for the Mec-Mec Gallery in Barcelona, which consisted of an imaginative re-creation of a 1950s "grand hotel". The following year he designed a prototype lamp. "Telepathic Friends", as he characteristically named the piece, demonstrated the way in which, for Mariscal, with his persistently ironic and playful view of the world, design was not a problem-solving exercise but rather a form of communication. This approach distanced him from the values of early Modernism, which held that objects should reflect only function.

Mariscal designed the "Alessandra" chair (right) in 1995 as part of a series called "Los Muebles Amorosos" manufactured by Moroso. The bold, cartoon-like form and expressive colours used in this piece characterize much of the designer's work.

FURNITURE AND INTERIORS

Mariscal's first interior design project came in 1978. Barcelona's Merbeye bar, with its fan seemingly slicing through one of the internal pillars, was, in many ways, a three-dimensional cartoon – as were many of his subsequent creations. In 1981 Fernando Amat, the owner of Vinçon, the leading design shop in Barcelona, asked Mariscal to put together an exhibition of furniture pieces. The items he produced – among them the "Gaidío" chair and the "Copa Luz" table – were quirky creations which abandoned all the constraints of rational Modernism. The Italian designer Ettore Sottsass (see pp.216–19) came to Barcelona to see the exhibition and invited Mariscal to participate in the first Memphis show that year in Milan. The "Hilton" trolley (opposite, below right) that he created for Memphis was among the first of Mariscal's designs to attract widespread public attention.

The second object to make an impact was the "Duplex" stool, with its asymmetrical shape and bright colours; it was designed in 1980 for the Duplex bar, and manufactured three years later by BD Ediciones de Diseño.

The sun and moon towers on the roof terrace of the Torres de Avila club (1990; above), designed with the architect Alfredo Arribas, with whom Mariscal collaborated on a number of bars.

A moulded glass toothbrush holder in the form of a stylized fish (below; 1997), made by the Barcelona firm Cosmic. Part of a range of bathroom items named "Peces" ("fish"), it is available in four colours.

From that point Mariscal created a number of objects and interiors which for many came to stand for the "new Spain". His "Very Formal Furniture" exhibition in 1983, for example, contained the "Spider" lamp, designed with Pepe Cortes, and the "Kabul" rug. In 1985 he produced a range of ceramics for Vinçon.

INTERNATIONAL RECOGNITION

By the end of the 1980s Mariscal had completed a large body of work, ranging from furniture and interiors to ceramics, textiles and visual identity. His background as a cartoonist and graphic designer remained constantly visible in the expressive shapes and identities of his objects and images. Indeed, Mariscal himself claimed that he produced images rather than furniture. In the Postmodern 1980s this not only proved a highly appropriate approach but also meant that his work received rapid international visibility. Mariscal's international reputation was reaffirmed by his design of the mascot for the 1992 Barcelona Olympics. Cobi the dog perfectly expressed the exuberant spirit of the "new Spain", while its creator was celebrated as an important catalyst in its visual expression.

The Hilton trolley (below; 1981), designed with Pepe Cortes. Its simple glass and metal forms echo early Modernism, but expressive elements were added in the exaggerated angle and coloured handles.

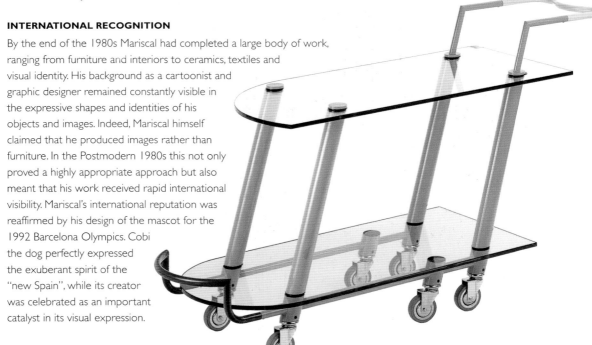

Ettore Sottsass' Memphis group, which showed its revolutionary work to the public for the first time in Milan in 1981, brought together the output of a number of talented individuals. Many of the young participants in the experiment – including Marco Zanini, Aldo Cibic, Matteo Thun, George Sowden, Nathalie du Pasquier, Martine Bedin and

Michele De Lucchi

Though he favours the radical rather than the mainstream, Michele De Lucchi has become internationally successful as a designer of furniture and products for domestic, retail and corporate projects.

Michele De Lucchi (b.1951) – went on to have independent careers as significant designers in their own right. De Lucchi has been particularly successful in bringing his intellectual approach to the mainstream areas of corporate and industrial design.

The "Cairo" table (below), made from tubular steel and varnished wood, was designed for the Memphis exhibition of 1986. It shows the way in which De Lucchi loves to inject a level of irony into design and to use it as a form of criticism and commentary. While referring openly, through a use of geometric forms and of bent metal, to the pioneering Modernism of the Bauhaus, it at once debunks that movement through the addition of decorative surface pattern and of an exotic name that suggests a background story rather than pure function.

TRAINING AND EARLY WORK

De Lucchi's personal style as a designer was well formed by the time he came into contact with Ettore Sottsass (see pp.216–19) in the mid-1970s. Trained as an architect at the University of Florence (1969–75) under the guidance of Adolfo Natalini, a founder member of the 1960s radical design group Superstudio, he felt the need to move outside the mainstream as a student. In Padua in 1973 he formed Gruppo Cavart, a student group that organized performance events, workshops and lively debates on design. Their provocative activities made a strong impact at a seminar on radical design held at Monselice two years later. In 1976 De Lucchi formed his own studio, Architetture e Altri Piaceri (Architecture and Other Pleasures), where he continued to work on conceptual rather than functional projects.

From the start of his career De Lucchi's thoughtful approach to design was expressed through deceptively simple visual and material means. While on the surface he combines form, colour, texture and pattern in a fun way, on a deeper level the designs represent a world of ideas, with ironic visual references to taste and culture.

ROLE IN ITALIAN DESIGN

Having worked in the studio of Gaetano Pesce (pp.224–5) in 1974, De Lucchi arrived in Milan in 1977 at the suggestion of Sottsass. There he worked on an exhibition and book with the theorist Andrea Branzi on the subject of Italian design of the 1950s. With Sottsass, in 1979, he collaborated on an office furniture project for Olivetti, consisting of co-ordinating pieces in blue and grey. His own designs from this year, for Studio Alchimia, were themselves clearly influenced by the 1950s. His table lamps "Sinvola" and "Sipernica", for example, playfully challenged the boundaries between good and bad taste, and high and low design. This innovative strategy was used even more effectively in his designs for the Memphis shows of the early 1980s, which he played a key role in organizing.

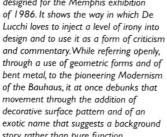

The "Horizon" bed (right) was designed and made for the 1984 Memphis exhibition. The design is typical of De Lucchi's early pieces for Memphis, which used brightly coloured plastic laminates and graphic black-and-white "Op Art" patterns. This less serious approach was part of a new modern design movement that went beyond the requirements of function to include wit and expression.

MEMPHIS

De Lucchi's designs from the early 1980s were typified by a playfulness, a strong use of imagery and an expressive and narrative content that took them beyond mere exercises in solving practical problems. He rejected the hard edges and sober colours of the new Functionalism, pinpointing instead the need for a softer, more innocent, child-like approach to design that reworked the past where appropriate and used form, texture and colour as parts of an expressive language. His metal "Oceanic" table light (1981) for Memphis, for instance, was in the shape of a stylized sea monster, a piece of 1960s-style "Op Art" in graphic black, yellow and white. In his numerous furniture designs of this period he developed this personal visual language to such a level of refinement that by the mid-1980s his work was widely recognized as that of a talented and, above all, highly individual designer.

The "Saltimbanco" chest (above) was designed with Mario Rossi in 1992 for Play Line. Its vibrant wooden curves show the designer's genius for creating simple yet expressive forms. Both utilitarian and playful, this piece is a mature version of some of De Lucchi's early Memphis designs.

After the success of Memphis, De Lucchi's client list rapidly expanded to include, among many others, the lighting manufacturers Fontana Arte and Artemide in Italy, the plastics firm Kartell (for which he designed desk accessories), and the furniture makers Bieffeplast in Germany. The size of his studio also grew over the next decade as he combined work for Olivetti (the Icarus office furniture project, 1983) with shop interiors (the Mandarin Duck store in Milan, 1988); corporate schemes (among them a project for the Deutsche Bank begun in the late 1980s); and furniture and products (including his "Tolomeo" desk lamp for Artemide, 1983).

Alongside this expansion of activities, however, and the necessity to develop increasingly sophisticated strategies for the many different kinds of design project that his studio took on, De Lucchi felt the need to work on a much more personal, innovative basis as well. In 1990 he established Produzione Privata, a small-scale production facility that allowed him to work on modest decorative objects in metal, glass and ceramics, and which provided him with creative fulfilment. In sharp contrast he has, since the mid-1990s, also acted as the Head of Olivetti's design department, one of the most influential design posts in Italian industry. It is this ability to combine an intellectual and personal approach to design with corporate and industrial projects that marks out De Lucchi as a key figure in late 20th-century design.

The "Antares" vase (right), made of blown glass for the Memphis exhibition of 1983. Like Sottsass, De Lucchi used blown glass because it is a flexible medium that allows the maker to create arresting images and shapes. With De Lucchi's characteristic irreverence, the traditional aspect of glass-blowing is overthrown by the visual impact of the vase's cartoon-like shape, which looks as if it could have been made of plastic.

Of the furniture and product designers who began to make their individual talents visible in the 1980s – including Jasper Morrison, Massimo Iosa-Ghini, Matteo Thun, Ron Arad, George Sowden, Daniel Weil, Michele De Lucchi, Nigel Coates, Bořek Šípek and Philippe Starck – Antonio Citterio (b.1950) was among the least demonstrative.

Antonio Citterio

In contrast to the more flamboyant pieces of, say, Arad and Šípek (see pp.256–7 and 234–5), his designs were characterized by being gentle and unassertive, and earned him a reputation for being attentive to detail, professional and uncompromising on every front.

Antonio Citterio's attention to detail in his work for a range of (mostly Italian) furniture manufacturers and for interior design projects have earned him a prominent reputation.

The "T-Chair" (below) was designed for Vitra in 1996 in collaboration with Glen Oliver Low. Its simple, functional forms are offset by the vivid stripes on the back, and by the green armrests.

ARCHITECTURAL APPRENTICESHIP

Born in Meda, north of Milan, Citterio graduated in architecture from the Polytechnic of Milan in 1972, although he had begun taking on projects as an industrial designer some five years earlier. On graduating he established a studio with Paolo Nava in Lissone; the two men were to remain close collaborators until 1981. The apprenticeship that Citterio served in the 1970s was intensive and rigorous. He worked with the architect Vittorio Gregotti on the restoration of the Brera Art Gallery in Milan and in 1973 began a collaboration with the furniture-manufacturing company B&B (formerly C&B) Italia, which produced a number of significant designs over the next two decades. By the early 1990s his clients included the Italian furniture/product companies Boffi, Flexform, Rivaplast, Kartell and Moroso, and the German furniture manufacturer Vitra. From 1987 he collaborated with his wife, the American designer Terry Dwan, with whom he designed showrooms for B&B Italia; offices and showrooms for Vitra in Germany and Paris; and an office furniture system for Olivetti. By the early 1990s they were working together in Japan, designing offices in Osaka and Tokyo.

INTERNATIONAL ACCLAIM

The early 1990s marked Citterio's first significant international achievements in furniture design. His elegant yet comfortable seating objects were among the most memorable exhibits at the Milan Furniture Fairs. Although he had worked on a number of interesting pieces before then – among them the "Diesis" armchair (1980; opposite, right) for B&B Italia, the "Max" divan (1983) and the "Phil" sofa (1985; both for Flexform) and the little anodized-aluminium "Enea" wall light (1987) for Artemide – his maturity and self-confidence reached a peak in 1990 with a series of chairs and sofas for B&B Italia named "Baisity", and, in the following year, with furniture items for Flexform, Vitra and Kartell. All the pieces were simple, elegant, neomodern solutions to the problem of seating, executed in steel, leather and fabric.

While the chairs and sofas were all characteristically handsome pieces, the folding tables and trolleys of 1990 for Kartell went further. The "Battista" trolley, for example, made from plastic, aluminium and steel, was not only visually elegant and professionally finished, but it also exuded a strong

The living area of a villa near Como (left); the interior was designed by Citterio and his wife, Terry Dwan. The open expanse – interrupted only by pillars and built-in shelving – is reminiscent of Modernist interiors of the 1920s, although the simple chairs have a slightly "retro" antique feel.

The "Diesis" armchair (below) was designed by Citterio with Paolo Nava in 1980, and manufactured by B&B Italia. One of Citterio's earliest production pieces, this easy chair – with its tubular steel frame and leather upholstery – was clearly indebted for its design to early Modernist precedents.

The "Mobil" plastic and metal storage system (below; 1994), designed in collaboration with Glen Oliver Low for Kartell. Citterio originally developed the design for his own office use.

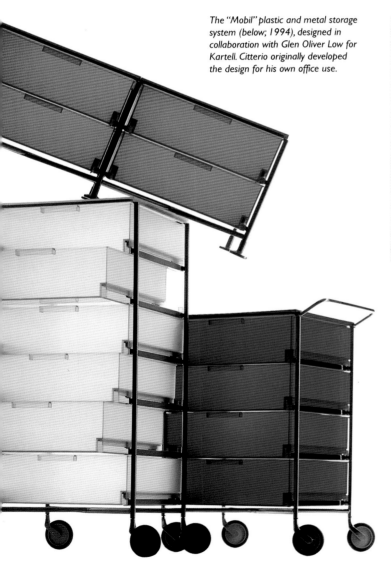

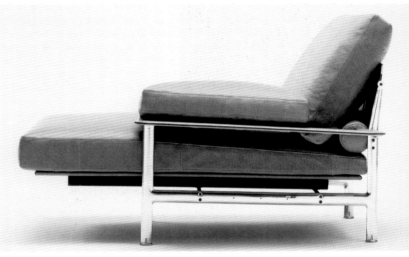

individualism – expressed primarily through the inclusion of an unusual metal mechanism which made it possible to extend the size of the trolley's top surface. The success was repeated on its partner object, a folding trolley named "Filippo".

ECLECTIC APPROACH

The appeal of Citterio's designs lies in their apparent simplicity. This is achieved by assiduous attention to detail, whether by the way in which the feet of his chairs and sofas meet the ground, the way in which "hi-tech" and "natural" materials are combined, or through the creation of appealing and durable images. Forms that recall the past – such as chairs with curved backs echoing the neoclassical Biedermeier style of the mid-19th century – mingle with stark, neomodern shapes and materials; the hand-made sits alongside the mass-manufactured. One range of leather chairs recalls traditional Lloyd Loom pieces, although the legs of Citterio's designs are capped with steel. This clever reworking of the old in combination with the new has distinguished Citterio's work in the 1990s.

The London-based Israeli designer Ron Arad (b. 1951) sees the designed object as a form of expression both for himself and – through the process of production and distribution – for the consumer, and in this sense works very much as a fine artist. His work is primarily about ideas. His designs for furniture using roughly finished materials

Ron Arad

The "Fantastic Plastic Elastic" chair (1997; below). In this neat design Arad balances his love of new materials and their visual effects with the commitment to organic form that distances him from early 20th-century Modernists.

From his involvement in the workshop manufacture of items that eschewed the slickness of factory production, Ron Arad has gone on to produce highly sophisticated goods and interiors for many international manufacturers.

such as metal and concrete were intended to echo the post-industrial urban decay of recession-hit Britain, while in his pieces incorporating salvaged elements he explored themes in common with artists such as Marcel Duchamp (who exhibited found objects as works of art). He has attracted international attention through extensive appearances at exhibitions around the world, and, more recently, through his interior design projects.

TRAINING AND EARLY WORK

Arad studied architecture from 1971–3 at the Jerusalem Academy of Art. He continued with his studies until 1979 at London's Architectural Association, where he came into contact with the ideas of Peter Cook (a member of the Pop architectural group Archigram), and also discovered the work of the Italian designer Gaetano Pesce (see pp.224–5). Arad's early career was influenced by an encounter with a British furniture entrepreneur called Dennis Groves, with whom he established One-Off, a small but successful business based in London. Here he became involved with constructing interior furniture structures from Kee Klamp (scaffolding-like pieces clamped together to create items such as bed structures and shelving), an initiative in sympathy with the 1980s style known as High-Tech.

Arad's breakthrough as a designer of note came in 1981 with his idea for "Rover" chairs – seats that used recycled leather seats from old Rover cars. He followed this up the same year with the "Transformer" seat, a granule-filled vinyl sack that could be moulded to the shape of its occupant's body. A year later, Arad's "Aerial" lamp exploited yet another type of ready-made technology – this time an electric car aerial – and his name began to appear in design magazines with some regularity.

DEVELOPING IDEAS

Still working from One-Off, although now alone and based in London's Covent Garden, he built up a furniture business through the 1980s. He used sheet steel and concrete in unexpected and surreal ways: the former for large easy chairs and the latter for hi-fi sets – for example, the distressed and semi-eroded "Concrete Stereo" (1984). Arad's reputation grew and he was asked to exhibit in Paris, in 1987, where he introduced a metal compacter to represent his preoccupation with urban decay. In the same year he also exhibited the compacter at the Kassel Documenta 8 in Germany, as well as showing his work at the Edward Totah gallery in London – the latter a venue normally reserved for fine artists.

The "Bookworm" bookcase (1992; above) was a characteristically simple idea. It was made, on a workshop basis, from one continuous piece of sheet metal curved back on itself three times.

A view (left) of the interior of the Belgo Noord bar and restaurant in north London, designed by Arad in 1994. The womb-like space is created by the curved, irregular wall surfaces and subtle lighting which comes partly from skylights.

DESIGN AND INTERIOR PROJECTS

From the late 1980s, a number of leading furniture manufacturers began to commission him to work on design projects. He also undertook interior projects, among them fashion shops in London and Milan, as well as the Tel Aviv Opera House foyer (1988; right). The Vitra company produced his "Well-tempered Chair", made of four pieces of tempered steel, bolted together and folded into shape; Arad designed wooden furniture for Sawaya & Moroni in Italy, and a glass-topped table for Zeev Aram in London. In 1989 his vinyl "Big Easy Red Volume" chair was produced by the Italian firm Moroso. For all these projects he began to produce more sophisticated designs in which he shed the rough, workshop appearance of earlier pieces.

In 1991 Arad received great acclaim at the Milan Furniture Fair, where the exhibition of the 12 brightly upholstered chairs that he had designed for Moroso further reduced his reputation as a "metal-basher". Through the 1990s he has continued to move in this direction, with his manufactured pieces incorporating a wide range of materials. In 1997 Arad became the Professor of Furniture Design at London's Royal College of Art, a confirmation of his status as a leading figure in the field.

The bronze amphitheatre staircase in the New Tel Aviv Opera House (right; 1988) designed in collaboration with Alison Brooks of Arad Associates. The dramatic space created by the glinting steps is one of Arad's most effective and important designs to date.

In what has to date been a short but very full career as a furniture and product designer, the Briton Jasper Morrison (b.1959) has made an enormous international impact. Ever since his remarkable and highly publicized graduation show at London's Royal College of Art in 1985, his commitment to practicality, simplicity and honesty in design – combined

Jasper Morrison

with an impeccable eye for elegant form and attention to manufacturing detail – has kept him in the limelight. Morrison is, however, a retiring person by nature, and in certain ways his furniture designs echo this desire to remain in the background. They are, in essence, anti-heroic, humbly evocative (although not directly emulative) of past masters, and strangely anonymous. Far from rendering them dull, their rigour and striking originality mark them out, and they come as a breath of fresh air at the end of a century that has witnessed the replacement of an austere and high-minded Modernism with the exuberance and stylistic eclecticism of Postmodernism.

Jasper Morrison has made an impact as an internationally respected and highly original designer in a very short time. Working with various European manufacturers – including Cappellini in Italy and Vitra in Germany – he has established himself as a minimalist furniture and product designer with an enormous amount to offer.

This plastic-and-metal bottle rack (below), designed in 1994 and manufactured by Magis in Italy, is available in a number of soft colours. Simple yet functional, the quality of the plastic used helps to transform what is a basic utility object into a desirable household item.

TRAINING AND EARLY WORK

Morrison began his training in 1979 at Kingston Polytechnic in Surrey, Britain, where he studied furniture design. On completing the course in 1982 he moved on to the Royal College of Art in London, also spending a period on a scholarship to study in Berlin, where he attended the Hochschule für Kunst. However, his professional reputation was established well before he had completed his studies, and preceding his graduation came the successes of his "Handlebar" table (1981), a construction of wood, two handlebars and a circular piece of glass; of some simple steel-rod stools designed for the London-based manufacturer Sheridan Coakley (1982); and of a flowerpot table (1983), comprising a pile of pots topped by a circle of glass, manufactured by the Italian company Cappellini.

By the time Morrison's work was shown in London at his final-year degree show at the Royal College of Art in 1985, he had an audience waiting – and the anticipation was well rewarded when he showed one of his most remarkable designs yet. Made of hardboard and wingnuts, his "Laundry Box" chair was innovative. Its simple form and construction had been engineered by a small company accustomed to putting together laundry boxes, and the chair – the batch production of which Morrison organized himself – established him as a highly original designer with a keen understanding of manufacturing processes and the ability to make straightforward, easily comprehensible and appealing design statements.

This plywood chair designed for Vitra (left; 1988) is not overtly radical yet it still has a very contemporary appeal. The ply in the seat has a considerable "give", making it comfortable as well as attractive.

The "Rug of Many Bosoms" (1985; right) has a surface pattern that is rare for Morrison, who prefers to let the structure and materials of his objects provide the decoration that he feels is appropriate.

INTERNATIONAL RECOGNITION

The following year saw the publication in various magazines of the interior that Morrison designed for himself in a West London flat, from which point his career took off internationally at an unprecedented pace. Commissions soon came from Italy and Germany, as did requests for him to participate in international exhibitions; these included the Kassel Documenta 8 (1987), where he showed a range of furniture items and created an interior for Reuters; an exhibition in Berlin (1988), where he produced some new household items; and the Milan Furniture Fairs from 1986 onwards, where he showed his latest designs. For the FSB company in Germany, Morrison designed a door-handle, and went on to provide a number of versions over subsequent years.

The "Universal" storage system designed for Cappellini (1989; below) consists of a range of cupboards and chests of drawers. They are united visually by scale and proportion, and by the keyhole opening in each drawer or door.

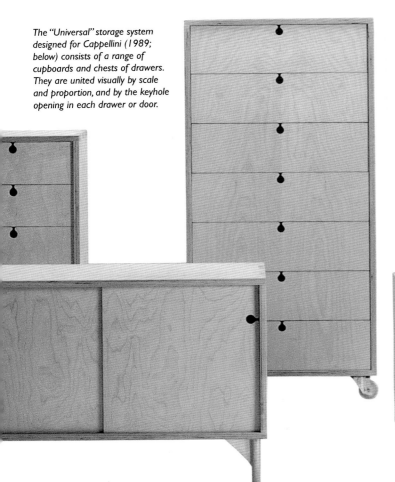

The Vitra company, also in Germany, commissioned several furniture pieces, the results of which have included an elegant plywood chair with an open back, a flat seat and subtly curved back legs (1988; above left); and, in the early 1990s, an upholstered sofa on four anodized-aluminium legs. In Italy, Cappellini was quick to recognize Morrison's enormous potential and, from the "Thinking Man's Chair" (a metal-framed lounge chair with pads for the hands; 1988) to his "Universal System" (a range of 25 beech plywood cupboards; 1993, left), the company has committed itself to this designer.

LATER WORK

Morrison has recently branched out from furniture into designing a tram for the city of Hanover in Germany, and clearly intends increasingly to enter the world of products. His commitment to the manufacturing process remains uppermost and, although materials themselves interest him greatly, it is those that allow easy, cheap production – such as plywood and aluminium – that appeal to him most.

While the prototyping of his products is an important stage of the whole design process for Morrison, he is clearly a designer rather than a craftsman, as it is the thought process that dominates his work. He is in tune with the values of early Modernism, yet he is also very much a part of 1990s' culture.

Bibliography

GENERAL STUDIES

Albera, G., and Monti, N. *Italian Modern: A Design Heritage* (New York, 1989)

Ambasz, E. (ed) *Italy: The New Domestic Landscape* (New York, 1972)

Art and Industry: A Century of Design in the Products We Use (London, 1982) exhibition catalogue

Baroni, D. *L'Oggetto Lampada* (Milan, 1981)

Byars, M. and Flinchum, R. (eds) *50 American Designers* (Washington, 1994)

Cooke, F. *Glass: Twentieth-Century Design* (New York, 1986)

Design Français: 1960–1990 (Paris, 1988) exhibition catalogue

Design Process: Olivetti 1908–1983 (Milan, 1983) exhibition catalogue

Doblin, J. *One Hundred Great Product Designs* (New York, 1970)

Dormer, P. *Design Since 1945* (London, 1993)

Fiell, C., and Fiell, P. *Modern Furniture Classics Since 1945* (London, 1991)

Fiell, C., and Fiell, P. *Modern Chairs* (Cologne, 1993)

Fossati, P. *Il design in Italia* (Turin, 1972)

Gregotti, V. *Il disegno del prodotto industriale: Italia 1860–1980* (Milan, 1982)

Heisinger, K. B. and Marcus, G. H. (eds) *Design Since 1945* (Philadelphia, 1983)

Heisinger, K. B., and Marcus, G. H. *Landmarks of Twentieth-Century Design* (New York, 1993)

Mathey, F. *Au bonheur des formes: design français 1945–1992* (Paris, 1992)

McFadden, D.R. *Scandinavian Modern Design 1880–1980* (New York, 1982)

McQuiston, L. *Women in Design: A Contemporary View* (New York, 1988)

Myerson, J., and Katz, S. *Conran Design Guides: Lamps and Lighting* (London, 1990)

Myerson, J., and Katz, S. *Conran Design Guides: Kitchenware* (London, 1990)

Opie, J. H. *Scandinavia: Ceramics and Glass in the Twentieth-Century* (New York, 1989)

Pansera, A. *Atlante del Design Italiano 1940–1980* (Milan, 1980)

Phillips, L. (intro) *Space and Environment: Furniture by American Architects* (New York, 1982)

Phillips, L. et al *High Styles, Twentieth-Century American Design* (New York, 1985)

Sparke, P. *An Introduction to Design and Culture in the 20th Century* (London, 1986)

Sparke, P. *Japanese Design* (London, 1987)

Sparke, P. *Design in Italy: 1870 to the Present* (New York, 1988)

Weston, R. *Modernism* (London, 1996)

Wilk, C. *Thonet: 150 Years of Furniture* (New York, 1980)

Zahle, E. (ed) *A Treasury of Scandinavian Design* (New York, 1961)

Zahle, E. *Scandinavian Domestic Design* (London, 1963)

CHAPTER 1

for pp.12–13:

Geretsegger, H. and Peintner, M. *Otto Wagner* (London, 1970)

Otto Wagner, Vienna 1841–1918: Designs for Architecture (Oxford, 1985) exhibition catalogue

for pp.14–15:

Garner, P. et el *The Amazing Bugattis* (London, 1979)

Die Bugatti (Hamburg, 1983)

for pp.16–17:

Ploegaerts, L. and Puttemans, P. *Henri van de Velde* (Brussels, 1987)

Sembach, K.-J. *Henri van de Velde* (London, 1989)

for pp.18–19:

Campbell, N. and Seebohm, C. *Elsie de Wolfe: A Decorative Life* (New York, 1992)

Smith, J.S. *Elsie de Wolfe: A Life in High Style* (New York, 1982)

for pp.20–21:

Frontisi, C. *Hector Guimard: Architectures* (Paris, 1985)

Ferre, F. and Rheims, M. *Hector Guimard* (New York, 1985)

for pp.22–23:

Greenhalgh, P. *Ephemeral Vistas: the Expositions Universelles, Great Exhibitions, and World's Fairs 1851–1939* (Manchester, 1988)

Silverman, D. L. *Art Nouveau in Fin-de-Siècle France: Politics, Psychology and Style* (California, 1989)

for pp.24–25:

Hanks, D.A. *The Decorative Designs of Frank Lloyd Wright* (New York, 1979)

for pp.26–29:

Crawford, A. *Charles Rennie Mackintosh* (London, 1995)

Kaplan, W. *Charles Rennie Mackintosh* (Glasgow, 1996)

for pp.30–33:

Buddensieg, T. et al *Industriekultur: Peter Behrens und die AEG 1907–1914* (Cambridge, MA, 1979)

Windsor, A. *Peter Behrens, Architect and Designer: 1868–1940* (London, 1981)

for pp.34–39:

Sekler, E.F. *Josef Hoffmann* (Salzburg, 1982)

Vergo, P. *Art in Vienna 1898–1918* (London, 1975)

Baroni, D. and D'Auria, A. *Josef Hoffmann e la Wiener Werkstätte* (Milan, 1981)

Schweiger, W.J. *Wiener Werkstätte: Kunst und handwerk 1903–1932* (Vienna, 1982)

CHAPTER 2

for pp.44–45:

Brunhammer, Y. *Jean Dunand, Jean Goulden* (Paris, 1973)

Garner, P. "The Lacquer Work of Eileen Gray and Jean Dunand", *Connoisseur* (March 1973)

Marcilhac, F. *Jean Dunand: His Life and Works* (London, 1991)

for pp.46–49:

Adam, P. *Eileen Gray: Architect-designer* (New York, 1987)

Garner, P. *Eileen Gray: Designer and architect* (Cologne, 1993)

for pp.50–51:

Camard, F. *Ruhlmann* (Paris, 1983)

Retrospective Ruhlmann (Musée des Arts Décoratifs, Paris, 1934) exhibition catalogue

Ruhlmann Centenary Exhibition (Foulk Lewis Collection, London, 1979) exhibition catalogue

for pp.52–53:

Brunhammer, Y. *Les années 25: Collection du Musée des Arts Décoratifs* (Paris, 1966)

Hillier, B. *Art Deco* (Minneapolis, 1971)

Duncan, A. *Art Deco* (London, 1988)

Battersby, M. *The Decorative Twenties* (London, 1969)

Battersby, M. *The Decorative Thirties* (London, 1971)

for pp.54–55:

Fisher, R. *Syrie Maugham* (London, 1978)

for pp.56–59:

Boman, M. (ed) *Estrid Ericson: Founder of Svenskt Tenn* (Stockholm, 1989)

Stritzler-Levine, N. (ed) *Josef Frank: Architect and Designer* (New York, 1966)

Wangberg-Ericcson, K. *Josef Frank, Livstrad i krigens skugga* (Stockholm, 1994)

for pp.60–61:

Batkin, M. *Wedgwood Ceramics 1846–1952: A New Appraisal* (London, 1983)

Taylor, D. "Keith Murray: A Modernist Designer in Glass, Ceramics and Metal", *Studies in the Decorative Arts* Vol. 1, no. 2 (New York, Spring 1992)

for pp.62–63:

Davidson, G. "Donald Deskey" in Byers, M. and Flinchum, R. *50 American Designers 1918–1968* (Washington, 1994)

Davies, K. *At Home in Manhattan: Modern Decorative Arts, 1925 to the Depression* (New Haven, 1983)

Hanks, D.A., and Toher, J. *Donald Deskey* (New York, 1987)

for pp.66–69:

Wilhelm Kåge: Gustavsberg (Stockholm, 1953) exhibition catalogue

for pp.72–73:

Myerson, J. *Gordon Russell, Designer of Furniture* (London, 1992)

Russell, G. *Designer's Trade: Autobiography of Gordon Russell* (London, 1968)

for pp.74–77:

Fleig, K. and Aalto, E. *Alvar Aalto: The Complete Work* (New York, 1992)

Schildt, G. *Alvar Aalto: The Early Years* (New York, 1984)

for pp.78–79:

Pritchard, J. *View from a Long Chair: The Memoirs of Jack Pritchard* (London, 1984)

for pp.80–81:

Herald, J. "A Portrait of Enid Marx", *Crafts*, no. 40 Sept. (London, 1979)

Utility Furniture and Fashion (Geffrye Museum, London, 1974) exhibition catalogue

Enid Marx (Camden Arts Centre, London, 1969) exhibition catalogue

CHAPTER 3

for pp.88–91:

Fitch, J.M. *Walter Gropius* (New York and London, 1960)

Franciscono, M. *Walter Gropius and the Creation of the Bauhaus in Weimar* (Illinois, 1971)

Gropius, I. *Walter Gropius: Buildings, Plans, Projects 1906–1969* (Massachusetts, 1972)

Gropius, W. *The New Architecture and the Bauhaus* (London, 1965)

Scheidig, W. *Crafts of the Weimar Bauhaus* (London, 1967)

The Bauhaus: Masters and Students (New York, 1988) exhibition catalogue

Whitford, F. *Bauhaus* (London, 1984)

for pp.92–93:

Blaser, W. *Mies van der Rohe: Furniture and Interiors* (London, 1982)

Ludwig Mies van der Rohe: Furniture and Furniture Drawings from the Design Collection and the Mies van der Rohe archive of MOMA (New York, 1977)

for pp.94–97:

Choay, F. *Le Corbusier* (New York, 1960)

De Fusco, R. *Le corbusier designer i mobili del 1929* (Milan, 1976)

Women in Design: Careers and Life Histories Since 1900 (Stuttgart, 1989) exhibition catalogue

for pp.98–101:

Baroni, D., and Bless, F. *The Furniture of Gerrit Thomas Rietveld* (New York, 1978)

Brown, T.M. *The Works of Gerrit Rietveld*

(Utrecht, 1958)

Kuper, M. and van Lijl, I. *Gerrit Th. Rietveld: The Complete Works 1888–1964* (Utrecht, 1992)

for pp.102–103:

El Lissitzky *Russia: An Architecture for World Revolution* (Cambridge, MA, 1970)

Frampton, K. "The Work and Influence of El Lizzitzky", *Architect's Yearbook* no. 12 (1968)

for pp.104–105:

Carrell, C., et al *The Rodchenko Family Workshop* (London, 1989)

Karginov, G. *Rodchenko* (London, 1979)

Quilici, V. (ed) *Rodchenko: The Complete Works* (London, 1986)

for pp.106–109:

Blake, P. *Marcel Breuer, Architect and Designer* (New York, 1949)

Droste, M. and Ludewig, M. *Marcel Breuer* (Cologne, 1992)

Wilk, C. *Marcel Breuer: Furniture and Interiors* (New York, 1981)

pp.114–115:

Eisenman, P. *Guiseppe Terragni* (Cambridge, 1978)

Marciano, A. F. *Guiseppe Terragni: Opera Completa 1925–1943* (Rome, 1988)

Schumacher, T.L. *Surface and Symbol: Guiseppe Terragni and the Architecture of Italian Rationalism* (London, 1991)

for pp.116–117:

Teague, W. D. *Design This Day: The Technique of Order in the Machine Age* (London, 1940)

for pp.118–119:

Appelbaum, S. *The New York World's Fair* (New York, 1977)

Meikle, J. *20th Century Limited: Industrial Design in America, 1925–39* (Philadelphia, 1979)

Pulos. A. *American Design Ethic: A History of American Industrial Design to 1940* (Cambridge, MA, 1983)

for pp.120–121:

Loewy, R. *Industrial Design* (New York, 1979)

Raymond Loewy: Pioneer of American Industrial Design (Munich, 1990) exhibition catalogue

The Designs of Raymond Loewy (Washington, 1976) exhibition catalogue

for pp.124–127:

Cantacuzina, S. *Wells Coates: A Monograph* (London, 1978)

Wells Coates, Architect and Designer (Oxford, 1979) exhibition catalogue

Thirties: British Art and Design Before the War (Hayward Gallery, London, 1980) exhibition catalogue

for pp.128–129:

Hennessey, W.J. *Russel Wright: American Designer* (Cambridge, MA, 1983)

Wright, R. and Wright, M. *A Guide to Easier Living* (New York, 1951)

for pp.130–131:

Dreyfuss, H. *Designing for People* (New York, 1955)

Flinchum, R. *Henry Dreyfuss: Industrial Designer* (New York, 1997)

for pp.132–133:

Ullen, J. "The Saab Saga" *Style Auto*, 36 (Turin, 1980)

Art and Industry (Conran Foundation, London, 1982) exhibition catalogue

CHAPTER 4

Jackson, L. *Contemporary: Architecture and Interiors of the 1950s* (London, 1994)

for pp.138–141:

Portoghesi, P,. and Pansera, A. *Gio Ponti alla Manifattura di Coccia* (Milan, 1982)

Ponti, L.L. *Gio Ponti: The Complete Work 1923–1978* (Cambridge, MA, 1990)

for pp.142–145:

Faber, T. *Arne Jacobsen* (Stuttgart, 1964)

for pp.146–147:

Branzi, A., and De Lucchi, M. *Design Italiano Degli Anni '50* (Milan, 1980)

Brino, G. *Carlo Mollino: Architecture as Autobiography* (London, 1987)

for pp.148–151:

Drexler, A. *Charles Eames: Furniture from the Design Collection* (New York, 1973)

Kirkham, P. *Charles and Ray Eames* (New York, 1996)

Neuhart, J., Neuhart, M., and Eames, R. *Eames Design* (New York, 1989)

for pp.154–155:

Abercrombie, S. *George Nelson: The Design of Modern Design* (Cambridge, MA, 1995)

Nelson, G. *On Design* (New York, 1979)

Nelson, G. *Problems of Design* (New York, 1957)

for pp.156–157:

Kuhner, R. A. *Eero Saarinen: His Life and Work* (Illinois, 1975)

Spade, R. *Eero Saarinen* (London, 1971)

for pp.160–161:

Moller-Nielsen, J. *Wegner: En Dansk Mobelkunstner* (Copenhagen, 1965)

for pp.162–163:

Conway, H. *Ernest Race* (London, 1982)

for pp.164–165:

Bryk, R. *Tapio Wirkkala* (Washington, 1956)

for pp.168–171:

Harris, J. *Lucienne Day: A Career in Design* (Manchester, 1993)

Jackson, L. *The New Look: Design in the Fifties* (London, 1991)

Lyall, S. *Hille: 75 Years of British Furniture* (London, 1981)

for pp.172–173:

Celant, G. *Marcello Nizzoli* (Milan, 1968)

for pp.174–175:

Bruce, G. "Eliot Noyes" in Byars, M. and Flinchum, R. (eds) *50 American Designers* (Washington, 1994)

Noyes, E. *Organic Design in Home Furnishing* (New York, 1941)

for pp.176–179:

Hans Gugelot: 1920–1965 (Bahnbrecher Systemdesign Munich, 1984) exhibition catalogue

Hochschule für Gestaltung Ulm: Die Moral der Gegenstande (Berlin, 1987) exhibition catalogue

for pp.180–181:

Bayley, S. (ed) *Sony Design* (London, 1982) exhibition catalogue

for pp.182–183:

Glancey, J. *Douglas Scott* (London, 1988)

for pp.184–187:

Brandes, U. *Dieter Rams, Designer: Die leise Ordnung der Dinge* (Göttingen, 1990)

Burckhardt, F. and Franksen, I. *Design: Dieter Rams* (Berlin, 1980)

for pp.188–189:

Kenneth Grange at the Boilerhouse: An Exhibition of British Product Design (Victoria & Albert Museum, London, 1983) exhibition catalogue

CHAPTER 5

for pp.194–195:

Ferrari, P. *Achille Castiglioni* (Milan, 1984)

for pp.196–197:

Dorfles, G. *Marco Zanuso: Designer* (Rome, 1971)

Zanuso, M. *Dunhill Industrial Design Lecture* (Melbourne, 1971)

for pp.198–201:

Pasca, V. *Vico Magistretti: Elegance and Innovation in Postwar Italian Design* (London, 1991)

for pp.202–203:

Katz, S. *Plastics: Common Objects, Classic Designs* (New York, 1984)

Sparke, P. *The Plastics Age* (Victoria & Albert Museum, London, 1990) exhibition catalogue

for pp.204–205:

Verner Panton (Copenhagen, 1986)

for pp.208–209:

Favata, I. *Joe Colombo and Italian Design of the Sixties* (London and Milan, 1988)

for pp.210–211:

McCarty, C. *Mario Bellini, Designer* (New York, 1987)

for pp.212–213:

Santini, P.C. *The Years of Italian Design: A Portrait of Cesare Cassina* (Milan, 1981)

for pp.214–215

Bayley, S. *Harley Earl and the Dream Machine* (New York, 1983)

for pp.216–219

Di Castro, F. (ed) *Sottsass' Scrapbook* (Milan, 1976)

Radice, B. *Ettore Sottsass: A Critical Biography* (New York, 1993)

Sparke, P. *Ettore Sottsass Jr.* (London, 1982)

for pp.224–225:

Vanlaethen, F. *Gaetano Pesce: Architecture, Design, Art* (New York, 1989)

Gaetano Pesce (Tel Aviv and New York, 1991) exhibition catalogue

CHAPTER 6

for pp.230–233:

ADI Annual 1976 (Milan, 1976)

Bangert, A. and Armer, K. M. *80s Style: Designs of the Decade* (New York, 1990)

for pp.234–235:

Hirst, A. *Metropolitan Home*, April (New York, 1990)

Lamarova, M. and Byers, M. *Boris Šípek: The Nearness of Far Architecture and Design* (Amsterdam, 1993)

for pp.236–237:

Frampton, K., and Rowe, C. *Five Architects: Eisenman, Graves, Gwathmay, Hejduk, Meier* (New York, 1972)

for pp.238–239:

Jencks, C. *The Language of Post-modern Architecture* (London, 1980)

Venturi, R. *Complexity and Contradiction in Architecture* (New York, 1966)

Radice, B. *Memphis: the New International Style* (Milan, 1981)

for pp.240–241:

Mobilier Japonais (Tokyo, 1985) exhibition catalogue

The Works of Shiro Kuramata: 1967–1981 (London, 1981) exhibition catalogue

for pp.242–243:

Pawley, M. *Eva Jiricna: Design in Exile* (London, 1990)

for pp.246–249:

Boissière, O. *Starck* (Cologne, 1991)

Nouvelles Tendances: les avant-gardes de la fin du XXme siècle (Paris, 1986) exhibition catalogue

for pp.250–251:

Coad. E. D. *Javier Mariscal: Designing the New Spain* (New York, 1991)

Julier, G. *New Spanish Design* (London, 1991)

for pp.252–253:

Buck, A. and Vogt, M. (eds) *Michele De Lucchi* (Berlin, 1993)

for pp.254–255:

Branzi, A. *The Hot House: The New Italian Design* (London, 1982)

Shimizu, F. and Thun, M. *The Descendants of Leonardo: The New Italian Design* (Tokyo, 1980)

Capella, J., and Larrea, Q. *Designed by Architects in the 1980s* (New York, 1988)

for pp.256–257:

Sudjic, D. *Ron Arad: Restless Furniture* (New York, 1989)

for pp.258–259:

Dormer, P. *Jasper Morrison: Designs, Projects and Drawings, 1981–1989* (London, 1990)

Manufacturers

Companies producing designer
objects today.

Ajeto Lindava 167, 47158 Czech
Republic. Produces designs by
Bořek Šípek.

Akaba SA Kale Nagusia 56, Lasarte
20160, Gipuzkoa, Spain. Produces
designs by Javier Mariscal.

Alessi SpA via Privata Alessi 6,
Crusinallo 28023, Novara, Italy.
Produces designs by Marianne
Brandt, Ettore Sottsass, Richard
Sapper, Michael Graves and
Philippe Starck.

Alterego 572 Egelantiersgracht,
Amsterdam, The Netherlands.
Produces designs by Bořek Šípek.

Ron Arad Studio 62 Chalk Farm
Road, London, NW1, UK. Produces
designs by Ron Arad.

Arflex SpA via Monte Rosa 27,
Limbiate 29951, Milan, Italy.
Produces designs by Marco Zanuso.

Arte srl via Nazario Sauro 34, Arosio
22060, Como, Ialy. Produces
designs by Marco Zanuso.

Artek Oy Ab Etelaesplanade 18,
FIN-00130, Helsinki, Finland.
Produced designs by Alvar Aalto.

Artemide SpA via Bergamo 18,
Pregnana Milanese 20010, Italy.
Produces designs by Vico
Magistretti, Ettore Sottsass, Richard
Sapper and Michele De Lucchi.

Avarte Oy Hie Kkakiventie 2, FIN-
00710, Helsinki, Finland. Produces
designs by Yryo Kukkapuro.

Av Mazzega srl via Vivarini 3,
Murano Venezia, Italy. Produces
designs by Michele De Lucchi.

B & B Italia SPA Strade Provinciale,
Padua, Italy. Produces designs by
Antoni Citterio.

Baroni & Associati Corso di Porta
Romana 122, Milan 20122, Italy.
Produces designs by Ron Arad.

Belux AG Bremgartnerstrasse 109,
Wohlen 5610, Switzerland.
Produces designs by Ron Arad.

Bernini G.B. Bernini SpA, Carate
Brianza, Italy. Produces designs by
Pier Giacomo and Achille Castiglioni.

Bigelli Marmi via Arceviese 26,
Senigállia 60019, Italy. Produces
designs by Ron Arad.

Braun Braun AG, Taunus, Germany.
Produces designs by Dieter Rams.

Cappellini Arte via Marconi 35,
Arosio 22060, Italy. Produces
designs by Shiro Kurumata and
Jasper Morrison.

Cassina SpA via L. Busnelli 1, Meda
20036, Milan. Produces designs by
Cassina, Charles Rennie
Mackintosh, Frank Lloyd Wright,
Gerrit Rietveld, Le Corbusier,
Charlotte Perriand, Pierre
Jeanneret, Mario Bellini, Vico
Magistretti, Gaetano Pesce and
Philippe Starck.

Castelli Anonima Castelli, Bologna,
Italy. Produces designs by Richard
Sapper.

Classicon Perchtinger Strasse 8,
Munich 81379, Germany. Produces
designs by Michele De Lucchi.

Cleto Munari Italy. Produces designs
by Ettore Sottsass.

Cosmic Barcelona, Spain. Produces
designs by Javier Mariscal.

De Padova Corso Venezia 14, Milan
20121, Italy. Produces designs by
Achille Castiglioni and Vico
Magistretti.

Driade SpA via Padana Inferiore 12,
29012 Fossadello di Caorso,
Piacenza, Italy. Produces designs by
Bořek Šípek and Philippe Starck.

Dux Mobel Sweden. Produces
designs by Bruno Mathsson.

Dyson Dual Cyclone Technology,
Dyson Appliances Ltd, Tetbury Hill,
Malmesbury, Wiltshire, SN16 0RP.
Produces the Dual Cyclone vacuum.

Evertaut & Hille (Idem Furniture)
Cross Street, Darwen, Lancashire
BB3 2PW, UK. Produces designs by
Robin Day.

Fiam Italia SpA Chiara del Vecchio,
Conseil, 38 Vitruvio, Milan 20124,
Italy. Produces designs by Ron Arad.

Flos SpA via Angelo Faini 2, Bovezzo
25073, Brescia, Italy. Produces
designs by Philippe Starck, and Pier
Giacomo and Achille Castiglioni.

Fritz Hansen A/S Allerodvej 8,
3450 Allerød, Denmark. Produces
designs by Arne Jacobsen, Vico
Magistretti, Hans Wegner and
Verner Panton.

Halifax srl via Furlanelli 96, Giussano
20034, Milan, Italy. Produces designs
by Antonio Citterio.

Herman Miller Herman Miller Inc.,
Zeeland, MI, USA. Produces designs
by George Nelson and Verner
Panton.

Ing C. Olivetti & Co. SpA 77 G.
Jervis, Ivrea 10015, Turin, Italy.
Produces designs by Michele De
Lucchi.

IBM (International Business Machines
Corporation), Old Orchard Road,
Armonk, New York 10504, USA.
Produces designs by Richard Sapper.

Iittala Glassworks Iittala, Finland.
Produces designs by Alvar Aalto,
Kaj Franck and Tapio Wirkkala.

Kartell SpA via dell Industrie 1,
Noviglio 20082, Milan, Italy.
Produces designs by Marco
Zanuso, Philippe Starck and
Antonio Citterio.

Kenwood Manufacturing Co. Ltd
New Lane, Havant, UK. Produces
designs by Kenneth Grange.

Knoll International Worcester
Street, New York, NY, USA.
Produces designs by Mies van der
Rohe, Marcel Breuer, Eero Saarinen
and Ettore Sottsass.

Le Klint Egstubben 13-15, DK-5270,
Odense N, Denmark. Produces
designs by Kaare Klint.

Logitech 6505 Kaiser Drive,
Fremont, CA 94555, USA. Produces
designs by frogdesign.

**Bruno Mathsson International
AB** S-331 27 Värnamo, Sweden.
Produces designs by Bruno
Mathsson.

Magis srl 15 Via Magnadola, Motto
de Lizenza 31045, Treviso, Italy.
Produces designs by Jasper
Morrison.

Mira-X SA CH-5034 Suhr,
Switzerland. Produces designs by
Javier Mariscal.

Mobles 114 Enric Granados,
Barcelona 08008, Spain. Produces
designs by Javier Mariscal.

Morphy Richards Talbot Road,
Mexborough, South Yorkshire, S64
8AJ, UK. Produces designs by
Kenneth Grange.

Motorola 50 E. Commerce Drive
North, MI, USA. Produces designs
by frogdesign.

Nani Marquina Bonavista 3,
Barcelona, Spain. Produces designs
by Javier Mariscal.

Olivetti via Lorenteggio 257, Milan
20152, Italy. Produces designs by
Mario Bellini, Ettore Sottsass and
Michele De Lucchi.

Packard Bell 1 Packard Bell Way,
Sacramento, CA 91362, USA.
Produces designs by frogdesign.

Philips Consumer Electronics
Alexanderstrasse 2, Hamburg
2000, Germany. Produces designs
by Ettore Sottsass.

Poltronova Poltronova SpA, Pistoia,
Italy. Produces designs by Ron Arad.

**Produzione Privata SAS e
Pintacuda** via Pallavinco 31, Milan
20145, Italy. Produces designs by
Michele De Lucchi.

Race Furniture, Ltd Bourton
Industrial Park, Bourton-on-the-
Water, Cheltenham,
Gloucestershire GL54 28Q, UK.
Produces designs by Ernest Race.

Rosenthal AG 43
Wittelsbacherstrasse, Selb 95100,
Germany. Produces designs by
Walter Gropius, Michele De Lucchi.

Royal Copenhagen Smallgade 45,
DK-2000 Frederiksberg, Denmark.
Produces designs by Arne Jacobsen.

Rudolph Rasmussen's Snedkerier
Nørrebrogade 45, 2200
Copenhagen NV, Denmark.
Produces designs by Kaare Klint.

Sambonet SpA 62 via XXVI Aprile,
Vercelli 13100, Italy. Produces
designs by Michele De Lucchi.

SCP Ltd 135–9 Curtain Road,
London EC2A 3BA, UK. Produces
designs by Jasper Morrison.

Sony Corporation 6–7–35
Kitashinagawa, Shinagawa-ku, Tokyo
141, Japan.

Steltman Editions 330 Spuistraat,
Amsterdam 1012 VX, The
Netherlands. Produces designs by
Bořek Šípek and Jasper Morrison.

Stelton Gl Vartov Vej 1, DK-2900
Hellerup, Copenhagen, Denmark.
Produces designs by Arne Jacobsen.

Steuben 717 Fifth Avenue, New
York, NY 10022. Produces designs
by W. D. Teague and Michael Graves.

D. Swarovski & Co. Wattens 6112,
Austria. Produces designs by Bořek
Šípek and Ettore Sottsass.

Svenskt Tenn Strandvägen 5, Box
5478, S-114 84 Stockholm.
Produces designs by Josef Frank.

Thomson Multimedia 9 Place des
Vosges, 92050 Paris la Défense,
Cedex France. Produces designs by
Philippe Starck.

Thonet Gebr. Thonet GmbH, PO
Box 1520, 3558 Frankenberg,
Germany. Produces designs by
Alvar Aalto and Marcel Breuer.

Tupperware PO Box 2353,
Orlando, Florida 32802, USA.
Produces the Tupperware designs
invented by Earl Tupper.

Venini SpA Fondata Vetrai 50,
Murano, Venice 30141, Italy.
Produces designs by Ettore Sottsass.

Vitra International AG
Klünenfeldstrasse 20, 4127
Birsfelden, Switzerland. Produces
designs by Charles Eames, Verner
Panton, Bořek Šípek, Jasper
Morrison, Antonio Citterio,
Michele De Lucchi and Ron Arad.

Wilkinson Sword Ltd
Cramlington, Northumberland,
NE23 8AW. Produces designs by
Kenneth Grange.

Zanotta SpA via Vittorio Veneto 57,
Nova Milanese 20054, Milan, Italy.
Produces designs by Achille
Castiglioni and Marco Zanuso.

Museums and design collections

Museums and collections housing displays of 20th-century design. Unless otherwise stated, the institutions listed house general decorative arts and design collections.

AUSTRALIA
National Gallery of Victoria, Melbourne
Powerhouse Museum, Sydney

AUSTRIA
Galerie Metropole, Vienna
Historisches Museum der Stadt, Vienna
Österreichisches Museum für Angewandte Kunst, Vienna

BELGIUM
Musée Royaux d'Art et d'Histoire, Brussels *Displays European decorative art and design to the Art Nouveau period.*
Museum voor Sierkunst en Vormgeving, Ghent *Includes Art Nouveau and Art Deco designs, works by Le Corbusier, and furniture, glassware, pottery and textiles to the present day.*

CANADA
Musée des Art Décoratifs, Montreal

DENMARK
Museum of Decorative Arts, Copenhagen *Houses 20th-century industrial design.*
Holmegaard Museum, Fensmark *Specializes in glass.*

FINLAND
Arabia Museum, Helsinki *Devoted to ceramics.*
Alvar Aalto Museum, Jyvaskyla *Focuses on the work of Alvar Aalto.*
Finnish Glass Museum, Riihimaki
Glass Museum, Iittala *Collection of locally manufactured glass, including works by Alvar Aalto and Kaj Franck. The Museum is attached to the Iittala glass factory.*
Museum of Applied Arts, Helsinki

FRANCE
Centre Georges Pompidou, Paris
Musée des Art Décoratifs, Paris
Musée d'Orsay, Paris *Includes furniture and applied art objects to the Art Nouveau period.*

GERMANY
Bauhaus Archiv, Museum für Gestaltung, Berlin *Displays the work of the Bauhaus, including designs made in the Bauhaus workshops, such as ceramics, textiles and furniture, and industrially produced objects.*
Bauhaus Museum, Kunstsammlungen zu Weimar *Focuses on the work produced under the State Bauhaus at Weimar, 1919–25.*
Deutsches Technik Museum, Berlin *Houses designs significant for their mechanical and scientific functions, including household and telecommunication appliances, computer and photographic technology, and aviation, road and rail transport.*
Kunstgewerbemuseum, Berlin
Kunstmuseum, Düsseldorf *Houses an extensive glass collection to the Art Nouveau period, plus contemporary studio glass, and applied art and industrial design of the 20th century.*
Museum für Angewandte Kunst, Cologne
Museum für Industriekultur, Nuremberg *Houses industrial design.*
Museum für Kunst und Gewerbe, Hamburg *Extensive collection of Art Nouveau designs, including many works exhibited at the 1900 World Fair, and applied art and industrial design of the modern period.*
Museum für Kunsthandwerk, Frankfurt am Main
Die Neue Sammlung Staatliches Museum für Angewandte Kunst, Munich *The largest museum of industrial design and a leading museum of 20th-century applied art and design.*
Ulmer Museum, Ulm *Includes a display of the Ulm Hochschule für Gestaltung.*
Vitra Design Museum, Weil am Rhein *Extensive collection of modern furniture design, including the estate of Charles and Ray Eames.*

ITALY
Museo della Ceramica, Laveno Mombello
Museo di Doccia, Florence
Museo Internazionale della Ceramiche, Faenza
Museo della Scala, Milan
Museo del Tessuto, Prato

THE NETHERLANDS
van Abbe Museum, Eindhoven
Boymans-van Beuningen Museum, Rotterdam
The Rietveld Schröder House, Centraal Museum, Utrecht *An example of De Stijl work, designed by Gerrit Rietveld in 1924.*
Nai Nederlands Architectuurinstituut, Rotterdam *The architectural collection includes examples of furniture designs.*
Stedelijk Museum, Amsterdam

NORWAY
Kunstindustrimuseet, Oslo *Houses industrial design.*
Nasjonalgalleriet, Oslo
Nordenfjeldske Kunstindustrimuseum, Trondheim *Houses industrial design.*

SWEDEN
Archive for Swedish Design, Kalmar
Nationalmusem, Stockholm
Gustavsberg Museum, Gustavsberg *Devoted to ceramics.*
Orrefors Glass Museum, Orrefors
Röhsska Konstslöjdmuseet, Gothenburg
Tekniska Museet, Stockholm

UNITED KINGDOM
Brighton Museum and Art Gallery *Includes displays of Art Nouveau and Art Deco design.*
City Museum and Art Gallery, Bristol
Broadfield Glass Museum, Kingswinford
Design Museum, London *Charts the development of design in mass production and displays examples of international contemporary design.*
Gallery of Modern Art, Glasgow *Includes design from 1945.*
Glasgow School of Art *Designed by C. R. Mackintosh.*
Hunterian Museum and Art Gallery, Glasgow *Displays designs by C. R. Mackintosh.*
London Transport Museum *Includes designs by Edith Marx and Douglas Scott.*
Manchester City Art Galleries
Royal Museum of Scotland, Edinburgh
Ulster Museum, Belfast *Includes displays of modern Irish and European design.*
Victoria & Albert Museum, London *Extensive collection of 20th-century design, including an installation of the office designed by Frank Lloyd Wright for his patron Edgar J. Kaufmann.*

Wedgwood Museum, Barlaston *Displays many 20th-century works designed for the Wedgwood pottery company.*
Whitworth Art Gallery, Manchester *Collection of wallpapers and textiles.*

UNITED STATES
Art Institute of Chicago
Brooklyn Museum of Art, New York
Busch-Reisinger Museum, Harvard University, Cambridge, MA *Houses international 20th-century design, including the archive of Walter Gropius.*
Cooper-Hewitt, National Museum of Design, New York
Corning Museum of Glass, Corning, NY *Extensive collection of glass to the present day. The museum is within the same complex as the Steuben factory.*
Denver Art Museum *Houses a collection of international 20th-century design.*
Huntington Art Gallery, San Marino, CA *The collection includes furniture and decorative art to 1930.*
Metropolitan Museum of Art, New York *Houses a broad collection of modern decorative arts and design.*
Museum of Fine Arts, Boston
Museum of Modern Art, New York
Philadelphia Museum of Art
Radio City Music Hall, New York *Interior designed in the Art Deco style by Donald Deskey.*
Studebaker National Museum, Indiana *Includes the work of Raymond Loewy.*

Glossary

Aesthetic Movement An English literary and artistic movement of the late 19th century founded on the ethos of "art for art's sake". The group was dedicated to the ideal of beauty and rejected the idea that art should have a social or moral purpose, in contrast to the Arts and Crafts Movement*.

"Anti-design" movement A movement that emerged in Italy during the later 1960s, following Ettore Sottsass's 1966 exhibition of furniture in Milan. The group rejected the formalist values of the neomodern* design movement in Italy and sought to renew the cultural and political role of design, believing that the original aims of Modernism had become no more than a marketing tool. In contrast to Modernism, the movement was founded on a belief in the importance of an object's social and cultural value as well as its aesthetic function. Employing all the design values rejected by Modernism, it embraced ephemerality, irony, kitsch*, strong colours and distortions of scale to undermine the purely functional value of an object, and question concepts of taste, and "good design". Sottsass spearheaded the activities which were carried out in individual groups; these were to consolidate as the Memphis group in the 1980s.

Anti-Modernism A movement originating in Italy through the activities of the Italian "Anti-design" movement*. By the end of the 1960s it had become an international concept as increasing numbers of designers rejected the formalist values of the Modern Movement*.

Art Deco The term widely used to describe the architectural and decorative arts style that emerged in France in the 1920s. It took its name from the 1925 Exposition Internationale des Arts Décoratifs et Industriels Modernes in Paris. Geometric forms and patterns, bright colours, sharp edges, and the use of expensive materials, such as enamel, ivory, bronze and polished stone are well-known characteristics of this style, but the use of other materials such as chrome, coloured glass and Bakelite* also enabled Art Deco designs to be made at low cost.

Art Nouveau A style of decorative art and architecture popular in Europe in the late 19th and early 20th centuries which is characterized by stylized curvilinear designs and organic forms. In Germany the style was called *Jugendstil*. Art Nouveau developed along two distinct lines: the rectilinear style pioneered by C. R. Mackintosh and seen in the work of the members of the Vienna Secession*, and the intricate curvilinear style of French and Belgian designers, such as Hector Guimard. Mackintosh's style of Art Nouveau was to influence the Wiener Werkstätte.

Arts and Crafts Movement An English aesthetic and social movement of the later 19th century, led by John Ruskin, William Morris, C.R. Ashbee and others, which sought to revive the importance of craftsmanship in a time of increasing mechanization and mass production. The ideal of the movement was to make well-designed and crafted objects available to all people, but because the objects were made by hand in workshops only wealthy patrons could afford to buy them. However, the movement did stimulate a drive for better standards in mass-production at the time, while its belief that good art and design could reform society, and its practice of rejecting showy decoration to concentrate on the simplicity of an object was to have a significant influence on exponents of the Modern Movement*, such as the designers associated with the German Bauhaus. The movement also influenced some 20th-century designers in Sweden, Finland and Germany to revive their own national styles.

Bakelite
The trade name of a plastic invented in 1907 by the chemist Leo H. Baekeland. It was the first plastic to be entirely synthetic. Cheap to manufacture and suitable for use in moulding processes, it became an ideal component for mass-consumer objects, such as the casings for telephones, radios and refrigerators.

Baroque A term used broadly in art and literature, it primarily refers to the style of art practised widely in Europe in the 17th and early 18th centuries during the Catholic Counter Reformation. It is a highly ornate style that in design and architecture is characterized by a lavish and dynamic use of materials.

Biedermeier A style of decorative arts popular in Germany and Austria in the 1820s to 1840s. Characterized by refined neoclassical* shapes, that display a simplicity of design and clean lines, the style was popular with the emerging middle-class. Austrian exponents of the Modern Movement*, such as the designers associated with the Wiener Werkstätte, were influenced by Biedermeier designs.

cantilever In architecture this term refers to the practice whereby a floor or horizontal structure projects out of a wall or vertical structure without a visible means of support. In design the term is used to describe a style of chair that has no back legs: the back of the seat is supported by the frame as the weight is distributed at the front of the chair. This style has been explored in the 20th century through the use of bent plywood, tubular steel and plastic.

Celtic style The artistic style of the people of Western Central Europe during the Iron Age. The highly accomplished metal work and the pottery are distinctive for their stylized, curvilinear surface decoration. The style was to influence C. R. Mackintosh and his circle in the later 19th century.

chrome A shiny, silver-coloured metallic element that became commercially available in 1925, proving to be ideal as a plate on other metals, such as tubular steel, for decorative purposes and to prevent corrosion. It immediately became popular and is now synonymous with much mass design of the 1920s and 1930s.

classical A term used broadly to describe a style of architecture, art and design that is created in, or that follows, the restrained style of classical antiquity and its adherence to accepted standards of form and craftsmanship.

classicism A style of architecture, art and design that is modelled on the ideals and style of the art of ancient Greece and Rome, displaying the qualities of restraint, harmony, proportion and reason, and adhering to accepted standards of form and craftsmanship. In the 18th century the style was interpreted as the movement known as neoclassicism*. The formal values of classicism have remained a constant source of inspiration for designers, particularly for those of the Modern Movement*.

Constructivism A Russian movement of artists, architects and designers who abandoned fine art traditions after the 1917 Russian Revolution in order to create art to serve the new social and political order. The exponents linked their work with mass production and industry, but although they designed furnishings and objects their ideas were never put into mass production. The main artists were Alexander Rodchenko, El Lissitzky and Kasimir Malevich. Avoiding the use of traditional art materials, they strove to make new art works by bringing different elements together, seen to strong effect in their posters created out of photomontage*. The movement was to have a strong influence on groups within the Modern Movement*, such as De Stijl* and the Bauhaus.

"Contemporary" style A style of modern furniture and furnishings made after World War II that was lighter, more expressive and playful than that of the pre-war Modern Movement*, and which reflected the greater optimism of the time. Characterized by organic shapes and a greater use of colour, the exponents of the style made use of technological advances and strove to make the designs more democratically accessible, as seen in the plywood chairs of Charles Eames.

Cubism An artistic movement developed by Pablo Picasso and Georges Braque from about 1907, in which the artists rejected traditional techniques for representing three-dimensional forms on a two-dimensional surface, such as canvas. Instead of using perspective and foreshortening to represent an object, Picasso and Braque depicted many different aspects of it simultaneously, thereby creating an image of differing planes that represented the object as seen from a variety of viewpoints. Cubism was to have a significant influence on art and design of the 20th century.

"Danish Modern" Movement A term used to describe the Modern Movement* as it emerged in Denmark after 1945, which was developed by designers such as Hans Wegner and Arne Jacobsen. Although the designers adopted many of the ideas of the German and French Modern Movements, they created works that were distinctive for their natural finishes and their traditional references.

De Stijl A group composed of architects, designers, painters, thinkers and poets founded in the Netherlands around a magazine of the same name in 1917. Under the leadership of the painter and architect Theo van Doesburg, the group aimed to break down the divisions between fine and applied arts in order to create a pure style of art, design and architecture that rejected natural forms in favour of abstract geometric forms.

Deutscher Werkbund An organization formed in Germany in 1907 to bridge the gap between industry and design. Composed of manufacturers, architects, designers and politicians, it campaigned for a style of design that it believed to be appropriate to the new industrial age, and argued for the moral and aesthetic importance of design, underlining its belief that practicality was the basis for expressing contemporary cultural values. It carried through some of the ideas of Art Nouveau* and applied them to industrial design.

eclecticism A term used to describe the practice of designers finding and incorporating ideas and influences from various styles and tastes into their work. In the 20th century it is a distinctive feature of Postmodernist design, allowing a freedom that has proved attractive to many designers.

Empire style A style of decorative arts and dress that emerged in Paris in the early 1800s, at about the time Napoleon I became Emperor, and spread through Continental Europe. It reflected an interest in ancient, particularly Egyptian, motifs.

faience Tin-glazed earthenware.

fibreboard A building material made of wood or other plant fibres compressed into boards.

fibreglass A strong, lightweight, structural material made from glass in fibrous form. It was developed commercially in the United States in the 1930s, and was used by designers such as Charles Eames, Arne Jacobsen and Joe Colombo to create chairs.

"form follows function" The phrase used widely to denote the Modernist principle that the form of an object or building should reflect the construction principles and materials from which it is made. This maxim was coined by the American architect Louis Sullivan in an essay of 1896 in reference to architecture. As a maxim for the Modern Movement*, its original meaning has been adapted to suggest that the idea of "utility" should determine an object's appearance.

Functionalism A term used broadly to refer to the principle that nothing is included in a design that does not enhance the object's purpose. The American architect Louis Sullivan is usually cited as the "founder" of Functionalism with his maxim "form follows function"*.

Futurism An Italian art movement founded in 1909 by the writer Filippo Tommaso Marinetti, which aimed to celebrate the machinery, speed and violence of the modern age. The paintings are characterized by a sense of movement and abstract, geometric forms. In book design the movement rejected traditional forms of typography and page design, seeking to find new forms to reflect their ideals.

Gothic A style of architecture and decorative arts, which developed in France in the mid-12th century to become the dominant style of Western Europe until the 16th century. The architecture is characterized by the use of pointed arches, rib vaults and flying buttresses in combination, while the decorative arts are distinctive for their lightness, elaborate forms and intricate surface decoration. It was a style that linked itself with the principles of Christianity and retained a strong spiritual content in its many revivals.

hardboard A stiff board made of compressed and treated wood pulp used in furniture manufacture.

High-Tech style A style of architecture and design that emerged in the 1980s, inspired by and embracing modern technology. It is characterized by visual simplicity, elegance and the use of industrial materials, or those made available through technological advances transferred to non-industrial settings. The term is also used more broadly to refer to the development in the Modern Movement* when designers began using new materials, such as glass, bricks, metals and plastics in favour of traditional materials; this is sometimes called the "industrial" style*.

Impressionism A movement in painting originating in France in the 1860s in which painters such as Claude Monet, Edgar Degas and Paul Renoir sought to record subjects as objectively as possible. Their paintings covered a broad spectrum of subjects, including nature, the fleeting effects of light, urban life and portraiture, which reflect the varied interests of the individual artists in the movement.

"industrial" style A term used broadly to refer to the development in the Modern Movement* when when designers began using new materials, such as glass, bricks, metals and plastics in favour of traditional materials. In the 1980s and 1990s the the style was interchangeable with that referred to as High-Tech*.

Jugendstil The name of the German and Scandinavian Art Nouveau* movement, which was characterized by its use of rectilinear forms. The name came from the *Jugend* magazine.

kitsch A term used to describe garish, pretentious or sentimental art and design. In the 20th century it has been seen to be the opposite of "good design". Since the 1960s some designers, such as Ettore Sottsass and the Memphis group, in rejecting the Modern Movement*, have deliberately incorporated kitsch elements into their work. The use of kitsch became widespread in the popular design styles of 1970s and 1980s.

melamine A plastic often used for laminate coatings, particularly on wooden kitchen surfaces, and to make tableware.

minimal A descriptive term for designs of the Modern Movement* that are characterized by a rejection of ornamentation in favour of simple elemental forms and structures.

Modern Movement A general term originally used by the architectural historian Nikolaus Pevsner in his influential book *Pioneers of the Modern Movement* (1936), to describe an international movement in architecture and design that emerged in Europe in the early decades of the 20th century. It was originally underpinned by a desire for a design ethos that reflected ideals of democracy and social reform, and a belief that the world of art and the manufacturing industry could be reconciled in order to provide all levels of society with well-designed, mass-produced goods. Early groups that were instrumental in the development of the Modern Movement include the Deutscher Werkbund* in Germany before World War I, and the De Stijl* group in the Netherlands after 1917. These principles were put into practice most notably, and with the most lasting influence, at the Bauhaus in Germany in the 1920s and early 1930s. The movement rejected the use of historical styles and unnecessary decoration, instead adhering to the principle "form follows function"*. It is more or less interchangeable with the term "Modernism".

neoclassicism A style of decorative arts and architecture that originated in the second half of the 18th century. With its rejection of the earlier Rococo*, it marked a revival of interest in the art and design of Classical antiquity and the qualities of restraint, harmony, proportion and reason. It is distinctive for its simple geometric forms, subdued colours and restrained decoration. The term is sometimes used broadly to describe designs that are created in, or that follow, this style.

neofunctionalism A design style of the post-World War II period the ethos of which emphasized geometrical simplicity and the removal of unnecessary detail. As expressed through the work of Hans Gugelot it was to lead on to a new visual minimalism in design. Its proponents claimed it to be "styleless" or "beyond style".

Neo-Liberty An Italian style of design that emerged in the late 1950s with the aim of reviving Italian Art Nouveau*. Through designing furnishings, lighting and interior design, exponents of the style such as Carlo Mollino sought to apply Art Nouveau to mass-produced objects and at the same time reintroduce a craft tradition to undercut the machine aesthetic of the Modern Movement*.

neomodernism An Italian design movement that emerged in the 1950s. Inspired by 1930s Rationalism*, it is characterized by minimal forms, but, unlike its predecessor, it was also characterized by a new alliance with the world of contemporary fine art, organic sculpture in particular.

"Novecento" movement A movement founded in Italy in the late 1920s which is characterized by a simplified neoclassical style of design. Although it was influenced by the decorative arts of France and Austria, it produced designs that were more overtly nationalistic than those of its contemporary architectural movement Rationalism*. The movement superseded Rationalism as the architectural style favoured by the Italian Fascists.

Op Art A style of abstract art of the 1960s. Through a variety of patterns it exploits optical effects to create illusions of movement and vibration. Leading exponents of the style were Bridget Riley and Victor Vasarely. The style found its way into 1960s interior, fashion and graphic design.

Perspex The trade name of a tough, light, and above all translucent, solid plastic which became commercially available in the later 1930s. It has great flexibility and a strong resistance to weathering, and is often used instead of glass. It can also be opaque.

photomontage A term applied to the practice of creating a new complete image out of different photographs or fragments of existing materials such as photographs, text and drawings. The technique was popularized by the Dada artists in Berlin and through the poster designs of the Russian Constructivists. It has been widely used in graphic design.

Plexiglass The trade name of a tough, light and solid plastic that can be manufactured as a translucent or opaque material. Its flexibility of handling is indicated by its use in the tableware designs of Marianne Brandt of the 1920s and for a seat design by Shiro Kurumata in the late 1980s.

Pointillism A technique that involves the application of paint on to a surface, such as canvas, in small dots of unmixed colour, which when viewed by the spectator blend optically. It was developed by Georges Seurat in the 1880s in an effort to achieve a depth of colour and a greater degree of light and vibrancy in his work.

Pop An art and design movement that developed during the 1960s responding to the general level of economic and technological optimism and finding inspiration in mass consumerism and popular culture. Rejecting Modernism, it sought to express the democratic spirit of the age, replacing Modernist values with its own aspirations of fun, change, variety, irreverence, and disposability.

Post-Impressionism A style of art of the late 19th and early 20th centuries, signalling a break from the naturalism of the Impressionists. Based on the work of such artists as Vincent Van Gogh, Paul Gauguin and Paul Cézanne, it was concerned with form and the expressive and symbolic potential of painting.

prefabrication The practice of manufacturing sections of a building, which are then assembled on site. It enables standardization of style and greater speed of construction. Prefabricated materials include reinforced concrete* panels, steel frames, windows and staircases.

Pre-Raphaelites A group of English artists and writers founded in 1848, who were united by their dislike of the academic and neoclassical art of the early 19th century. They sought to return to the values of Gothic and Early Renaissance painting. William Holman Hunt, Dante Gabriel Rossetti and John Everett Millais were the chief painters in the group. They often painted biblical and literary subjects, and their style was characterized by strong colours and minute attention to detail. Although the original group began to disband in the 1850s, the name continued to be applied to the later pictures of Rossetti and the work of Edward Burne Jones and William Morris, who used scenes from medieval romances in his furniture designs. As a result the name became associated with a kind of romantic escapism.

Purism An artistic movement of the early 20th-century, founded by Le Corbusier and the painter Amédée Ozenfant. Arising out of a rejection of Cubism*, it drew inspiration from the mathematical precision of machinery. It emphasized the purity of geometric form and marked a return to the representation of recognizable objects.

Rationalism The name of the Italian Modern Movement* that emerged in 1926 in the work of a group of architects known as the "Group of Seven" and became popular in the 1930s. Influenced by Modernists in Germany and France it sought to make the most economic use of materials and space. For a short period the work of the movement reflected the revolutionary and socialist aims of the early Italian Fascist party, but it was to prove too radical and international in character, and was superseded by "Novecento"*. Rationalism was to influence Italian design in the years immediately following 1945.

reinforced concrete Concrete manufactured with metal bars or wire embedded within it to increase its tensile strength.

retro A term used to describe designs that imitate or adopt characteristics of earlier styles, as seen in the Sharp "QT50" radio cassette player of 1986.

Rococo A style of architecture and design that flourished in France, southern Germany and Austria in the first half of the 18th century, which is characterized by light colours, scroll work, shell motifs and a sense of playfulness. It was to influence the French Art Nouveau movement.

Secession The name taken by several groups of artists in Germany and Austria who broke away from the official academies in the 1890s to pursue their own artistic aims and organize their own exhibitions. The first Secession was in Munich in 1892. This was followed by the Vienna Secession* in 1897, and by the Berlin Secession in 1899.

slipware The name for lead-glazed earthenware, on to which slip – a mixture of fine clay and water – has been applied as relief decoration.

space-age A style that draws its inspiration from the field of space exploration. It was a popular style in fashion, furniture and interior design in the 1960s.

streamform A decorative style used by American designers in the 1930s and 1940s. As for streamlining*, streamform objects have an aerodynamic appearance, whatever their function: they tend to be shaped into a teardrop form and to have chrome highlight decoration. It was visible in architecture, the decorative arts and products.

streamlining A form of styling that emerged in the 1930s, through the work of American designers such as Raymond Loewy. It was used to make objects – vehicles, household appliances and electrical equipment – appear unified and modern and to increase their consumer appeal. Streamlined objects are often characterized by an aerodynamic appearance, with blunt, rounded and smoothly finished forms, and chrome highlight decoration. The style remained popular through to the 1950s. Since this time streamlining has sometimes been used to design vehicles that create the least resistance to motion, as seen in the British 125 high-speed train designed by Kenneth Grange.

Swedish Modern A tradition-based yet essentially modern style, it is characterized by the use of natural materials in preference to those such as tubular steel, a material synonymous with the Modern Movement*. The objects were well-designed, inexpensive to manufacture and affordable for most people. This style dominated international taste in domestic interior design after World War II.

Symbolism An international artistic movement of the late 19th century, with close links to the Symbolist movement in French poetry. In contrast to the naturalism of Impressionism, it sought to express emotions and states of mind through colour and form, often drawing on literary or occult subject-matter.

"truth to materials" The edict of the Arts and Crafts Movement* that the forms of objects should reflect the materials from which they are made. It was to influence designers of the Modern Movement*, including those at the Bauhaus in Germany and Gordon Russell in Britain.

Vienna Secession A group of painters, architects and designers in Vienna, headed by Gustav Klimt, and including Josef Hoffmann and Joseph Maria Olbrich, who broke away from the Vienna Academy of Fine Arts in 1897 to organize their own avant-garde exhibitions. They aimed to break down the divisions between architecture and the fine and decorative arts.

Index

Acknowledgments

The author would like to thank Barbara Berry at the Royal College of Art; staff and students of the joint Victoria & Albert/Royal College of Art History of Design Course; John Small; and everyone at Mitchell Beazley. The publisher would like to thank Frankie Leibe, Jane Royston, Kirsty Seymour-Ure, Emma Shackleton and Sarah Yates for their invaluable help in the preparation of this book.

The publisher would like to thank the following for their kind permission to reproduce photographs for use in this book.

Key b bottom, **c** centre, **l** left, **r** right, **t** top

Front jacket Ron Arad Associates (Photograph by Armin Linke); **back jacket t** Verner Panton, **c** Bridgeman Art Library (Private Collection/DACS 1998), **b** Studio De Lucchi; **inside flap portrait** Octopus Publishing Group Ltd (Tommy Candler) **7** Herman Miller, Inc; **11** AKG, London; **12t** Philippe Garner, **b** Angelo Hornak; **13tl** AKG, London, **tr** Sotheby's Picture Library, **b** Victoria & Albert Museum; **14t** Philippe Garner, **b** Christie's Images; **15t** Philippe Garner, **b** Christie's Images; **16t** Philippe Garner, **b** Vitra Design Museum; **17tl** E.T. Archive, **tr** Sotheby's Picture Library, **b** Christie's Images; **18t** Sotheby's Picture Library (Cecil Beaton), **b** Elsie de Wolfe ('The House in Good Taste', New York, The Century Co, 1916.); **19t** Derry Moore, **b** Elsie de Wolfe ('The House in Good Taste' The Century Co, New York, 1916); **20t** Collection Kharbine-Tapabor, **b** Collection Kharbine-Tapabor; **21tl** Scope (Noel Hautemaniere), **tr** Christie's Images, **br** Christie's Images; **22** Christie's Images; **23t** Philippe Garner, **b** Bridgeman Art Library (Giraudon/Musee Carnavalet, Paris), **c** Collection Kharbine-Tapabor (©ADAGP, Paris and DACS, London, 1988); **24t** The Frank Lloyd Wright Archives, **bl** Cassina S.P.A. (Romano Fotografie. ARS, NY and DACS, London 1998), **br** Christie's Images (ARS, NY and DACS, London 1998); **25tl** Paul Rocheleau, **tr** Christie's Images (ARS, NY and DACS, London 1998), **b** Cassina S.P.A. (Andrea Zani. ARS, NY and DACS, London 1998); **26t** Glasgow School of Art Collection, **b** Christie's Images; **27t** Christie's Images, **b** The Glasgow Picture Library; **28t** Hunterian Art Gallery, University of Glasgow (Mackintosh Collection, Mark Fiennes), **b** Bridgeman Art Library (The Fine Art Society, London); **29tl** The Glasgow Picture Library, **tr** The Glasgow Picture Library, **b** Glasgow School of Art Collection; **30t** AKG, London, **b** G. M. Pfaff AG (DACS 1998); **31tl** AEG Hausgerate GmbH (DACS 1998), **tr** Sotheby's Picture Library (DACS 1998), **b** Sotheby's Picture Library (DACS 1998); **32t** Sotheby's Picture Library (DACS 1998), **b** Sotheby's Picture Library (DACS 1998); **33 l** AKG, London, **r** AKG, London; **34** Philippe Garner, **t** Bridgeman Art Library (Osterreichisches Nationalbibliothek, Vienna), **b** Vitra Design Museum; **35 l** AKG, London (Osterreichisches Museum fur angewandte Kunst), **r** Philippe Garner; **36t** Angelo Hornak, **b** Christie's Images; **37t** Victoria & Albert Museum, **b** Philippe Garner; **38t** Christie's Images, **b** Sotheby's Picture Library; **39tl** Philippe Garner, **tr** Christie's Images, **b** Sotheby's Picture Library; **43** Sotheby's Picture Library; **44** Christie's Images (ADAGP, Paris and DACS, London 1998), **t** Roger-Viollet, **b** Christie's Images (ADAGP, Paris and DACS, London 1998); **45t** Christie's Images (ADAGP, Paris and DACS, London 1998), **b** Sotheby's Picture Library (ADAGP, Paris and DACS, London 1998); **46t** Philippe Garner, **b** Christie's Images; **47t** Philippe Garner, **b** Bridgeman Art Library (Private Collection); **48t** Victoria & Albert Museum, **b** Bridgeman Art Library (Private Collection); **49t** Sotheby's Picture Library, **b** Vitra Design Museum; **50t** Roger-Viollet, **b** Christie's Images; **51tl** Philippe Garner, **tr** Christie's Images, **b** Christie's Images; **52t** Jean-Loup Charmet, **tl** Roger-Viollet, **b** Philippe Garner; **53tr** Jean-Loup Charmet, **b** Philippe Garner; **54t** Sotheby's Picture Library (Cecil Beaton), **b** National Monuments Record (Crown copyright); **55tl** Derry Moore;, **tr** The Conde Nast Publications Ltd (Anthony Denney), **br** Philippe Garner; **56t** Svenskt Tenn (Lennart Nilsson), **b** Vitra Design Museum; **57tl** AKG, London, **tr** Svenskt Tenn, **b** Svenskt Tenn; **58t** Svenskt Tenn, **b** Svenskt Tenn; **59r** Svenskt Tenn, **tl** Svenskt Tenn; **60t** The Wedgwood Museum, **b** WORSHIPFUL COMPANY OF GOLDSMITHS,; **61** The Wedgwood Museum, **t** Broadfield House Glass Museum, **b** The Wedgwood Museum; **62t** Corbis UK Ltd (Bettman/UPI), **b** Christie's Images; **63** Christie's Images, **t** Corbis UK Ltd, **b** Christie's Images; **64t** Rud. Rasmussens Snedkerier Aps, **b** DANSKE KUNSTINDUSTRIMUSEET, (Ole Woldbye); **65tl** Le Klint, **tr** DANSKE KUNSTINDUSTRIMUSEET, (Ole Woldbye), **b** Rud. Rasmussens Snedkerier Aps; **66t** AB Gustavsberg, **b** Victoria & Albert Museum; **67t** Nordiska Museet, **b** Statens Konstmuseer; **68t** Victoria & Albert Museum, **bl** Victoria & Albert Museum, **br** AB Gustavsberg; **69t** Statens Konstmuseer, **b** Victoria & Albert Museum; **70t** AB Orrefors Glasbruk, **b** Svenskt Tenn; **71tl** Nordiska Museet, **tr** Victoria & Albert Museum, **b** Keramiskt Centrum; **72** Christie's Images, **t** The Gordon Russell Trust;, **b** Christie's Images; **73t** The Gordon Russell Trust, **b** Christie's Images; **74t** artek, **b** Sotheby's Picture Library; **75t** Philippe Garner, **b** Artek; **76t** Iittala, **bl** Vitra Design Museum, **br** Artek; **77t** Corbis UK Ltd (Bettmann/UPI), **b** Artek; **78t** Heals, **bl** Vitra Design Museum, **br** Christie's Images; **79t** Philippe Garner, **b** Victoria & Albert Museum; **80t** Mathsson International AB, **b** Mathsson International AB; **81t** Mathsson International AB;, **b** Mathsson International AB; **82t** The Royal Society for the encouragement of Arts, Manufactures and Commerce, London (The Faculty of Royal Designers for Industry), **bl** © The Post Office 1998, Reproduced by kind permission of the Post Office, All Rights Reserved, **br** Enid Marx; **83tl** London Transport Museum, **tr** The Whitworth Art Gallery, University of Manchester; **87** AKG, London; **88** BAUHAUS-ARCHIVE, **t** BAUHAUS-ARCHIVE, **b** Rosenthal; **89t** BAUHAUS-ARCHIVE, **b** AKG, London; **90t** AKG, London, **b** Victoria & Albert Museum; **91t** AKG, London, **bl** AKG, London (DACS 1997), **br** Victoria & Albert Museum (DACS 1998); **92t** BAUHAUS-ARCHIVE, **bl** Knoll (The Mies van der Rohe Collection, Tubular Brno Chair, courtesy of Knoll), **br** Christie's Images (DACS 1998); **93t** Esto Photographics (Scott Frances), **b** AKG, London (Erich Lessing); **94b** Cassina S.P.A. (Oliviero Venturi. ADAGP, Paris and DACS, London 1998), **t** Charlotte Perriand (Pierre Jeanneret); **95t** Fondation Le Corbusier, **b** Charlotte Perriand (Pierre Jeanneret. ADAGP, Paris and DACS, London 1998); **96t** Fondation Le Corbusier, **b** Cassina S.P.A. (Mario Carrieri. ADAGP, Paris and DACS, London 1998) **97t** Cassina S.P.A. (Oliviero Venturi. ADAGP, Paris and DACS, London 1998), **bl** Hulton Getty Picture Collection, **br** Christie's Images (ADAGP, Paris and DACS, London 1998); **98t** Centraal Museum Utrecht (Rietveld Schroder Archive/DACS 1998), **b** Christie's Images (DACS 1998); **99t** Centraal Museum Utrecht (DACS 1998), **b** Octopus Publishing Group Ltd (DACS 1998); **100t** Cassina S.P.A. (DACS 1998), **b** Christie's Images (DACS 1998); **101t** Sotheby's Picture Library (DACS 1998), **b** Centraal Museum Utrecht (Rietveld Schroder Archive/Jannes Finders/DACS 1998) **102t** Stedelijk Van Abbe Museum, Eindhoven, **b** Christie's Images (DACS 1998); **103t** Stedelijk Van Abbe Museum, Eindhoven (DACS 1998), **bl** CHRISTIE'S IMAGES, (DACS 1998), **br** Bridgeman Art Library (Private Collection/DACS 1998); **104t** Society for Cooperation in Russian & Soviet Studies, **bl** Society for Cooperation in Russian & Soviet Studies, **br** Society for Cooperation in Russian & Soviet Studies; **105t** AKG, London (Moscow, Lenin Library, Erich Lessing), **b** Christie's Images; **106t** BAUHAUS-ARCHIVE, (DACS 1998), **b** Sotheby's Picture Library (DACS 1998); **107** Officina Alessi (DACS 1998), **t** Sotheby's Picture Library (DACS 1998), **b** Christie's Images (DACS 1998); **108t** BAUHAUS-ARCHIVE, **bl** Victoria & Albert Museum, **br** Philippe Garner; **109t** BAUHAUS-ARCHIVE, **b** AKG, London; **110t** Victoria & Albert Museum, **bl** Victoria & Albert Museum, **br** Sotheby's Picture Library; **111** Pedro E. Guerrero; **112t** Victoria & Albert Museum, **b** BAUHAUS-ARCHIVE, (Erich Consemuller); **113** Victoria & Albert Museum, **t** BAUHAUS-ARCHIVE, **b** Christie's Images; **114t** Centro Studio Guiseppe Terragni, **b** Centro Studio Guiseppe Terragni; **115t** Centro Studio Guiseppe Terragni, **b** Centro Studio Guiseppe Terragni; **116t** Corbis UK Ltd (Bettmann/UPI), **b** Corning Museum of Glass (Copyright 1985. Gift of Steuben Glass.); **117** Advertising Archives, **t** Henry Ford Museum and Greenfield Village, **b** CHRISTIE'S IMAGES; **118** Corbis UK Ltd (Library of Congress); **119tl** Statens Konstmuseer, **tr** Corbis UK Ltd (Library of Congress), **br** Corbis UK Ltd (Bettmann), **bl** E.T. Archive; **120** Corbis UK Ltd (Bettmann/UPI), **t** AKG, London; **121tl** AKG, London, **tr** AKG, London; **122tl** AKG, London, **tr** AKG, London; **122bl** AKG, London; **123** AKG, London; **124t** Design Council/DHRC, University of Brighton, **b** Victoria & Albert Museum; **125tl** Philippe Garner, **tr** Royal Institute of British Architects;, **b** Royal Institute of British Architects; **126t** Design Council/DHRC, University of Brighton (Leonard G Taylor, AIBP), **bl** Royal Institute of British Architects, **br** Victoria & Albert Museum; **127br** Royal Institute of British Architects; **128t** Corbis UK Ltd (Bettmann/UPI), **b** Octopus Publishing Group Ltd; **129tl** Syracuse University, The George Arents Research Library for Special Collections, **tr** Syracuse University, The George Arents Research Library for Special Collections, **b** Syracuse University, The George Arents Research Library for Special Collections; **130t** Corbis UK Ltd (Bettmann/UPI), **bl** AKG, London, **br** Advertising Archives; **131t** Julius Shulman, **b** The Thermos Company; **132t** SAAB, **b** SAAB; **133t** SAAB, **bl** SAAB, **br** CHRISTIE'S IMAGES,; **137** Herman Miller, Inc; **138t** Archivio Gio Ponti, **b** Agenzia Fotografica Luisa Ricciarini, Milan; **139** Index, **t** Agenzia Fotografica Luisa Ricciarini, Milan; **140t** Index, **b** Christie's Images; **141t** Archivio Gio Ponti, **b** Octopus Publishing Group Ltd (Ian Booth); **142** Fritz Hansen, **t** Fritz Hansen, **b** Octopus Publishing Group Ltd; **143tl** Royal Copenhagen (Georg Jensen Silversmiths), **tr** Fritz Hansen; **144tl** Fritz Hansen, **tr** Octopus Publishing Group Ltd (Tim Ridley), **b** Fritz Hansen; **145t** Royal Institute of British Architects, **b** Stelton; **146t** Archivio Carlo Mollino, **b** Christie's Images; **147t** Victoria & Albert Museum, **bl** Archivio Carlo Mollino, **br** Christie's Images; **148t** Herman Miller, Inc, **b** CHRISTIE'S IMAGES,; **149tl** Julius Shulman, **tr** Herman Miller, Inc, **b** Victoria & Albert Museum; **150t** Octopus Publishing Group Ltd (Tim Ridley), **b** Herman Miller, Inc; **151t** Herman Miller, Inc, **b** Herman Miller, Inc; **152b** Fritz Hansen; **153tl** Philippe Garner, **tr** Victoria & Albert Museum, **bl** Christie's Images, **br** Victoria & Albert Museum; **154t** Herman Miller, Inc (Melissa Brown), **b** Herman Miller, Inc (Rooks Photography); **155tl** Herman Miller, Inc, **tr** Octopus Publishing Group Ltd (Tim Ridley), **b** Herman Miller, Inc; **156t** Knoll, **b** Octopus Publishing Group Ltd (Tim Ridley); **157tl** Victoria & Albert Museum, **tr** Corbis UK Ltd (Bettmann), **b** Esto Photographics (Ezra Stoller); **158t** Ittala, **b** Octopus Publishing Group Ltd (Ian Booth); **159tl** Iittala, **tr** Iittala, **b** Victoria & Albert Museum; **160t** Fritz Hansen, **b** Octopus Publishing Group Ltd (Ian Booth); **161** Fritz Hansen, **t** Bridgeman Art Library, **b** Octopus Publishing Group Ltd (Ian Booth); **162t** Design Council/DHRC, University of Brighton, **b** Octopus Publishing Group Ltd (Ian Booth); **163** Race Furniture Limited, **t** Race Furniture Limited, **b** Race Furniture Limited; **164t** Iittala, **bl** Victoria & Albert Museum, **br** Christie's Images; **165** Iittala, **t** Corning Museum of Glass, **b** Christie's Images; **166t** Agenzia Fotografica Luisa Ricciarini, Milan, **b** Octopus Publishing Group Ltd (Ian Booth); **167t** Agenzia Fotografica Luisa Ricciarini, Milan, **bl** Agenzia Fotografica Luisa Ricciarini, Milan, **br** Archivio Gio Ponti; **168t** Advertising Archives, **b** Robin and Lucienne Day; **169** Robin and Lucienne Day (Hille International); **169t** Robin and Lucienne Day, **b** Robin and Lucienne Day; **170** Robin and Lucienne Day, **t** Robin and Lucienne Day, **b** Robin and Lucienne Day; **171tl** Robin and Lucienne Day, **tr** Robin and Lucienne Day; **172t** Archivio Storico of Olivetti, Ivrea, Italy, **b** Olivetti (UK); **173** Agenzia Fotografica Luisa Ricciarini, Milan, **t** Archivio Storico of Olivetti, Ivrea, Italy, **br** Agenzia Fotografica Luisa Ricciarini, Milan (Roberto Schezen) **174t** New Canaan Historical Society, **b** Corbis UK Ltd (Bettmann/UPI); **175** New Canaan Historical Society, **t** IBM, **b** Science & Society Picture Library, Science Museum; **176t** Braun, Germany, **b** Octopus Publishing Group Ltd (Ian Booth); **177tl** Ulmer Museum/HfG-Archiv, **tr** Braun,

Germany, **b** Ulmer Museum/HfG-Archiv; **178t** Ulmer Museum/HfG-Archiv, **b** Ulmer Museum/HfG-Archiv; **179** Professor Herbert Lindinger, **t** Ulmer Museum/HfG-Archiv, **b** Professor Herbert Lindinger; **180t** Sony United Kingdom Limited, **tl** Advertising Archives, **b** Science & Society Picture Library, Science Museum (NMPFT); **180b** Advertising Archives; **181tr** Advertising Archives; **182t** The Royal Society for the encouragement of Arts, Manufactures and Commerce, London (RDI Archive), **b** The Royal Society for the encouragement of Arts, Manufactures and Commerce, London (RDI Archive); **183tl** London Transport Museum (John Somerset Murray), **tr** The Royal Society for the encouragement of Arts, Manufactures and Commerce, London (RDI Archive), **b** London Transport Museum; **184t** Braun, Germany, **b** Design Council Slide Collection, Manchester Metropolitan University (Boilerhouse); **185t** Braun, Germany, **b** Design Council Slide Collection, Manchester Metropolitan University (Boilerhouse), **t** Philippe Garner, **b** Braun, Germany; **186b** Neil Austin; **188t** Pentagram Design Limited, **b** Pentagram Design Limited; **189tl** Pentagram Design Limited, **tr** Pentagram Design Limited, **b** Pentagram Design Limited; **193** Verner Panton; **194t** Studio Arch. Castiglioni, **b** Zanotta, S.p.A. (Mauro Masera); **195tl** Flos, **tr** Octopus Publishing Group Ltd, **b** Bernini S.p.a.; **196t** Design Council/DHRC, University of Brighton, **b** Zanotta, S.p.A. (Aldo Ballo); **197** Zanotta, S.p.A. (Aldo Ballo), **tr** Zanotta, S.p.A. (Mauro Masera), **b** Octopus Publishing Group Ltd (Ian Booth); **198t** Fritz Hansen, **b** Vico Magistretti; **199tl** Vico Magistretti, **tr** Vico Magistretti; **200tl** Vico Magistretti, **tr** Vico Magistretti, **b** Vico Magistretti; **201** Vico Magistretti; **202t** Pentagram Design Limited, **b** Studio Joe Colombo, Milano; **203tl** Katz Collection, **tr** Private Collection, **b** Tupperware; **204t** Verner Panton, **bl** Octopus Publishing Group Ltd (Ian Booth), **br** Verner Panton; **205t** Verner Panton, **b** AKG, London; **206t** Studio Nurmesniemi Ky (Rauno Traskelin), **bl** Studio Nurmesniemi Ky, **br** Studio Nurmesniemi Ky; **207t** Studio Nurmesniemi Ky, **b** Studio Nurmesniemi Ky; **208t** Studio Joe Colombo, Milano, **b** Philippe Garner; **209tl** Studio Joe Colombo, Milano, **tr** Philippe Garner, **b** Studio Joe Colombo, Milano; **210t** Mario Bellini Associati;, **b** Mario Bellini Associati, **tl** Mario Bellini Associati, **tr** Mario Bellini Associati, **b** Mario Bellini Associati; **212** Cassina S.P.A. (Bella e Ruggeri), **bl** Cassina S.P.A. (Bella & Ruggeri); **213tl** Cassina S.P.A., **tr** Cassina S.P.A. (Aldo Ballo), **b** Cassina S.P.A. (Aldo Ballo); **214t** Copyright 1978 G. M. Corp. Used with permission from the G. M. Media Archives, **b** Copyright 1978 G. M. Corp. Used with permission from the G. M. Media Archives; **215tl** Copyright 1978 G. M. Corp. Used with permission from the G. M. Media Archives, **tr** Advertising Archives, **b** Copyright 1978 G. M. Corp. Used with permission from the G. M. Media Archives; **216t** Design Council/DHRC, University of Brighton, **b** Octopus Publishing Group Ltd (Andy Johnson & Rish Durka); **217t** Ettore Sottsass, **bl** Ettore Sottsass; **217br** Ettore Sottsass; **218t** Ettore Sottsass (Santi Caleca), **b** Ettore Sottsass; **219t** Ettore Sottsass, **b** Ettore Sottsass (Aldo Ballo); **220t** Hulton Getty Picture Collection, **tr** Victoria & Albert Museum, **b** Philippe Garner (Domus, Editoriale Domus – Rozzano (MI) Italy); **221tl** Hulton Getty Picture Collection, **b** Philippe Garner; **222t** Philippe Garner (Archigram), **b** Philippe Garner; **223t** Philippe Garner, **b** Philippe Garner (Domus); **224t** Gaetano Pesce, **b** Gaetano Pesce; **225tl** Gaetano Pesce, **tr** Gaetano Pesce, **b** Gaetano Pesce; **229** AKG, London (Laurent Limot); **230t** Richard Sapper (Serge Libiszewski), **b** Artemide; **231t** Richard Sapper, **b** Richard Sapper (Aldo Ballo); **232t** Richard Sappe, **b** Richard Sapper; **233tl** Richard Sapper, **tr** Richard Sapper (Mario Carrieri), **b** Richard Sapper (Aldo Ballo); **234t** Studio Sipek (Erwin Olaf), **b** Studio Sipek/Vitra; **235t** Studio Sipek/Leon Gulikers, **bl** Studio Sipek/Vitra, **br** Studio Sipek/Courtesy Steltman Galleries, Amsterdam/New York, Leon Gulikers; **236t** Michael Graves, **b** Michael Graves (Paschall/Taylor); **237t** Michael Graves (William Taylor), **bl** Michael Graves, **br** Michael Graves; **238** Studio de Lucchi, **bl** Dyson Appliances Ltd, **br** Avarte; **239t** Octopus Publishing Group Ltd (Courtesy of Charles Jencks/James Merrell), **b** Victoria & Albert Museum; **240t** Kuramata Design Office, **b** Kuramata Design Office (Mitsumasa Fujitsuka); **241t** Kuramata Design Office (Mitsumasa Fujitsuka), **bl** Kuramata Design Office (Mitsumasa Fujitsuka), **br** Kuramata Design Office; **242** Eva Jiricna Architects Limited, **t** Eva Jiricna Architects Limited, **b** Eva Jiricna Architects Limited (Alistair Hunter); **243tl** Eva Jiricna Architects Limited (Alistair Hunter), **tr** Arcaid (Richard Bryant, 1994); **244** frogdesign inc. (Dietmar Henneka), **t** frogdesign inc., **bl** frogdesign inc. (Victor Goico), **br** Esslinger Design (Dietmar Henneka); **245t** frogdesign inc. (Dietmar Henneka), **br** frogdesign inc. (Victor Goico); **246t** Flos, **b** Flos; **247t** Arcaid (Earl Carter/Belle), **bl** Arcaid (Richard Bryant), **br** Arcaid (Richard Bryant); **248t** AKG, London (Laurent Limot), **b** Thomson; **249t** Arcaid (Simon Kenny/Belle), **bl** Flos, **br** Thomson; **250t** Estudio Mariscal, **b** Estudio Mariscal; **251t** Estudio Mariscal, **bl** Estudio Mariscal, **br** Estudio Mariscal; **252** Studio de Lucchi, **t** Studio de Lucchi, **b** Studio de Lucchi; **253t** Studio de Lucchi, **b** Studio de Lucchi; **254t** Antonio Citterio, Architetto (Gitty Darugar), **b** Antonio Citterio, Architetto (Hans Hansen); **255** Antonio Citterio, Architetto (Luciano Svegliado), **t** Antonio Citterio, Architetto (Gionata Xerra), **b** Antonio Citterio, Architetto (Miro Zagnoli); **256t** Ron Arad Associates, **b** Ron Arad Associates; **257tl** Ron Arad Associates (C. Kicherer), **tr** Ron Arad Associates (Christopher Kicherer), **b** Ron Arad Associates (G Dagon); **258** Jasper Morrison, **t** Jasper Morrison, **b** Jasper Morrison; **259tl** Jasper Morrison, **tr** Arcaid (Richard Bryant)